DIALECT
GEOGRAPHY OF
SYRIA-PALESTINE,
1000–586 B.C.E.

W. RANDALL GARR

upp UNIVERSITY OF PENNSYLVANIA PRESS · PHILADELPHIA

Designed by Adrianne Onderdonk Dudden

Copyright © 1985 by the University of Pennsylvania Press
All rights reserved

Library of Congress Cataloging in Publication Data

Garr, W. Randall.
  Dialect geography of Syria-Palestine, 1000–586 B.C.

  Bibliography: p.
  Includes index.
  1. Semitic languages—Dialects—Syria.   2. Semitic
languages—Dialects—Palestine.   3. Syria—Languages.
4. Palestine—Languages.   I. Title.
PJ3079.G37   1984   492   84-3639
ISBN 0-8122-7927-1

Printed in the United States of America

*For my mother
and the memory of my father*

CONTENTS

ACKNOWLEDGMENTS

It is a great pleasure to acknowledge and thank those who have contributed so much to this study. Gary Beckman, Benjamin Foster, William Hallo, and William Labov kindly offered methodological and bibliographical advice. Stephan Bennett, Elise Crosby, Tremper Longman III, and Glenn Schwartz helped me with linguistic and historical issues. I am also grateful to Isidore Dyen for his many hours of counsel and tutoring on the problems of dialect geography.

I am grateful as well to several scholars for sharing their unpublished work: Jo Ann Hackett, Joseph Healey, Joseph Naveh, Robert Ratner, Jeffrey Tigay, Manfred Weippert, and Clifford Wunderlich.

I greatly appreciate the technical assistance I received in preparing the manuscript. I wish to thank Maureen Draicchio and Ulla Kasten for advice on the preparation of the manuscript, and Walter Gamboa and David Lawson for patiently preparing the maps. Mrs. Erwin Raisz kindly allowed me to use her late husband's Landform Map as the base of the maps presented here.

I thank the many people who have read earlier versions of this study. Jeffrey Blakely, Henry Hoenigswald, Stanislav Segert, Robert Wilson, and Ziony Zevit read the manuscript thoroughly and corrected many errors which would otherwise have passed unnoticed. I owe a special debt to Stephen Kaufman, whose detailed comments and insistence on precision forced me to rethink several issues raised in this study.

I thank Laura Kalman for reading every word of this book in its several forms, several times, and for offering sound and good-humored criticism on a subject about which she would have preferred to remain ignorant.

Most of all, I wish to thank Franz Rosenthal and Marvin Pope. Professor Pope introduced me to the study of Northwest Semitic dialects and increased my interest in comparative and historical linguistics. Professor Rosenthal, who suggested this topic of study, has been a model of scholarly craftsmanship; he has consistently shown the rewards of a command of all aspects of Semitic linguistics. I thank both teachers for their encouragement and guidance.

Finally, I thank Yale University and the National Foundation for Jewish Culture for their generous financial support during my years of graduate study, and the University of Pennsylvania Research Foundation for defraying publication costs.

ABBREVIATIONS

ABL	Robert Francis Harper, *Assyrian and Babylonian Letters Belonging to the Kouyunjik Collection of the British Museum.*
ADAJ	*Annual of the Department of Antiquities of Jordan.*
ADD	C. H. W. Johns, *Assyrian Deeds and Documents.*
AF	Franz Rosenthal, *Die aramaistische Forschung seit Th. Nöldeke's Veröffentlichungen.*
AfO	*Archiv für Orientforschung.*
AION	*Annali dell'Istituto orientale di Napoli* (Nuova Serie).
AJBA	*Australian Journal of Biblical Archaeology.*
AJSL	*American Journal of Semitic Languages and Literatures.*
Akk.	Akkadian.
ANET[3]	James B. Pritchard (ed.), *Ancient Near Eastern Texts Relating to the Old Testament.* 3rd ed. with Supplement.
AOAT	Alter Orient und Altes Testament.
AoF	*Altorientalische Forschungen.*
Arab.	Arabic.
ArOr	*Archiv Orientální.*

Arsl.T.	Arslan Tash Phoenician texts.
AS	*Anatolian Studies.*
ASOR	American Schools of Oriental Research.
AUSS	*Andrews University Seminary Studies.*
BA	*Beiträge zur Assyriologie und semitischen Sprachwissenschaft* (1889–1927); *The Biblical Archaeologist* (1938–).
BASOR	*Bulletin of the American Schools of Oriental Research.*
BH	Biblical Hebrew.
Bibl	*Biblica.*
BiOr	*Bibliotheca Orientalis.*
BJPES	*Bulletin of the Jewish Palestine Exploration Society.*
B-L	Hans Bauer and Pontus Leander, *Historical Grammatik der hebräischen Sprache des Alten Testamentes.*
BMAP	Emil G. Kraeling (ed.), *The Brooklyn Museum Aramaic Papyri.*
BMB	*Bulletin du Musée de Beyrouth.*
Bus.	Buseirah ostracon.
BZAW	Beiheft zur Zeitschrift für die alttestamentliche Wissenschaft.
C	*Consonant.*
CBQ	*Catholic Biblical Quarterly.*
CIS	Corpus Inscriptionum Semiticarum.
Cit.	Amman Citadel Inscription.
CTA	Andrée Herdner, *Corpus des tablettes en cunéiformes alphabétiques découvertes à Ras Shamra-Ugarit de 1929 à 1939.*
EA	El-Amarna.
EHO	Frank M. Cross and David N. Freedman, *Early Hebrew Orthography.*
EI	*Eretz-Israel.*
ESA	Epigraphic South Arabian.
Eth.	Ethiopic.
Fekh.	Fekheriyeh Aramaic inscription.
GAG	Wolfram von Soden, *Grundriss der akkadischen Grammatik.*
GKC	*Gesenius' Hebrew Grammar,* edited by E. Kautzsch and A. E. Cowley. 28th ed.

GvG	Carl Brockelmann, *Grundriss der vergleichenden Grammatik der semitischen Sprachen*. 2 vols.
H	Hadad inscription (KAI 214).
Hesh. Ost.	Heshbon ostracon.
HTR	*Harvard Theological Review*.
HUCA	*Hebrew Union College Annual*.
IEJ	*Israel Exploration Journal*.
IJAL	*International Journal of American Linguistics*.
JANES	*Journal of the Ancient Near Eastern Society of Columbia University*.
JAOS	*Journal of the American Oriental Society*.
JBL	*Journal of Biblical Literature*.
JCS	*Journal of Cuneiform Studies*.
JJS	*Journal of Jewish Studies*.
JKF	*Jahrbuch für kleinasiatische Forschung*.
JNES	*Journal of Near Eastern Studies*.
JNSL	*Journal of Northwest Semitic Languages*.
JPOS	*Journal of the Palestine Oriental Society*.
JSS	*Journal of Semitic Studies*.
KAI	Herbert Donner and Wolfgang Röllig, *Kanaanäische und aramäische Inschriften*. 3 vols.
KAI	Ibid. (text number).
Lach.	Lachish letter.
Lg.	*Language*.
MDOG	*Mitteilungen der Deutschen Orient-Gesellschaft*.
Mur.	Murabbaʿât Hebrew inscription.
MUSJ	*Mélanges de l'Université Saint-Joseph*.
MVÄG	Mitteilungen der Vorderasiatisch-Aegyptischen Gesellschaft.
NESE	*Neue Ephemeris für Semitische Epigraphie*.
NP	Neo-Punic inscription (see KAI 3: 74–77).
NSI	George A. Cooke, *A Text-Book of North-Semitic Inscriptions*.
NWS	Northwest Semitic.
O	Object.
OLP	*Orientalia Lovaniensia Periodica*.
OLZ	*Orientalistische Literaturzeitung*.
Or	*Orientalia* (Nova series).

Or Ant	*Oriens Antiquus.*
P	Panammu inscription (KAI 215).
PAPhS	*Proceedings of the American Philosophical Society.*
PEFQS	*Palestine Exploration Fund, Quarterly Statement.*
PEQ	*Palestine Exploration Quarterly.*
PN	Personal name.
PPG	Johannes Friedrich, *Phönizisch-Punische Grammatik.*
PPG²	Johannes Friedrich and Wolfgang Röllig, *Phönizisch-Punische Grammatik.* 2nd ed.
QDAP	*Quarterly of the Department of Antiquities of Palestine.*
RA	*Revue d'Assyriologie et d'archéologie orientale.*
RB	*Revue biblique.*
RHR	*Revue de l'histoire des religions.*
RS	*Revue sémitique.*
RSF	*Rivista di studi fenici.*
RSO	*Rivista degli studi orientali.*
S	Subject.
SBLMS	Society of Biblical Literature, Monograph Series.
Sf.	Sfire inscription (KAI 222–224).
Sir.	Tell Siran bottle inscription.
SMS	*Syro-Mesopotamian Studies.*
UT	Cyrus H. Gordon, *Ugaritic Textbook.*
UT	Ibid. (text number).
V	Verb.
V	Vowel.
VESO	William F. Albright, *The Vocalization of the Egyptian Syllabic Orthography.*
VT	*Vetus Testamentum.*
VTS	Vetus Testamentum, Supplement.
WO	*Die Welt des Orients.*
WZKM	*Wiener Zeitschrift für die Kunde des Morgenlandes.*
ZA	*Zeitschrift für Assyriologie und verwandte Gebiete.*
ZAW	*Zeitschrift für die alttestamentliche Wissenschaft.*
ZDMG	*Zeitschrift der Deutschen Morgenländischen Gesellschaft.*
ZDPV	*Zeitschrift des Deutschen Palästina-Vereins.*
ZS	*Zeitschrift für Semitistik und verwandte Gebiete.*

CHAPTER ONE

INTRODUCTION

Dialectal variation in a given area is not only a linguistic phenomenon but also a by-product of historical, political, and socioeconomic forces. Other factors also influence dialect formation, be they the physical contours of the land (for example, mountains), political boundaries, trade routes, or religious taboos. Dialectal variation results from a complex of factors which affect, either directly or indirectly, human communication.[1]

The area under examination is Syria-Palestine, between 1000 and 586 B.C.E. This period was selected for several reasons. First, it marks the beginning and end of the Israelite state; 1000 B.C.E. is a convenient date for the beginning of the Davidic rule, and 586 B.C.E. marks the fall of Jerusalem.[2] The dates chosen thus represent the time during which Israel was a political and military entity. Second, something of the history of Syria-Palestine during this period is known.[3] The alliances of the individual nations, their battles, their social and economic contacts—these types of human interaction affect linguistic contact between peoples. Third, these dates were chosen for the purely practical reason of including as many texts as possible in this study. The larger the data base, the greater the possibility of drawing accurate linguistic conclusions from the available inscriptions. Thus the period 1000–586 B.C.E. provides an acceptable chronological frame from both the historical and linguistic viewpoint.

The relationship among the Northwest Semitic speech forms[4] of Syria-Palestine from 1000 to 586 B.C.E. is complex. In this relatively small area, there appear to be a number of discrete speech forms. While some speech forms cluster into groups, as for example the Aramaic-speaking communities in the North, others appear idiosyncratic, as for example the dialect of Deir Alla. By assembling all available data, it should be possible to classify each speech form and explain the linguistic relationship among the NWS dialects.

In the past, linguistic classification of the NWS dialects has yielded differing results. For example Albright[5] subdivided Canaanite into northern (the area around Ugarit),[6] eastern (Syrian desert to Sinai, and parts of Palestine), southern (Phoenicia, and most of Syria-Palestine), and Hebraic branches (Jerusalem). In his Phoenician grammar, Harris[7] adopted Albright's basic classification but divided the area into North (Ugarit), Middle (Phoenicia), and South (southern Syria, and Palestine). And Segert[8] proposed the divisions into northern (Ugarit), inland (Hebrew/Israel), coastal (Phoenicia), and peripheral inland groups (Ammon, Moab, and Edom). These scholars either adduced one linguistic feature to support their classification or adduced no linguistic features at all; in the latter case, their general survey of the material led them to their particular classification.

Classification of the individual NWS dialects has been equally idiosyncratic. Examination of the Deir Alla dialect has yielded classifications as Old Aramaic,[9] Ammonite,[10] South Canaanite,[11] Midianite,[12] and Gileadite.[13] Samalian has been classified as a local Aramaic[14] and as an independent dialect.[15] Similarly, Ammonite is seen to be South Canaanite[16] or North Arabic.[17] Many of the variations in the classification of the individual dialects have resulted from the actual choice of linguistic features deemed dialectally significant for classification.

In all these cases, the classificatory scheme is methodologically constrained. Either the classification proceeds from an impressionistic inspection of the material.[18] Or, the classification is based upon those particular linguistic elements selected for examination.[19] The lack of methodological controls in both cases has made resultant classifications highly subjective.[20]

The method and results of dialect geography produce a new perspective on the interrelationship and classification of the NWS dialects. Dialect geography is, in effect, the study of linguistic differentiation and interrelation in a given area at a given time.[21] It seeks a planar layout[22] of all linguistic features which differentiate speech areas. Dialect geography seeks an aerial view of linguistic differentiation by plotting all dialectally significant linguistic features on a map.

On the one hand, dialect geography traces individual linguistic features throughout a region.[23] An isogloss, or linguistic boundary line, is then drawn between the areas where one feature is found and those where a different feature occurs. The isoglosses of all features mapped can then be compared to see how the distribution of isoglosses varies throughout the area. At this level, dialect geography enables the scholar to see the interrelationships between the dialects.

On the other hand, however, dialect geography is, according to Bloomfield, "the study of local differentiations in a speech-area."[24] The focus shifts from the examination of linguistic features and their distribution to the description of individual dialect regions. Each speech area is characterized by its unique distribution, and combination, of features.[25] Dialect geography "seeks to provide an empirical basis for conclusions about the linguistic variety that occurs in a certain locale."[26] At this level, dialect geography enables the scholar to characterize the individual dialects.

In its utilization of every linguistic feature differentiating speech areas, dialect geography seeks a complete data base in determining dialectal relationship. All features, whether phonological, morphological, syntactic, or lexical, are charted on maps, provided that each feature sets off one dialectal region from another. The features themselves are of equal importance; no one differentiating feature is, *a priori*, more important than another.[27] The planar presentation of all such features in an area is a goal of dialect geography.

Some of the results of dialect geographical studies are important in a classification of the NWS dialects. Studies of dialect geography have shown that linguistic changes spread from one area to another, through different types of human contact.[28] A number of changes may originate in a single place and slowly diffuse to outlying regions. Areas where such changes cluster are linguistic centers; outlying areas which display some, but not all, of the changes are marginal, or peripheral.[29] An area which did not receive changes is isolated as a dialect island; conversely, a dialect island is one where a number of changes occurred but did not spread outward.[30] Further, areas which accept changes of two linguistic centers, or lie midway between them linguistically, are transitional, since they bear characteristics of both centers.[31]

Three[32] scholars have been especially important in the application of dialect geography to Syria-Palestine.[33] Bergsträsser[34] is methodologically most conservative. In his study of modern, spoken Arabic dialects in Syria-Palestine, he has presented the spread of relevant linguistic data on individual maps. He has also correlated physical and social boundaries with linguistic (dialectal) divisions.[35] Bergsträsser has avoided classification and dialect characterization altogether[36] but has presented the spread of dialectally significant linguistic elements—phonological, morphological, syntactic, and lexical—throughout Syria-Palestine.

Harris expanded Bergsträsser's scope of inquiry in his *Development of the Canaanite Dialects*.[37] His book is properly a "linguistic history" of Syria-Palestine; Harris' principal concern is diachrony. Instead of presenting a static picture of the distribution of linguistic elements in a restricted area, as Bergsträsser intended,[38] Harris traced the development and diffusion of linguistic changes throughout the history of the Canaanite language group. In his concluding analysis, however, Harris returned to the synchronic domain of dialect geography and briefly characterized "the resultant dialects" which emerged in the course of the linguistic development.

Harris predicated a division of the Canaanite dialects upon a detailed analysis of the linguistic evidence. This linguistic history suggested, according to Harris, a dialectal division into coastal (Ugarit, Samʾal, and Phoenicia) and inland groups (Hebrew, Moab, and Hamat[39]).[40] Coastal dialects were the more innovative, since many changes occurred there. Inland dialects tended to be conservative, for they not only produced few convergent changes but also did not accept every change which took place on the coast.[41] Like Bergsträsser, Harris based his linguistic divisions upon linguistic data, instead of upon an impressionistic survey of the evidence. Unlike Bergsträsser, however, Harris qualitatively evaluated the linguistic evidence and proposed a linguistic classification based upon the types of linguistic changes apparent in each area.

Rabin[42] synthesized the work of Bergsträsser and Harris, while expanding its scope still further. Like Bergsträsser's, Rabin's study is synchronic, "ignoring the time factor and treating the various dialects as coexisting each in the location in which we first encounter it. . . ."[43] Like Harris, Rabin applied the methodology and concepts of dialect geography to Semitic (as for example innovative and conservative areas [central and marginal] and transitional areas). On the basis of the particular distribution of linguistic elements, Rabin sought a new classification of the Semitic languages. He divided them into northern marginal (Fertile Crescent), southern marginal (Aksum influence), and central areas (Mediterranean to Arabia).[44]

Each of these scholars has had his methodological successors. Garbini's *Il semitico di nord-ovest*[45] most closely approximates Bergsträsser's approach to dialectology. In this book, Garbini traced individual phonological, accentual, and morphological features which differentiate the Northwest Semitic dialects. Like Bergsträsser, Garbini assembled and examined every linguistic feature deemed dialectally significant in NWS.[46] Unlike Bergsträsser, though, Garbini's goal was the characterization of the individual dialects in a historical frame.

Harris' concluding classification of coastal vs. inland Canaanite has gained only one partial supporter. Segert[47] adopted a classification approximating Harris', dividing the Canaanite dialects into northern, coastal, inland, and peripheral inland groups. But the similarity between Segert's and Harris' divisions was largely coincidental; Harris based his conclusions upon linguistic features, whereas Segert's divisions were, in effect, largely geographical in nature.

Methodologically, however, several scholars have followed Harris' lead in distinguishing between conservative and innovative dialect(al area)s. Rabin was the first to apply this method to the classification of the Semitic languages in general. Diakonoff[48] also applied this method to the Semitic languages, but he concluded that they could be accurately divided into northern peripheral (Akkadian), northern central (NWS), southern central (Arabic dialects), and southern peripheral groups (South Arabian and Ethiopic). And finally, Garbini[49] followed Rabin by pinpointing the innovative area of the Semitic languages in Syria-Palestine itself, but attributed the innovative impulse to a progressive "Amoritization." According to

Garbini,[50] Rabin's "central axis" corresponded to a proposed Amorite-Aramaic-Arabic language group.

« »   « »

This study employs much of the methodology which scholars have previously used. It has two goals. The first, following Bergsträsser, is the isolation and presentation of all dialectally significant linguistic features. Any feature, whether phonological, morphological, or syntactic, which divides Syria-Palestine into dialect regions is traced throughout the first-millennium NWS dialects. The result is a tabular display of the distribution of features throughout the dialects.

Whereas phonology, morphology, and syntax are employed in the dialectal analysis, it is impossible to analyze the lexicon for this purpose.[51] Although such an analysis is potentially valid for first-millennium NWS, the extant texts do not offer sufficient lexical material to make possible an interdialectal analysis. Lexical comparison should be based upon a standardized list of core vocabulary items found in all cultures at all times—the Swadesh list.[52] Yet few of the lexical items in the Swadesh list appear in the preserved texts. Without complete Swadesh lists for each dialect, lexical comparison becomes inexact. Although a lexical analysis may be used in the future, with the discovery of additional texts, it is not feasible at present.

While the first goal of this study is the presentation of distinctive dialect features in first-millennium NWS, the second is the classification of the extant dialects on the basis of these features. The focus shifts from the distribution of features themselves to the composition of the individual dialects. The features will be analyzed in order to produce a classificatory scheme based on the totality of linguistic features present. Like Harris and Rabin, then, this study seeks to produce a linguistic classification based upon an analysis of significant diagnostic linguistic features. The result is an organic classificatory scheme of NWS dialects in Syria-Palestine in the early first millennium B.C.E.

« »   « »

In this study, "Syria-Palestine" is used in its widest sense. It includes not only ancient Israel (Palestine) and the Aramean states

(Syria), but also the Transjordanian states of Ammon, Moab, and Edom, the coastal city-states of Phoenicia, as well as the polyglottal communities on the northern periphery, as for example Karatepe (Syria-Anatolia) and Arslan Tash (Syria-Mesopotamia). "Syria-Palestine" designates all areas west and north of the Syrian desert in which a Northwest Semitic dialect was spoken.

In this sense, Syria-Palestine was a geographical unit.[53] It was set within the confines of the Mediterranean Sea (west), the desert (east and south) and the northern mountain ranges. Yet the area was not physically homogeneous. Mountains, rivers, valleys, deserts, forests, and other physical features divided Syria-Palestine into numerous geographical subunits. Within a short distance, the topography could vary considerably. In general, the terrain is rough and dry.

The topography of Syria-Palestine did not promote easy communication. The land itself was composed of small geographical subunits disconnected from other subunits; its effect was to isolate instead of to facilitate communication. People tended not to move about freely but stayed in their own region. Communication tended to be local.[54]

Topography also contributed to the appearance of independent local governments throughout Syria-Palestine. In pre-Davidic times, the area was characterized by numerous, city-state, political systems governed by local chiefs. In the Aramean and Phoenician city-states, Edom, and Israel, government was local and independent. Centralization, and national unity, developed somewhat later in certain parts of the region, notably in Jerusalem. The overall picture of Syro-Palestinian government is political segmentation.[55]

Trade routes served to counterbalance this tendency to fragmentation.[56] Two principal trade routes cut through the area longitudinally, and a series of lesser routes bridged the eastern and western extremes. The *Via Maris* connected Phoenicia, Israel, and Judah through its various branches. The King's Highway traversed Transjordan from Damascus, through Ammon and Moab, to Edom. Other routes ran between larger cities in the interior and provided a complex network of trade and communication.

The western seaports, the eastern trade stations, and all other points on the edge of these routes were extremely important in the linguistic development of Syria-Palestine. Since these areas lay on the periphery, their inhabitants communicated with foreigners, ex-

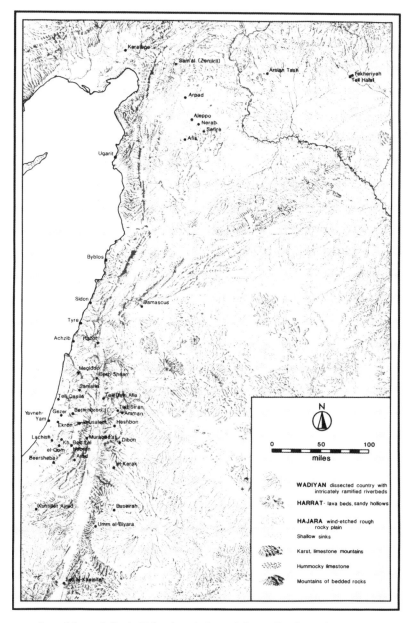

MAP 1:   Map of Syria-Palestine (adopted from Erwin Raisz' Landform Map of the Near East).

changed both commodities and ideas, and served not only as commercial centers but as cultural centers as well. Through travel and trade along these routes, new ideas and ways were brought to the interior. In this way, the obstacles of the topography and polity were partially overcome. Although communication was essentially local, new forms of speech gradually filtered through the land as a result of these traveling traders.

« »   « »

Dialect geography is usually concerned with the recording and mapping of current speech patterns.[57] Dialect geographers are able to talk to their informants, elicit a number of responses, and record the different responses from each speaker. The informants themselves are carefully selected. They should be native to the area examined without having traveled a great deal, they should have been schooled in their own communities, and they should speak the dialect of their particular community.[58] In eliciting responses, the dialect geographer tries to engage the informant in a natural, unselfconscious speech; he wants to capture the everyday, common speech pattern.[59]

Similarly, the choice of communities examined is important. A variety of community types ensures a variety of informants.[60] Native speech patterns are best seen in long-settled, nonurban, sedentary communities; the absence of newcomers guards against serious external linguistic influence, while the sedentary nature of the community itself keeps speech patterns native and internal. A community may be located in a variety of places—for example in the hills or on a plain—which will likewise affect settlement and speech patterns. Of course, social structure within each community has its effect on speech patterns as well.[61]

The procedure in studying urban dialectology is more unsure.[62] The representativeness of the informants of native speech patterns becomes uncertain because of the size and complexity of the community. The "normal" speech of the larger communities is difficult to capture; socially, culturally, and economically stratified societies produce a variety of speech patterns. Because of the diversity of informants, many factors complicate a study of dialect geography in urban areas.

The method of gaining linguistic information must be modified when treating an ancient period.[63] Informants cannot be questioned. Communities and native speakers cannot be selected firsthand for investigation. It may be impossible to isolate nonlinguistic factors affecting speech habits, as for example class and occupation. In other words, the linguistic investigator is largely dependent upon the preserved sources.

These sources are written. Linguistic information, then, is gained through the intermediary of the written language. Phonetic differences in speech, exact phonetic realizations of phonemes, and regional language variation must be filtered through the camouflage of the written language.[64] Although the written and spoken languages were not necessarily different,[65] the conventional practices of orthography did tend to obscure individual linguistic differences among speakers.[66] The written language, then, had a leveling effect.

The texts themselves are not consistent. There are royal inscriptions, commemorative and funerary inscriptions, graffiti, letters, and other kinds of documents, each written for a different purpose and by people of different backgrounds and classes.[67] The representativeness of such texts, vis-à-vis the entire population, is uncertain. Further, since some texts are literary and designed to be preserved into future generations, individual linguistic differences may have been suppressed. The requirements of the standard literary language can, in many cases, have superseded the speech form of the speaker.[68] Many dialectal differences, then, cannot be recovered.

Further, the dates of the texts vary considerably. The Gezer Calendar is dated to the tenth century B.C.E., and the Old Byblian inscriptions are roughly contemporary. The Mesha inscription is mid-ninth century. The Hadad and Panammu inscriptions date from a century later. And the Lachish letters are sixth-century documents. These texts, then, are not contemporary in the strictest sense.

The scribal intermediary also complicates the recovery of linguistic data. Since scribes were school-trained, they wrote in the literary, educated language of the elite, not that of the common individual. Further, a scribe may have written texts in his native tongue as well as that of another; for example, the "Aramaic" scribal practices in the Arslan Tash Phoenician texts suggest that the scribe was not Phoenician but Aramean.[69] Scribes were also imported from the outside to write royal inscriptions and other documents.[70] Thus the scribe brings new problems to the use of the epigraphic material for dialectological study. The possible nonrepresentativeness of the inscriptions, then, is a warning against attaching too much importance to each document.

Native speech patterns may be difficult to recover on the basis of the extant texts. In several communities, at least two different dialects may have been spoken concurrently. For example, both Aramaic texts and texts of another, unidentified dialect were found in Deir Alla.[71] Aramaic and Phoenician texts were found in Arslan Tash. Akkadian and Aramaic texts appeared in Tell Fekheriyeh. Karatepe shows Phoenician and Hittite texts. And Samʾal witnesses texts in Phoenician, Aramaic, and the local Samalian dialect. It is unclear, then, whether native speakers were multilingual or whether only the scribes were versed in different speech forms.

Transplanted languages also present difficulties to linguistic analysis.[72] The degree to which the transplanted language represents the speech form of the homeland and the degree to which it has changed in its new environment are immediate problems. For example, commercial interests brought the Phoenicians far afield to areas where no Semitic language was spoken. The Phoenician of Karatepe represents such a transplantation; the Phoenician language had been carried to far-off Anatolia.[73] Ironically, in the case of Phoenician, transplantations constitute the largest bulk of standard Phoenician linguistic data.

The difficulties in evaluating the linguistic material of first-millennium Syria-Palestine are unquestionable. In order to obviate some of these difficulties, it is best to assemble NWS linguistic evidence from all extant texts. Although the texts are unevenly distributed throughout the area, they provide the greatest clue to speech patterns. It is impossible to conduct a random sample[74] or a selective, systematic survey[75] on the basis of the present data base, since the texts are relatively few. Within these limitations, only a complete assembly of texts can provide the basis for a dialect map of Syria-Palestine.

The inscriptions themselves provide the largest, and most valuable, data base for a study of Syro-Palestinian dialect geography in the first millennium B.C.E. Since the provenience and date of the texts are known for the most part, they can be used as evidence of a particular community's speech form. Thus inscriptions are the primary linguistic source in this study.

If, however, direct evidence for a particular linguistic feature is missing from epigraphic sources, other material must be consulted. Personal names may reflect native speech patterns and therefore may be helpful in dialectal study. For example, Hallo and Tadmor[76] have noted "the earliest evidence for the sound-shift â > ô" in the personal name $^{m}DUMU$-ḫa-nu-ta; the element ḫa-nu-ta, [ʿanōt],[77] is a doublet of *ʿanāt. Bauer[78] has made a synthetic study of Hebrew personal names in order to show the different phonological, morphological, and lexical influences they reflect. And Rabin[79] has shown that biblical personal names conform to the Barth-Ginsberg law. Personal names, then, may fill the gap when epigraphic material yields no linguistic information.

Where no contemporary linguistic data are available, later linguistic material may be consulted. For example, if a certain feature does not appear in the extant Phoenician texts of 1000–586 B.C.E., the evidence of Punic may be used as indirect testimony of the feature in the older linguistic phase. Similarly, if a feature does not appear in the extant epigraphic Hebrew texts, Masoretic Hebrew may be adduced as evidence. But, in this case, Masoretic Hebrew is used with caution. It does not represent one Hebrew dialect but probably a mixture of dialect traditions.[80] Further, some regular features of Masoretic Hebrew, such as anaptyxis in *$qVtl$- nouns, are demonstrably late;[81] the projection of late features into the early first millennium B.C.E. would be a false inference. Thus biblical Hebrew evidence can be used only when it is apparently representative of the earlier language as well.

Scholars have also employed place names in linguistic analysis. The changes reflected in a place name may reflect changes in the native, spoken language. Gelb,[82] for example, distinguished second-millennium Canaanite (Palestine and Phoenicia) from Amorite (Amurru, Alalakh, and Ugarit) on the basis of place names ending in -ūna/i vs. -ānu; according to Gelb, the ū of -ūna/i reflects the Canaanite correspondence *á:[ó]. Friedrich[83] claimed that the vowel shift *ā > [ō] reached the Phoenician coast only by the eighth century, pointing to the place names Ba-ʾ-li-ra-si (Shalmaneser III, 858–824) and Ba-ʾ-li-ṣa-pu-na (Tiglath-Pileser III, 747–727) as proof.

Yet place names do not necessarily reflect current speech patterns. Because a place name may be much older than contemporary speech, it may reflect an older language phase.[84] And, the interpretation of individual names often differs among scholars,[85] making the linguistic analysis of a name difficult.

Not all linguistic sources are equally reliable. For the purpose of Syro-Palestinian dialect geography, inscriptions offer the most secure linguistic material. They also represent the most complete collection of linguistic material preserved from this early period. Personal names can fill in needed gaps in the epigraphic data, as can the evidence from later sources. Later sources, of course, can provide only the basis for linguistic inferences in previous history. Finally, place names are used sparingly, only in the absence of more reliable evidence. For the present study, linguistic data must be collected from all available sources and used discriminately.

« »   « »

What follows is a list of linguistic features which differentiate the first-millennium Northwest Semitic dialects. Texts within each dialect are grouped under their conventional dialect names: Phoenician, Aramaic, Samalian,[86] Ammonite, Deir Alla, Moabite, Edomite, and Hebrew. This procedure follows traditional classification of the texts[87] and facilitates an easy comparison of dialects. Wherever possible, dialectal subgroupings are isolated, as for example Byblian Phoenician when it differs from standard Phoenician, the speech form of most Phoenician-speaking communities. Frequently, the Old Aramaic texts differ from one another on particular linguistic features; in these cases, the dialectal differences within each dialect are fully treated. Dialect headings are used for convenient reference and are not prejudicial to the final classification scheme in Chapter 5.

The dialects are presented in a certain geographical order. Beginning on the western coast (Phoenicia), the route proceeds north (Aram; Sam'al), through Transjordan and back toward Palestine (Israel and Judah). Unless otherwise noted, Phoenician, Aramaic, Samalian, Moabite, and Hebrew texts are cited according to the readings of *KAI*. Wherever necessary, however, the readings of *KAI* have been corrected according to more recent studies. Well-known texts in those dialects not included in *KAI* are cited according to the *editio princeps* and any later studies.[88] Ammonite,[89] Deir Alla,[90] and Edomite[91] texts are also cited according to the *editio princeps*. Bibliographic citations are provided for less well-known texts.

Notes to Chapter 1

1. Leonard Bloomfield, *Language* (New York: Holt, Rinehart & Winston, 1933), p. 343; André Martinet, "Diffusion of Language and Structural Linguistics," *Romance Philology* 6 (1952): 5; and Joseph H. Greenberg, *Essays in Linguistics* (Chicago: The University of Chicago Press, 1957), p. 54.

2. On the problem of dating the fall of Jerusalem, see David N. Freedman, "The Babylonian Chronicle," *BA* 19 (1956): 55 n. 20; and B. Oded, "Judah and the Exile," in *Israelite and Judaean History*, ed. John H. Hayes and J. Maxwell Miller (Philadelphia: The Westminster Press, 1977), pp. 474–475.

3. Although a comprehensive history of Syria-Palestine during the first millennium B.C.E. remains to be written, the history of several individual states has appeared. For Aram, see André Dupont-Sommer, *Les araméens*, L'orient ancien illustré, vol. 2 (Paris: A. Maisonneuve, 1949), and Abraham Malamat, "The Aramaeans," in *Peoples of Old Testament Times*, ed. D. J. Wiseman (Oxford: Oxford University Press, 1973), pp. 134–155. For Sam'al, see Benno Landsberger, *Sam'al. Studien zur Entdeckung der Ruinenstaette Karatepe*, Veröffentlichungen der türkischen historischen Gesellschaft, Series 7, no. 16 (Ankara: Türkische historische Gesellschaft, 1948). For Ammon, see George M. Landes, "Ammon, Ammonites," in *The Interpreter's Dictionary of the Bible*, 4 vols. (Nashville/New York: Abingdon Press, 1962), 1:108–114, and B. Oded, "Ammon, Ammonites," in *Encyclopaedia Judaica*, 16 vols. (Jerusalem: Keter Publishing House, 1971–1972), 2:853–859. For Edom, see Manfred Weippert, "Edom. Studien und Materialien zur Geschichte der Edomiter auf Grund schriftlicher und archäologischer Quellen" (Inaugural-Dissertation, Eberhard-Karl-Universität, 1971). And for Israel, see the standard histories.

4. For the term, see Edward Sapir, "Dialect," in *Encyclopaedia of the Social Sciences*, ed. Edwin R. A. Seligman and Alvin Johnson, 15 vols. (New York: Macmillan Co., 1930–1935), 5:123–126. In this study, "speech form" and "dialect" (see recently I. M. Diakonoff, "Earliest Semites in Asia. Agriculture and Animal Husbandry According to Linguistic Data [VIIIth–IVth Millennia B.C.]," *AoF* 8 [1981]: 24 n. 1) are interchangeable.

5. William F. Albright, "The Northwest-Semitic Tongues before 1000 B.C.," in *Atti del XIX congresso internazionale degli orientalisti . . . 1935* (Rome: Tipografia del Senato, G. Bardi, 1938), p. 448. Cf. idem, "Recent Progress in North-Canaanite Research," *BASOR* 70 (1938): 21.

6. Albright used "North-Canaanite" as a synonym for Ugaritic already in his first two publications on Ugaritic. See "New Light on Early Canaanite Language and Literature," *BASOR* 46 (1932): 17, 19, and "The North-Canaanite Epic of 'Al'êyân Ba'al and Môt," *JPOS* 12 (1932): 185.

7. Zellig S. Harris, *A Grammar of the Phoenician Language*, American Oriental Series, vol. 8 (New Haven: American Oriental Society, 1936), p. 7 with n. 31.

8. Stanislav Segert, *A Grammar of Phoenician and Punic* (Munich: C. H. Beck, 1976), §§12.36, 12.38.

9. For example, J. Hoftijzer, "Interpretation and Grammar," in *Aramaic Texts from Deir ʿAlla*, ed. J. Hoftijzer and G. van der Kooij. Documenta et Monumenta Orientis Antiqui, vol. 19 (Leiden: E. J. Brill, 1976), p. 300; and Joseph A. Fitzmyer, "[Review of Hoftijzer and van der Kooij, eds., *Aramaic Texts*]," *CBQ* 40 (1978): 94.

10. Jonas C. Greenfield, "[Review of Hoftijzer and van der Kooij, eds., *Aramaic Texts*]," *JSS* 25 (1980): 251.

11. Jo Ann Carlton (Hackett), "Studies in the Plaster Text from Tell Deir ʿAllā" (Ph.D. dissertation, Harvard University, 1980), pp. 186–189; and idem, "The Dialect of the Plaster Text from Tell Deir ʿAlla," *Or* 53 (1984): 64.

12. Alexander Rofé, *The Book of Balaam* (*Numbers 22:2–24:25*), Jerusalem Biblical Studies, vol. 1 (Jerusalem: Simor, 1979), pp. 69–70 (in Hebrew).

13. Joseph Naveh, "[Review of Hoftijzer and van der Kooij, eds., *Aramaic Texts*]," *IEJ* 29 (1979): 136 (one alternative).

14. So, for example, Greenfield, "Dialect Traits in Early Aramaic," *Leshonenu* 32 (1968): 363, 361 (in Hebrew); idem, "The Dialects of Early Aramaic," *JNES* 37 (1978): 94; and Fitzmyer, "The Phases of the Aramaic Language," in idem, *A Wandering Aramean: Collected Aramaic Essays*, SBLMS, vol. 25 (Missoula: Scholars Press, 1979), p. 77 n. 30.

15. So, for example, Johannes Friedrich, *PPG*, p. 162; idem, "Zur Stellung des Jaudischen in der nordwestsemitischen Sprachgeschichte," in *Studies in Honor of Benno Landsberger . . . 1965*, Assyriological Studies, vol. 16 (Chicago: The University of Chicago Press, 1965), p. 429; and Giovanni Garbini, "Studi aramaici—1–2," *AION* 19 (1969): 7.

16. Frank M. Cross, "Ammonite Ostraca from Heshbon: Heshbon Ostraca IV–VIII," *AUSS* 13 (1975): 17–18.

17. Garbini, *Le lingue semitiche. Studi di storia linguistica* (Naples: Istituto orientale di Napoli, 1972), p. 107 (one alternative).

18. Isidore Dyen, "[Review of Dahl, *Malgache et maanjan*]," *Lg.* 29 (1953): 580.

19. L. Gauchat, "Gibt es Mundartgrenzen?" *Archiv für das Studium der neueren Sprachen und Literaturen* 111 (1903): 378.

20. Harris, *Development of the Canaanite Dialects*, American Oriental Series, vol. 16 (New Haven: American Oriental Society, 1939), p. 98 n. 8; and William G. Moulton, "Structural Dialectology," *Lg.* 44 (1968): 456.

21. Gotthelf Bergsträsser, "In Sachen meines 'Sprachatlas,'" *ZS* 1 (1922): 220–221; Hans Kurath, *Studies in Area Linguistics* (Bloomington/London: Indiana University Press, 1972), p. 75; and J. K. Chambers and Peter Trudgill, *Dialectology* (Cambridge: Cambridge University Press,

1980), p. 24. Cf. Sabatino Moscati, *The Semites in Ancient History* (Cardiff: University of Wales Press, 1959), p. 99; and Franz Rosenthal, "[Review of Friedrich, *PPG*]," *JAOS* 72 (1952): 172.

22. Dyen (private communication).

23. Cf. Harris, *Development*, p. 16.

24. Bloomfield, *Language*, p. 321.

25. Ibid., p. 325.

26. Chambers and Trudgill, *Dialectology*, p. 24.

27. Ibid., p. 112; and Lawrence M. Davis, "Dialectology and Linguistics," *Orbis* 26 (1977): 25.

28. Bloomfield, *Language*, p. 323.

29. See, for example, Harris, *Development*, p. 1.

30. See Charles F. Hockett, *A Course in Modern Linguistics* (New York: Macmillan Publishing Co., 1958), p. 481; and Raimo Anttila, *An Introduction to Historical and Comparative Linguistics* (New York/London: Macmillan Publishing Co./Collier Macmillan Publishers, 1972), p. 294.

31. Pavle Ivić, "On the Structure of Dialectal Differentiation," *Word* 18 (1962): 43; and Anttila, *Introduction*, p. 298.

32. Albright never published his dialect maps of third-millennium Palestine, mentioned in "Notes on Early Hebrew and Aramaic Epigraphy," *JPOS* 6 (1926): 82 n. 15.

33. See also Sever Pop, *La dialectologie. Aperçu historique et Méthodes d'enquêtes linguistiques,* Université de Louvain, Récueil de travaux d'histoire et de philologie, 3ᵉ Série, Fascicules 38/39, 2 vols. (Louvain/Gembloux: [private]/J. Duculot, 1950), esp. 2:1091–1100.

34. Bergsträsser, "Sprachatlas von Syrien und Palästina," *ZDPV* 38 (1915): 169–222; cf. idem, *ZS* 1 (1922): 218–226.

35. See especially his methodological statement, *ZS* 1 (1922): 220–221.

36. Ibid., p. 220.

37. Harris, *Development*.

38. Bergsträsser, *ZS* 1 (1922): 220.

39. Although Harris included the Zkr inscription in his study of Canaanite (see *Development*, p. 18), the language of this text is generally classified as Old Aramaic.

40. Ibid., p. 98. Cf. H. L. Ginsberg, "[Review of Harris, *Development*]," *JBL* 59 (1940): 550.

41. Harris, *Development*, p. 98.

42. Chaim Rabin, "The Origin of the Subdivisions of Semitic," in *Hebrew and Semitic Studies Presented to Godfrey Rolles Driver,* ed. D. Winton Thomas and W. D. McHardy (Oxford: Oxford University Press, 1963), pp. 104–115.

43. Ibid., p. 106.

44. For criticism of Rabin's method, see Joshua Blau, "Hebrew and North West Semitic: Reflections on the Classification of the Semitic Languages," *Hebrew Annual Review* 2 (1978): 22 n. 2.

45. Garbini, *Il semitico di nord-ovest,* Quaderni della sezione linguistica degli Annali, vol. 1 (Naples: Istituto universitario orientale di Napoli, 1960).

46. See also Haim Blanc, *Communal Dialects in Baghdad*, Harvard Middle Eastern Monographs, vol. 10 (Cambridge: Harvard University Press, 1964) for methodological similarities.

47. See n. 8 above.

48. Diakonoff, *Semito-Hamitic Languages. An Essay in Classification* (Moscow: Nauka Publishing House, 1965), pp. 11–12.

49. Garbini, *Le lingue*, pp. 15, 36.

50. Ibid., p. 15.

51. For recent attempts at lexical analysis in Semitic, see Rabin, "Lexicostatistics and the Internal Divisions of Semitic," in *Hamito-Semitica*, ed. James and Theodora Bynon. Janua Linguarum, Series Practica, vol. 200 (The Hague/Paris: Mouton, 1975), pp. 85–99; Diakonoff, "Linguistic Data on the History of the Most Ancient Speakers of Afrasian Languages," *Africana* 10 (1975): 117–130 (in Russian); and Dyen, "Lexicostatistics: Present and Prospects," in *Lexicostatistics in Genetic Linguistics II: Proceedings of the Montreal Conference . . . 1973*, ed. Isidore Dyen and Guy Jucquois. Cahiers de l'Institut de Linguistique de Louvain, vol. 3, pt. 5–6 (Louvain: Imprimerie Orientaliste, 1976), pp. 20–21, 25.

52. Morris Swadesh, "Lexico-statistic Dating of Prehistoric Ethnic Contacts with Special Reference to North American Indians and Eskimos," *PAPhS* 96 (1952): 452–463; and idem, "Towards Greater Accuracy in Lexicostatistic Dating," *IJAL* 21 (1955): 121–137.

53. Moscati, *The Semites*, p. 76; and Masao Sekine, "The Subdivisions of the North-West Semitic Languages," *JSS* 18 (1973): 206. Cf. Albright, "Some Canaanite-Phoenician Sources of Hebrew Wisdom," in *Wisdom in Israel and in the Ancient Near East*, ed. M. Noth and D. Winton Thomas. VTS, vol. 3 (Leiden: E. J. Brill, 1955), p. 2. For the following discussion, see Yohanan Aharoni, *The Land of the Bible: A Historical Geography*, trans. A. F. Rainey. 2nd ed. (Philadelphia: The Westminster Press, 1979).

54. Harris, *Development*, p. 14; and Blau, "Some Difficulties in the Reconstruction of 'Proto-Hebrew' and 'Proto-Canaanite,'" in *In Memoriam Paul Kahle*, ed. Matthew Black and Georg Fohrer. BZAW, vol. 103 (Berlin: A. Töpelmann, 1968), p. 41.

55. Harris, *Development*, pp. 13–14.

56. Kurath, *Studies*, p. 95.

57. See the discussion in Chambers and Trudgill, *Dialectology*, pp. 15–23.

58. Kurath, *Handbook of the Linguistic Geography of New England*, 2nd ed. (New York: AMS Press, 1973), pp. 41, 49; idem, *Studies*, p. 12; and Chambers and Trudgill, *Dialectology*, pp. 33–35.

59. Kurath, *Handbook*, pp. 45, 48.

60. See ibid., pp. 39, 49; idem, *Studies*, pp. 10–11; and Hockett, *Course*, p. 483.

61. Bloomfield, *Language*, p. 345; and Chambers and Trudgill, *Dialectology*, pp. 54–55. See also William Labov, *Sociolinguistic Patterns*, Conduct and Communication, no. 4 (Philadelphia: University of Pennsylvania Press, 1972).

62. Chambers and Trudgill, *Dialectology*, pp. 55–59.

63. See also the study of Middle English cited in Hockett, *Course*, p. 473.

64. Bloomfield, *Language*, pp. 293, 294, 296; Ernst Pulgram, "The Nature and Use of Proto-Languages," *Lingua* 10 (1961): 24; and Anttila, *Introduction*, p. 43.

65. Cf. the recent study by Gary Rendsburg, "Evidence for a Spoken Hebrew in Biblical Times" (Ph.D. dissertation, New York University, 1980).

66. Theodora Bynon, *Historical Linguistics* (Cambridge: Cambridge University Press, 1977), pp. 183, 214. See also Segert, "Aufgaben der biblisch-aramäischen Grammatik," *Communio Viatorum* 1/2–3 (1958): 130.

67. See, for example, B. S. J. Isserlin, "Epigraphically attested Judean Hebrew, and the question of 'upper class' (Official) and 'popular' speech variants in Judea during the 8th–6th centuries B.C.," *AJBA* 2/1 (1972): 197–203.

68. Bloomfield, *Language*, pp. 483, 484; Pulgram, "Spoken and Written Latin," *Lg.* 26 (1950): 459; and Bynon, *Historical Linguistics*, p. 193. See also Rosenthal, "[Review of Harris, *Development*]," *Or* 11 (1942): 181–182; and idem, *JAOS* 72 (1952): 172.

69. Naveh, "[Review of Friedrich and Röllig, *PPG*²]," *JAOS* 93 (1973): 589; Cross, "Leaves from an Epigraphist's Notebook," *CBQ* 36 (1974): 486 n. 4; and Wolfgang Röllig, "Die Amulette von Arslan Taş," *NESE* 2 (1974): 28.

70. See, for example, Albrecht Goetze, "Cilicians," *JCS* 16 (1962): 53–54 n. 45.

71. Naveh, *IEJ* 29 (1979): 136; P. Kyle McCarter, "The Balaam Texts from Deir ʿAllā: The First Combination," *BASOR* 239 (1980): 50; and Hackett, *Or* 53 (1984): 58.

72. Kurath, *Studies*, pp. 104–105, with modern examples on pp. 107–121.

73. Irene J. Winter, "On the Problems of Karatepe: The Reliefs and Their Context," *AS* 29 (1979): 136–140, esp. pp. 138–139.

74. Harris, *Development*, p. 17.

75. Cf. Kurath, *Studies*, pp. 1–2.

76. William W. Hallo and Hayim Tadmor, "A Lawsuit from Hazor," *IEJ* 27 (1977): 4–5.

77. Square brackets indicate the reconstructed pronunciation of words and phonemes.

78. Hans Bauer, "Die hebräischen Eigennamen als sprachliche Erkenntnisquelle," *ZAW* 48 (1930): 73–80.

79. Rabin, "Archaic Vocalisation in Some Biblical Hebrew Names," *JJS* 1 (1948): 22–26.

80. See, for example, Harris, *Development*, p. 23; and Alexander Sperber, *A Historical Grammar of Biblical Hebrew* (Leiden: E. J. Brill, 1966).

81. Harris, *Development*, p. 80.

82. I. J. Gelb, "The Early History of the West Semitic Peoples," *JCS* 15 (1961): 42.

83. Friedrich, "Kanaanäisch und Westsemitisch," *Scientia* 84 (1949): 222, 223 n. 1.

84. Bloomfield, *Language*, pp. 339–340; and Kurath, *Studies*, p. 59. See also Wolfram von Soden, "Zur Einteilung der semitischen Sprachen," *WZKM* 56 (1960): 180.

85. Compare, for example, Gelb (*JCS* 15 [1961]: 43–44), Chaim Brovender ("Hebrew Language. Pre-Biblical," in *Encyclopaedia Judaica*, 16:1564), and Malamat ("Northern Canaan and the Mari Texts," in *Near Eastern Archaeology in the Twentieth Century*, ed. James A. Sanders [Garden City, N.Y.: Doubleday & Co., 1970], p. 174 n. 14).

86. For the use of Samalian as a dialect name, see Greenfield, *Leshonenu* 32 (1968): 359 n. 6; and Helga and Manfred Weippert, "Die 'Bileam'-Inschrift von *Tell Dēr ʿAllā*," *ZDPV* 98 (1982): 85 n. 31.

87. Edomite texts are recognized by find-spot, the appearance of *Qôs* personal names, and to a lesser extent by the script. On the latter, see Naveh, "The Scripts of Two Ostraca from Elath," *BASOR* 183 (1966): 27–30.

88. PHOENICIAN: For the second Arslan Tash inscription, see André Caquot and R. du Mesnil du Buisson, "La seconde tablette ou 'petite amulette' d'Arslan-Tash," *Syria* 48 (1971): 396, 403, and 392 fig. 1, 393 fig. 2A; and Röllig, *NESE* 2 (1974): 29.

For "Byblos 13," see Jean Starcky, "Une inscription phénicienne de Byblos," *MUSJ* 45 (1969): 257–273; and Cross, "A Recently Published Phoenician Inscription of the Persian Period from Byblos," *IEJ* 29 (1979): 40–44.

For Plautus' "Poenulus," see W. M. Lindsay, "The Carthaginian Passages in the 'Poenulus' of Plautus," *The Classical Review* 12 (1898): 361–364; and Maurice Sznycer, *Les passages puniques en transcription latine dans le "Poenulus" de Plaute*, Etudes et commentaires, vol. 65 (Paris: C. Klincksieck, 1967).

ARAMAIC: For the recently discovered bilingual text from Tell Fekheriyeh, see Ali Abou Assaf, "Die Statue des HDYSʿY, König von Guzana," *MDOG* 113 (1981): 3–22; Ali Abou-Assaf, Pierre Bordreuil, and Alan R. Millard, *La statue de Tell Fekherye et son inscription bilingue assyro-araméenne* (Paris: Editions Recherche sur les civilisations, 1982), pp. 23–60; and the study by Stephen A. Kaufman, "Reflections on the Assyrian-Aramaic Bilingual from Tell Fakhariyeh," *Maarav* 3 (1982): 137–175.

For the Tell Halaf ostraca, see Friedrich, "Denkmäler mit westsemitischer Buchstabenschrift," in *Die Inschriften vom Tell Halaf*, ed. J. Friedrich et al., AfO Beiheft, vol. 6 (Berlin: [private], 1940), pp. 71–78; and Rainer Degen, "Die aramaeischen Tontafeln vom Tell Halaf," *NESE* 1 (1972): 50–56.

For the words of Ahiqar, see A. E. Cowley, ed., *Aramaic Papyri of the Fifth Century B.C.* (Oxford: Oxford University Press, 1923), pp. 212–220.

MOABITE: For the Kerak fragment, see William L. Reed and Fred V. Winnett, "A Fragment of an Early Moabite Inscription from Kerak," *BASOR* 172 (1963): 1–9; and Freedman, "A Second Mesha Inscription," *BASOR* 175 (1964): 50–51.

HEBREW: For the Ajrud texts, see Zeev Meshel, *Kuntillet ʿAjrud. A Religious Centre from the Time of the Judaean Monarchy on the Border of Sinai,* The Israel Museum Catalogue no. 175 (Jerusalem: Israel Museum, 1978).

For the Arad texts, see Aharoni, *Arad Inscriptions* (Jerusalem: The Bialik Institute and the Israel Exploration Society, 1975) (in Hebrew); and Rainey, "Three Additional Hebrew Ostraca from Tel Arad," *Tel Aviv* 4 (1977): 97–102.

For the texts from Khirbet Beit Lei, see Naveh, "Old Hebrew Inscriptions in a Burial Cave," *IEJ* 13 (1963): 84 (Text A), 86 (Texts B and C), 79 ("Beit Lei"); and Cross, "The Cave Inscriptions from Khirbet Beit Lei," in *Near Eastern Archaeology*, pp. 301 (Text A) and 302 (Texts B and C).

For the Lachish letters, see Harry Torczyner et al., *Lachish I (Tell ed Duweir). The Lachish Letters,* The Wellcome Archaeological Research Expedition to the Near East Publications, vol. 1 (London/New York/Toronto: Oxford University Press, 1938), pp. 19–183; and David Diringer, "Early Hebrew Inscriptions," in Olga Tufnell et al., *Lachish III (Tell ed Duweir). The Iron Age,* The Wellcome-Marston Archaeological Research Expedition to the Near East, vol. 3, 2 vols. (London/New York/Toronto: Oxford University Press, 1953), 1:331–338 (letters 1–18); Diringer, in *Lachish III,* 1:338–339; Ginsberg, "Lachish Ostraca New and Old," *BASOR* 80 (1940): 12–13 (letters 19–21); and David Ussishkin, "Excavations at Tel Lachish—1973–1977, Preliminary Report," *Tel Aviv* 5 (1978): 81–88 (letters 24–30).

For Murabbaʿât 17, see J. T. Milik, "Textes hébreux et araméens," in P. Benoit et al., *Les grottes de Murabbaʿât,* Discoveries in the Judaean Desert, vol. 2 (Oxford: Oxford University Press, 1961), pp. 95–97.

For the el-Qom texts, see William G. Dever, "Iron Age Epigraphic Material from the Area of Khirbet El-Kôm," *HUCA* 40–41 (1969–1970): 151–174.

For the Tell Qasile texts, see Benjamin Maisler, "Two Hebrew Ostraca from Tell Qasîle," *JNES* 10 (1951): 266–267.

For a new edition of the Samaria ostraca, see Ivan T. Kaufman, "The Samaria Ostraca: A Study in Ancient Hebrew Palaeography," 2 vols. (Ph.D. dissertation, Harvard University, 1966), 1:141–147 (transliterations) and vol. 2 (photographs).

89. The Amman Citadel inscription was published by Siegfried H. Horn, "The Amman Citadel Inscription," *ADAJ* 12–13 (1967–1968): 81–83; idem, "The Ammān Citadel Inscription," *BASOR* 193 (1969): 2–13. See

also William J. Fulco, "The ʿAmmān Citadel Inscription: A New Collation," *BASOR* 230 (1978): 39–43.

For the Amman Statue inscription, see R. D. Barnett, "Four Sculptures from Amman," *ADAJ* 1 (1951): 34–36; and Aharoni, "A New Ammonite Inscription," *IEJ* 1 (1950–1951): 219–222.

For the Amman Theater inscription, see R. W. Dajani, "The Amman Theater Fragment," *ADAJ* 12–13 (1967–1968): 65–67; and Fulco, "The Amman Theater Inscription," *JNES* 38 (1979): 37–38.

For the Siran bottle inscription, see Fawzi Zayadine and Henry O. Thompson, "The Ammonite Inscription from Tell Siran," *Berytus* 22 (1973): 115–140; and idem, "The Tell Siran Inscription," *BASOR* 212 (1973): 5–11. See also Cross, "Notes on the Ammonite Inscription from Tell Sīrān," *BASOR* 212 (1973): 12–15.

For the Heshbon ostraca, see Cross, "An Ostracon from Heshbon," *AUSS* 7 (1969): 223–229 (no. 1); idem, "Heshbon Ostracon II," *AUSS* 11 (1973): 126–131 (no. 2); idem, *AUSS* 13 (1975): 1–20 (nos. 4–8); and idem, "Heshbon Ostracon XI," *AUSS* 14 (1976): 145–148 (no. 11).

90. Hoftijzer and van der Kooij, eds., *Aramaic Texts*, pp. 173–178, 267, and plates 1–15, 19b, 20–23. See also Carlton (Hackett), "Studies," pp. 40–41. The lineation and reconstruction of Combination I follow André Caquot and André Lemaire, "Les textes araméens de Deir ʿAlla," *Syria* 54 (1977): 193–194.

91. Complete references are given when individual texts are cited.

CHAPTER TWO

PHONOLOGY

1. The correspondences of *$\underline{d}$.

PHOENICIAN: צ, as in ארץ "land, country" (Karatepe A I 4.9.18, etc.) and יצא "to go out" (Arsl.T. 1:26, 2:3). Although there is no evidence for the correspondence of *$\underline{d}$ in Old Byblian, the appearance of ארץ in Yehawmilk 10 suggests that צ represented *$\underline{d}$ in Byblian as well. Since *$\underline{d}$ had merged with *$\d{s}$ in Ugaritic,[1] the phoneme *$\underline{d}$ was lost throughout the Canaanite dialects at a very early date.

ARAMAIC: ק, as in ארק(א) "(the) land, country" (Zkr B 26; Br-Rkb 1:4, 2:2; Sf. I A 26.28; Fekh. 2; etc.), רקה "to appease" (Sf. III 6, etc.), מרק "sickness" (Fekh. 9), and קרק "to flee" (Sf. III 4.19.19/20).[2] Kutscher[3] also cited the personal name *Ra-qi-a-nu*[4] and its variant *Ra-ḫi-a-nu* (*ANET*[3], p. 283).[5] The exact phonetic value of Old Aramaic ק < *$\underline{d}$ is not known.[6]

The only exception to this systematic correspondence is חצר "green grass" (Sf. I A 28).[7]

SAMALIAN: ק, as in ארק "land, country" (H 5; P 5, etc.), מוקא "rising (sun)" (P 13.14), and רקה "to delight in" (H 18.22).

The only exception to the systematic correspondence of $*\d{d}$:ק is צרי "my enemies" (H 30), cognate to Arabic [ḍarra] "to harm, injure."[8] The other word adduced as an exception to this correspondence, שמרג "to fall sick" (P 16), from the root $*mr\d{d}$,[9] is doubtful for two reasons: (1) the causative in Samalian is -ה not -ש. The morpheme itself, or the entire word, would have been borrowed; and (2) there is no parallel to the alleged correspondence $*\d{d}$:ג in either Samalian or Aramaic. The parallel cited by Dion,[10] following Kutscher[11]—Syriac גחך "to laugh"—does not prove the point, since גחך, like other Semitic verbs of laughing,[12] is onomatopoetic.

AMMONITE: צ, as in צאן "sheep" (Hesh. Ost. 4:2.7.10).[13]

DEIR ALLA: ק, as in קרק "to flee" (I 15).[14] Whatever the pronunciation of the Deir Alla ק was,[15] the representation of $*\d{d}$ by ק strongly aligns the Deir Alla dialect with Old Aramaic and Samalian.

MOABITE: צ, as in ארץ "land, country" (Mesha 5/6, etc.) and צאן "sheep" (Mesha 31).

EDOMITE: No evidence.

HEBREW: צ, as in רחץ "washing" (Sam. Ost. 19:3, 54:2/3, etc.), מוצא "spring" (Shiloah 5), and חמץ "vinegar" (Arad 2:7).

The Northwest Semitic dialects spoken between 1000 and 586 B.C.E. exhibit two graphic correspondences of $*\d{d}$. In Phoenician, Ammonite, Moabite, and Hebrew, $*\d{d}$ is represented by צ. Old Aramaic, Samalian, and the Deir Alla dialect use a different grapheme, ק, to represent $*\d{d}$. This graphic representation suggests that $*\d{d}$ had merged with a sibilant in Phoenician, Ammonite, Moabite, and Hebrew. In Old Aramaic, Samalian, and the Deir Alla dialect, $*\d{d}$ had merged with a uvular. Further refinement of this twofold dialectal distinction along phonetic lines is not possible at present.

2. The correspondences of $*\d{\underline{d}}$.

PHOENICIAN: ז [z], as for example the Byblian relative -ז (Ahirom 1; Yehimilk 1, etc.) and the demonstrative pronoun זן "this" (Ahirom 2; Ahirom Graff. 3, etc.), and זבח "(to) sacrifice" (Karatepe A II 19, C IV 2.4, etc.). The original phoneme $*\d{\underline{d}}$ was lost in the earliest Phoenician texts and had merged with $*z$.[16]

ARAMAIC: ז [ḏ], as in אחז "to grasp, seize" (Br-Rkb 1:11; Fekh. 19), זחל "to fear" (Zkr A 13; Sf. II C 6), the relative זי (passim),

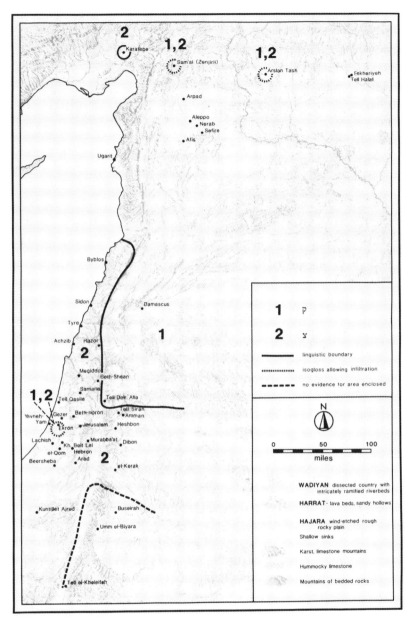

MAP 2: The correspondences of *ḏ.

etc.[17] ז in the Old Aramaic texts was bivalent, corresponding to both
*$\underline{d}$ and *z. The double pronunciation of Old Aramaic ז is inferred
from the representation of *$\underline{d}$ by both ז and ד in Imperial Aramaic
texts.[18] The shift of *$\underline{d}$ > ד could not have occurred had *$\underline{d}$ not
remained an independent phone(me) in this early period.[19] There is
also the possibility, however, that *$\underline{d}$ had merged with [z]/*z in Old
Aramaic and that the Imperial Aramaic ז < *$\underline{d}$ originated in another
dialect strain.

SAMALIAN: ז, as, for example, in אחז "to grasp, seize" (H 3,
etc.; P 11), זהב "gold" (P 11), the relative particle ז(י) (H 1.3.4.22,
etc.), etc.[20] The phonetic value of ז < *$\underline{d}$ is uncertain; the phoneme
*$\underline{d}$ may have been independent (as in Old Aramaic)[21] or may have
merged with [z] (as in Phoenician dialects).[22] Also, the possibility
of foreign influence on the phonetic realization of ז < *$\underline{d}$ cannot be
excluded.

AMMONITE: ז [(?)], as in the PN ירחעזר (Amman Statue) and אלעזר
(seal of נדבאל).[23]

DEIR ALLA: No evidence.[24] The relative/genitive particle זי (Clay
Text 1) < *$\underline{d}$ is probably Aramaic.[25] The examples of *$\underline{d}$ cited by
Hoftijzer,[26] נזית (Vd 2) and פחזי[27] (II 8), are ambiguous since the
etymology is uncertain in each case.[28]

MOABITE: ז [(?)], as in זאת "this" (fem. sing.) (Mesha 3) and אחז
"to capture" (Mesha 11.14, etc.). The phonetic value of ז < *$\underline{d}$ is
unknown. Cf. Samalian above.

EDOMITE: ז [(?)], in the PN בעזראל.[29] The phonetic value of
Edomite ז is uncertain.[30]

HEBREW: ז [z], as in the PN אחז (Sam. Ost. 2:5), זהב "gold"
(Silwan B 1), זה "this" (masc. sing.) (Lach. 6:2; Yavneh-Yam 1:9;
Arad 13:2), etc.

According to the available evidence, the correspondences of *$\underline{d}$
divide the NWS dialects into two parts. Old Aramaic, in all probability, preserved an independent phoneme, *$\underline{d}$. In Phoenician and
Hebrew, *$\underline{d}$ was lost and had merged with *z. In each of the remaining dialects, it is unknown whether *$\underline{d}$ was independent or had
been lost to another phoneme.

Although Phoenician and Hebrew jointly lost *$\underline{d}$ to *z, the
merger may have occurred independently in each dialect.[31] Since
*$\underline{d}$ > [z] also occurred in Akkadian and Ethiopic, the loss of *$\underline{d}$ in
Phoenician and Hebrew may not be an exclusively shared innovation

but parallel, independent developments. Alternatively, $*\underline{d} > $ [z] in NWS may have arisen by mutual contact and linguistic diffusion. The geographical proximity of the NWS dialects exhibiting the merger argues for the second alternative.[32]

3.   The correspondences of $*\underline{t}$.

PHOENICIAN: צ [ṣ], as in חצר "courtyard" (Arsl.T. 1:7).

One possible exception to this correspondence is the place name צר "Tyre" $< *\underline{t}or$, transcribed in Greek as Τυρος. While some scholars[33] have claimed that the representation of $*\underline{t}$ by T indicates that $*\underline{t}$ was still an independent phoneme in Phoenician, the evidence is dubious. Either the representation of $*\underline{t}$ by T reflects a sole remnant of [ṭ] in an old place name, or T results from foreign influence on the transmission of the place name.[34] In either case, there is no other evidence that $*\underline{t}$ persisted as an independent phoneme in Phoenician.

ARAMAIC: צ [ṭ], as in רץ "to run" (Br-Rkb 1:8) and נצר "to protect" (Sf. I B 8, C 15.17; Nerab 1:12.13; Adon 8).[35] In the later Imperial Aramaic texts, ט becomes the standard representation of $*\underline{t}$.[36] Thus, as in the case of $*\underline{d}$, the later phases of the Aramaic dialects indicate that the old phoneme had not been lost.

SAMALIAN: צ* [(?)]. The only possible evidence of $*\underline{t}$ is the PN ברצר (P 1.3.20.20), if it is composed of בר "son" + $*\underline{t}r$ "rock."[37] Although no certain examples of $*\underline{t}$ occur in the Samalian texts, the phoneme would be represented by צ, as in both Aramaic and Phoenician dialects; its phonetic value, however, remains unknown.

AMMONITE: No evidence.

DEIR ALLA: צ [(?)], as in עצה "advice" (II 9) and יעץ "to advise" (II 9). Hoftijzer[38] claimed that $*\underline{t}$ was still an independent phoneme on the basis of the orthographic variation in representing this phoneme. He cited עטם (I 7) cognate to Arabic [ʿaẓuma] "to be vast, powerful"[39] and עצם (VIIc 3), from the same root. Yet the new readings of the Balaam text show עלם in I 7, not עטם.[40] There is, then, no orthographic variation in the representation of $*\underline{t}$. $*\underline{t}$ always corresponds to צ. Its phonetic value is unknown.

MOABITE: צ [(?)], as in צהרם "noon" (Mesha 15). In the absence of both transcriptions of Moabite and knowledge of later phonetic developments in this dialect, it is impossible to suggest the phonetic value of Moabite צ $< *\underline{t}$.

EDOMITE: No evidence.

HEBREW: צ [ṣ], as in קץ "summer" (Gezer Cal. 7), עצמת "bones" (Silwan B 2), etc. Both biblical and epigraphic texts show that *ṭ̣ and *ṣ́ have completely merged; there is no trace of an independent phoneme *ṭ̣.

The resultant dialect map is similar to that of *ḏ. In Phoenician and Hebrew, *ṭ̣ and *ṣ́ have merged into צ; the phoneme *ṭ̣ was lost. In Aramaic dialects, however, this phoneme was preserved. But by the fifth century, *ṭ̣ was becoming obsolete and had merged with ט [ṭ].

Whether Samalian, Ammonite, Deir Alla, Moabite, and Edomite had an independent phoneme *ṭ̣, as did Aramaic, or lost it, as did Phoenician and Hebrew, is unclear. The representation of this phoneme by צ in these dialects makes any judgment about the phonetic value impossible. Both the Canaanite and Aramaic dialects utilized צ to represent different sounds.

4. The correspondences of *ṯ.

PHOENICIAN: ש [š], as in משפט "judgment" (Ahirom 2), ישב "to sit, dwell" (Karatepe A I 11, etc.; Kilamu 14), and שמנה "8" (Arsl.T. 1:17/18). The phoneme *ṯ had already merged with [š] and had been lost by the time of the earliest Phoenician texts.[41]

Bauer and Leander,[42] however, objected that *ṯ was preserved through late Phoenician times. They noted, in support, that Plutarch explicitly relates the Phoenician pronunciation of "ox"—Hebrew שור—as θωρ, not as the expected *σωρ. Yet Friedrich[43] and Harris[44] suggested that Plutarch's θωρ does not represent the actual Phoenician pronunciation of שר*, but rather the Aramaic pronunciation [tôr]. Thus, there are no exceptions to the complete loss of *ṯ in Phoenician dialects.

ARAMAIC: ש [t], in all Aramaic-speaking communities except that of Tell Fekheriyeh. Thus *ṯ is represented as ש in Samal (ישב "to sit, dwell" [Br-Rkb 1:5 = Sf. III 7.17] and שלשן "30" [KAI 219:3]), Sfire (שבר "to break" [Sf. I A 38], שו(ו)ב "to return" [Sf. III 6, etc.], and שאת/ן "ewe(s)" [Sf. I A 21.23]), and Aleppo (אשר "place; trace" [Zkr B 15.16 (partially restored) = Sf. I A 5, etc.]). In the recently published Aramaic text from Tell Fekheriyeh, however, *ṯ appears as ס (e.g., עסר "riches" [l. 2], יסב "to sit, dwell" [ll. 5.16], חדס "(a)new" [l. 11], and סאון "ewes" [l. 20]).[45] As Kaufman has stated,[46] this ס does not represent a different phonetic correspondence of *ṯ, but only a different graphic representation. The use of ס rather than the standard ש in representing [ṯ] may result from the influence of Assyrian, where *š:[s].

The persistence of an independent phoneme [ṯ] is suggested by the spelling of the PN עתרסמך (Sf. I A 1, etc.), pronounced ['Attar-] < *ʿAṯtar-. Had *ṯ merged with [š], as in Phoenician dialects, the name would have appeared as עשתרסמך*;[47] cf. biblical Hebrew עשתרת and Akkadian Ištar. This particular form in Sfire could not have arisen had *ṯ/[ṯ] not been an independent phone(me).

For the supposed form ירת in Sf. I C 24, see Chapter 3, no. 16a.

SAMALIAN: ש [(?)], as in אשר "place" (H 27.27.32), ישב "to sit, dwell" (H 8.15, etc.), etc.[48] The graphic correspondence of *ṯ:ש, found in both Phoenician and Aramaic dialects, does not indicate any dialectal affinity.[49] Without transcriptions, Samalian ש is dialectally ambiguous.

AMMONITE: ש [(?)], as in דשא "grass" (Hesh. Ost. 4:9) and שתע "to fear" (Cit. 6).[50] The exact phonetic value of ש is unknown.

DEIR ALLA: ש [(?)], as in שמ(ה) "there, thither" (II 7.13.14), משפט "judgment" (II 17), etc.[51] It is unclear whether the phoneme *ṯ was lost, as in Phoenician dialects, or was retained, as in Old Aramaic dialects. Orthographically, Deir Alla ש < *ṯ could be interpreted in either way.

MOABITE: ש [(?)], as in שלשן "30" (Mesha 2), ירש "to occupy" (Mesha 7), and ישב "to sit, dwell" (Mesha 8.8/9, etc.). This grapheme is also phonetically ambiguous, as in Samalian, Ammonite, and the Deir Alla dialect.

EDOMITE: No evidence.[52]

HEBREW: ש [š], as in שלש "3" (Shiloah 2), אשר "(relative particle)" (Silwan B 1.2; Lach. 2:6, etc.), and חדש "month" (Arad 7:3/4). By the time of the earliest Hebrew text, *ṯ had already been lost and had merged with *š/[š]. The Hebrew epigraphic texts offer no evidence bearing on Speiser's[53] claim that in one Hebrew dialect, *ṯ was realized as [s].

The merger of *ṯ and *š did not occur simultaneously in Phoenician and Hebrew.[54] Rather, it occurred some four centuries earlier in Phoenician than in Hebrew. On the basis of this timetable, it is evident that the merging of *ṯ and [š] began in Phoenician and then spread into Palestine, finally reaching Hebrew centuries later. Phoenician was therefore the linguistic innovator from which Hebrew received the change.

The correspondences of *$\underline{t}$ divide the first-millennium NWS dialects into two groups. Old Aramaic preserved an independent phoneme *$\underline{t}$, whereas *$\underline{t}$ had merged with *$\check{s}$ in Phoenician and Hebrew. It appears that the change *$\underline{t}$ > [š] gradually diffused through Palestine.[55] The dialectal status of Samalian, Ammonite, Deir Alla, Moabite, and Edomite, in this respect, is unknown.

5.   The correspondences of *$\acute{a}$.

PHOENICIAN: [ṓ], as inferred from the second-millennium transcriptions *Bi-(ʾa)-ru-ta* (VESO X C 4.5) and *ḫu-mi-tu* "wall" (EA 141:44).[56] The shift *$\acute{a}$ > [ṓ] continued throughout the history of the Phoenician dialects, as the transcriptions *A-ḫu-ut-mi-il-ki* (ADD 894:5) < *$\ast^{\circ}A\underline{h}\acute{a}t$- and Punic *dobrim* "saying" (Poen. 935) < *$d\acute{a}bir\bar{\imath}m$-demonstrate.[57] Although evidence for the correspondence *$\acute{a}$:[ṓ] is based on transcriptions from different places and periods, the consistency with which *$\acute{a}$ changed to [ṓ] indicates that this correspondence applied to *all* Phoenician dialects from the El-Amarna period on.[58]

ARAMAIC: *[ā́]. Although there is no direct evidence for the treatment of *$\acute{a}$ in this period, the later Aramaic dialects (biblical Aramaic and Syriac especially) suggest that *$\acute{a}$ remained stable in the early period.[59]

SAMALIAN: *[ā́], as in the place name *Sam-al, Sa-am-al-la*;[60] cf. Hebrew שמאול.[61] The Samalian texts themselves, however, offer no direct evidence that *$\acute{a}$ corresponded to [ā́].

AMMONITE: [ṓ (?)]. In all probability, Ammonite underwent the change of *$\acute{a}$ > [ṓ], as seen in one Ammonite PN.[62] Since, in Phoenician, the change *$\acute{a}$ > [ṓ] was patterned after the older shift *$\acute{a}$ > [ṓ],[63] it can be inferred that, like Phoenician, Ammonite also modified *$\acute{a}$ > [ṓ].[64] This vocalic change may also be evidenced in the place name עמ(ו)ן [ʿAmmṓn] and in the divine name "Milkom."

In Akkadian texts,[65] however, "Ammonites" appears as *Am-ma-na-aia*; the correspondence *$\acute{a}$:[ṓ] is absent. Yet this form of the gentilic probably does not reflect actual Ammonite pronunciation but is rather an Akkadian form. The foreign name was adapted to Akkadian phonetic patterns;[66] in Akkadian *$\bar{a}$ remained [á].[67] Thus the evidence suggests that in Ammonite *$\acute{a}$:[ó].

DEIR ALLA: No evidence.

MOABITE: [(?)]. The evidence of Akkadian transcriptions is ambiguous since the Moabite PN *Ka-am-mu-su-na-ad-bi* (*ANET*[3], p. 287), with apparent *$\acute{a}$:[ó], contrasts with the PNs *Ka-ma-as-ḥal-ta-a* (*ANET*[3], p. 298) and *Sa-la-ma-nu* (*ANET*[3], p. 282).[68] These names, then, cannot alone serve to posit the correspondence *$\acute{a}$:[ó] in Moabite.

Blau[69] used indirect evidence to find the correspondence of *$\bar{a}$ in Moabite. According to him, the first person sing. perfect תי- bears [ī] on analogy to the independent pronoun [ʾanōkī]. The final [ī] on [ʾanōkī], however, results from the following development: *ʾanáku (as in Akkadian and Ugaritic) > *ʾanōkǔ > (via dissimilation) [ʾanōkī]. Thus Blau hypothesized that [ī] of the suffix תי- indicates the existence of *$\acute{a}$:[ó] in Moabite.

Yet the verbal suffix [tī] does not appear only in dialects which exhibit the correspondence *$\acute{a}$:[ó]. In Amorite, for example, the first person sing. perfect ended in [ti],[70] but *$\acute{a}$:[á]. The verbal suffix [tī] in Moabite, then, need not imply the correspondence *$\acute{a}$:[ó]. Thus it is preferable to revert to the traditional explanation of [ī]; [ī] in [tī] derives from an analogy with the first person sing. possessive suffix [ī].[71] The suffix תי-, then, does not point to the existence of *$\acute{a}$:[ó] in Moabite.

EDOMITE: No evidence. Bauer,[72] however, suggested that *$\acute{a}$:[ó] in Edomite, on the basis of the personal name עכבור (Gen. 36:38.39) < *-bār and possibly the place name "Edom" itself.

HEBREW: [ó], already in the El-Amarna period (e.g., *aḫ-ru-un-nu* "last" [EA 245:10 (Megiddo)] and *sú-ki-ni* "agent" [EA 256:9])[73] and continuing throughout the biblical texts. There is, however, no direct evidence from the epigraphic texts which suggests that *$\acute{a}$:[ó].

The correspondence *$\acute{a}$:[ó] appears in Phoenician dialects, Ammonite, and in Hebrew. In Old Aramaic and probably Samalian, *$\bar{a}$ was preserved as [á]. The treatment of *$\bar{a}$ in Moabite, Deir Alla, and in Edomite is unknown.

On the basis of geographical location—adjacent to Hebrew in the South—it is possible that Edomite followed the pattern of Phoenician, Ammonite, and Hebrew and exhibited the correspondence *á:[ó]. The situation in Moabite and Deir Alla is more difficult to infer because each dialect shares diagnostic traits with both Phoenician-Hebrew and with Aramaic dialects. Additional evidence is needed to decide this issue.

6.   The correspondences of *â.[74]

PHOENICIAN: [ó], whether *â had contracted from *a> (as Pun. nasot "I bore" [Poen. 947] < *naśấtī < *naśá>tī)[75] or from the syncope of the semi-vowels y or w (as in the PNs Bu-di-ba-al [ANET[3], p. 296] < *bâd < *bali-yad[76] and Ḫi-ru-um-mu [ANET[3], p. 283] < *râm < *rawam).[77] Although nasot is attested in the late phase of Phoenician, the form is probably old;[78] cf. similarly the Greek ρω < *rấš < *rá>š. The correspondence *á:[ó] presumably appeared in both Byblian and standard Phoenician, although the innovating dialect of the correspondence cannot be determined. That the correspondence is systematic, occurring without exception,[79] suggests that all Phoenician dialects participated in the shift *á > [ó].

ARAMAIC: *[â], as inferred from the later Aramaic dialects. Even in those Aramaic dialects which exhibit the correspondence *á:[ó], *á does not shift to [ó]. Old Aramaic, then, probably preserved *â throughout.

SAMALIAN: *[â (?)], as inferred from the preservation of *â. Since the correspondence *á:[ó] is based upon the prior change *á:[ó],[80] the absence of *á:[ó] in Samalian suggests the absence of *á:[ó] as well.

AMMONITE: [ó], in the PN Pu-du-il [Pᵊdō-ᵓēl] mentioned in the annals of Sennacherib and Essarhaddon.[81] If this name is composed of the elements פדה "to ransom" (third person masc. sing. perfect) + the divine name "El," the transcription Pu-du-il indicates that, as in Phoenician dialects, the vowel *â < *aya shifted to [ō] (u in the transcription). The development of the name, then, is *Padâ-ᵓil[82] > *Padô-ᵓil > [Pᵊdô-ᵓēl].[83] Ammonite reflects the correspondence *á:[ó], if *á resulted from the syncope of an intervocalic semi-vowel. Whether *á < *a> also shifted to [ó], as in Phoenician, is unclear.

DEIR ALLA: No evidence.

MOABITE: No evidence.

EDOMITE: No evidence.

HEBREW: [ṓ], if *ā́ was derived from the absorption of ˀ into the preceding *a in a doubly closed syllable, as in BH ראש "head" and צאן "sheep."[84] Otherwise, *ā́ < *aˀ corresponded to [ā́], as in ל"א qal perfects.[85] When *ā́ resulted from the contraction of *aya and *awa, however, *ā́ became [ā́], as in the third person masc. singular perfect of final weak verbs in BH. Yet there is no direct evidence for the correspondences of *ā́ in the epigraphic texts themselves; such correspondences can only be inferred from other, non-epigraphic sources.

On the basis of the available evidence, Aramaic dialects (and probably Samalian) preserved *ā́ as [ā́] in all cases. In Phoenician dialects, *ā́ shifted to [ṓ] consistently, whether *ā́ was derived from the contraction of *aˀ > *ā́ or from the intervocalic syncopation of *aya/*awa > *ā́. Ammonite followed the Phoenician pattern, for the shift *ā́ > [ṓ] is apparent when *ā́ resulted from the syncope of *aya/*awa > *ā́. There is no evidence for the treatment of *aˀ > *ā́ in Ammonite, although this *ā́ too probably shifted to [ṓ]. At present, then, it is impossible to determine the vowel in Ammonite צאן "sheep" (Hesh. Ost. 4:2.7.10).

Hebrew, at least as attested in the Masoretic text, lay midway between the two linguistic extremes represented by Aramaic (complete preservation of *ā́:[ā́]) and Phoenician dialects (complete transformation of *ā́ to [ṓ]). When *ā́ resulted from the contraction of *aˀ in a doubly closed syllable, *ā́ shifted to [ṓ]. When *ā́ resulted from the syncopation of an intervocalic y or w, *ā́ became [ā́]. The former case follows the Phoenician pattern; the latter follows the Aramaic pattern. The treatment of *ā́ in Hebrew thus varied depending upon the development and environment of *ā́.

7. The correspondences of *á.

PHOENICIAN: [ṓ], in nominal formations, as in the PNs Ba-ˀa-al-ma-lu-ku (ANET[3], p. 296) < *malā́k < *malák, Ia-a-tu-na (Nabu-naid 33.5) < *yatán, and Pun. -λαβον "white" < *labán.[86] In Phoenician dialects, *á was stress-lengthened to *ā́ and thence shifted to [ṓ]; cf. *ā́:[ṓ] in Phoenician.[87]

In verbal forms, however, *á was preserved as [á], as, for example, in the PNs Mil-ki-a-ša-pa (ANET[3], p. 291 [Byblos])[88] and

Ilu-ya-ta-a-nu (ABL 1112:8). While these forms may indicate a general dialectal variant to the correspondence *á*:[ó],[89] another, more specific explanation is available. The evidence conforms to that of BH: tonic lengthening occurs in nouns (incl. PNs) but not in verbs.[90] Those forms in Phoenician with [ó] were treated as nouns, those with [á] were treated as verbs.

ARAMAIC: *[á], as inferred from the later Aramaic dialects.[91]

SAMALIAN: *[á (?)], although evidence is lacking.

AMMONITE: No evidence.

DEIR ALLA: No evidence.

MOABITE: [*ā̆], if the evidence of the place name "Moab," Akk. *Mu/a-ʾa-b(a)* (*ANET*[3], pp. 282, 287, etc.) is to be normalized [Mōʾāb].[92] Whether *á* was stress-lengthened, as in Phoenician and Hebrew, is unknown.

EDOMITE: [ā̆], as in the PNs [Baʿal-ḥānān] (Gen. 36:38, etc.) and *Qauš-malaku* (*ANET*[3], p. 282). The quantity of the vowel, however, is unknown.

HEBREW: As inferred from the Masoretic vocalization, *á* in nouns was stress-lengthened, whereas in verbs it remained [á].[93] Although there is no evidence for the quantity of this vowel in the epigraphic texts, the consistency with which BH treats nominal vs. verbal *á* suggests that the Masoretic rules were operative in the epigraphic texts as well.

The evidence of those NWS dialects that show the correspondence of *á* suggests an initial twofold division among the dialects. In Phoenician and Hebrew, *á* was stress-lengthened to [ā̆] in nominal forms only. In Aramaic, and probably also in Samalian, *á* was preserved as [á] under all circumstances, whereas in Phoenician and Hebrew it was preserved as [á] only in verbal forms. Thus Phoenician and Hebrew constitute a single dialect group, which exhibits stress-lengthening, as opposed to the other first-millennium NWS dialects which attest to the correspondence *á*:[á]. The dialectal status of Ammonite, the Deir Alla dialect, Moabite, and Edomite, in this respect, is unknown.

Within the Phoenician-Hebrew group, Phoenician shows a further phonological development. Whereas *á* in Hebrew nominal forms was only stress-lengthened to [ā̆], in Phoenician *á* was stress-lengthened to *ā̆* and was then treated as an originally long, accented *ā̆*, becoming [ó]. Hebrew distinguished *ā̆* from *ā́* and *á*; the first always shifted to [ó], the second shifting only when *ā́* resulted from *aᵓ in a doubly closed syllable, and the third retaining its quality but lengthening to [ấ] in nouns but remaining [á] in verbs. In Phoenician, however, all three vowels became [ố], with the exception of verbal *á:[á]. The phonological correspondence *ā́:[ố] in Phoenician therefore extended to nearly all *a*-vowels under the accent.

The consistency with which Phoenician applied the correspondence *ā̊:[ố] suggests that the change began in this dialect. From this point, the change spread to different parts of Syria-Palestine. *ā́:[ố] reached Ammonite and Hebrew; *á:[ố] reached Ammonite, and nominal *á:[ấ] reached only Hebrew. The further modification of *á > *ā́ > [ố] never spread beyond Phoenicia itself. The source of these changes, then, was Phoenician.

8.   The correspondences of *aw* and *ay*.

PHOENICIAN: [ô]/[ê], as in, for example, עלך [ʿalêkā̃] "upon you" (Bronze Spat. 5), בת [bêt] "house, temple" (Yehimilk 1, etc.), לל [lêl(ê/ā)] "night" (Karatepe A II 17), ים [yôm] "day" (Yehimilk 5; Kilamu 12; Karatepe A I 5, etc.), and ען [ʿên] "eye" (Arsl.T. 2:2.4; cf. לען [li-ʿênê] "before" [Yehawmilk 10]).[94] The contraction of both diphthongs had already occurred by the El-Amarna period, for both Ugaritic and the Amarna letters from Syria reflect these contractions.[95] In the first-millennium Phoenician dialects, diphthongs contracted in both medial and final positions, whether stressed or not.[96]

Cross and Freedman, however, found an exception to diphthong contraction in the third person masc. sing. perfect of final weak verbs in Old Byblian.[97] They vocalized עלי "he attacks" (Ahirom 2), בני "he built" (Yehimilk 1; Shiptibaal 1), and חוי "he restored" (Yehimilk 2) as [ʿalay], [banay], and [ḥawway], respectively. Yet internal and comparative evidence suggest the vocalization [ʿalaya], [banaya], and [ḥawwa/iya].[98] Thus *aw* and *ay* contracted without exception throughout the Phoenician dialects.

ARAMAIC: [aw]/[ay], as in יום [yawm] "day" (Sf. I A 12, etc.; Nerab 2:3.4; Fekh. 7), או [ʾaw] "or" (Sf. I B 27, etc.; Zkr B 21), בית [bayt] "house, dynasty" (Zkr B 9.12; Hama 7 A 923 + 7 A 538 [partially restored]; Br-Rkb 2:3.4; Fekh. 8, etc.), and שמין [šamayn] "heaven" (Zkr B 25; Sf. I A 11, etc.; Fekh. 2). In general, *aw* and *ay* were retained in both medial and final positions.[99]

The only[100] real exception to the preservation of these diphthongs lay in the morphological distinction between certain "long" and "short" imperfects of final weak verbs.[101] In the "short" im-

perfect—i.e., in those forms derived from *yaqtul—the final diphthong was preserved; it was marked by ־י. In the "long" imperfect,
this diphthong contracted and was represented by ־ה.[102]

The oft cited[103] form בניהֹם [bênayhum] "between them" in Sf.
III 18.18.19 remains unexplained. If the original form was *bayn, as
all comparative evidence indicates,[104] the absence of י is notable.[105]
So too בת "house" in Fekh. 17.[106]

SAMALIAN: [aw]/[ay] when in medial position, and [ô]/[aw] and
[ê] in final position. [aw] in medial position occurs in, for example,
הושב(ת) [hawṯ/šib(t[u/i])] "I/he settled" (H 19; P 19) and מודד [maw-
dad] "friend" (H 24.27);[107] medial [ay] occurs in בית [bayt] "house,
dynasty" (H 9; P 2, etc.), עין [ʿayn] "eye" (H 30.32), and היטבה
[hayṭibih (?)] "he made it better" (P 9). Final [ê] may appear in לילא
[laylê] "night" (H 24) < *laylay.[108] Original final *aw is represented
by ־ו, as in או "or" (H 16.25, etc.); it is unclear, however, whether
the original diphthong contracted, like final *ay, or was preserved,
like medial *aw. The orthography itself is ambiguous in this case.

In every instance that an original diphthong is expected, it is
orthographically represented, except in two cases. The form יומי
"my days" occurs in P 10.18, while in H 9 ימי "my days" appears.
Similarly, the expected איחיה "his brothers" appears in H 27.28,
while in H 30 and P 17 איחה "his brothers" is found. In the case of
ימי:יומי, scholars[109] generally noted that the marking and nonmarking
of the original diphthong signifies that the diphthong had either contracted or was in the process of contracting. It is also possible,
however, that Samalian had two, competing, plural forms of יום*
"day."[110] The first, represented by ימי, is the extended plural of a
NWS monosyllabic singular noun. It is characteristic of the NWS
dialects that *qVtl- singular nouns form their plural as *qatal-.[111]
Thus Samalian [yawm] "day" had *yawam- as its plural, from which
intervocalic waw was lost,[112] producing *yaam > *yâm-. The masc.
plural morpheme [ū] was added to *yâm, resulting in [yâmū] for the
nominative plural corresponding to ימי; cf. BH יָמִים. The other plural
form, יומי, developed differently. The singular noun, יום*, was used
as the base of the plural, to which was added the masc. plural morpheme. The result is [yawm]-singular → [yawmū]-plural, the nominative corresponding to יומי. This second plural formation resembles
Old Aramaic יומן "days" (Sf. II C 17; Fekh. 7). For similarly competing forms, cf. biblical Aramaic רָאשִׁין "heads" (Dan. 7:6) < *riʾš
and רָאשֵׁיהֹם "their heads" (Ezr. 5:10) < *raʾaš-.

In the case of איחיה and איחה, the difference in the orthography may reflect a grammatical difference in the two nouns. In Samalian, the nominative masc. pl. morpheme was [ū], and the oblique [ī].[113] איחיה, with the ending [ī], is in the oblique case, whether genitive (H 27) or accusative (H 28). איחה, however, is nominative, as is obvious from the words in apposition to it, זכרו "males" (H 31) and מלכו "kings" (P 17). The orthographic difference between איחיה and איחה therefore reflects a difference in morphology.[114] איחיה and איחה are different forms and are not different spellings of the same word. Therefore neither ימי nor איחה exemplifies incipient diphthong contraction in Samalian.

AMMONITE: [aw]/[ê], as in יומת [yawmōt] "days" (Sir. 7) and מות- [mawt] "death" (seal of ענמות).[115] *ay, however, contracted in both medial (e.g., ין [yên] "wine" [Hesh. Ost. 4:7.8]) and final positions (e.g., בן [banê/ī][116] "the sons of" [Sir. 1.2, etc.]). The different treatment of *aw and *ay is paralleled in Attic Greek where, according to Sturtevant,[117] final *au̯ was preserved and *ai̯ contracted to [ē].

DEIR ALLA: [aw]/[ay], in both medial and final positions.[118] [aw] occurs, for example, in מועד [mawʿid] "counsel" (I 6), מות [mawt] "death" (II 13.14), and או [ʾaw] "or" (II 9); [ay] appears in בית [bayt] "house, dynasty" (II 6, etc.), לילה [laylā] "night" (I 1), בני [banay] "the sons of" (II 8), etc.[119] Since internal matres lectionis do not appear in these texts,[120] the semi-vowels י and ו mark uncontracted diphthongs.

The only exception to the preservation of these diphthongs in Deir Alla, as in Old Aramaic, lies in the distinction between "long" and "short" imperfect forms of the third person masc. sing. final weak qal verbs.[121] The diphthong was preserved in the "short" imperfect, י- [ay], but the diphthong contracted to [ê] (ה-) in the "long" imperfect.[122]

MOABITE: [aw] > [au̯] > [ô]/[ay] > [ai̯] > [ê]. The evidence of the Mesha stone suggests that these diphthongs were in a state of flux.[123] Uncontracted diphthongs are found in one gentilic (הדיבני [had-Daybōnī] "the Dibanite" [Mesha 1/2]) and one place name (חורנן [Hawrōnān (?)] [Mesha 31.32]). Diphthong contraction, however, was the general rule in Moabite, as, for example, in השעני [hôšiʿannī] "he saved me" (Mesha 4), ואשב [wā-ʾôšib] "and I settled" (Mesha 13), ללה [lêlā] "night" (Mesha 15), מאתן [maʾtên] "200" (Mesha 20), and לפני [li-panê] "before" (Mesha 13.18).[124] Whereas, then, original diphthongs were pronounced in place names, the spoken language had diphthong contraction.

The link between these phonetic extremes is represented by a pair of words in which one lacks a marker of the original diphthong while the other marks the original diphthong. In בת "house, dynasty" (Mesha 7.23) and בית (Mesha 25), the first form points to diphthong contraction; the *yodh* of the second form, however, suggests the presence of the diphthong **ay*. Whereas, then, Moabite place names have uncontracted diphthongs and the rest of the language shows general diphthong contraction, the doublet בית:בת suggests that contraction was not complete by the late ninth century. Although the Mesha inscription reflects a dialect in which diphthongs had, for the most part, contracted, vestigial uncontracted forms do appear.

EDOMITE: [aw] > [ô]/[(?)]. Evidence for the diphthong **aw* is found only in the divine name קוס,[125] which is vocalized as [Qaus]/[Qauš] in Akkadian[126] and as *Q3ws* in Egyptian.[127] Both vocalizations indicate that, at least through the seventh century, the diphthong in the divine name did not contract. By the Persian period, however, the diphthong had contracted, as in the PNs *Qusuyada* (Darius) and *Qusuyahab* (Artaxerxes I).[128] The diphthong, then, contracted within two centuries.

At present, there is no evidence for the correspondence(s) of **ay* in Edomite.

NORTHERN HEBREW (North of Jerusalem): [ô]/[ê], as in קץ [qêṣ] "summer" (Gezer Cal. 7), ין [yên] "wine" (Sam. Ost. passim), and חרן [Ḥôrān (?)] "Horan" (Tell Qasile 2). Northern Hebrew thus followed the pattern of diphthong contraction already evident in Ugaritic and in the Amarna letters from north Palestine.[129]

The only exception to diphthong contraction in northern Hebrew is the form בית in Tell Qasile 2 and the Beth-Shean ostracon.[130] The *yodh* would seem to indicate the presence of a diphthong, contrary to the general phonological trend in northern Hebrew. This exception may be explained in several ways, however. The *yodh* may be a *mater lectionis* for [ê]; there are, however, no parallels to this usage. The form may have been borrowed, or may have spread, from a dialect that did not contract diphthongs, as, for example, southern Hebrew.[131] Finally, since בית is part of a place name in both instances, the form may not reflect current speech patterns but those of an earlier, nonmonophthongizing dialect.[132] Whatever the

explanation, the form בית does not conform to the pattern of diphthong contraction in northern Hebrew.[133]

SOUTHERN HEBREW (Jerusalem and the South): [aw]/[ay], as in
עוד [ˤawd] "still" (Shiloah 1.2; Arad 1:5, 2:7), מוצא [mawṣāʾ]
"spring" (Shiloah 5), יין [yayn] "wine" (Arad 1:3.9, etc.; Lach. 25),
and בית [bayt] "house, dynasty" (Beer-Sheba Ost. 1:4;[134] Silwan B
1; Mur 17 A 1). These diphthongs were uncontracted in both medial,
and presumably final, positions.[135] With respect to final diphthongs,
however, the orthographic pattern in these texts is of no help since
final long vowels are marked; whether contracted or not, a semi-
vowel would appear in the orthography. Thus the consistent appearance of medial diphthongs suggests the presence of final diphthongs.

Two forms,[136] however, may reflect diphthong contraction in
the southern Hebrew dialect. The first is the place name תלד [Tôlād]
< *Tawlad.[137] This spelling is surprising, since the place itself was
located in south Judah. But it is likely that the reading תלד is er-
roneous.[138] In this case there is no contracted diphthong.

The other possible instance of diphthong contraction is reflected
in the form of the word "day." While the form ים appears throughout
the southern Hebrew texts,[139] it is striking that יום*, comparable to
[yawm] in Old Aramaic and Ammonite, never appears.[140] There are
two explanations: (1) as in all Semitic languages,[141] BH had two
forms of "day," *yawm > יום [yôm] and *yam > ימים [yāmīm]/ימי-
[yᵊmê]. The appearance of ים "day" in the southern Hebrew epigraphic texts, then, would suggest that, at one time, Hebrew had a
form *yam > [yām][142] in the singular as well.[143] (2) ים was indeed
pronounced [yôm], as in BH [yôm] < *yawm. This form had to be
borrowed from a diphthong-contracting dialect, probably from
northern Hebrew. In either case, the form ים in southern Hebrew
does not violate the rule that, in this dialect, all diphthongs were
pronounced.[144]

The first-millennium NWS dialects reflect various degrees of
diphthong contraction and noncontraction. At one extreme, Phoenician dialects and northern Hebrew contracted the diphthongs *aw
and *ay in both medial and final positions. At the other extreme,
Old Aramaic, the Deir Alla dialect, and southern Hebrew preserved
these diphthongs in both positions. In Old Aramaic and the Deir Alla
dialect, however, the diphthong contracted in the "long" imperfect

of some final weak forms. The treatment of *ay and *aw in Samalian resembles that of Old Aramaic and Deir Alla, except that *ay in final position contracted to [ê]; this contraction is perhaps attributable to the influence of Phoenician in Samal at this time.

Those dialects which lay on the periphery of Aramaic- and Canaanite-speaking peoples show greater variation in the treatment of original diphthongs. In Ammonite, [aw] was preserved in medial (and final?) position, whereas *ay contracted to [ê] in both. In Edomite, the only evidence for original diphthongs suggests that *aw, preserved as late as the eighth-seventh centuries, contracted to [ô] by the fifth century B.C.E. Finally, *aw and *ay in Moabite were in the process of contracting; place names preserved the original diphthongs, while the spoken language reflects a distinct tendency to contract diphthongs.

Two models can account for this distribution. Monophthongization may have originated in Phoenicia, and thence spread to northern Israel, later to Ammon, Moab, and finally reached Edom centuries later. Alternatively, monophthongization developed independently in several dialects as it did, for example, in Akkadian. As a result, it is unclear whether monophthongization is a shared innovation in NWS. The distribution of the phenomenon, however, suggests a Phoenician origin.[145]

9.   The treatment of *n + consonant.

BYBLIAN: Within the word, *nun* always assimilated to the following consonant, as for example in אדת "lady" (Elibaal 2; Shiptibaal 4) < *ʾadōnt[146] and מג/פשת "offerings, possessions" (Bronze Spat. 4.5) < *ngś or *npš. The only exception to this rule is that *nun* did not assimilate to a following laryngeal,[147] as for example תנחל "you will inherit" (Bronze Spat. 4).

Nun assimilated to the following consonant even between words, as for example ביחמלך "son of Yehimilk" (Shiptibaal 3; Elibaal 1 [partially restored]) < *bin + Yehimilk and בכלבי "son of Kalbay" (ʿAbdo) < *bin + Kalbay. This particular assimilation was restricted to בן + PN, when the two words were pronounced in sandhi and when the initial letter of the second letter was not a laryngeal; cf. בן אחרם "son of Ahirom" (Ahirom 1) and בן אלבעל "son of Elibaal" (Shiptibaal 2). The assimilation of *bin to the following

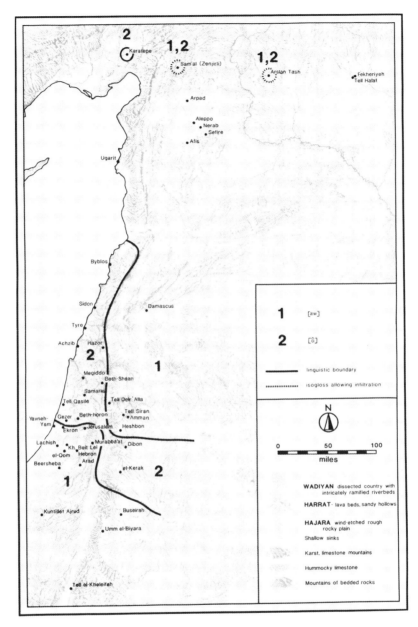

MAP 3: The correspondences of *aw*.

word did not continue into later Byblian, for by the fifth century the form בן יחרבעל appears (Yehawmilk 1).

STANDARD PHOENICIAN: *Nun* assimilated to the following consonant only within a word, as for example יסע [yissaˁ] "he rips out" (Karatepe A III 15.17) < *yinsaˁ, יזק [yâzziq] "he damages" (Kilamu 14) < *yânziq, and possibly[148] כת [kattī] "I was" (Kilamu 6.10.10.11).

ARAMAIC: *Nun* always assimilated to the following consonant within a word, as for example אפין [ʾappayn] "face" (Sf. I A 28.42, III 2) < *ʾanp-, ואשא [wā-ʾaśśaʾ] "and I raised" (Zkr A 11; see also Sf. I B 39, etc.) < *ʾanśaʾ, and יסחו [yassᵊḥū] "may they remove" (Nerab 1:9) < *yansᵊḥū.[149] The preposition מן "from" did not assimilate to the following consonant (e.g., Zkr A 10.10, etc.; Sf. I A 30, B 8, etc.).[150]

Although several exceptions have been adduced to the rule, they are not convincing. For example, Fitzmyer[151] tentatively saw an unassimilated *nun* in תנתע (Sf. I B 29). Yet the division of words in this line is very difficult, and the proposed etymology of תנתע < *ntḏ violates the regular Aramaic correspondence of *ḏ:ק as well.[152] Similarly, the forms תנצר "you protect" and ינצר "it will be protected" in Nerab 1:12.13[153] may either be *peal* or *pael* conjugations. If *peal*, י/תנצר would be the only instance where *nun* failed to assimilate to the following consonant; cf. יסחו "may they remove" (Nerab 1:9). Yet it is also possible that the forms are *pael*, in which case the preservation of the *nun* could be explained by a vowel between the *nun* and *ṣade* ([yᵊnaṭṭer (?)]). Thus, there is no clear evidence for an exception to the rule of the assimilation of *nun* to the following consonant in Old Aramaic.

SAMALIAN: Within a word, *nun* always assimilated to the following consonant, as for example יתנו "they will give" (H 4) < *ntn, את [ʾatt(a)] "you" (H 33) < *ʾantă, חטה [ḥiṭṭā] "wheat" (H 6; P 6.9) < *ḥinṭā, and possibly מת [mit(t)] "indeed" (H 12.13, etc.) < *mint.[154] The *nun* of מן "from" never assimilated to the initial consonant of the following word (P 2.4.7, etc.).[155] The nonassimilation in this case may be attributable to the word divider separating the preposition from the word. Assimilation of *nun*, then, was only word-internal; cf. Byblian.

The only possible exception to this rule is the form of the infinitive לנצב "to erect" (H 10). This example is ambiguous, however,

since the form may be a *pael*,[156] or a *peal* infinitive with a vowel
between the first and second radicals.[157]

AMMONITE: Although the evidence is scarce, it appears that *nun*
assimilated to the following consonant within a word (as in the PN
הצלאל [Sir. 2] < *nṣl). The *nun* of מן "from" did assimilate to a
following consonant, even if that consonant were a laryngeal (as in
מאלת "from Elath" [Hesh. Ost. 4:4]).[158]

DEIR ALLA: *Nun* assimilated to the following consonant within
a word, as in תטפן "they drip (?)" (II 35.36) < *ntp.[159] The *nun* of
מן "from," however, did not assimilate (I 3.13; II 8.8.8).[160]

MOABITE: *Nun* assimilated to the following consonant within a
word, as for example שת [šat(t)] "year" (Mesha 2.8) < *šant and
ואשא [wā-ʾaśśaʾ] "and I raised" (Mesha 20.30) < *nśʾ. The *nun* of
מן "from" assimilated to a following laryngeal, as in מעלם "always"
(Mesha 10) < *min + **ʿō/ālǎm*.[161] The existence of the form בן.
[כמש]ית "son of Kemosh-yat" (Mesha 1) demonstrates that, unlike
Old Byblian, *nun* did not assimilate between words.

EDOMITE: No certain evidence. An example of the preposition
*מן may appear in the Umm el-Biyara Ostracon, l. 2 מעדר "from
ʿAdr."[162] The preposition *מן, then, would have assimilated to the
following word, even if that word began with a laryngeal.

HEBREW: *Nun* always assimilated to the following consonant
within a word (e.g., הכו [hikkū] "they struck" [Shiloah 4] < *nkh
and תתן [tittin] "you shall give" [Arad 1:10] < *ntn). Also, the *nun*
of מן "from" assimilated to a following consonant (e.g., מיין [miy-
yayn] "of wine" [Arad 1:9] < *min + *yayn*, etc.), even if it were
a laryngeal (e.g., מאתך [mē-ʾittāk] "from you" [Arad 5:2, 6:2] < *min
+ *ʾitt*- and מערד [mē-ʿᵃrād] "from Arad" [Arad 24:12] < *min +
ʿArad).

While the final *nun* of *ntn "to give" assimilated to the following
consonant in the perfect (e.g., ונתת "and you will give" [Arad 2:7/8]
< *natant-), the *nun* of other ל"ן verbs did not assimilate in the
perfect, as in BH שכנתי "I dwelt" and ישנתי "I am asleep."[163] Although no such ל"ן verbs appear in epigraphic Hebrew, it is inferred
from BH that this exception was present in the epigraphic texts as
well.

All the dialects exhibit assimilation of *nun* to a following nonlaryngeal consonant, when that consonant was part of the same word

as the *nun*. In Ammonite, Moabite, Edomite, and Hebrew, this assimilation extended to laryngeals as well. In Byblian, however, a
following laryngeal obstructed the assimilation. Similarly, the assimilation of *nun* in מן "from" occurred in Ammonite, Moabite,
Edomite, and Hebrew as an extention of the assimilation of *nun*
within a word. In Old Aramaic, Samalian, and the Deir Alla dialect,
the *nun* of מן "from" did not assimilate.

It is doubtful, however, that these instances of assimilation reflect a shared innovation; *nun* assimilates to a following consonant
in several Semitic languages.[164] The assimilation of *nun*, then, is
most likely a case of independent development in the NWS dialects.[165]

Two idiosyncratic innovations, however, can be isolated.
Only[166] in Old Byblian did *nun* assimilate to the following consonant
of a following word, in the construction **bin* "son" + PN. Hebrew
is also unique since in this dialect alone the *nun* of ל״נ verbs did not
assimilate to a following consonant; cf. possibly standard Phoenician
כת [kattī] "I was" < **kantī*.[167] Thus, the assimilation of *nun* between
words distinguishes Old Byblian (in **bin* + PN), and the failure of
the third radical of ל״נ verbs to assimilate distinguishes Hebrew.

10.   The dissimilation of emphatics.

PHOENICIAN: Not in Phoenician (e.g., קץ "extremity" [Karatepe
A I 14.21] and קצר "harvest" [Karatepe A III 2, C IV 5]).

ARAMAIC: The evidence suggests that initial **q* + emphatic dissimilated to כ + emphatic, as in כיצא "the summer" (Br-Rkb 1:19)
< **qayṭ* and כטל "to kill" (Nerab 1:11) < **qṭl* < **qṭl*.[168] See the
later forms כציר "harvest" and הכצר "to harvest (?)" (Ahiqar 127),
and כצפה "anger" (Ahiqar 101).[169] When **q* was medial, it did not
assimilate, as לקט "to collect" (Fekh. 22).

The distribution of this dissimilation suggests that it was a general, Aramaic phonetic trait. While in later dialects, particularly
Mandaic,[170] dissimilation of *qoph* became characteristic of eastern
Aramaic,[171] in the early period dissimilation occurred in both western (Samal) and eastern (Nerab) Syro-Palestinian Aramaic texts. At
this period, then, dissimilation of initial *qoph* in the presence of an
emphatic does not indicate any dialectal affinities with either East
or West; cf. also the sporadic appearance of this dissimilation in
later western Aramaic.[172]

SAMALIAN: Evidence uncertain. If Ginsberg[173] is correct in interpreting קשתה (H 26.32) as "his truth," this word would constitute evidence that emphatics could dissimilate in Samalian. The Samalian form would agree with that of Syriac [quštā], as opposed to Mandaic [kuštā] in which the first radical dissimilated. Yet while Ginsberg's new interpretation accords well with the context of H 26, it does not fit the military context of H 32 (hence the traditional meaning "his bow" is justified there).

AMMONITE: No evidence.

DEIR ALLA: Probably not in Deir Alla (e.g., קקן "constraint" [I 14] < *ḏwq).[174] There is, however, no word in the Deir Alla texts which begins with *qoph and is followed by an emphatic.

MOABITE: No evidence.

EDOMITE: No evidence.

HEBREW: Not in Hebrew (e.g., קץ "summer" [Gezer Cal. 7] and קצר "to harvest" [Yavneh-Yam 1:3.4.10]).

The dissimilation of emphatics is found in Old Aramaic, and possibly in Samalian. The meager evidence suggests that this dissimilation was restricted to initial *qoph* + emphatic consonant. In Old Aramaic, the *qoph* dissimilated to *kaph*; in Samalian, the following emphatic dissimilated. In terms of distribution, the dissimilation of emphatics is found in both northern and central regions. In the later Aramaic dialects, however, it occurs most commonly in Mandaic (East Aramaic), but is also found sporadically in western dialects as well; the Samalian form קשת* has a parallel only in Syriac. While the dissimilation of emphatics was a specifically Aramaic innovation,[175] it was not particular to one Aramaic-speaking community.

11. Anaptyxis.

PHOENICIAN: Incipient anaptyxis in words whose middle radical was a laryngeal,[176] as especially in PNs containing the element בעל (*Ba-ʾa-lu* [*ANET*[3], pp. 290–292, 297]; *Ba-ʾa-al-ma-lu-ku* [*ANET*[3], p. 296], etc.[177]). Perhaps the transcription of the PN שפטבעל as *Si-pí-it-ti-bi-ʾi-il* (*ANET*[3], pp. 282, 283)[178] indicates that anaptyxis began to spread from middle laryngeal nouns to other, strong nouns.[179]

ARAMAIC: At least incipient anaptyxis, as seen in the contrast between צדה [ṣadê] "owl" (Sf. I A 33) < *ṣady and גדה [gadê] "kid" (Sf. II A 2) < *gady, over against צבי "gazelle" (Sf. I A 33) < *ṭaby.[180] While all three nouns are *qatl- formations of final weak roots, the vacillation between final ה- and י- indicates different phonetic realizations. The forms with final he suggest that the vowel was [ê]; in other words, *gady gained a secondary vowel between the second two radicals, *gadiy, which contracted to [gadê].[181] The form אריה "lion" (Sf. II A 9) also presupposes anaptyxis since it is traceable from *ʾaryiy[182] > [ʾaryê]. צבי, however, either preserves the older form with its final weak consonant, or it represents a different set of phonological changes from those in צדה and גדה. Cf., for example, BH בְּכֹה "weeping" vs. בְּכִי "weeping."[183] The available evidence, then, suggests that anaptyxis was operative in at least its beginning stages.

SAMALIAN: Apparently not in Samalian, as for example שבי "captives" (collective singular)[184] (P 8) < *šiby. The examples adduced by Dion[185] to demonstrate anaptyxis—חבא (H 20), חרא (H 23), and חמא (H 33)—are semantically and morphologically difficult; anaptyxis cannot be proven by these examples alone. Finally, Poebel[186] and Dion[187] explained שי "likeness, similitude" (H 18) as derived from *šiwy > *šiwiy > (syncopation of intervocalic waw) *šiiy > [šî]; anaptyxis must be assumed if the development of this noun is to be traced correctly. Yet in this case as well, שי may mean "gift"[188] (BH שי) and need not involve anaptyxis at all. Thus there is no unambiguous example of anaptyxis in Samalian.

AMMONITE: No evidence.

DEIR ALLA: No evidence.

MOABITE: No evidence.

EDOMITE: No evidence.

HEBREW: Probably not in the early period. Anaptyxis apparently began at a later time, as reflected, in its early stage, by Septuagint transcriptions.[189]

From the evidence at hand, only Phoenician and Aramaic show signs of anaptyxis in the eighth-seventh centuries B.C.E. Yet the relationship between anaptyxis in these two dialects is unclear. Anaptyxis may have developed independently in both dialects (cf. later Hebrew) or may have spread from one to the other (cf. the geographical contiguity of Phoenician and Aramaic). However, the history of the phenomenon itself,[190] suggesting a universal Semitic tendency to break up consonant clusters, as well as the strong isogloss between Aramaic and Phoenician dialects, indicate that anaptyxis probably arose independently in these two dialects.[191]

12. The prothetic ʾaleph.[192]

BYBLIAN: No evidence.

STANDARD PHOENICIAN: If the prothetic aleph appears in אגדד "band" (Karatepe A I 15),[193] this example is unique in standard Phoenician. It is also possible, however, that אגדד represents an *ʾaqtūl nominal formation. In that case, the prefixed aleph was not a phonetic feature but part of the nominal pattern.

In the later Phoenician dialects, particularly in Cyprian, the prothetic aleph commonly occurred before sibilants, as for example אשנם "two" (KAI 32:3) < *šnêm and the demonstrative pronoun אז "this" (KAI 31:1, 32:2, etc.) < *z.[194] In the early period, the only example of prothetic aleph before a sibilant is the relative אש < *š.[195] In this case, however, the prothetic aleph also marked a syntactic difference: while אש was the relative particle, ש was the genitive.[196] The prothetic aleph in אש, then, was phonemic.

ARAMAIC: Only in אשם "name" (Sf. I C 25, II B 7) < *šm[197] (cf. שם "name" [Zkr C 2.2; Nerab 1:10, 2:3]) and the place name אזרן (Fekh. 13) < *Zarani (Fekh. Akkadian text, l. 20). The pronunciation of the place name, however, is uncertain. Either it was [ʾAzarani][198] or perhaps [ʾAzrani] < *Zrani;[199] the latter vocalization presumes the loss of the initial unaccented vowel. The present evidence, then, suggests that the prothetic aleph appeared in Old Aramaic only before sibilants in (?) initial consonant clusters. Admittedly, two lone examples do not constitute a phonetic rule.

SAMALIAN: Only in isolated instances—אשם "name" (H 16.21), אגם "also" (P 5), and אסנב "two-thirds mina" (P 6). In אשם, the prothetic aleph broke up the initial consonant cluster *šm by making the cluster noninitial. The aleph in אסנב was not, as some scholars believed,[200] part of the conjunction [wa], since there is no definite proof that Samalian had a conjunction וא beside the regular -ו.[201] Rather, the aleph broke up an initial consonant cluster *sneb < Akkadian sinepû; the Akkadian word, probably with stress on the ultima, lost the first syllable since its short vowel in an open syllable was two positions away from the accent. In this way, the reduction of the vowel created a consonant cluster, which in turn was broken up by a prothetic *aleph*.[202] Finally, the *aleph* in אגם remains unexplained, since the form גם "also" appears in H 8.9 and P 16.[203]

AMMONITE: Possibly in אשחת "cistern" (Sir. 5) and את/סחר "(?)" (Sir. 4).[204] The reading of the second word, however, is uncertain. Thompson and Zayadine[205] read the second letter as *taw* and derived the noun from *ḥwr*. Cross[206] read the second letter *samekh* and interpreted the word as "wall (of circumnavigation)" < *sḥr*. While both readings require the presence of a prothetic *aleph*, Cross' אסחר would suggest that in Ammonite, as in Cyprian Phoenician, prothetic *aleph* was attached only to sibilants; see also the relative particle אש < *š. Nevertheless, it is possible that the *aleph* in אשחת and את/סחר was part of the nominal formation (*aqtul, *aqtal, *aqtil, etc.).

DEIR ALLA: Only in אפרח "chick" (I 8). While Hoftijzer[207] interpreted the *aleph* as part of a broken plural formation, such broken plurals are uncommon in NWS.[208] Indeed, comparison with BH אפרח suggests that the *aleph* was merely phonetic. In this case, the *aleph* broke up an initial consonant cluster.

MOABITE: Only in אשוח "cistern" (Mesha 9.23 [partially restored]). Since the vocalization of this word is not known, the exact function of the *aleph* is uncertain.[209] It is suspected, however, that it broke up an initial consonant cluster.

EDOMITE: No evidence.

HEBREW: There are no examples of the prothetic *aleph* in epigraphic Hebrew. The evidence of Masoretic Hebrew, however, suggests that in epigraphic Hebrew too, the prothetic *aleph* arose in order to break up initial consonant clusters. In Hebrew, moreover, there is no special connection between the prothetic *aleph* and initial sibilants.

Initial consonant clusters are unstable in all the Semitic languages and are commonly broken up by prothesis.[210] The prothetic *aleph* appears throughout the NWS dialects. In standard Phoenician and Old Aramaic, the scanty evidence suggests that the prothetic *aleph* was not a regular phonetic feature. In Ammonite, and possibly Moabite, as well as in later Phoenician dialects, the prothetic *aleph* was attracted to sibilants; in Old Aramaic too, both examples of the prothetic *aleph* preceded sibilants. In the Deir Alla dialect and Masoretic Hebrew, there was no special connection between the prothetic *aleph* and initial sibilants.

13. *CV ᵓ > [CV̂].

PHOENICIAN: The *aleph* was lost, at least in speech, when it was syllable-closing[211] (e.g., *ra²š > *râš > [rōš] = Greek ρω, and Punic *nasot* "I bore" [Poen. 947] < *naśa²tī). Although the *aleph* was lost in the spoken language, it was still written, as for example צאן [ṣōn] "sheep" (Karatepe A III 9, etc.), ראש [rōš] "head" (Kilamu 15.16), and the later Byblian form קראת [qarōtī] "I called" (Yehawmilk 7).

ARAMAIC: There are only two alleged examples of the loss of *aleph* in Aramaic. The first, אהבד "I shall destroy" (Sf. II C 5), thought by some[212] to reflect the syncope of syllable-closing *aleph* in its beginning stages, is rather a scribal error for אהאבד which does appear in Sf. II C 4.[213] The other example is בירא "well (?)" (Sf. I B 34) < *bi²r, where a syllable-closing *aleph* would have quiesced, producing a long vowel.[214] Yet even though the latter example is possible, syllable-closing *aleph* was otherwise retained in both verbs (e.g., פ"א *peal* imperfects) and nouns (e.g., ראש "head"). The lone example of בירא, then, is counterbalanced by the otherwise consistent preservation of *aleph* in all positions.

SAMALIAN: The only possible instance of the loss of postvocalic *aleph* is קרני "he summoned me" (H 13), if the verbal root is *qrᵓ.[215] In no other instance, however, was the *aleph* lost, as for example in פ"א verbs (יאחז "he seizes" [H 15, etc.], יאמר "he will say" [H 17, etc.], and לאכל "to eat" [H 23]).[216]

AMMONITE: No evidence of the loss of *aleph*. In both cases of syllable-closing *aleph*—צאן "sheep" (Hesh. Ost. 4:2.7.10) and דשא "grass" (Hesh. Ost. 4:9)—the *aleph* is retained in the orthography. Whether it persisted in the spoken language is unknown.

DEIR ALLA: No evidence of the loss of *aleph* from the consonantal text, for example יאנש "he will weaken" (II 10), ויאמר "and he said" (I 4/5), and ראש "head" (II 11).

MOABITE: There are two probable, and one possible, instances of the loss of *aleph*. רש "chief" (Mesha 20) is probably cognate to the common Semitic *ra²š; the *aleph* had therefore been absorbed into the preceding [a].[217] The other likely candidate is בר "cistern" (Mesha 24.25). Whether this word is cognate to BH באר < *bi²r[218] or to BH בור < bu²r,[219] the outcome is identical; syllable-closing *aleph* was lost in the Moabite word. That syllable-closing *aleph* was not always lost, however, is proven by צאן "sheep" (Mesha 31).[220] The latter, however, is probably a historical spelling.

Finally, it is possible that *aleph* was lost in רית "spectacle (?)" (Mesha 12), if the root is *$*r^{\jmath}y$.[221] Yet the nominal pattern of this word is thoroughly obscure. Would the supposed *aleph* have been syllable-opening or syllable-closing?

EDOMITE: No evidence.

HEBREW: Postvocalic *aleph* was lost in, for example, לקרת "toward" (Shiloah 4) = BH לקראת.[222] *Aleph* is present in, for example, ראש "head" (Shiloah 6). Like BH, then, syllable-closing *aleph* was absorbed into the preceding vowel in epigraphic Hebrew;[223] the appearance of etymological *aleph* in forms such as ראש is attributable to historical spelling.

With respect to the loss of postvocalic *aleph*, the first-millennium NWS dialects fall into two groups. In the Deir Alla dialect and Old Aramaic (except for one possible example), etymological *aleph* was always preserved in syllable-closing position. Ammonite is the only overall Canaanite dialect which preserved *aleph* in all texts, although the quiescence of this consonant might have begun in the spoken language.

In Phoenician, Moabite, and Masoretic Hebrew, the syllable-closing *aleph* was lost. This syncope was (presumably) consistent in all three dialects, although only in Moabite and Hebrew did the loss of *aleph* enter the written language as well. In Samalian too, postvocalic *aleph* might have been absorbed into the preceding vowel. Since the consonantal quality of *aleph* had weakened severely in several Semitic languages,[224] the syncope of *aleph* in NWS reflects a general Semitic phenomenon. The loss of syllable-closing *aleph*, then, might have developed independently in the individual NWS dialects.

14.   The aphaeresis of *ʾaleph*.

BYBLIAN: Initial *aleph* was not lost (see examples below).

STANDARD PHOENICIAN: In Phoenician personal names, there was a tendency to drop initial *aleph* when it began an open syllable two positions away from the accent, as for example *Ḥi-ru-um-mu* (*ANET*[3], p. 283) = חרם (KAI 31:1) < אחרם [ʾAḥīrōm] (Ahirom 1) and *Tu-ba-ʾ-lu* (*ANET*[3], p. 287) < תבעל[א] (Ahirom 1).[225] Whether this aphaeresis was a regular feature of the spoken language, however, cannot be determined.

ARAMAIC: Loss of initial *aleph* occurred only in the numeral "one" חד (Sf. I B 26.26, etc.; Br-Rkb 1:13) < *ʾaḥad* (as in Arabic and Ugaritic). Cf., in contrast, אנש "man" (Sf. III 16 [plural]; Fekh. 9.14) and אשרת "sanctuary" (Sf. I B 11) < Akk. *aširtu*.

Since aphaeresis of *aleph* was restricted to a single word, it cannot have been a regular phonetic feature of the dialect. In some way, the aphaeresis was peculiar to this numeral.[226] Perhaps the loss of *aleph* was conditioned by the construction "one" + bound plural noun, as for example חד מלכן "one king" (Sf. I B 26; Br-Rkb 1:13) and חד מלכי ארפד "one of the kings of Arpad" (Sf. III 1). The initial syllable of *ʾaḥad*, both open and removed from the principal stress of the construct phrase, was lost in this very unstable position. Whatever the origin of this aphaeresis, however, the form [ḥad] < *ʾaḥad* became characteristic of all Aramaic dialects.[227]

SAMALIAN: Loss of initial *aleph* occurred only in the numeral "one" חד (H 15.27; P 5), as in Old Aramaic and Deir Alla;[228] no other noun shows this aphaeresis, as the form אנש "man" (P 23) suggests. It is unclear, however, whether the form חד was borrowed from Aramaic or participated in the same innovation as in Aramaic (cf. H 27.27 and P 5). Nevertheless, the restriction of this aphaeresis to חד is notable. See, similarly, Deir Alla.

AMMONITE: No evidence. The alleged attestation of the numeral "one," חד*, in the phrase כחד אכחד (Cit. 3)[229] does not exist. Rather, כחד אכחד is an inf. absolute + imperfect of the root *kḥd* "to destroy."[230]

DEIR ALLA: Initial *aleph* was lost only in the numeral "one" חד (II 10). Cf., perhaps, אנפה "heron" (I 8) < BH אנפה.

MOABITE: *Aleph* was not lost in initial position (e.g., אחר "after" [Mesha 3]).

EDOMITE: No evidence.

HEBREW: Loss of initial *aleph* occurred only in נחנו "we" (Lach. 4:10/11) < BH אנחנו.[231] In view of the common BH [ʾanaḥnū], the epigraphic form appears to have lost the initial *aleph*. Yet in comparison with other Semitic forms of this pronoun, for example Arabic [naḥnu], Akk. *nīnu,* and Eth. [nəḥna], the epigraphic form is historically correct; the reconstructed Proto-Semitic form does not have an initial *aleph*.[232] And, since there is no other example of the first person plural independent pronoun in epigraphic Hebrew, it is unclear whether this form was the common one or whether an initial *aleph* (cf. BH) was indeed lost. Nevertheless, the loss of an initial

ʾ + short vowel in an open, unaccented syllable is consistent with the general pattern of the other NWS dialects.

Initial ʾ + short vowel, in an open, unaccented syllable is subject to aphaeresis in the first-millennium NWS dialects. On the basis of the present evidence, the aphaeresis was absent from Byblian and Moabite, whereas it occurred, to different degrees, in standard Phoenician, Old Aramaic, Samalian, the Deir Alla dialect, and (?) Hebrew. In standard Phoenician, this process was most prominent, for PNs often lost this syllable when it lay two positions away from the accent. In Old Aramaic, Samalian, and the Deir Alla dialect, loss of initial *aleph* was restricted to the numeral "one" חד < *ʾaḥad*; in Samalian and Deir Alla, though, it is unclear whether this loss of initial *aleph* reflects an innovation shared with Old Aramaic or whether חד was borrowed from Old Aramaic. Nevertheless, given the restricted nature of this aphaeresis to a single word, the form חד connects these three dialects as one dialectal group. Finally, loss of initial *aleph* may have occurred in Hebrew, only in the pronoun "we" נחנו.

15. The syncope of *yodh* between short vowels (except *wa* + impf.).

BYBLIAN: The only evidence pertains to the syncope in originally final position. In ל"י verbs, intervocalic *yodh* did not syncopate, as for example עלי [ʿalaya] "he attacks" (Ahirom 2), בני [banaya] "he built" (Yehimilk 1; Shiptibaal 1), and חוי [ḥawwa/iya] "he restored" (Yehimilk 2).

STANDARD PHOENICIAN: Syncope was regular in final position, as in final weak perfect verbs (e.g., חז [ḥazō] "he saw" [Kilamu 11.11.12] < *ḥazâ < *ḥazaya).[233] In initial position, however, the evidence is mixed. In the causative conjugation, intervocalic *yodh* was lost in the imperfect (e.g., יזק "he damages" [Kilamu 14] < *יינזק), whereas in the preposition "through" both forms appear (e.g., *ba-di-u* [EA 245:35] = בד [bōd] [KAI 60:1] vs. ביד [Kilamu 6; cf. l. 13]).

A possible exception to the syncope of intervocalic *yodh* is ליפתח "may it be opened" (Arsl.T. 1:22/23).[234] Whether the prefixed ל- be vocalized [lū], [li], or [lu], the effect is identical: the *yodh* remains. Yet new readings of this text have shown that this form does not exist. In its stead, אליפתח should be read.[235] Intervocalic *yodh*, then, syncopated everywhere except in the preposition ביד "through" (Kilamu 6).

ARAMAIC: Syncope was regular in final weak perfect verbs, as for example [ה]ות [hawât] "it became" (Sf. III 24) < *hawaya-t. In initial position, *yodh* did not syncopate in ביד [ba/i-yad] "through" (Zkr A 12), but syncopation occurred when the precative *lamedh* was followed by the third person jussive (as for example להוי "may he be" [Fekh. 12] < *li-yihway, לאכלו "may they eat" [Fekh. 22] < *li-yaʾkulū, etc.).[236]

SAMALIAN: Intervocalic *yodh* syncopated in final weak perfect verbs, as for example הות [hawât] "it was/fell" (P 2) < *hawaya-t and perhaps שתא "it drank" (H 9) < *šataya. In initial position, however, the *yodh* did not always syncopate. It did not syncopate in ביד [ba/i-yad] "in the hand of" (H 2.4.8), [י]ביאד "in Yʾdy" (H 25), etc. It did syncopate when precative -ל was attached to third person imperfect verbs, as in למנע [limnaᶜ] "may he prevent" (H 24) < *li-yimnaᶜ and לבתשה "may they pound him" (H 31) < *li-yaktušū-.[237]

AMMONITE: The evidence indicates that intervocalic *yodh* syncopated in final weak perfect verbs, as for example בנה [banō] "he built" (Cit. 1) < *banâ < *banaya.[238] In the preposition "from, through," the *yodh* was retained in the PN בידאל[239] but was lost in the PN בדאל.[240]

DEIR ALLA: Intervocalic *yodh* syncopated in final weak perfect verbs, as for example שהה [šahâ (?)] "it is desolate" (II 14) < *šahaya. The presence of *yodh* in שתיו (I 10), however, does not fall into this category since *yodh* was followed by a long vowel.[241]

MOABITE: Intervocalic *yodh* syncopated in final weak perfect verbs, as for example בנה [banâ (?)] "he built" (Mesha 18) < *banaya. No other example of the syncopation of intervocalic *yodh* appears.

EDOMITE: There is no evidence to indicate whether intervocalic *yodh* syncopated in final weak verbs. Initial *yodh*, however, might have been lost in בד "from, through" < *ba/i-yad, which forms part of a PN in Ost. 6043:2[242] (partially restored) and which might have been an independent preposition in the Umm el-Biyara ostracon.[243]

HEBREW: Intervocalic *yodh* was syncopated in final weak perfect verbs, as for example היה [hāyâ] "it was" (Shiloah 1) < *hayaya and עשה [ᶜāśâ] "he did" (Lach. 4:3) < *ᶜaśaya. Intervocalic *yodh* did not syncopate in initial position (e.g., ביד "through" [Arad 17:9; cf. the restored passages in Arad 16:5/6 and 24:13/14]).[244]

In varying degrees, intervocalic *yodh* was syncopated in all first-millennium NWS dialects. Standard Phoenician, Aramaic, Samalian, Ammonite, the Deir Alla dialect, Moabite, and Hebrew have lost the final *yodh* in the perfect of final weak verbs. In Byblian Phoenician, however, this final *yodh* was preserved.

The form of the composite preposition יד + ב also differed within the dialects. In Samalian-Phoenician, Aramaic, Samalian, and Hebrew, intervocalic *yodh* did not syncopate. In later Phoenician and Edomite, the *yodh* disappeared. Ammonite shows examples of each spelling. Perhaps the different forms are traceable to different vocalizations of the preposition -ב.[245]

Finally, an initial *yodh* in verbal forms was lost in standard Phoenician, Old Aramaic, and Samalian. In standard Phoenician, the *yodh* of the causative conjugation was lost in all imperfect forms. In Aramaic and Samalian, the *yodh* of the third person jussive forms was lost following the precative *lamedh*. The phonetic environment in Aramaic and Samalian was apparently identical, whereas that of Phoenician was probably different.

16.   The syncope of intervocalic *he*.

BYBLIAN: Only the *he* of the third person masc. sing. suffix attached to singular nouns was syncopated in Byblian.[246] The syncopation occurred between the tenth and ninth centuries. In the Ahirom inscription, intervocalic *he* was present in the suffix, as for example אבה [ʾabī-hū] "his father" (l. 1), משפטה [mašpaṭi-hū] "of his judgment" (l. 2), and מלכה [mulki-hū] "of his dominion" (l. 2); cf. שתה [šōtahū] "he placed him" (l. 1). One century later the *he* was lost, as in אדתו [ʾadōttaw, -tô] or [ʾadōttiw] "his lady" (Elibaal 2; Shiptibaal 4) < *ʾadōttahŭ̆ or *-tihŭ̆; the quality of the connecting vowel is unknown. Cf. also the fifth-century form זרע [zarʿaw, -rô] "his seed" (Yehawmilk 15) < *zarʿahŭ̆.[247]

Intervocalic *he* did not syncopate when the definite article followed the conjunction -ו "and." Although the evidence is late, the forms והערפת "and the portico" (Yehawmilk 6) < *wa-ha . . . and והעפת "and the bird" (Yehawmilk 5) < *wa-ha . . . demonstrate that, in Byblian, *h* of the definite article was not lost after *wa "and."

STANDARD PHOENICIAN: The *he* of the third person possessive and objective suffixes was lost when attached to consonantal endings, as for example שם [šmô] "his name" (Karatepe A III 14.16) < *-a-hŭ, שם [šmâ] "its name" (Karatepe A II 10.18) < *-a-hă, and ישבם [yôšibōm] "(I) made them settle" (Karatepe A I 20) < *-a-humu. If, however, a vowel preceded the suffix, the resultant form was י- for the singular and נם- for the plural suffixes.[248]

The definite article *he* was lost after the prepositions -ב and -ל (e.g., במקמם "in the places" [Karatepe A II 3] < ה + ב*) and after the conjunction -ו "and"[249] (e.g., ועם "and this people" [Karatepe A III 7/8, C IV 7] < ה + ו* and וזבח "and the sacrifice" [Karatepe C IV 2] < ה + ו*, etc.).[250]

ARAMAIC: Intervocalic *he* did not syncopate in Old Aramaic. The supposed exceptions to this rule are, in fact, uncertain. While, for example, the causative form יסכר "he will hand over" in Sf. III 3, without the causative *he*, may reflect the syncopation of intervocalic *he* (cf. the correct יהסכר in Sf. III 3),[251] יסכר is most likely a scribal error.[252] The other, more celebrated example of this syncope in the third person masc. sing. suffix וה-[253] is likewise questionable;[254] in no other NWS dialect was the *he* syncopated in this suffix.[255]

The only real exception to the rule of nonsyncopation is in Fekh.-Aramaic, where the third person plural suffixes on sing. nouns were ם- (Fekh. 4.4) and ן- (Fekh. 3.5), masc. and fem.[256]

SAMALIAN: Syncopation of intervocalic *he* occurred only in the imperfect of the causative conjugation (e.g., יקם [yâqim] "he will erect" [H 28] < *yu/a-haqim and יזכר [yâzkir (?)] "he will mention" [H 16] < *yu/a-hazkir).[257] The *he* in the third person suffixes did not syncopate (e.g., אבה "his father" [H 29; P 2, etc.] and ידיה "his hands" [H 29]).

AMMONITE: It is unclear whether, or to what extent, intervocalic *he* syncopated in Ammonite. There are, for example, no occurrences of the definite article -ה preceded by the prepositions -ב or -ל; but the definite article did not syncopate after *wa* "and" (e.g., וה.גנת "and the garden" [Sir. 4] and והאת/סחר "and the (?)" [Sir. 4]). There are also no examples of the causative stem in the imperfect.[258]

It is likely that intervocalic *he* was retained in the third person suffixes. Nevertheless, all suffixed forms are not completely understood. If, for example, כרה "its laver (?)" (Cit. 5) contains the third person masc. sing. suffix on a masc. sing. noun,[259] the final *he* marks

the suffix. And according to the orthographic pattern of this inscription, this *he* is most likely consonantal. Cf. similarly Cross'[260] reading אכחֹד[ה]וֹ "I shall extirpate him" (Cit. 3).

DEIR ALLA: Intervocalic *he* was syncopated in the causative imperfect (example uncertain).[261] *He* of the third person suffixes, however, was retained in the singular (e.g., לבבה "his heart" [II 12] and
עמה "his people" [I 4, II 17]) and plural (only on prepositions, e.g.
להם "to them" [I 5]). In the plural suffix attached to sing. nouns,
the form was -ם < *-a-humu[262] (e.g., בלבבם "in their heart" [II
12][263]). Cf. Hebrew.

MOABITE: Intervocalic *he* syncopated when the definite article
was preceded by an enclitic preposition (e.g., בקר "in the city"
[Mesha 11] < *bi/a-haq-qīr),[264] and when the causative particle *he*
was preceded by a personal pronoun of the imperfect (e.g., ואשב
"and I brought back" [Mesha 12] < שב + ה + א*).

It is unclear, however, whether *he* syncopated in third person
sing. suffixes. According to Harris,[265] intervocalic *he* has syncopated. He vocalized ארצה "his land" (Mesha 5/6) as [ʾarṣô] <
*arṣahŭ; for final *he* as [ô], he adduced the name נבה "Nebo"
(Mesha 14) = BH נבו. Yet the exact value of the final *he* in נבה as
a transcription of Akkadian "Nabu" is uncertain, especially in view
of the spelling נבא in Sf. I A 8;[266] there are no other certain examples
of Moabite ה- with the value [ô].[267] Further, the *he* of the third person
masc. sing. suffix was present on masc. plural nouns (e.g., ימה "his
days" [Mesha 8] and רשה "its chiefs" [Mesha 20]; cf. שעריה "its
gates" [Mesha 22]). Thus, since there is no syncopation of the suffixed *he* on plural nouns, it is uncertain whether the suffixed *he* on
sing. nouns syncopated either. There remain, then, two possibilities:
(1) syncopation of *he* did not occur in the Moabite third person
suffixes, comparable to the situation in Old Aramaic and probably
Samalian;[268] or (2) intervocalic *he* syncopated after an *a*-vowel (e.g.,
[ʾarṣô] < *-ahŭ) but remained after long/contracted vowels (e.g.,
[yômôh] < *-awh < *-awhŭ),[269] comparable to standard Phoenician
and Hebrew. On the basis of the orthography, either alternative is
possible.

EDOMITE: No evidence.

HEBREW: Intervocalic *he* was syncopated when the prepositions
-ב, -ל, and -כ preceded the definite article (e.g., בצר "in the rock"
[Shiloah 3] < צר + ה + ב* and לשר "to the officer" [Yavneh-Yam
1:12] < שר + ה + ל*), and in the *hiphil* imperfect (e.g., ישמע "may

he cause to hear" [Lach. 2:1, 3:2, etc.] < *yu/a-hašmiᶜ). After the conjunction *wa, however, the definite article did not syncopate.

Syncopation of intervocalic he in the third person suffixes is a more complicated issue.[270] In general, the third person masc. sing. suffix lost he after short a (e.g., [ע]בדה) [ᶜabdô] "his servant" [Lach. 2:5] < *-aw < *-ahŭ and אמתה [ᵃmātô] "his maidservant" [Silwan B 2] < *-aw < *-ahŭ; similarly the objective suffix, לקחה [lᵊqāḥô] "he took him" [Lach. 4:6] < *-aw < *laqaḥ + a + hŭ and שלחה "he sent it" [Lach. 3:21] < *šalaḥ + a + hŭ); after accented connecting vowels, the he was retained (e.g., the objective suffix on ויעלהו "and he brought him up" [Lach. 4:6/7]). Similarly, the third person plural suffix lost intervocalic he after short a (e.g., ימם [yômām] "their day" [Ajrud] < *-ahem < *-a-humu and אתם [ᵓōtām] "them" [Arad 3:6] < *-ahem < *ᵓōt + a + humu; so too the objective suffix in והבקידם [wᵊ-hibqīdām (?)] "and he will hand them over" [Arad 24:14/15] < *hibqīd + a + humu), except in the monoconsonantal prepositions (e.g., להם "to/for them" [Arad 1:8] < *lahumu); intervocalic he was retained after long vowels (no examples from the epigraphic texts).

Two problematic forms, however, remain. In רעו "his fellow" (Shiloah 3), the third person masc. sing. suffix appears as waw instead of he. Although Cross and Freedman[271] vocalized the form [reᶜew], such a suffix [ew] would be anomalous on final weak roots; cf. BH רֵעֵהוּ "his fellow" and ויעלהו (Lach. 4:6/7). Rather, the final waw in רעו is an alternate spelling for the third person masc. sing. suffix ה-. The form, then, should be vocalized [rēᶜô] < *reᶜ + ahŭ. The base of רעו was *riᶜ, in contrast to the final weak root in BH.[272] Cf. the suffixed forms of BH שדה "field."

The other problematic form is the third person masc. sing. suffix on masc. plural nouns. Whereas most scholars[273] posited syncope of he in this suffix, it is unnecessary to trace the development of the suffixed form in this fashion. Such a derivation does not accord with the other forms of the suffix in the NWS dialects.

Intervocalic he in the first-millennium NWS dialects syncopated in different degrees. All NWS dialects with a prefixed definite article lost the article when it was preceded by a monoconsonantal preposition. In standard Phoenician, the definite article was lost after the conjunction *wa "and" as well. Standard Phoenician, then, extended the application of a general phonetic rule.

Of those dialects which had *he* as the causative prefix, *he* was lost in imperfect forms in Samalian, Deir Alla (?), Moabite, and Hebrew. In contrast, causative *he* was consistently preserved in Old Aramaic. Old Aramaic was therefore conservative in this respect.

The treatment of intervocalic *he* varied most in the third person pronominal suffixes. On the basis of the present evidence, this *he* did not syncopate in Old Byblian, Old Aramaic (except at Fekheriyeh), and (probably) Moabite; preservation of intervocalic *he* may have been the rule in Samalian, Ammonite, and the singular suffix in Deir Alla as well. In contrast to these dialects, intervocalic *he* was lost in later Byblian ו- [aw, ô] < *-a-hŭ, standard Phoenician suffixes attached to consonantal endings, and in the third person plural suffix in the speech of Fekheriyeh and Deir Alla (attached to consonants). If this characterization is correct, the singular suffix in Fekh.-Aramaic and Deir Alla followed the Old Byblian-Old Aramaic pattern (preservation), while the plural suffix followed standard Phoenician (syncope).

He of the third person suffixes in Hebrew and standard Phoenician behaved differently. In Hebrew, *he* syncopated after *a*, but it was preserved after long or accented vowels. In standard Phoenician, however, *he* syncopated when the suffix was attached to a consonant (e.g., [ô] < *-ahŭ). But when attached to a vocalic ending, *he* was replaced by *yodh* in the singular suffixes and by *nun* in the plural. The derivation of the syncopated form, however, is identical in both dialects: *-ahŭ > [ô] (sing. suff.), and *-a-humu > [ām] (Hebrew) and [ōm] (standard Phoenician) (plural suff.). Whereas, then, the development of the suffixes with syncopated *he* unites Hebrew and standard Phoenician, the synchronic rules for choosing the syncopated or nonsyncopated suffix were idiosyncratic in each dialect.

17.   The palatalization of ה*.

BYBLIAN: No palatalization, for example משפטה "of his judgment" and מלכה "of his rule" (Ahirom 2). There is no example of the causative particle in this dialect.

STANDARD PHOENICIAN: ה* changed to י in the presence of an *i*-vowel.[274] Palatalization of ה* was restricted to third person sing. pronominal suffixes (e.g., למ-נערי [li-min-naʿūrê-yū/ī][275] "from his youth" [Kilamu 12] < *-ê-hŭ < *-ay-hŭ and צרתי [ṣarōti-yū/ī] "of his co-wives" [Arsl.T. 1:17] < *-i-hŭ)[276] and the *yiphil* causative stem (i.e. [yip'il] < *hip'il; cf. EA 256:7 ḫi-iḫ-bi-e "he hid" with prefixed *i*-vowel in the perfect causative). This palatalization did not extend to the independent pronouns of the third person.[277]

ARAMAIC: No palatalization, since the causative prefix and pronominal suffixes of the third person were formed with *he*.

SAMALIAN: No palatalization.

AMMONITE: No palatalization.

DEIR ALLA: No palatalization.

MOABITE: No palatalization.

EDOMITE: No evidence.

HEBREW: No palatalization.

Palatalization of *he* to *yodh* was a strictly Phoenician phonetic phenomenon, occurring only in the presence of [i] and *i*-grade vowels. Within Phoenician, it was restricted to standard Phoenician. This palatalization occurred only in one set of pronominal suffixes and the causative particle; it did not spread to the third person independent pronouns.

18a. The correspondences of final *-át.

BYBLIAN: No evidence.[278]

STANDARD PHOENICIAN: *-át was preserved in absolute fem. sing. nouns (e.g., עלמת ['almōt] "lass" [Kilamu 8] < *-át < *-át and אלת ['ilōt] "goddess" [Arsl.T. 1:1] < *-át < *-át).

ARAMAIC: [ā] in abs. fem. sing. nouns (e.g., לחיה "bad" [Sf. I A 26] and מאה "100" [Fekh. 20.20.21.22]).

The only possible exceptions are in the nouns מרמת "rebellion" (Sf. III 22) and שאת "ewe" (Sf. I A 21). Yet neither noun contained an original ending *-át. מרמת is derived from *marmay + at > [marmāt].[279] שאת probably developed from *ṭaʾ + t > [ṭaʾt].[280] Neither form, then, constitutes an exception to the shift *-át > [ā] in absolute feminine singular nouns.

SAMALIAN: [ā] in abs. fem. sing. nouns (e.g., חטה "wheat" [H 6; P 6.9] and שערה "barley" [H 6; P 6.9]).

AMMONITE: *-át was preserved in abs. fem. sing. nouns (e.g., גנת [gannat (?)] "garden" [Sir. 4] and אשחת "cistern" [Sir. 5]).

DEIR ALLA: *-át changed to ה- [ā] in the abs. fem. sing. noun (e.g., אנפה "heron" [I 8] and כהנה "priestess" [I 11]).

MOABITE: *-át was preserved in abs. fem. sing. nouns (e.g., רית "spectacle (?)" [Mesha 12] and המסלת "the highway" [Mesha 26]).

EDOMITE: No evidence.

HEBREW: *-át had shifted to [ā́] in the abs. fem. sing. noun (e.g., הנקבה "the tunnel" [Shiloah 1], (ה)ברכה "(the) pool" [Shiloah 5; Arad 28:7], and הרעה "the evil thing" [Arad 40:15]).

To a certain extent, all the NWS dialects exhibit the tendency to shift final *-át > [ā́].[281] This change appeared in Old Aramaic, Samalian, Deir Alla, and Hebrew. *-át was preserved in standard Phoenician, Ammonite, and Moabite. Since, however, the correspondence *át:[ā́] was not an exclusively shared innovation,[282] its appearance resulted from independent development or diffusion.

18b. The correspondences of *-at.

BYBLIAN: Final *-at was preserved in the pronoun האת [hu²at (?)] "he" (Yehimilk 2). There is no direct evidence for *-at of the third person fem. sing. perfect; in later Byblian, however, it had changed to [ā][283] (e.g., שמע [šam(a)ʿā] "she heard" [Yehawmilk 3.8]).

STANDARD PHOENICIAN: *-at was preserved in the pronoun המת [humat (?)] "they" (Kilamu 13; Karatepe A I 17). It was not preserved in third person fem. sing. perfect verbs (e.g., [?] כרת [kar(a)tā] "she made a covenant" [Arsl.T. 1:10] < *karatat).

ARAMAIC: *-at was preserved in the third person fem. sing. perfect, as for example שבת "it returned" (Sf. III 25).

SAMALIAN: *-at was preserved in third person fem. sing. perfect verbs, as for example כברת "it was abundant" and אכלת "it ate" (P 9).

AMMONITE: No evidence.

DEIR ALLA: *-at was preserved in the third person fem. sing. perfect verb, as for example חרפת "it reproached" (I 7/8) and הקרקת "it chased" (I 15). Adverbial *-at, however, became [ā], as in שמה "there, thither" (II 13.14) < *ṭamat.[284]

MOABITE: No evidence.

EDOMITE: No evidence.

HEBREW: *-at changed into [ā] in adverbs (e.g., שמה "there" [Lach. 4:8; Arad 24:20]), and presumably in the third person plural independent pronoun (BH המה) and the third person fem. sing. perfect (although there is no epigraphic evidence).

In final weak verbs, however, final *t of the third person fem. sing. perfect was preserved, as in הית [hāyât] "there was" (Shiloah 3).[285] The *t was preserved in this form, in contrast to other examples of *-at > [ā], because it was preceded by a long, contracted vowel. The form הית developed from *hayaya-t > *hayayat > [hāyât].[286] Cf. the Old Aramaic fem. sing. nominal form in [ât].

*-at of the third person fem. sing. perfect was preserved in Old Aramaic, Samalian, and the Deir Alla dialect. In standard Phoenician, Hebrew, and later Byblian, it shifted to [ā]. The deictic/adverbial ending *-at, however, was preserved in Byblian and standard Phoenician, in contrast to its change to [ā] in Deir Alla and Hebrew. Thus, like the correspondences of *-át, *-at probably developed independently in the different NWS dialects.

19. Case endings.

BYBLIAN: Final short vowels may have been preserved in this dialect. The evidence, however, is indirect. The third person masc. sing. perfect of final weak verbs ended in -י. For example, בני "he built" (Yehimilk 1; Shiptibaal 1) was probably pronounced [banaya], with final [a];[287] since final short vowels did not drop in verbal forms, it is inferred that they did not drop in nouns.[288] Further, the *nota accusativi* does not appear in these texts. Since the appearance of this particle coincided with the loss of final short vowels—in order to distinguish between subjective and objective nouns after the morphological distinction disappeared[289]—the absence of this particle in Old Byblian suggests that a grammatical distinction between the cases was preserved.

There is no evidence of the presence of plural case distinctions. The masc. plural morpheme, -ם, does not indicate whether a vocalic distinction was preserved between nominative and oblique cases.

STANDARD PHOENICIAN: It is unclear whether cases were preserved in this dialect. On the one hand, an orthographic distinction was maintained between "my" when attached to masc./fem. sing. nominative/accusative nouns and when attached to the corresponding genitive noun; in the former case, the orthography is -∅ [ī] while in the latter it is -י [iya (?)]. Similarly in the masc./fem. third person sing. suffixes, -∅ vs. י-. This orthography suggests that case distinctions, at least in the singular noun, were preserved.[290]

On the other hand, the appearance of the *nota accusativi* אית in Karatepe A 1 3, III 3, etc., suggests that the distinction between nominative and accusative nouns was lost. Further, the thesis concerning the orthographic distinction between nominative/accusative and genitive sing. nouns may be unsound. Instead of reflecting the actual pronunciation of the language, the orthography may have been historical. In other words, by the time of these texts, the Phoenician orthography could have been standardized and may have reflected mere orthographic convention instead of actual pronunciation;[291] cf. the spelling of the PN [Kilamû] as כלמו < *-*muwa*. It remains ambiguous, then, whether final short vowels were or were not pronounced.[292]

As in Byblian, there is no evidence for the distinction between nominative and oblique plural nouns in standard Phoenician.

ARAMAIC: Final short vowels were probably lost in Old Aramaic. The absolute fem. sing. nominal ending ה- [ā] could have arisen only after the final vowel of *-*ātu* was lost, producing *-*āt*, and finally [ā].[293] Note also the appearance of the *nota accusativi* אית.

SAMALIAN: Case vowels were present in masc. plural nouns but not in masc./fem. sing. or fem. plural nouns.[294] In masc. plural nouns, the nominative ended in [ū] (e.g., מלכו "kings" [P 17] and אלהו "gods" [H 2]), and the oblique case ended in [ī] (e.g., באבני "with stones" [H 31.31] and קדם.אלהי "before the gods" [P 23]). The loss of the short case vowels, however, is demonstrated by the form of the abs. fem. sing. nominal ending ה- < *-*āt* < *-*ātu* and also by the transcription of the PN *Pa-na-am-mu-u* (*ANET*[3], pp. 282, 283) < *-*muwa*.[295]

AMMONITE: No evidence. The preservation of final *-*āt* in abs. fem. sing. nouns does not necessarily indicate the presence of final short vowels, since *-*āt* is an intermediate stage between *-*ātu* (as in Ugaritic and Akkadian) and [ā] (as in Hebrew, etc.).

DEIR ALLA: Final short vowels were probably lost in the Deir Alla dialect. The abs. fem. sing. nominal ending [ā] could have arisen only after final short vowels were lost.

MOABITE: There were probably no case endings in Moabite, since the *nota accusativi* was frequently employed.

EDOMITE: No evidence.

HEBREW: Case endings were lost throughout Hebrew, as the appearance of the *nota accusativi* and the abs. fem. sing. nominal morpheme ‏ה-‎ < *-*át* < *-*átu* indicate.

The only possible exception to the loss of case vowels in Hebrew is the form ‏ירחו‎ in the Gezer Calendar, ll. 1.1.2. Ginsberg,[296] for example, suggested that the final *waw* marked [ō], derived from *$\bar{a}$ of the nominative dual ending. Garbini[297] believed that the *waw* marked the old nominative plural [ū]. Yet the ending of this noun remains enigmatic. No certain conclusions can be based on this form alone.

Case endings were, for the most part, lost throughout the first-millennium NWS dialects.[298] Only Byblian and, to a lesser extent, standard Phoenician may have preserved case endings in the singular noun; they do not, however, appear to have retained case distinctions in the masc. plural. In the opposite manner, Samalian preserved case distinctions in the masc. plural, although the singular endings were lost. All other contemporary NWS dialects had lost both singular and plural case endings.

Notes to Chapter 2

1. See Zellig S. Harris, *Development of the Canaanite Dialects*, American Oriental Series, vol. 16 (New Haven: American Oriental Society, 1939), p. 35; and Cyrus H. Gordon, *UT* §5.6. The correspondence *d:ẓ in UT 75 (= CTA 12) constitutes a special problem. See Joshua Blau, "On Problems of Polyphony and Archaism in Ugaritic Spelling," *JAOS* 88 (1968): 525.

2. Other examples are listed by Rainer Degen, *Altaramäische Grammatik der Inschriften des 10.–8. Jh. v. Chr.*, Abhandlungen für die Kunde des Morgenlandes, vol. 38/3 (Wiesbaden: Franz Steiner, 1969), §13.

3. Eduard Y. Kutscher, "Aramaic," in *Linguistics in South West Asia and North Africa*, Current Trends in Linguistics, vol. 6 (The Hague/Paris: Mouton, 1970), p. 353.

4. Louis D. Levine, *Two Neo-Assyrian Stelae from Iran*, Royal Ontario Museum Art and Archaeology Occasional Paper 23 (Toronto: The Royal Ontario Museum, 1972), p. 18 (col. II, l. 4).

5. Wherever possible, cuneiform evidence will be cited to Pritchard's *ANET*.

6. See the discussions by Manfred Weippert, "Menahem von Israel und seine Zeitgenossen in einer Steleninschrift des assyrischen Königs Tiglathpilesar III. aus dem Iran," *ZDPV* 89 (1973): 46–47 n. 83; and Richard C. Steiner, *The Case for Fricative-Laterals in Proto-Semitic*, American Ori-

ental Series, vol. 59 (New Haven: American Oriental Society, 1977), pp. 38–41. Cf. Stephen A. Kaufman, "The Enigmatic Adad-Milki," *JNES* 37 (1978): 105 with n. 20.

7. Degen, *Grammatik*, §13, Anm.; and John C. L. Gibson, *Textbook of Syrian Semitic Inscriptions*, 3 vols. (Oxford: Oxford University Press, 1971–1982), 2:39. Cf. Blau, "'Weak' Phonetic Change and the Hebrew *śîn*," *Hebrew Annual Review* 1 (1977): 69–70 with n. 6.

8. George A. Cooke, *NSI*, pp. 170–171; Gibson, *Textbook*, 2:76; and Steiner, *Fricative-Laterals*, p. 150. See below, no. 3.

9. So Kutscher, in *Linguistics in South West Asia*, p. 354; and Paul-E. Dion, *La langue de Yaʾudi* (Waterloo, Ont.: The Corporation for the Publication of Academic Studies in Religion in Canada, 1974), p. 97.

10. Dion, *La langue*, p. 97.

11. Kutscher, in *Linguistics in South West Asia*, p. 354.

12. For example, Akkadian *ṣâḫu*, Eth. [šaḥaqa], BH צחק/שחק, Arab. *ḏḥk*, Chr.-Pal./Jewish Aramaic דחיק, חאיך, and חיך. Cf. Steiner, *Fricative-Laterals*, pp. 111–120.

13. Felice Israel, "The Language of the Ammonites," *OLP* 10 (1979): 144.

14. The complete list is given by J. Hoftijzer, "Interpretation and Grammar," in *Aramaic Texts from Deir ʿAlla*, ed. J. Hoftijzer and G. van der Kooij. Documenta et Monumenta Orientis Antiqui, vol. 19 (Leiden: E. J. Brill, 1976), p. 283; and Jo Ann Carlton (Hackett), "Studies in the Plaster Text from Tell Deir ʿAllā" (Ph.D. dissertation, Harvard University, 1980), p. 135 (with significant differences). Cf. Joseph Naveh, "[Review of Hoftijzer and van der Kooij, eds., *Aramaic Texts*]," *IEJ* 29 (1979): 135–136; and Jonas C. Greenfield, "[Review of Hoftijzer and van der Kooij, eds., *Aramaic Texts*]," *JSS* 25 (1980): 250–251, who doubt this correspondence. Yet their only substantive counterproposal—to derive יקחן (I 11) from *lqḥ "to take"—does not fit the context. See Helga and Manfred Weippert, "Die 'Bileam'-Inschrift von *Tell Dēr ʿAllā*," *ZDPV* 98 (1982): 98.

15. See Carlton (Hackett), "Studies," pp. 36, 164–165; and idem, "The Dialect of the Plaster Text from Tell Deir ʿAlla," *Or* 53 (1984): 61, for the logical possibilities.

16. Harris, *Development*, p. 36; and idem, *A Grammar of the Phoenician Language*, American Oriental Series, vol. 8 (New Haven: American Oriental Society, 1936), p. 20.

17. See Degen, *Grammatik*, §11, for the list.

18. Cf. Hans H. Schaeder, *Iranische Beiträge I*, Schriften der Königsberger Gelehrten Gesellschaft, Geisteswissenschaftliche Klasse, vol. 6, pt. 5 (Halle an der Saale: Max Niemeyer, 1930), pp. 242–246, esp. p. 244.

19. H. L. Ginsberg, "Psalms and Inscriptions of Petition and Acknowledgement," in *Louis Ginzberg Jubilee Volume*, 2 vols. (New York: The American Academy for Jewish Research, 1945), 1:161 n. 8; and Joseph A. Fitzmyer, *The Aramaic Inscriptions of Sefîre*, Biblica et Orientalia, vol. 19 (Rome: Pontifical Biblical Institute, 1967), p. 150.

20. See Dion, *La langue*, p. 93; and Johannes Friedrich, *PPG* §8*a, for a complete list.

21. So, for example, D. H. Müller, "Die altsemitischen Inschriften von Sendschirli," *WZKM* 7 (1893): 115–116.

22. Friedrich, *PPG* §8*a; and idem, "Zur Stellung des Jaudischen in der nordwestsemitischen Sprachgeschichte," in *Studies in Honor of Benno Landsberger . . . 1965,* Assyriological Studies, vol. 16 (Chicago: The University of Chicago Press, 1965), p. 427.

23. N. Avigad, "Ammonite and Moabite Seals," in *Near Eastern Archaeology in the Twentieth Century,* ed. James A. Sanders (Garden City, N.Y.: Doubleday & Co., 1970), p. 288; Pierre Bordreuil, "Inscriptions sigillaires ouest-sémitiques. I. Epigraphie ammonite," *Syria* 50 (1973): 185, no. 25; and Ruth Hestrin and Michal Dayagi-Mendels, *Inscribed Seals* (Jerusalem: Israel Museum, 1979), p. 129. Israel (*OLP* 10 [1979]: 144 with n. 5) also cited the PN עזראל (Francesco Vattioni, "I sigilli ebraici," *Bibl* 50 [1969]: 377, no. 170).

There is no evidence for the merger of *ḏ and ד, against Garbini's claim (*Le lingue semitiche. Studi di storia linguistica* [Naples: Istituto orientale di Napoli, 1972], p. 100). The PN דבלכס is probably composed of the elements כס + דבל, as Albright has already noted ("Notes on Ammonite History," in *Miscellanea Biblica B. Ubach,* ed. R. M. Díaz. Scripta et Documenta, vol. 1 [Barcelona: Imprenta-Escuela, 1953], p. 134 n. 19), not of the relative *ḏ > ד + ב + לבס "who is in *Lbs*" suggested by Garbini. In any case, the Ammonite relative particle was אש, not ד < *ḏ (see Chapter 3, no. 3).

24. Carlton (Hackett), "Studies," p. 135.

25. So, for example, Naveh, *IEJ* 29 (1979): 136. See above, Chapter 1, p. 11.

26. Hoftijzer, in *Aramaic Texts,* p. 283.

27. See the new reading proposed by Kaufman, "[Review of Hoftijzer and van der Kooij, eds., *Aramaic Texts*]," *BASOR* 239 (1980): 73.

28. See, for example, the discussion of פחזי (II 8) in Carlton (Hackett), "Studies," pp. 97–98.

29. G. R. Driver, "Seals from ʿAmman and Petra," *QDAP* 11 (1944): 82.

30. Cf. Israel, "Miscellanea idumea," *Rivista biblica italiana* 27 (1979): 180.

31. Blau, "Some Difficulties in the Reconstruction of 'Proto-Hebrew' and 'Proto-Canaanite,'" in *In Memoriam Paul Kahle,* ed. Matthew Black and Georg Fohrer. BZAW, vol. 103 (Berlin: A. Töpelmann, 1968), p. 39. See also Franz Rosenthal, *AF,* pp. 69–70 n. 2; and Albrecht Goetze, "Accent and Vocalism in Hebrew," *JAOS* 59 (1939): 451 n. 64.

32. See Hans Kurath, *Studies in Area Linguistics* (Bloomington/London: Indiana University Press, 1972), p. 157.

33. For example, *B-L* §2g′; and Hans Bauer, *Zur Frage der Sprachmischung im Hebräischen. Eine Erwiderung* (Halle an der Saale: Max Niemeyer, 1924), pp. 31–33. Cf. Garbini, *Il semitico di nord-ovest,* Quaderni della sezione linguistica degli Annali, vol. 1 (Naples: Istituto universitario orientale di Napoli, 1960), pp. 32–33.

34. See the summary in Harris, *Development*, p. 40.

35. Degen, *Grammatik*, §11.

36. Pontus Leander, *Laut- und Formenlehre des Ägyptisch-Aramäischen* (1928; reprint ed., Hildesheim: Georg Olms, 1966), §2a.

37. So, tentatively, Dion, *La langue*, p. 94. Alternatively, the element צר may be cognate with Arabic [ḍarra], as in צרי "my enemies" (H 30).

38. Hoftijzer, in *Aramaic Texts*, pp. 283–284.

39. Ibid., p. 197.

40. So Carlton (Hackett), "Studies," pp. 40, 69 with n. 33; Baruch A. Levine, "The Deir ʿAlla Plaster Inscriptions," *JAOS* 101 (1981): 197; and P. Kyle McCarter, "The Balaam Texts from Deir ʿAllā: The First Combination," *BASOR* 239 (1980): 51, 54.

41. Harris, *Development*, pp. 40–41.

42. *B-L* §2g'; and Bauer, *Zur Frage*, p. 33.

43. Friedrich, "Zum Phönizisch-Punischen," *ZS* 2 (1923): 2–4.

44. Harris, *Grammar*, pp. 3–4 with n. 15, 20 n. 3.

45. Ali Abou-Assaf, Pierre Bordreuil, and Alan R. Millard, *La statue de Tell Fekherye et son inscription bilingue assyro-araméenne* (Paris: Editions Recherche sur les civilisations, 1982), pp. 43–44, 60.

46. Kaufman, "Reflections on the Assyrian-Aramaic Bilingual from Tell Fakhariyeh," *Maarav* 3 (1982): 146–147.

47. Presuming, of course, that עתרסמך was not an inherited spelling of the name.

48. See the list in Dion, *La langue*, pp. 93–94.

49. Friedrich, *PPG* §8*a; and idem, in *Studies . . . Landsberger*, p. 427.

50. Further examples are given by Israel, *OLP* 10 (1979): 144, to which add: PN בקש (seal of בקש [Hestrin and Dayagi-Mendels, *Inscribed Seals*, p. 130]) and PN שעל (seals of מתא [in ibid., p. 137], פלטי [ibid., p. 136], and שעל [ibid., p. 135]).

51. Further examples listed by Carlton (Hackett), "Studies," p. 136; and Hoftijzer, in *Aramaic Texts*, p. 283.

52. Cf. Israel, *Rivista biblica italiana* 27 (1979): 180.

53. E. A. Speiser, "The Shibboleth Incident (Judges 12:6)," *BASOR* 85 (1942): 10–13.

54. Harris, *Development*, pp. 40–41, 62–64, and the chronological chart.

55. Cf. p. 26 above.

56. Harris, *Development*, pp. 43–44.

57. Additional examples in Friedrich and Röllig, *PPG*² §§79a–79b.

58. Harris, *Grammar*, p. 35. Cf. P. Swiggers, "[Review of Segert, *Grammar*]," *Lingua* 50 (1980): 383.

59. The problem, however, lies in the development of *ā̆ in later, post-Christian Aramaic dialects in Syria-Palestine. The shift *ā̆ > [ō], as found in Phoenician and Hebrew, is characteristic of western Aramaic dialects—notably western Syriac, Maʿlūla, and Christian Palestinian Aramaic. Several explanations are possible. In the early period, *ā̆ was retained in Aramaic-

speaking areas and only later changed to [ō] under the influence of the older Canaanite vowel-shift (through spread or borrowing) or through independent, parallel development. Another possibility is that, since the Aramaic shift *á > [ó] is restricted to western dialects, there was already a dialectal boundary between western (*á > [ó]) and eastern ([á]) regions in the early period. Proof is lacking until further evidence can be adduced to support one explanation. See Chaim Rabin, "The Origin of the Subdivisions of Semitic," in *Hebrew and Semitic Studies Presented to Godfrey Rolles Driver*, ed. D. Winton Thomas and W. D. McHardy (Oxford: Oxford University Press, 1963), p. 109; and Blau, in *In Memoriam Paul Kahle*, p. 36.

60. See Benno Landsberger, *Sam'al. Studien zur Entdeckung der Ruinenstaette Karatepe*, Veröffentlichungen der türkischen historischen Gesellschaft, Series 7, no. 16 (Ankara: Türkische historische Gesellschaft, 1948), p. 22 n. 43, for complete citations.

61. See also Ran Zadok, "West Semitic Personal Names in the Murašû Documents," *BASOR* 231 (1978): 74.

62. See below, no. 6.

63. Harris, *Development*, pp. 43–45, 61–62.

64. Cf. Israel, "Un'ulteriore attestazione dell'evoluzione fonetica ā > ō nel semitico di nord-ovest," *RSF* 7 (1979): 159–161; and Ziony Zevit, *Matres Lectionis in Ancient Hebrew Epigraphs*, ASOR Monograph Series, vol. 2 (Cambridge: ASOR, 1980), p. 25 n. 44.

65. See the list in Simo Parpola, *Neo-Assyrian Toponyms*, AOAT, vol. 6 (Kevelaer/Neukirchen-Vluyn: Butzon & Bercker/Neukirchener Verlag des Erziehungsvereins, 1970), pp. 16, 76.

66. Cf. Stanislav Segert, *A Grammar of Phoenician and Punic* (Munich: C. H. Beck, 1976), §21.91.

67. Sabatino Moscati, ed., *An Introduction to the Comparative Grammar of the Semitic Languages*, Porta Linguarum Orientalium, New Series, vol. 6 (Wiesbaden: Otto Harrassowitz, 1969), §8.70.

68. Zadok, "Historical and Onomastic Notes," *WO* 9 (1977): 41.

69. Blau, "Short Philological Notes on the Inscription of Mešaʿ," *Maarav* 2 (1980): 147–148.

70. I. J. Gelb, "La lingua degli Amoriti," *Atti della Accademia nazionale dei Lincei. Rendiconti della Classe di scienze morali, storiche e filologiche*, Series VIII, vol. 13/3–4 (1958): 157 (§3.3.6.2.1).

71. Carl Brockelmann, *GvG* 1:§262e.

72. Bauer, "Die hebräischen Eigennamen als sprachliche Erkenntnisquelle," *ZAW* 48 (1930): 74.

73. Harris, *Development*, p. 44.

74. Contraction is marked by a circumflex (ˆ), except in the case of [ō] < *awa/*aya/*aʾ (cf. [ô] < *aw). A macron (ˉ) marks originally long, or stress-lengthened, vowels.

75. Harris, *Grammar*, p. 31; idem, *Development*, p. 73; and Friedrich and Röllig, *PPG*^{2} §80b.

76. Friedrich and Röllig, *PPG*^{2} §80a; cf. Harris, *Development*, pp. 56–57. For *bali*, see Brockelmann, *GvG* 1:§252bα; and Rosenthal, "[Review of Gordon, *Ugaritic Grammar*]," *Or* 11 (1942): 176–177, 177 n. 2.

77. Friedrich and Röllig, *PPG*² §78d, with other examples.
78. Harris, *Grammar*, p. 31 n. 17.
79. Possible exceptions may be Pun. *anech* "I" (Poen. 995) (see Friedrich and Röllig, *PPG*² §79c) and *corathi* "I called" (Poen. 930) (Harris, *Grammar*, p. 31 n. 17).
80. See n. 63 above.
81. References given by Frank M. Cross, "Leaves from an Epigraphist's Notebook," *CBQ* 36 (1974): 494 n. 50. Cf. idem, "Notes on the Ammonite Inscription from Tell Sīrān," *BASOR* 212 (1973): 14 n. 17.
82. Cf. the Murašu PN *Padā-yaw*, cited by Cross, *CBQ* 36 (1974): 494 n. 55, and BH PNs פדהאל (Num. 34:28) and פדהצור (Num. 1:10, 2:20, etc.).
83. For a different explanation, see Cross, *BASOR* 212 (1973): 13; and Zadok, *WO* 9 (1977): 53–55.
84. Brockelmann, *GvG* 1:§§37fβ,γ. Cf. Gotthelf Bergsträsser, "Mitteilungen zur hebräischen Grammatik," *OLZ* 26 (1923): 255. See also the Palestinian El-Amarna forms *ru-šu-nu* "our head" (EA 264:18) and *sú-ú-nu* "sheep" (EA 263:12). The [ō]-vowel in BH יאכל "he will eat" and יאחז "he will seize," however, is of a different origin.
85. *B-L* §§25b–c. See also Harris, *Development*, p. 73, and no. 13 below.
86. Harris, ibid., p. 61. Other examples are cited by Harris, *Grammar*, pp. 25, 34–35, and by Friedrich and Röllig, *PPG*² §§78a.c (exceptions listed on p. 30 n. 1).
87. See Harris, *Development*, pp. 60–62.
88. Cf. P. Kyle McCarter and Robert B. Coote, "The Spatula Inscription from Byblos," *BASOR* 212 (1973): 20 n. 17.
89. Friedrich and Röllig, *PPG*², p. 30 n. 1; Segert, *Grammar*, §§54.212.1–2; and Swiggers, *Lingua* 50 (1980): 383.
90. Ginsberg, "[Review of Harris, *Grammar*]," *JBL* 56 (1937): 139; Brockelmann, "[Review of Harris, *Grammar*]," *OLZ* 40 (1937): 528; and Harris, *Development*, p. 72.
91. See above, no. 5.
92. Harris, *Development*, p. 61 (citing only [Mô²āb]).
93. Ginsberg, *JBL* 56 (1937): 139.
94. Harris, *Grammar*, p. 37; idem, *Development*, pp. 29–32; and Frank M. Cross and David N. Freedman, *EHO*, pp. 13–19.
95. Harris, *Development*, pp. 29–30, 31.
96. Ginsberg, "The Northwest Semitic Languages," in *Patriarchs*, ed. B. Mazar, The World History of the Jewish People, vol. 2 ([New Brunswick, N.J.]: Rutgers University Press, 1970), p. 108; and Cross and Freedman, *EHO*, p. 19.
97. Cross and Freedman, *EHO*, pp. 14, 15.
98. See below, nos. 15, 19, and Chapter 3, nos. 23b, 23h.
99. See Degen, *Grammatik*, §7.
100. On the form of גדה "kid" (Sf. II A 2), צדה "owl" (Sf. I A 33), and אריה "lion" (Sf. II A 9), cited by Degen (*Grammatik*, §19b) as examples of monophthongization, see no. 11 below. For לילה "night" (Sf. I A 12),

see BH and Deir Alla לילה "night" (see pp. 117, 158, n. 253). The final alleged example of monophthongization in Old Aramaic, אלן "these" (Sf. I A 7.7.38, etc.), posited by Kutscher (*A History of Aramaic*. Part 1: *Old Aramaic, Jaudic, Official Aramaic [Biblical Aramaic excepted]* [Jerusalem: Akadamon, 1972], p. 12 [in Hebrew]) does not necessarily end in an original diphthong (see Chapter 3, no. 2c, especially the alternate explanation).

101. Degen, "Die Präfixkonjugationen des Altaramäischen," in *XVII. Deutscher Orientalistentag . . . Würzburg. Vorträge*, ed. Wolfgang Voigt. ZDMG Supplementa, vol. 1, pt. 2 (Wiesbaden: Franz Steiner, 1969), pp. 701–706; and idem, *Grammatik*, §19. See below, Chapter 3, no. 23d.

102. If, however, these imperfects are derived from *yabniyu/*yabniy, this exception disappears.

103. Fitzmyer, *Sefire*, pp. 116, 146; Degen, *Grammatik*, p. 62 n. 39a; Kutscher, *A History of Aramaic*, p. 12; and *KAI* 2:269–270.

104. Brockelmann, *GvG* 1:§252bθ.

105. See, however, Klaus Beyer, "[Review of Degen, *Grammatik*]," *ZDMG* 120 (1970): 200.

106. Abou-Assaf et al., *La statue*, pp. 34, 46.

107. מֹשָׁב "throne" (H 8.15, etc.; P 2) is a different form altogether. See Ginsberg, "The Classification of the North-West Semitic Languages," in *Akten des vierundzwanzigsten internationalen Orientalisten-Kongresses . . . 1957*, ed. Herbert Franke (Wiesbaden: Franz Steiner, 1959), p. 257; and idem, in *Patriarchs*, p. 119. See also below, Chapter 3, no. 21a.

108. See Friedrich, *PPG* §§2*,6*; and Dion, *La langue*, pp. 57–58, 72–80, for further examples (although with different analyses and conclusions).

109. Friedrich, *PPG* §4*; Dion, *La langue*, pp. 72–73; and idem, "The Language Spoken in Ancient Sam'al," *JNES* 37 (1978): 116 n. 9.

110. Cf. Merton E. Sherman, "Systems of Hebrew and Aramaic Orthography: an Epigraphic History of the Use of *matres lectionis* in Non-biblical Texts to *circa* A.D. 135" (Ph.D. dissertation, Harvard University, 1966), p. 32 n. 61.

111. Harris, *Development*, p. 9 with nn. 14 and 15.

112. See Dion, *La langue*, pp. 122–123.

113. See below, no. 19, and Chapter 3, no. 6a.

114. Dion, *La langue*, pp. 145–148.

115. Dion, "Notes d'épigraphie ammonite," *RB* 82 (1975): 27. For the seal, see Garbini, *Le lingue*, p. 99 n. 13.

116. For the masculine plural construct ending, see Chapter 3, no. 6b.

117. Sturtevant, *Pronunciation of Greek and Latin*, pp. 142, 148, cited in Harris, *Grammar*, p. 37 n. 43.

118. Hoftijzer, in *Aramaic Texts*, pp. 284–285, 222 n. 104; Carlton (Hackett), "Studies," p. 50 n. 8; and idem, *Or* 53 (1984): 63.

119. Additional examples given by Hoftijzer, in *Aramaic Texts*, pp. 284–285; and by Carlton (Hackett), "Studies," pp. 137–138.

120. Hoftijzer, in *Aramaic Texts*, p. 285; and Carlton (Hackett), "Studies," p. 138.

121. See above, pp. 35, 69 n. 101.

122. See above, n. 102.

123. Cf. Rosenthal, "[Review of Cross and Freedman, *EHO*]," *JAOS* 73 (1953): 47; and Cross and Freedman, *EHO*, p. 42.

124. See the lists in Cross and Freedman, *EHO*, p. 43. Cf. Segert, "Die Sprache der moabitischen Königsinschrift," *ArOr* 29 (1961): 212–213.

125. On *Qôs*, see Israel, *Rivista biblica italiana* 27 (1979): 184–191.

126. Ibid., p. 186.

127. B. Oded, "Egyptian References to the Edomite Deity Qaus," *AUSS* 9 (1971): 47–50.

128. Beyer, *Althebräische Grammatik* (Göttingen: Vandenhoeck & Ruprecht, 1969), p. 29.

129. Harris, *Development*, pp. 29–32.

130. Published by N. Tzori, "A Hebrew Ostracon from Beth-Shean," *Yediot* 25 (1961): 145–146 (in Hebrew).

131. Cf. André Lemaire, *Inscriptions hébraïques*, Tome 1: *Les ostraca*, Littératures anciennes du Proche-Orient, vol. 9/1 (Paris: Les Editions du Cerf, 1977), p. 254.

132. See above, p. 12.

133. Cross and Freedman, *EHO*, p. 48 with n. 20a. Cf. Zevit, *Matres Lectionis*, p. 15.

134. The Beer-Sheba ostraca were published by Yohanan Aharoni, "The Hebrew Inscriptions," in *Beer-Sheba I. Excavations at Tel Beer-Sheba, 1969–1971 Seasons*, ed. Y. Aharoni (Tel Aviv: Tel Aviv University Institute of Archaeology, 1973), pp. 71–78. Cf. the reading by Lemaire, *Inscriptions*, pp. 271–272.

135. Cross and Freedman, *EHO*, p. 57.

136. Another possible exception is עֹר in a text from Tell Ajrud (published by Zeev Meshel, "Kuntilat ʿAjrud, 1975–1976," *IEJ* 27 [1977]: 53). If this is the same word as עיר "city" in Arad 24:16/17 and Lach. 4:7, 18:2, a diphthong may have contracted. In this case, however, the original diphthong was probably *iy* (Bergsträsser, *Hebräische Grammatik*, 2 vols. [Leipzig: F. C. W. Vogel, 1918–1929], 1:§17i), not *ay* (cf. Cross and Freedman, *EHO*, p. 55). See also אש "man" (Shiloah 2.2.4; cf., e.g., Sf. II B 16 and H 34) vs. איש "man" (Arad 40:7.8; Lach. 3:9/10).

On קל "voice" (Shiloah 2), see קל "voice" (Sf. I A 29; and Deir Alla I 8), and Paul Joüon, *Grammaire de l'hébreu biblique* (Rome: Pontifical Biblical Institute, 1923), p. 189 n. 3.

137. See, for example, Zevit, *Matres Lectionis*, pp. 19, 24.

138. Lemaire, *Inscriptions*, p. 272.

139. For example, Shiloah 3; Lach. 2:3, etc.; Arad 1:4, etc.

140. The reading יום[ה], accepted by *KAI* (2:200), is probably incorrect. In its stead, read אסמ, following Naveh, Cross, Lemaire, and Pardee.

141. See Theodor Nöldeke, *Neue Beiträge zur semitischen Sprachwissenschaft* (Strassburg: Karl J. Trübner, 1910), pp. 133–135, for the comparative evidence.

142. For Hebrew, *á:[å]*, see no. 7 above.

143. Ginsberg, "Notes on the Lachish Documents," *BJPES* 3 (1935): 79 (in Hebrew); William F. Albright, "Ostracon C 1101 of Samaria," *PEFQS* 1936: 215 n. 1; and Cross and Freedman, *EHO*, pp. 50, 53 with n. 40.

144. Cf. Anson F. Rainey, "The Word 'Day' in Ugaritic and Hebrew," *Leshonenu* 36 (1972): 187–189 (in Hebrew); and Zevit, *Matres Lectionis*, pp. 21, 24.

145. Cf. Ginsberg, in *Patriarchs*, p. 108.

146. Or the form may be derived from *ʾad-at.

147. Friedrich and Röllig, *PPG*² §58b; *KAI* 2:5; and Albright, "The Phoenician Inscriptions of the Tenth Century B.C. from Byblus," *JAOS* 67 (1947): 157 n. 39.

148. The extent of assimilation of *nun* in final *nun* verbs is uncertain. Since כת "I was" is the only example of this particular assimilation in standard Phoenician during this period, additional examples are needed to ensure that this assimilation was regular. Not only is the verb "to be" generally irregular in many languages, but different verbs behaved differently in this regard (cf. BH נתתי "I gave" vs. שכנתי "I dwelt").

149. Additional examples are given by Degen, *Grammatik*, §20; and Segert, *Altaramäische Grammatik* (Leipzig: VEB Verlag Enzyklopädie, 1975), §3.7.5.

150. Cf. Fitzmyer, *Sefire*, p. 187.

151. Ibid., p. 150.

152. Degen, *Grammatik*, p. 14 n. 63.

153. See Segert, *Grammatik*, §5.7.4.1.

154. Dion, *La langue*, p. 107; and Landsberger, *Samʾal*, p. 69 n. 176 (one possibility).

155. Gibson, *Textbook* 2:62.

156. J. Halévy, "Nouvel Examen des inscriptions de Zindjirli," *RS* 7 (1899): 345.

157. Rosenthal, *Die Sprache der palmyrenischen Inschriften und ihre Stellung innerhalb des Aramäischen*, MVÄG, vol. 41, pt. 1 (Leipzig: J. C. Hinrichs'sche Buchhandlung, 1936), p. 60; Friedrich, *PPG* §19*; and Dion, *La langue*, pp. 105, 215. See below, Chapter 3, no. 19a.

158. Israel, *Rivista biblica italiana* 27 (1979): 181 with n. 31.

159. Hoftijzer, in *Aramaic Texts*, p. 292.

160. Ibid., pp. 294, 300.

161. Segert, *ArOr* 29 (1961): 211.

162. Crystal-M. Bennett, "Fouilles d'Umm el-Biyara. Rapport préliminaire," *RB* 73 (1966): 399; and Israel, *Rivista biblica italiana* 27 (1979): 180.

163. Harris, *Development*, pp. 39–40.

164. Brockelmann, *GvG* 1:§61a.

165. Goetze, "Is Ugaritic a Canaanite Dialect?" *Lg.* 17 (1941): 129 n. 20; and Blau, "Hebrew and North West Semitic: Reflections on the Classification of the Semitic Languages," *Hebrew Annual Review* 2 (1978): 35.

166. B. Maisler (של התפתחותו ושלשלת מגבל הפניקיות הכתובות" הכתב האלפבית הפניקי-העברי", *Leshonenu* 14 [1946]: 173) cited some non-

Phoenician examples of this phenomenon; see also Friedrich and Röllig, *PPG*[2], p. 39 n. 3. I know of no other examples of this particular assimilation in the NWS epigraphic texts.

167. See n. 148. In Ugaritic as well, *nun* did not assimilate in this position (Gordon, *UT* §9.45).

168. Comparative evidence indicates that the root was originally *qtl* (as in Arabic, Samalian, and Sfire-Aramaic); *qtl* became *$qṭl$* by assimilation of the *taw* to the emphatic *qoph*, as in Hebrew and Imperial Aramaic (see Brockelmann, *GvG* 1:§54h). From the intermediate *$qṭl$*, the *qoph* dissimilated to *kaph* in contiguity to the following emphatic, thus: *$qṭl$* > *$qṭl$* > בטל.

169. Segert, *Grammatik*, §3.7.2.2.2.

170. Nöldeke, *Mandäische Grammatik* (1875; reprint ed., Darmstadt: Wissenschaftliche Buchgesellschaft, 1964), §42.

171. Kutscher, in *Linguistics in South West Asia*, p. 365.

172. Ibid.; and Greenfield, "Dialect Traits in Early Aramaic," *Leshonenu* 32 (1968): 364 (in Hebrew).

173. Ginsberg, in *Akten . . . 1957*, p. 256; and idem, in *Patriarchs*, p. 119.

174. Hoftijzer, in *Aramaic Texts*, pp. 218, 283; André Caquot and André Lemaire, "Les textes araméens de Deir ʿAlla," *Syria* 54 (1977): 201; Carlton (Hackett), "Studies," pp. 85, 135; and Weippert and Weippert, *ZDPV* 98 (1982): 100 n. 123.

175. Kaufman, *The Akkadian Influences on Aramaic*, Assyriological Studies, vol. 19 (Chicago/London: The University of Chicago Press, 1974), p. 122.

176. Harris, *Grammar*, pp. 33–34; idem, *Development*, p. 80; and Friedrich and Röllig, *PPG*[2] §§75b, 96b.

177. Additional examples are given by Harris, *Grammar*, pp. 88–90.

178. Friedrich and Röllig, *PPG*[2] §75b.

179. Thus, while the Akkadian spellings *Ba-ʾa-lu/al-* may be an attempt to represent consonantal ʿ, the form *Si-pí-it-* exhibits true anaptyxis.

180. Kutscher, *A History of Aramaic*, p. 13.

181. For *iy* > [ê] (ה-) see Degen, *Grammatik*, §19b.

182. See Brockelmann, *GvG* 1:§93u.

183. See Joseph L. Malone, "Wave Theory, Rule Ordering, and Hebrew-Aramaic Segolation," *JAOS* 91 (1971): 44–66, esp. pp. 59–62 (on the Hebrew phenomenon).

184. *KAI* 2:227.

185. Dion, *La langue*, pp. 60–61.

186. Arno Poebel, *Das appositionell bestimmte Pronomen der 1. Pers. Sing. in den westsemitischen Inschriften und im Alten Testament*, Assyriological Studies, vol. 3 (Chicago: The University of Chicago Press, 1932), p. 47 n. 1 (implied derivation).

187. Dion, *La langue*, pp. 56, 104, 124.

188. So, for example, *KAI* 2:220 (one possibility).

189. Bergsträsser, *Hebräische Grammatik* 1:§23h.

190. Speiser, "Secondary Developments in Semitic Phonology: An Application of the Principle of Sonority," *AJSL* 42 (1926): 145–169; and I. M. Diakonoff, "Problems of Root Structure in Proto-Semitic," *ArOr* 38 (1970): 453–480.

191. Cf. Malone, *JAOS* 91 (1971): 66.

192. *B-L* §61mε.

193. So, for example, *KAI* 2:41; and Segert, *Grammar*, §36.511.

194. Friedrich and Röllig, *PPG*² §95a.

195. See Stanley Gevirtz, "On the Etymology of the Phoenician Particle אש," *JNES* 16 (1957): 125 n. 12.

196. Harris, *Grammar*, pp. 63–64; and Friedrich and Röllig, *PPG*² §310.2. See below, Chapter 3, no. 3, and Chapter 4, no. 3a.

197. Degen, *Grammatik*, §22. See Goetze, *JAOS* 59 (1939): 444 n. 36 on the Proto-Semitic form of (א)שם "name."

198. Kaufman, *Maarav* 3 (1982): 162.

199. Cf. Abou-Assaf et al., *La statue*, p. 85.

200. For example, Ginsberg, "Aramaic Studies Today," *JAOS* 62 (1942): 236 with n. 34; Kaufman, *Akkadian Influences*, p. 103 n. 361; and Dion, *La langue*, p. 116.

201. Rosenthal, "[Review of Dion, *La langue*]," *JBL* 95 (1976): 154.

202. For the etymology of *sinepû*, see Goetze, "Number Idioms in Old Babylonian," *JNES* 5 (1946): 202 n. 81; and the bibliography cited by Kaufman, *Akkadian Influences*, p. 103 n. 361.

203. While some scholars have sought a prothetic *aleph* in וארקן "and favor" (H 13), it is preferable to read ואדרו "and strength" (with Joseph P. Healey, "The Archaic Aramaic Inscriptions from Zinjirli" [Ph.D. dissertation, Harvard University, 1981], p. 9). This reading not only clears up the phonetic difficulty of the prothetic *aleph* but also provides better sense.

204. See recently M. Baldacci, "The Ammonite Text from Tell Siran and North-West Semitic Philology," *VT* 31 (1981): 367.

205. Henry O. Thompson and Fawzi Zayadine, "The Tell Siran Inscription," *BASOR* 212 (1973): 10, and "The Works of Amminadab," *BA* 37 (1974): 17 (one possibility).

206. In ibid.

207. Hoftijzer, in *Aramaic Texts*, p. 203 with n. 54.

208. Brockelmann, *GvG* 1:§190, Anm. 2.

209. Cf. Segert, *ArOr* 29 (1961): 219–220.

210. Brockelmann, *GvG* 1:§82a.

211. Harris, *Grammar*, pp. 30–31; idem, *Development*, pp. 42–43, 73; and Friedrich and Röllig, *PPG*² §13a.

212. For example, André Dupont-Sommer, *Les inscriptions araméennes de Sfîré (stelès I et II)*, Extrait des Mémoires présentés par divers savants à l'Académie des Inscriptions et Belles-Lettres, vol. 15 (Paris: Imprimerie Nationale, 1958), pp. 120–121; and *KAI* 2:263 (one possibility).

213. Degen, *Grammatik*, pp. 19 n. 76, 25, 66 n. 46, 71–72 n. 64; Fitzmyer, *Sefire*, pp. 91, 144 (one possibility); and Segert, *Grammatik*, §3.7.8.5.3 (one possibility).

214. Fitzmyer, *Sefîre*, p. 70.

215. So Cooke, *NSI*, p. 167; *KAI* 2:219; and Dion, *La langue*, p. 213.

216. Although Dion (*La langue*, p. 120) also cited רש "head" < *raʾš in P 12, the passage is broken and does not yield clear sense.

217. Cf. Harris, *Development*, pp. 42–43.

218. Ibid., p. 73 (one possibility); and Segert, *ArOr* 29 (1961): 219.

219. Harris, *Development*, p. 73 (alternate derivation). Cf. *B-L* §25b.

220. Cf. Bauer, *Zur Frage*, pp. 29–30; and idem, "[Review of Dhorme, *Langues*]," *OLZ* 36 (1933): 318.

221. So, for example, Cooke, *NSI*, p. 11.

222. Albright, "A Reëxamination of the Lachish Letters," *BASOR* 73 (1939): 21 n. 35. Cf. Gibson, *Textbook* 1:23.

223. Harris, *Development*, pp. 42, 43, 73.

224. See Brockelmann, *GvG* 1:§45, for comparative evidence.

225. Albright, "Notes on Early Hebrew and Aramaic Epigraphy," *JPOS* 6 (1926): 79; Harris, *Grammar*, pp. 31–32; and Friedrich and Röllig, *PPG*[2] §94.

226. In Syriac, initial *aleph* + short vowel in an unaccented, open syllable is consistently reduced to zero, as for example [ḥātā] "sister" < *ʾaḥātā and [nāš] "man" < *ʾunāš (Nöldeke, *Kurzgefasste syrische Grammatik*, 2nd ed. [1898; reprint ed., Darmstadt: Wissenschaftliche Buchgesellschaft, 1966], §32; and Brockelmann, *GvG* 1:§89lo).

227. Brockelmann, *GvG* 1:§89lo.

228. Friedrich, *PPG* §9*; and Segert, *Grammatik*, §3.7.8.6.1. Cf. Dion, *La langue*, p. 118; and idem, *JNES* 37 (1978): 116.

229. So Albright, "Some Comments on the ʿAmmân Citadel Inscription," *BASOR* 198 (1970): 39; and A. van Selms, "Some Remarks on the ʿAmmān Citadel Inscriptions," *BiOr* 32 (1975): 8.

230. So, for example, William J. Fulco, "The ʿAmmān Citadel Inscription: A New Collation," *BASOR* 230 (1978): 42.

231. Cf. Harris, *Development*, pp. 78–79.

232. Brockelmann, *GvG* 1:§104bα; and Garbini, *Il semitico*, p. 88 n. 1.

233. Harris, *Development*, pp. 56–57; and Segert, *Grammar*, §§35.731, 54.463. Cf. Goetze, *JAOS* 59 (1939): 450 n. 62, on the vocalization.

234. So read by *KAI* 2:46; and Albright, "An Aramaean Magical Text in Hebrew from the Seventh Century B.C.," *BASOR* 76 (1939): 9–10 with n. 36.

235. So Frank M. Cross and Richard J. Saley, "Phoenician Incantations on a Plaque of the Seventh Century B.C. from Arslan Tash in Upper Syria," *BASOR* 197 (1970): 46 with nn. 29–30; and Röllig, "Die Amulette von Arslan Taş," *NESE* 2 (1974): 19, 25.

236. Abou-Assaf et al., *La statue*, p. 34.

237. See Rosenthal, *Die Sprache*, pp. 54–55. Cf. Dion, *La langue*, pp. 123–124; and idem, *JNES* 37 (1978): 116 n. 14.

238. Cf., e.g., Albright, *BASOR* 198 (1970): 38, and below, Chapter 4, no. 11.

239. For references see Naveh, "The Ostracon from Nimrud: An Ammonite Name-List," *Maarav* 2 (1980): 167 with nn. 31–34.

240. Avigad, "Two Ammonite Seals Depicting the *Dea Nutrix*," *BASOR* 225 (1977): 64–65.

241. For this verbal form, see Chapter 3, no. 23c.

242. Nelson Glueck, "Ostraca from Elath," *BASOR* 82 (1941): 3–6; and idem, "Tell el-Kheleifeh Inscriptions," in *Near Eastern Studies in Honor of William Foxwell Albright*, ed. Hans Goedicke (Baltimore/London: The Johns Hopkins Press, 1971), p. 229.

243. See n. 162 above; and Israel, *Rivista biblica italiana* 27 (1979): 183.

244. Lemaire (*Inscriptions*, p. 50), however, found the syncopated form ‏בד-‎ in the PN ‏בדיו‎ (Sam. Ost. 58:1). Yet the reading is uncertain; Lemaire's *b* may be *p*. See Ivan T. Kaufman, "The Samaria Ostraca: A Study in Ancient Hebrew Palaeography," 2 vols. (Ph.D. dissertation, Harvard University, 1966), 1:144.

245. See above, n. 76.

246. For possible *hiphil* imperfects in Old Byblian, see below, Chapter 3, no. 16c.

247. Friedrich, "Kleinigkeiten zum Phönizischen, Punischen und Numidischen," *ZDMG* 114 (1964): 226; and Segert, *Grammar*, §51.233.2.

248. Cross and Freedman, "The Pronominal Suffixes of the Third Person Singular in Phoenician," *JNES* 10 (1951): 228–230. See below, Chapter 3, nos. 9b, 9d, 10b–10c.

249. Thomas O. Lambdin, "The Junctural Origin of the West Semitic Definite Article," in *Near Eastern Studies . . . Albright*, p. 328.

250. Cf., however, the later form ‏והאדמם המת‎ "and those people" (Eshmunazor 22).

251. Cf., for example, Dupont-Sommer, *Sfiré*, pp. 120–121.

252. Degen, *Grammatik*, pp. 19 n. 79, 25, 66 n. 46; and Segert, "Zur Schrift und Orthographie der altaramäischen Stelen von Sfire," *ArOr* 32 (1964): 121.

253. So Cross and Freedman, *EHO*, p. 29; Segert, *Grammatik*, §3.8.1.7; and recently Fitzmyer, "The Phases of the Aramaic Language," in idem, *A Wandering Aramean: Collected Aramaic Essays*, SBLMS, vol. 25 (Missoula: Scholars Press, 1979), pp. 82–83 n. 95.

254. Degen, *Grammatik*, §36 (end).

255. See below, Chapter 3, no. 10b.

256. Abou-Assaf et al., *La statue*, p. 29.

257. Friedrich, *PPG* §25*b; *KAI* 2:219, 222; and Dion, *La langue*, pp. 121, 201.

258. Cf. Coote, "The Tell Siran Bottle Inscription," *BASOR* 240 (1980): 93; and Baldacci, *VT* 31 (1981): 367.

259. So Cross, "Epigraphic Notes on the Ammān Citadel Inscription," *BASOR* 193 (1969): 19 with n. 15; and Raphael Kutscher, "A New Inscription from ʿAmman," *Qadmoniot* 5 (1972): 28 (in Hebrew).

260. Cross, *BASOR* 193 (1969): 17.

261. Hoftijzer, in *Aramaic Texts*, p. 293; and Carlton (Hackett), "Studies," p. 146.

262. *B-L* §25r.

263. So read by Carlton (Hackett) ("Studies," p. 41) and Levine (*JAOS* 101 [1981]: 200). Hoftijzer (in *Aramaic Texts*, pp. 174, 236) and Caquot and Lemaire (*Syria* 54 [1977]: 205) read בלבב.מנ, in which case this suffix would disappear.

264. Segert, *ArOr* 29 (1961): 218; and Friedrich and Röllig, *PPG*² §18.1.

265. Harris, *Development*, p. 55. See already Nöldeke, *Die Inschrift des Königs Mesa von Moab* (Kiel: Schwers'sche Buchhandlung, 1870), p. 32.

266. Rosenthal, *JAOS* 73 (1953): 47.

267. Cross and Freedman, *EHO*, pp. 36, 43.

268. Ibid., pp. 37 with n. 7, 38, 41.

269. For this derivation, see below, Chapter 3, no. 10b.

270. See the discussion in Brockelmann, *GvG* 1:§§105fε, gε; and *B-L* §§25l–v.

271. Cross and Freedman, *EHO*, p. 50.

272. See Harris, *Development*, p. 55; and Zevit, *Matres Lectionis*, p. 20.

273. For example, Brockelmann, *GvG* 1:§40l; and *B-L* §25l. Cf. Cross and Freedman, *EHO*, pp. 47, 54–55 with n. 42.

274. Harris, *Development*, pp. 54–55; and Segert, *Grammar*, §35.61.

275. See Chapter 3, nos. 9b, 10b.

276. See Friedrich and Röllig, *PPG*² §§234–238, for additional examples.

277. It is possible that palatalization of *he* in the suffixes influenced the same change in the causative prefix. As Speiser has shown ("The 'Elative' in West-Semitic and Akkadian," *JCS* 6 [1952]: 81–82 with n. 4; and "The Terminative-Adverbial in Canaanite-Ugaritic and Akkadian," *IEJ* 4 [1954]: 108–115), the pronominal suffixes, causative prefix, and third person independent pronouns are etymologically related. A phonetic change which occurred in one of these elements may have spread to another. In this case, however, it did not spread to the independent pronouns. Cf. Garbini, *Le lingue*, p. 70.

278. The examples which Friedrich and Röllig (*PPG*² §227) adduced to show the preservation of *-át in Old Byblian—מחנת "camp" and נחת "peace" (Ahirom 2)—are unclear. Because מחנת is derived from a final weak root, the form may have developed from *maḥnay-at > *maḥnât > [maḥnōt]; a simple ending *-at may not be in question. Further, נחת may have ended in *-t like BH *naḥt-, not in *-át.

279. Degen, *Grammatik*, p. 49 n. 12.

280. Alternatively, שאת is derived from *ṭa'aw + at (cf. Arabic) > [ṭa'ât]. See, however, Chapter 3, no. 7.

281. Blau, "The Parallel Development of the Feminine Ending -at in Semitic Languages," *HUCA* 51 (1980): 27. See ibid., pp. 17–27 for a complete discussion, including Arabic evidence.

282. Ibid.

283. For the vocalization, see Charles R. Krahmalkov, "On the Third Feminine Singular of the Perfect in Phoenician-Punic," *JSS* 24 (1979): 25–28. See also n. 233 above.

284. Cf. Ugaritic *tmt* "there, thither."

285. Harris, *Development*, pp. 58–59.

286. Bergsträsser, *Hebräische Grammatik* 2:§30r.

287. See above, no. 15, and below, Chapter 3, no. 23b.

288. But cf. Blau, in *In Memoriam Paul Kahle*, pp. 37–38.

289. Idem, *Maarav* 2 (1980): 157.

290. Segert, *Grammar*, §52.42.

291. Harris, *Grammar*, pp. 36 n. 37, 61.

292. Cf. Segert, *Grammar*, §52.43; and A. M. Honeyman, "Phoenician Inscriptions from Karatepe," *Le Muséon* 61 (1948): 49 n. 10.

293. Friedrich, "Der Schwund kurzer Endvokale im Nordwestsemitischen," *ZS* 1 (1922): 10.

294. Ibid., pp. 7–10.

295. Dion, *La langue*, pp. 101–102.

296. Ginsberg, "[Review of Diringer, *Le iscrizioni*]," *ArOr* 8 (1936): 146.

297. Garbini, "Note sul 'calendario' di Gezer," *AION* 6 (1954–1956): 123–130.

298. Moscati, "Il semitico di nord-ovest," in *Studi orientalistici in onore di Giorgio Levi Della Vida*, Pubblicazioni dell'Istituto per l'Oriente, no. 52. 2 vols. (Rome: Istituto per l'Oriente, 1956), 2:217; idem, "Sulla posizione linguistica del semitico nord-occidentale," *RSO* 31 (1956): 231; and Harris, *Development*, p. 100.

CHAPTER THREE

MORPHOLOGY[1]

1a. The independent pronouns:
The first person singular.

PHOENICIAN: אנך (Kilamu 1, etc.; Karatepe A I 1, etc.). Evidence for this pronoun in Byblian appears only in later texts (e.g., Yehawmilk 1; KAI 11, etc.).

ARAMAIC: אנה (Zkr A 2, etc.; Sf. II C 8, etc.; Br-Rkb 1:1.20, 2:1, etc.).

SAMALIAN: אנך[2] (H 1; P 19).

AMMONITE: No evidence.

DEIR ALLA: No evidence.

MOABITE: אנך (Mesha 1.2.21, etc.).

EDOMITE: No evidence.

HEBREW: The only form of this pronoun in the epigraphic texts is אני (Arad 88:1; Beit Lei A 1 [partially restored][3]); the final [ī] was transferred from the first person sing. pronominal suffix.[4] The other form frequently found in the Masoretic text, אנכי, does not appear in the epigraphic texts.

The West Semitic dialects exhibit two forms of the first person sing. independent pronoun. In Phoenician, Samalian, and Moabite, it was אנך; cf. Akk. *anāku*. The specifically West Semitic innovation,[5] **anā, appeared in Aramaic (אנה) and Hebrew (אני); cf. Arabic and Eth. [ʾanā]. The form of the pronoun in Ammonite, Deir Alla, and Edomite is unknown.

1b.   The second person masculine singular.

PHOENICIAN: את* [ʾattā], attested only in the later Phoenician inscriptions (KAI 13:3; Eshmunazor 4.20).

ARAMAIC: את, as in Sf. III 11.20 and Nerab 1:5, 2:8. It is unclear, however, whether the pronoun was pronounced [ʾatt], without a final vowel, or [ʾatta], with a final short vowel.[6]

SAMALIAN: את (H 33). As in Old Aramaic, the Samalian pronoun was pronounced either [ʾatt] or [ʾatta].[7] Cf. the doublet זנה "this" (P 22) and זן "this" (H 1.14.16; P 1.20), where the final vowel was not represented in the orthography of the second form.[8]

AMMONITE: No evidence.

DEIR ALLA: No evidence.

MOABITE: No evidence.

EDOMITE: No evidence.

HEBREW: אתה, in Beit Lei B, according to Naveh's reading.[9] Whether this form does or does not appear in the epigraphic texts, however, is practically irrelevant, since the Masoretic *qʾre* consistently shows [ʾattā]. אתה, then, was the Hebraic form of the second person masc. sing. independent pronoun.

The second person masc. sing. independent pronoun is derived from **antă.[10] In Phoenician and Hebrew, the pronoun was [ʾattā] < **antā. The Samalian and Aramaic form, however, was either [ʾatta], or [ʾatt], like the later Aramaic dialects. In either case, the alternate base **antă appeared in Samalian and Old Aramaic. Both the Phoenician-Hebrew and Aramaic-Samalian pronouns were inherited.

1c.   The third person masculine singular.

BYBLIAN: One pronoun was הא (Ahirom 2), pronounced [huʾa] and later, presumably, [hū(ʾ)]. A second form of the pronoun, האת, also appears in Yehimilk 2.

STANDARD PHOENICIAN: הא* [hū(ʾ)],[11] as inferred from the later Phoenician texts.

ARAMAIC: הא [hū(ʾ)] (Sf. I A 37, etc.; Br-Rkb 1:17, etc.).

Although Dupont-Sommer[12] has argued for a second form of this pronoun, הו, in Sf. III 22 והו יחלפה "and he will replace him," Milik[13] and others[14] suggested a more plausible word-division והוי חלפה "and be his successor." The only form of the third person masc. sing. independent pronoun in Old Aramaic was הא.

SAMALIAN: הא (H 22.30; P 11.22). The pronunciation of this form is uncertain.

AMMONITE: No evidence.

DEIR ALLA: הא (I 1).[15] It is possible, however, that this word is the interjection "behold" [haʾ].[16]

MOABITE: הא (Mesha 6). The pronunciation was either [hū(ʾ)] or [huʾa (?)].

EDOMITE: No evidence.

HEBREW: הא (Arad 40:12). The *aleph* had probably lost its consonantal value, so that the pronoun was pronounced [hū], as in biblical Hebrew.[17]

The form אה is common to all first-millennium dialects which exhibit this pronoun. The dialects were differentiated according to its phonetic variants. Only Old Byblian had [huʾa], since final short vowels were probably not yet lost in this dialect;[18] in the other dialects, the form was [hŭʾ]. In the course of the first millennium, the final *aleph* was lost as well.

Whereas the common form of this pronoun was הא, Old Byblian alone preserved a second pronoun האת; cf. ESA and perhaps Eth.[19] This form is parallel to the third person plural independent pronoun המת "they" in standard Phoenician.[20] Perhaps the preservation of this pronoun was a Phoenician trait.

1d.   The third person masculine plural.

PHOENICIAN (including Byblian?): המת (Kilamu 13; cf. Karatepe A I 17).[21] That this pronoun was not restricted to the northern Phoenician periphery is proven by its appearance in later Cyprian (KAI 43:5 [fem. plural]) and Sidonian dialects (Eshmunazor 11.22 [both demonstrative]).

ARAMAIC: הם (Sf. I B 6) and [ה]מו (Zkr A 9). There is no apparent semantic or syntactic difference between these two forms. The short form of this pronoun was not productive in the later Aramaic dialects.

SAMALIAN: No evidence.

AMMONITE: No evidence.

DEIR ALLA: No evidence.

MOABITE: No evidence.

EDOMITE: No evidence.

HEBREW: הם* [hēm], as inferred from the biblical texts. BH also had the form הֵמָּה, cognate with Phoenician המת. Neither form is found in the epigraphic Hebrew texts.

As in other Semitic languages, these dialects exhibit several forms of the third person masculine plural independent pronoun. Phoenician (regularly?) used המת as its subjective pronoun; cf. also BH המה and ESA *hmt*.[22] A short form, הם, appeared (presumably) in epigraphic Hebrew; in Old Aramaic, the independent pronoun was restricted to the dialect of Sfire. The other form, [ה]מו, is found in Zkr as well as in the later Aramaic dialects; cf. Arabic and ESA.

2a. The demonstrative pronouns: "This" (masc. sing.).

BYBLIAN: זן (Ahirom 2; Ahirom Graff. 3).[23] Later Byblian had both זן (Yehawmilk 4.5.12, etc.) and ז (Yehawmilk 4.5.10, etc.).

STANDARD PHOENICIAN: ז [(?)] (Kilamu 14.15; Karatepe A III 14.15.18).

ARAMAIC: זנה (Zkr A 17, etc.; Br-Rkb 1:20; Sf. I A 36, etc.; Adon 8[24]).

SAMALIAN: זן (H 1.14.16; P 1.20) and זנה (P 22). These two forms of the pronoun probably reflect different spellings of the same demonstrative [dinā, zinā];[25] cf. the spellings of the relative particle as זי (H 1) and ז(מ) (H 3.4.22).

AMMONITE: No evidence. van Selms,[26] however, believed to have uncovered the masc. sing. demonstrative in לך (Cit. 1), comparable to Arabic [ḏālika] "this." Yet as most scholars have recognized,[27] it is preferable to understand this form as the dative preposition -ל "to, for" + second person masc. sing. suffix "you." Not only does this interpretation fit the context better than the demonstrative, but a specifically Arabic etymology need not be invoked.

DEIR ALLA: No evidence.

MOABITE: No evidence.

EDOMITE: No evidence.

HEBREW: זה [ze] (Arad 13:2; el-Qom 1:3; Yavneh-Yam 1:9; Shiloah 1, etc). It is also possible that this demonstrative is attested in Hazor 3,[28] if the reading בת ז{.}ה "this house/*bath*" is correct.

Two forms of the masc. sing. demonstrative pronoun "this" appear in the first-millennium NWS dialects. The "short" form, $*d$ + vowel, is attested only in standard Phoenician and Hebrew. A longer form, with *nun* as the second consonant, appears in Old Byblian, Old Aramaic, and Samalian. In later Byblian, however, the "short" form competed with the older זן.

It is difficult to decide the extent to which shared innovation accounts for this distribution. The Semitic languages show demonstrative pronouns derived from $*d$- and from $*d$-n,[29] so that both bases may be reconstructed for Proto-Semitic. In NWS, however, $*d$ appears to be restricted to the Canaanite group.

2b. "This" (fem. sing.).

BYBLIAN: זא*, as inferred from later Byblian inscriptions (Yehawmilk 6.12).

STANDARD PHOENICIAN: ז (Karatepe A II 9.17, III 15).

ARAMAIC: זא (Sf. I A 35.37, III 9) and זאת (Fekh. 15).[30]

SAMALIAN: זא (H 18).

AMMONITE: No evidence.

DEIR ALLA: No evidence.

MOABITE: זאת (Mesha 3).

EDOMITE: No evidence.

HEBREW: זאת (Silwan B 1.3; Lach. 6:10; Arad 40:14/15 [partially restored]).

All forms of the fem. sing. demonstrative pronoun are derived from $*d\bar{a}$.[31] This form was preserved in standard Phoenician. In Byblian (?), Old Aramaic (excluding Fekh.), and Samalian, a secondary, syllable-closing *aleph* appeared on the pronoun.[32] In addition to this syllable-closing *aleph*, a final *-t* also appeared in the Moabite, Hebrew, and Fekh.-Aramaic demonstrative; cf. Ethiopic.[33] Because of this distribution, the *t*-forms may have been common inheritances[34] or parallel, independent developments.

2c.   "These" (common plural).

BYBLIAN: אל (Yehimilk 3).

STANDARD PHOENICIAN: אל*, as inferred from the later Phoenician texts (Eshmunazor 22; CIS I 14.5, etc.).

Rosenthal[35] and Caquot[36] have suggested that this demonstrative appears in Arsl.T. 1:3; the former read אלה, the latter אלו. Yet the reading and context of the passage in question are too unclear to provide any certain evidence of this demonstrative.

ARAMAIC: אל (Zkr A 9.16, B 8) and אלן (Sf. I A 7.7.38, etc.). The second form, with final *nun,* arose on analogy with the singular זנה; the *nun* of the singular form was transferred to the plural.[37] Cf. biblical Aramaic דך "that" (sing.) and אלך "those" (plural). Alternatively, the *nun* was borrowed from the nominal plural morpheme ‎ן-.

SAMALIAN: אל (H 29).

AMMONITE: No evidence.

DEIR ALLA: Evidence uncertain. Hoftijzer[38] and Caquot and Lemaire[39] identified אל (I 2) as the demonstrative plural, whereas Hackett[40] and others[41] interpreted it as the divine name "El." It is not possible to decide between these alternatives at present.[42]

MOABITE: No evidence.

EDOMITE: No evidence.

HEBREW: No evidence from the epigraphic texts. In BH, this demonstrative is אֵלֶּה.

All first-millennium NWS dialects exhibit a demonstrative plural pronoun derived from *ʾ*i/ull.*[43] Whereas nearly all dialects had the same consonantal formation of the demonstrative, the vocalization differed slightly from dialect to dialect. The later Punic transcription, *ily* "these" (Poen. 938), suggests that the Phoenician demonstrative was pronounced approximately [ʾillē]. This final vowel, however, was not an innovation shared exclusively by Phoenician and Hebrew; it also appears in Arabic and later Aramaic dialects.[44]

Yet in terms of first-millennium NWS dialect grouping, Phoenician and BH share one form, and Aramaic-Samalian another.

The major deviation, or innovation, away from the common NWS אל was the addition of a final *nun* in Sfire-Aramaic, on analogy with either the final *nun* of the masculine singular demonstrative or the nominal plural morpheme ן-. This particular analogy was unique to Old Aramaic, among the first-millennium NWS dialects.[45]

3.   The relative pronoun/particle.

BYBLIAN: ז- [zu, zi (?)] (Ahirom 1; Yehimilk 1; Elibaal 1; Ship-tibaal 1). In later Byblian, ז- died out, and another relative, אש, appeared (Yehawmilk 2, etc.; KAI 11).

STANDARD PHOENICIAN: אש (Kilamu 15; Karatepe A I 15.19, etc.; Arsl.T. 1:16, 2:4).

ARAMAIC: זי [dī] (Zkr A 1.16, etc.; Br-Hdd 1.4; Sf. I A 5.7, etc.; Fekh. 1.5, etc.).[46] In Halaf Ost. 1 Obv. 5, the relative was written defectively as ז,[47] like the construction זלי "my, mine" in the Assur Ost. 13.[48]

SAMALIAN: זי [dī, zī] (H 1), written defectively in the construction מז "whatever" (H 3.4.22)[49] and in Kilamu Scepter 1 ז.[50]

AMMONITE: אש (Hesh. Ost. 4:6).[51]

DEIR ALLA: No evidence.

Although Hackett[52] found the Deir Alla relative in אש (I 1), the context and syntax of the passage suggest the meaning "man."[53] A relative particle זי[54] is also uncertain; in Clay Text 1 it is probably Aramaic,[55] and in fragment Vf 3 the reading is too uncertain.

MOABITE: אשר (Mesha 29).

EDOMITE: No evidence.

HEBREW: אשר (Lach. 3:5; Arad 40:5, etc.; Mur 17 A 2; Silwan B 1.2; etc.).[55a] There is no direct evidence of a relative ש- in the epigraphic texts.

The relative particle of the first-millennium NWS dialects was formed from three different roots. Byblian Phoenician, Old Aramaic, and Samalian formed the relative from *$\underline{d}$. Standard Phoenician and Ammonite formed a group which used *$\underline{t}$ as the base for the relative particle. And Moabite and Hebrew used a (construct?) form of the noun *$^\text{ʾ}a\underline{t}ru$ "place" as the relative; cf., possibly, *ašar* in EA[56] and *ʾa\underline{t}r* once in Ugaritic.[57] Whereas *$\underline{d}$[58] and *$\underline{t}$[59] are Proto-Semitic

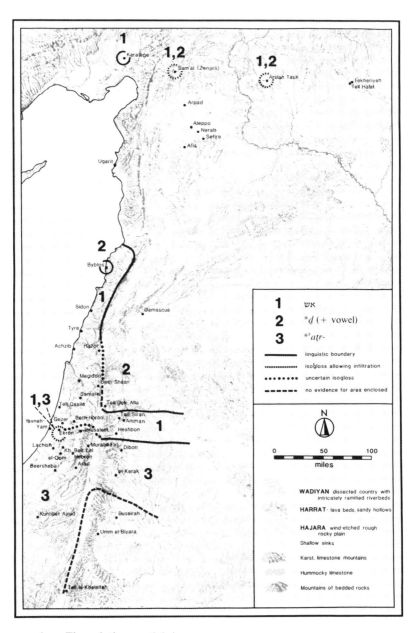

MAP 4:   The relative particle/pronoun.

relative particles, Moabite and Hebrew jointly recycled the old noun "place" in this new manner. This use of *ᵓaṯru "place," then, was an innovation shared exclusively by Moabite and Hebrew among the first-millennium NWS dialects.

4. The personal, interrogative pronoun.

PHOENICIAN: מי [miya, mī] (Kilamu 11.12.13.15). Cf. EA mi-ya "who" (EA 85:63, 94:12, 116:67).[60]

ARAMAIC: מן [man] (Zkr B 21, etc.; Sf. II B 9, etc.; Fekh. 10.16).

SAMALIAN: מן [man (?)] (H 15).

AMMONITE: מ [mī], in the PN מכמאל [Mī-kamō-ᵓĕl] (seal[61]).[62]

DEIR ALLA: מן [man (?)] (II 12), if the line is to be read בלבב.מן.נאנח.[63] If, however, the line is read בלבבם.נאנח,[64] the pronoun מן disappears.[65]

MOABITE: No evidence.

EDOMITE: No evidence.

HEBREW: מי [mī] (Lach. 2:3, 5:3, 6:2, 7:2 [partially restored], 9:2 [partially restored]).

The NWS dialects employed two personal, interrogative pronouns. Old Aramaic, Samalian, and possibly Deir Alla used the common Semitic pronoun *man.[66] Phoenician, Ammonite, and Hebrew, however, jointly innovated by using a new form *miya.[67] These latter three dialects, then, constituted a single dialectal group not only within NWS but also within the other Semitic languages as well.

5. The form of the definite article.

PHOENICIAN: -ה (e.g., הבתם "the houses" [Yehimilk 2],[68] הקרת "the city" [Karatepe A II 9.17, etc.], המלכם "the kings" [Kilamu 9/10], and הנסך "the weaver" [Achzib][69]). The definite article was followed by consonantal gemination, as inferred from the late Punic forms עממקם [ammaqōm] "the places" (KAI 173:5) < *ha(m) + maqōm[70] and possibly הגגפם [haggāpīm] "the fences" (CIS I 340) < *ha(g) + gāpīm.[71]

ARAMAIC: א- [āᵓ] (e.g., נצבא "the stele" [Br-Hdd 1; Zkr A 1, etc.], ארקא "the land" [Br-Rkb 1:4; Adon 2], דמותא "the image" [Fekh. 1.15], etc.).

Two exceptions to the designation of the definite article by postpositive aleph have been adduced, both involving the use of postpositive *he*. The first is מלכה (Hama 7 A 923 + 7 A 538), which Garbini[72] and Donner and Röllig[73] interpreted as "the king." Yet, as Degen[74] has suggested, מלכה should be interpreted either as "his king" or "queen"; the final *he* was not the definite article.

The other exception is the form אחרה (Nerab 1:13), which Cooke[75] interpreted as "another," comparable to later Aramaic אוחרנא; the final *he* would represent the usual postpositive *aleph* of the definite article. Yet the form is better interpreted as אחר + adverbial [ā], in the sense of "in the future";[76] cf. לאחרה "in the future" (Nerab 2:8), with pleonastic *lamedh*. This interpretation better fits both the context and syntax of the inscription. The only definite article in Old Aramaic, then, was postpositive א- [āʾ].

SAMALIAN: There is no evidence of a written definite article in Samalian;[77] all examples of a suffixed *aleph* corresponding to a definite article are uncertain.[78] Yet it is impossible to verify Schaeder's[79] thesis that Samalian had a suffixed definite article [ā] which was never present in the orthography. Until a written form of the definite article appears, it is preferable to follow the majority of scholars and to deny the existence of the definite article in this dialect.

AMMONITE: ה-, as in הכרם "the vineyard" (Sir. 4) and ה.גנת "the garden" (Sir. 4).

DEIR ALLA: There is no certain evidence of a definite article in these texts.[80] Hoftijzer[81] suggested that it was א-, based on the reading ובשכמתא.אל "and in these mountainous regions (?)" in I 2. Caquot and Lemaire,[82] as well as McCarter,[83] agreed that the definite article in Deir Alla was א-, but they read I 2 as כמלן[י]א.אל "according to these words." Yet Hackett's[84] reading כמשא.אל "like an oracle of El" is also plausible. In that case, the final *aleph* was a root letter. McCarter[85] further cited זי שרעא "of the gatekeeper" (Clay Text 1) and אבן שרעא "the gatekeeper's stone" (Clay Text 2) as proof of a suffixed definite article א- in the Deir Alla spoken dialect. Yet in addition to the uncertainty of equating the dialect of the Clay Texts with that of the plaster texts, שרעא may be a personal name ending in the hypocoristicon [ō].[86] Finally, the suggested definite article in אחראה "in the future (?)" (I 2)[87] is grammatically difficult.[88]

MOABITE: ה-, as in הארץ "the land" (Mesha 29.31), הקר "the city" (Mesha 12.24.24), and היערן "the forests" (Mesha 21).[89]

EDOMITE: ה-, as in המלך "the king" (Bus. 386;[90] seal of קוסענל[91]).[92]

HEBREW: ה-, as in הנקבה "the tunnel" (Shiloah 1), הצבא "the army" (Lach. 3:14), and הים "the day, today" (Arad 1:4, 24:19). Presumably the definite article in epigraphic Hebrew was pronounced like its Masoretic counterpart, [ha] + gemination of the following consonant.

The definite article is a morphological innovation which appeared during the early first millennium B.C.E.[93] It did not develop in Samalian. In the other dialects, however, it appeared either as a prefixed *he* (+ gemination of the following consonant) or a suffixed [ā']. The article *he* is found in Phoenician dialects, Ammonite, Moabite, Edomite, and in Hebrew. [ā'] is found only in Old Aramaic. The form of the definite article in the Deir Alla dialect is still unknown.

6a. The noun: The ending of the absolute dual and masculine plural.

PHOENICIAN: ם-, as in מלכם "kings" (Ahirom 2; Kilamu 5.6, etc.), מקמם "places" (Karatepe A I 14.17, II 3), and שמם "Heaven" (Yehimilk 3; Karatepe A III 18). In the Arslan Tash dialect, however, the ending was ן-, as in קדשן "Holy Ones" (Arsl.T. 1:12) and ללין "night demons" (1:20);[94] the cultic terms בן אלם "divinities" (Arsl.T. 1:11) and שמם "Heaven" (Arsl.T. 1:13) are borrowed, or inherited, religious vocabulary and do not reflect local speech patterns.[95]

ARAMAIC: ן-, as in מלכן "kings" (Zkr A 5; Br-Rkb 1:10.13, etc.), אלהן "gods" (Zkr B 9; Sf. I A 30, etc.; Fekh. 14.4), and שמין "heaven" (Sf. I A 26, etc.; Fekh. 2; Adon 3; Zkr B 25 [partially restored]).

SAMALIAN: The ending of the nominative masc. plural was ו- [ū], and the oblique was י- [ī].[96] The ending of the oblique dual was י- also, as in בלגרי "at the feet" (P 16) and ידיה "his hands" (H 29); in both cases, however, the nouns are bound, not absolute.

AMMONITE: ם-, as in אלם "gods" (Cit. 6) and the later form חבלם "ropes" (Hesh. Ost. 11:4); cf. רבם "great" (masc. plural) (Sir. 7).[97]

DEIR ALLA: ן-, as in אלהן "gods" (I 1.1.5, etc.), חכמן "wise men" (I 11), and שמין "heaven" (I 6).

MOABITE: ן-, as in ימן "days" (Mesha 5), שלשן "30" (Mesha 2), and מאתן "200" (Mesha 20).

EDOMITE: No evidence.

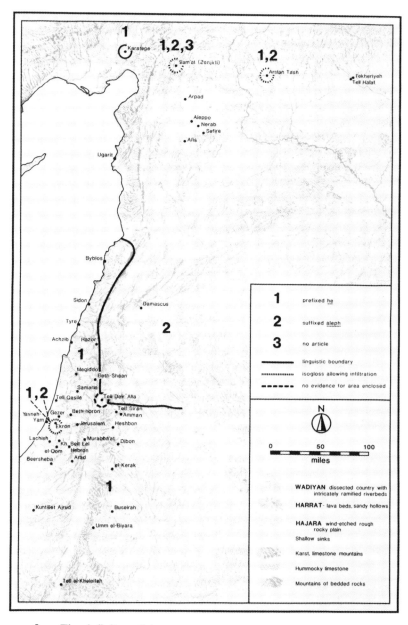

MAP 5:   The definite article.

HEBREW: ם-, as in חמרם "asses" (Arad 3:5), חצבם "hewers" (Shiloah 4), שנים "2" (Arad 7:7), and מאתים "200" (Shiloah 5).

Like all Semitic languages, the absolute dual and masculine plural end in a long vowel, long vowel + *n*, or long vowel + *m*.[98] As in Akkadian masc. plural nouns, Samalian forms terminated in a simple long vowel. Nunation was added in Aramaic, Deir Alla, Moabite, and the Phoenician dialect of Arslan Tash; the origin of this -*n* is uncertain. And in Phoenician dialects (except at Arslan Tash), Ammonite, and Hebrew, these nominal forms ended in -*m*; this -*m* was transferred from the mimation of singular nouns. In view of the Akkadian and Samalian evidence, both mimation and nunation may have been secondary developments.[99]

6b.   The ending of the masculine plural construct.

PHOENICIAN: -∅ [ê], as for example in בן גבל "the gods of Byblos" (Yehimilk 4.7), פן.ש "the face of a sheep" (Kilamu 11), and בן אלם "divinities" (Arsl.T. 1:11). For the ending [ê], see the Greek transcriptions ΦΑΝΕ ΒΑΛ "Face of Baal" (KAI 175:2) and ΦΕΝΗ ΒΑΛ "Face of Baal" (KAI 176:2/3).[100]

ARAMAIC: י- [ay], as for example בתי [bâttay] "the houses of" (Zkr B 9; Sf. II C 2/3, etc.) and עדי [ʿa/eday] "the treaty of" (Sf. I A 1, etc.), etc.

SAMALIAN: There was no special form for the masc. plural construct noun.[101] The ending was either [ū] or [ī], depending upon the syntax of the *nomen regens*; when the noun was the grammatical subject, it ended in [ū], and when it was the object or followed a preposition, it ended in [ī].[102]

AMMONITE: -∅ [(?)], as in בן "the sons of" (Sir. 1.2.3; Theater 2 [?]). The vocalization of this ending, however, is uncertain. Either it was *[ê] < *ay, as in Phoenician and (northern) Hebrew, or *[ī].[103] Since the masculine plural construct may have originally been *-ī in NWS,[104] it is unknown whether the original *-ī was retained in Ammonite or was replaced by the dual construct *-ay (as in Phoenician, Hebrew, and Aramaic).

DEIR ALLA: י- [ay], as in אפרחי.אנפה "chicks of the heron" (I 8) and בני.אש "men" (II 8); cf. משכבי.עלמיך "your eternal bed" (II 11).

MOABITE: י- [ê (?)], as in אסרי "prisoners of" (Mesha 25/26), ימי "the days of" (Mesha 8), and לפני "before" (Mesha 13.18); cf. שעריה

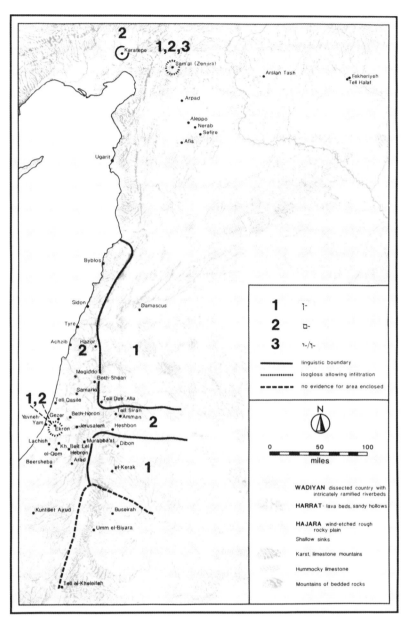

MAP 6:   The ending of the absolute dual and masculine plural noun.

"its gates" (Mesha 22), in which the *yodh* suggests the reflex of an original diphthong *ay*.

EDOMITE: No evidence.

HEBREW: The evidence comes only from the southern dialect, where the masc. plural construct ended in ‎י- [ay], as for example ‎בני "the sons of" (Arad 16:5, 49:1.2, etc.), ‎ספרי "the letters of" (Lach. 6:4), and ‎דברי "the matters of" (Lach. 6:5). Since diphthongs did not contract in the southern Hebrew dialect,[105] it is probable that the masc. plural construct ending *ay* did not contract either. There is no reason, then, to accept the conclusion of Dion[106] that this ending ‎י- was pronounced [ê], as in Phoenician, Ammonite, and Moabite. In northern Hebrew, however, this morpheme would have been pronounced *[ê].

The masc. plural construct ending is an innovation within NWS. In Samalian, the morpheme had not yet developed; the nominal ending depended upon the syntax of the noun itself and not on its relation to its following modifier. An old ending *-ī may have appeared in Ammonite, but the evidence is uncertain. The common NWS masc. plural ending *-ay, however, is found in Phoenician, Aramaic, Deir Alla, Moabite, Hebrew, and possibly in Ammonite. This morphological innovation, then, was shared by most, if not all, NWS dialects in Syria-Palestine proper.

6c. The ending of the absolute feminine singular.

BYBLIAN: ‎ת- [ōt], as in ‎מחנת [maḥnōt] "camp" (Ahirom 2), and [t], as in ‎נחת [naḥt (?)] "peace" (Ahirom 2).[107]

STANDARD PHOENICIAN: ‎ת- [ōt][108] (see examples in Chapter 2, no. 18a). In later Phoenician, "year" appears as ‎שת < *šan-t (KAI 19:5, 52:4, 60:1, etc.).

ARAMAIC: ‎ה- [ā] (see examples in Chapter 2, no. 18a). Other endings included [ât] (as in ‎מרמת [marmât] "rebellion" [Sf. III 22]) and possibly [t] (as in ‎שאת [taʾt (?)] "ewe" [Sf. I A 21]).

SAMALIAN: ‎ה- [ā] (see examples in Chapter 2, no. 18a). A fem. sing. abstract form in ‎ו- [ū] also appeared in this dialect (e.g., ‎כברו "greatness" [H 11] and ‎אברו "strength" [H 15.21]).[109]

AMMONITE: ‎ת- [at (?)] (see examples in Chapter 2, no. 18a).

DEIR ALLA: ‎ת- [ā] (see examples in Chapter 2, no. 18a).

MOABITE: ת-. The ending was vocalized [t] in שת [šat(t)] "year" (Mesha 2.8) < *šant, and perhaps in משמעת [ma/išmaʻt] "subjects" (Mesha 28); cf. BH משמעת. The ending was vocalized [ăt] in המסלת [ham-masillăt] "the highway" (Mesha 26) and [īt] in שחרת [šaḥrīt] "morning" (Mesha 15). Three pronunciations [t], [ăt], and [īt], then, are concealed behind one consonantal ending ת-.[110]

EDOMITE: No evidence.[111]

HEBREW: ה- [ā] (see examples in Chapter 2, no. 18a). Other abs. fem. sing. endings included ת-, vocalized [t] (as in שת [šat(t)] "year" [Sam. Ost., passim] < *šan-t; cf. BH *šan-at) and [īt] (as in העשרת [hā-ʻśīrīt] "the tenth" [Sam. Ost. 1:1, etc.] and רבעת [rᵊbīʻīt] "fourth" (Lach. 29]), and a form in ית- [īt (?), iyyāt] (בתשעית "on the ninth" [Lach. 20:1]).

The basic form of the abs. fem. sing. noun ended in *-át in all first-millennium NWS dialects. This *-át was preserved, with different pronunciations, in Phoenician dialects, Ammonite, and Moabite; in Aramaic, Samalian, the Deir Alla dialect, and Hebrew, *-át changed to [ấ] in this nominal form. This distribution of the correspondence *-át:[ấ] does not indicate the geographical (or dialectal) source of this innovation. Indeed, the appearance of *-át:[ấ] in several Semitic languages suggests that it occurred independently in NWS.[112]

Other feminine singular endings varied from dialect to dialect. Samalian alone preserved the abstract ending [ū], which is also found in later Aramaic dialects. A feminine ת- is found in Old Byblian נחת, in (northern?) Hebrew, Moabite, and later Phoenician שת, and possibly in Old Aramaic שאת; the simple addition of [t] to a *CaC base may have been a northern, Syro-Palestinian linguistic feature. Finally, Hebrew and Moabite shared the ending [īt], while Hebrew may have contained a ballast form of this ending under the guise of ית-.

6d.   The ending of the absolute feminine plural.

PHOENICIAN: ת- [ōt] < *āt, as in שנת [šanōt] "years" (Karatepe A III 6) and חמית [ḥōmiy(y)ōt] "walls" (Karatepe A I 13.17). For the vocalization, see *alonuth* "goddesses" (Poen. 930),[113] where -*uth* represents the Phoenician ending [ōt] < *āt.

ARAMAIC: There were two abs. fem. plural endings in Old Aramaic. One was ת- [āt], as in לחית [laḥyāt] "evil" (Sf. I C 20, III 2). The other was ן- [ān], as for example שאן "ewes" (Sf. I A 23), [מהי]נקן "wetnurses" (Sf. I A 21), and מעינן "wells" (Sf. I A 12); cf. סאון "ewes" (Fekh. 20) and נשון "women" (Fekh. 21.22).[114] In Sfire, the two endings may have marked a distinction between feminine plural adjectives ([āt]) and nouns ([ān]).[115]

The ending in [ān] was a secondary innovation in Aramaic, formed on analogy with the abs. masc. plural ending [īn].[116] The analogy followed a proportional model:

[tāb] "good" (masc. sing.) : [tāb-ī-n] "good" (masc. pl.)
[ṭābā] "good" (fem. sing.) : *ṭāb-ā- "good" (fem. pl.)

The final *nun* became the sign of plurality and was transferred from the abs. masc. plural to the abs. fem. plural. The form, therefore, became [ṭābān] and replaced the older [ṭābāt].

SAMALIAN: ת- [āt], as in קירת [qīrāt] "cities" (H 10; P 4), קתילת [qatīlāt] "killed (women)" (P 8), and חרבת "wasted (cities)" (P 4).

AMMONITE: ת- [ōt], as in מבאת "entrances" (Cit. 1) and יומת "days" (Sir. 7).

DEIR ALLA: No evidence.

While Hoftijzer[117] believed he isolated three examples of the abs. fem. plural, each example is dubious. The alleged fem. plural ת- in ‏את.אתיחדו[   ] (I 5) is to be read ‏[   ]ן.[118] The plural form, ארנבן "hares" (I 9), is not the feminine plural of *ארנבה but the masculine plural of sing. ארנב (cf. Old Aramaic, Arabic, and Akkadian).[119] Finally, the form קקן "constraint" (I 14) does not conceal an abs. fem. plural; the *nun* is probably a nominal suffix *ān attached to the middle weak root *ḏwq.[120] There are, then, no certain examples of the abs. fem. plural in the Deir Alla texts.

MOABITE: ת- [(?)], as in גברת "women" (Mesha 16) and רחמת "children" (Mesha 17).

EDOMITE: No evidence.

HEBREW: ת- [ōt], as in האגנת "the basins" (Arad 1:10) and אמת "cubits" (Shiloah 2).

All the first-millennium NWS dialects exhibit final ת- for the singular of the abs. fem. plural. The old form, [āt], as in Akkadian and Arabic, was preserved in Old Aramaic and Samalian; those dialects which had the systematic correspondence *ā́:[ṓ] had the ending [ōt]—i.e. Phoenician dialects, Ammonite, and Hebrew.

The only deviation from the use of final *taw* as the sign of the abs. fem. plural was in Old Aramaic. There, the *nun* of the abs. masc. plural was transferred to the abs. fem. plural. The Sfire texts document this change from [āt] to [ān]; in these texts alone, both endings appear in complementary distribution. In the later Aramaic dialects, however, [ān] dominated.

7. The plural formation of final weak nouns.

PHOENICIAN: Final weak nominal plurals ended in **iy(y)ōt*, **iy(y)īm*, or **iy(y)īn*, as for example קצית [qaṣiy(y)ōt] "extremities" (Karatepe A I 14) < קצת [qaṣīt] (Karatepe A I 21, B 1), חמית [ḥōmiy(y)ōt] "walls" (Karatepe A I 13.17), and ללין [lêliy(y)īn] "night demons" (Arsl.T. 1:20). In Ugaritic, a similar plural appeared, as in *ḥmyt* "the walls of" (CTA 32:28) and perhaps *qrytm* "two cities" (CTA 3:B:7).

ARAMAIC: As in later Aramaic dialects,[121] final weak nouns ended in **awwā-* + fem. plural morpheme, as for example מחנות [maḥnawwāt] "camps of" (construct) (Zkr A 9)[122] and סאון [ta'awwān] "ewes" (Fekh. 20). Cf. נשון [našawwān] "women" (Fekh. 21.22), in which the root was considered final weak.[123]

A special plural formation of final weak nouns did not appear at Sfire. In the Aramaic dialect of that community, the simple nominal plural morpheme was added to the singular base. So, for example, שאן "ewes" (Sf. I A 23) < sing. שאת (Sf. I A 21) was analyzed as **ta'* + suffix, not as a final weak root.[124] Cf. similarly נשי "the women of" (Sf. I A 41), which also coincides with the general Aramaic plural formations in these nouns.

SAMALIAN: All evidence suggests that the plural of final weak nouns was the same as that of regular, strong nouns. For example, מחנת "camps" (P 13.16), if plural,[125] should be vocalized [maḥnāt], in contrast to Old Aramaic מחנות-. Similarly, משות [mašwāt] "(?)" (P 21) is derived from **mašway* + *at* (sing.) > **mašwaat* > **[maš-wāt][126]* → [mašwāt (?)] (plural). The pattern for the plural of final weak nouns, then, followed that of regular, strong nouns.

AMMONITE: No evidence.

DEIR ALLA: No evidence. The etymology and meaning of שדין (I 6.5 [partially restored]) is still uncertain; if derived from a final weak root, it is possible that this form reflects a plural formation **iy(y)īn* comparable to that of ללין in Arsl.T. 1:20.

MOABITE: Final weak nouns followed the pattern of regular, strong nouns, as for example חמת [ḥōmā/ōt] "walls" (Mesha 21.21 [both construct]). Cf. Phoenician חמית.

EDOMITE: No evidence.

HEBREW: Final weak nouns followed the pattern of regular, strong nouns, as inferred from plural forms in the Masoretic text (e.g., חמת [ḥōmōt] "walls," etc.).

The form of the plural in final weak nouns divided the first-millennium NWS dialects into two groups. In Samalian, Moabite, and Sfire-Aramaic the plural morpheme was attached to the nominal singular base. In Phoenician and Old Aramaic (excluding Sfire), a special plural formation appeared, *iy(y)- + plural in the former and *awwā- + fem. plural in the latter. These two northern dialect groups deviated from the common NWS pattern.

On the one hand, Phoenician and Old Aramaic (excepting Sfire) were united by special plural formations of final weak nouns. On the other, the actual plural form itself differed between them. Phoenician leveled all final weak nouns to yodh (*iy[y]-), and Aramaic leveled them to waw (*awwā-). Despite the difference in outcomes, however, these dialects constituted one group in their use of a plural formation for final weak nouns different from that of regular, strong nouns.

8. The attaching of possessive suffixes to feminine plural nouns.

BYBLIAN: In all probability, the suffix was attached to fem. plural nouns in the same manner as it was attached to masc./fem. sing. nouns. One example is מג/פשת "my offerings/possessions" (Bronze Spat. 5), where the noun appears to be plural;[127] the first person sing. suffix was -∅ [ī]. Had the suffix been attached in the same manner as it was to masc. plural nouns, the form would have been *מג/פשתי* with the suffix pronounced [ay(ya)].[128] Further, in the inscriptions from the mid-tenth century onward, שנתו "his years" (Yehimilk 5; Elibaal 3; etc.) ended in the same suffix [aw, ô] as אדתו "his lady" (Elibaal 2; Shiptibaal 4) and זרעו "his seed" (Yehawmilk 15); cf., however, ימו "his days" (Yehawmilk 9), with a different pronunciation.[129] All evidence is admittedly ambiguous with respect to the suffix on these fem. plural nouns. Nevertheless, comparison with other dialects strongly suggests that the suffix was attached to fem. plural nouns in the same manner as to masc./fem. sing. nouns.

STANDARD PHOENICIAN: In all probability, the suffix was attached directly to the noun, without an intervening vowel [ê].[130] The first person sing. suffix was written ‑י on fem. plural nouns only when the noun stood in the genitive (e.g., בימתי "in my days" [Karatepe A II 1.5, etc.]; cf. later וקרא אנך את רבתי "and I called my lady" [Yehawmilk 2/3], where רבתי was in the genitive following the preposition את[131]). Similarly, the third person sing. suffix attached to fem. plural nouns appeared as ‑י in ושבע.צרתי "and his seven co-wives" (Arsl.T. 1:17). But here too צרתי was in the genitive case following ושבע.[132] In each example, then, it was the genitive construction which demanded the suffix ‑י on fem. plural nouns. There is no evidence that the fem. plural noun had a binding vowel [ê] before the suffix.

ARAMAIC: The suffix was attached directly onto the fem. plural noun in the same manner as onto masc./fem. sing. nouns (e.g., בנתה "his daughters" [Sf. I A 24] and מחנות.הם "their camps" [Zkr A 9]). Cf. the corresponding masc. plural nouns with a connecting diphthong (e.g., בנוה "his sons" [Sf. I A 5, etc.] and בתיהם "their houses" [Sf. II C 16]).

SAMALIAN: The evidence is ambiguous. Both examples of the fem. plural noun + suffix tentatively suggested by Dion[133]—אמרתה "his command(s)" (H 26.32) and גברתה "his strength" (H 32)—may have been fem. sing. nouns just as well.[134]

AMMONITE: No evidence.[135]

DEIR ALLA: No evidence.

MOABITE: The scanty evidence suggests that, like Aramaic and Phoenician, the suffix was directly attached to fem. plural nouns.[136] The form מגדלתה [magdalā/ōtẵh] "its towers" (Mesha 22) contrasts with the only other example of the third person fem. sing. suffix on a plural noun, שעריה "its gates" (Mesha 22). Whereas Cross and Freedman[137] saw the identical suffix in both forms, the example of Phoenician and Aramaic suggests that the two forms are to be examined individually. יה‑ is derived from the masc. plural construct ending *ay + suffix, whereas ה‑ is, like the suffix on sing. nouns, the simple suffix added directly onto the noun. The Moabite form would therefore tally with that of the other NWS dialects, with the exception of Hebrew.

EDOMITE: No evidence.

HEBREW: As inferred from BH, the suffixes were attached to fem. plural nouns in the same manner as to masc. plural nouns: a binding vowel [ê] was transferred from the masc. to the fem. plural suffixed form,[138] probably on the following model:

> [bānīm] "sons" : [bān-ê-hā] "her sons"
> [bānōt] "daughters" : *banōt- -hā "her daughters"

The connecting vowel [ê] was inserted in the fem. plural paradigm on analogy with the masc. plural suffixed noun. In the southern dialect the connecting vowel would have been *[ay], as in לפניך [li-pānayk(a)] "before you" (Arad 7:6); in the northern dialect it would have been the monophthong [ê] (no certain examples).

The evidence suggests that the general NWS pattern for appending suffixes onto fem. plural nouns was noun + suffix of the masc./fem. sing. noun. Since, like masc. and fem. sing. nouns, the fem. plural ended in a simple consonant, the suffix could have been attached directly onto the noun (perhaps with a short, connecting vowel). This pattern appeared in Aramaic, Moabite, and probably Phoenician.

A second formation was attested only in Hebrew. On analogy with the suffixed masc. plural noun, the fem. plural suffixed noun borrowed the connective *[ay]/[ê] and inserted it between the fem. plural noun and suffix. Like other cases of proportional analogy, this transference was idiosyncratic, restricted to a single dialect, and did not spread to other dialects.

9a. The form of the possessive suffix attached to "singular" nouns: The first person singular.

BYBLIAN: -∅ [ī], when the noun was in the nominative/accusative, and י- [iya (?)], when the noun was in the genitive case. While there is no direct evidence from Byblian of this period, later texts show that the distinction between [ī] and [iya (?)] was maintained (e.g., קל [qōlī] "my voice" [Yehawmilk 3.8], as direct object of שמע "she heard" vs. על פן פתחי [pittūḥiya (?)] "of my inscription" [Yehawmilk 5], as genitive governed by a prepositional phrase).[139]

STANDARD PHOENICIAN: -∅ [ī], when the noun was in the nominative/*accusative[140] case (e.g., וכן.אב [ʾabī] "and my father was" [Kilamu 3]), and י- [iya (?)], when the noun was in the genitive case (e.g., בת אבי [ʾabīya (?)] "my father's house" [Kilamu 5; cf. l. 9 = Karatepe A I 11] and בת אדני [ʾadōniya (?)] "my lordly houses"[141] [Karatepe A I 10]). In later standard Phoenician, the written form י- was pronounced [ī] and was standardized for all cases.[142]

ARAMAIC: י- [ī], regardless of construction, as for example אבי [ʾabī] "my father" (Br-Rkb 1:4, etc.; Sf. II B 8, etc. [all genitive]), לחמי [laḥmī] "my food" (Sf. I B 38 [accusative]), etc.[143]

SAMALIAN: י- [ī], regardless of construction, as for example משבי [mattabī, maššabī] "my throne" (H 15.20 [both genitive]), אבי [ʾabī] "my father" (H 8; P 10 [both genitive]; P 6.8.10 [all nominative]), etc.

AMMONITE: No evidence.

DEIR ALLA: י- [ī], attested only in לבי [libbī (?)] "my heart (?)" (II 32).

MOABITE: י- [ī], regardless of construction, as for example אבי [ʾabī] "my father" (Mesha 3 [genitive]; l. 2 [nominative]).

EDOMITE: No evidence.

HEBREW: י- [ī], regardless of construction, as for example כצאתי [kᵊṣē(ʾ)tī] "when I left" (Arad 16:3 [genitive]), אדני [ʾadōnī] "my lord" (Arad 18:1; Lach. 2:1, etc. [all genitive]; Arad 21:3 [nominative]), etc.

Most of the first-millennium NWS dialects had [ī] for the possessive suffix of the first person sing. on sing. nouns. This ending appeared regardless of the syntax of the base noun; after the loss of final short vowels, the suffix on genitive nouns ([iya(?)]) had merged with its nominative/accusative counterpart ([ī]).

Only the Phoenician dialects preserved this distinction between [ī] and [iya (?)]. Like Ugaritic[144] and Akkadian,[145] the Phoenician dialects show [iya (?)] on the genitive noun and [ī] on the nominative/accusative. Even after short, final vowels had been lost in NWS, standard Phoenician continued to preserve, at least orthographically, the distinction between the different forms of the possessive pronoun. Later, one orthographic form and one pronunciation became standardized for all cases. Like the other NWS dialects, then, Phoenician ultimately used the single ending י- [ī] for the first person sing. possessive suffix.

9b. The third person sing. suffix, masculine and feminine.

BYBLIAN: Masc. ה- [hū] in the oldest inscription, as for example
אבה [ʾabīhū] "his father" (Ahirom 1). In the course of the tenth
century, however, the Byblian suffix changed to ו- [aw, ô], as for
example אדתו [ʾadōttaw, -tô][146] "his lady" (Elibaal 2; Shiptibaal 4)
and שנתו [šanōtaw, -tô] "his years" (Yehimilk 5; Elibaal 3; Shiptibaal
5).[147]

Fem. ה-* [hā], as inferred from the late Byblian form מספנתה
"its roof" (Yehawmilk 6).

Another suffix, ן- [nnū (?)] < *n-hŭ, is found only on monoconsonantal prepositions in later Byblian texts (e.g., בן [bi/annū (?)]
"in it" [KAI 9 A 3]). In the earlier texts, however, there is no example of a preposition + third person masc./fem. sing. suffix. Two
hypotheses can explain the appearance of this form in the later dialect: (1) ן- occurred in the older phase of the dialect but is as yet
unattested. In this case, ן- would have been native to this dialect;
or (2) ן- spread from standard Phoenician (where it is attested already
in the eighth century) to later Byblian. In this second case, ן- was
not an indigenous form but spread, or was borrowed, from the neighboring dialect. Since later Byblian shows a number of borrowings
from standard Phoenician, the second hypothesis is preferable.

STANDARD PHOENICIAN: Masc. The ending was -∅ [ô] < *-ahŭ if
the suffix did not follow a vowel, as for example שם [šmô] "his
name" (Karatepe A III 14.16, C IV 16 [accusative]) and ראש [rōšô]
"his head" (Kilamu 15.16 [accusative]). If the suffix followed a
vowel, especially the genitive vowel [i], the ending was י- ([yū][148]
or [yī][149]), as for example in צרתי [ṣarōtiyū/ī] "of his co-wives"
(Arsl.T. 1:17), לתתי [li-tittiyū/ī] "that he may give" (Karatepe A III
4), and עד מבאי "until its setting" (Karatepe A I 5, II 3). See the
identical distribution of the first person sing. possessive suffix on
"singular" nouns.

The distinction between the suffixed [ô] and [iyū/ī] had begun
to deteriorate by the late eighth century B.C.E.[150] In Karatepe A III
14.16, C IV 16, the text reads ושת שם "and sets up his name ([šmô]),"
whereas in C IV 18, the text reads ושת שמי, with the same meaning.[151]
Either שמי is an orthographic error, or the form of the suffix after
the genitive vowel [i] was beginning to predominate over the other
form [ô]. Cf., in this respect, the competition between forms of the
first person sing. suffix [ī] and [iya (?)].

Fem. Like its masc. counterpart, the ending was -∅ <
*-ahă, if the governing noun ended in a consonant, as for example
שמ [šmâ] "its name" (Karatepe A II 10.18 [accusative]). If, however,
the governing noun ended in a vowel, the suffix was -י < *i-yā <
*-i-hă[152] (no examples from this period).

The fem. sing. suffix appeared as -ן [nnā (?)] < *n-hă only on
monoconsonantal prepositions, as for example בן [bi/annā (?)] "in
it (the city)" (Karatepe A II 18, III 8).[153]

ARAMAIC: Masc. -ה [ih (?)] < *i-hŭ, as for example ידה [yadih
(?)] "his hand" (Sf. I B 27, III 2), בנתה [banātih (?)] "his daughters"
(Sf. I A 24), etc. The vocalization is inferred from the later Aramaic
dialects which consistently exhibit a form of *ih as this suffix. Like
the standard Phoenician suffixes "my" [iya (?)] and "his/her" [iyū/ī,
iyā], the connecting vowel between the noun and the suffix was the
genitive [i]. In Aramaic, however, the genitive case became standardized as the connecting vowel for this suffix; in Phoenician, the
use of the connecting [i] was subject to the syntax of the noun.

Fem. -ה [ah(a)] < *a-hă, as for example עמה ['ammah(a)]
"its people" (Sf. I A 29, etc.), כלה [kullah(a)] "all of it" (Sf. I A 5),
etc. The exact pronunciation of the suffix is unknown. Either the
original *ahă was preserved or it was shortened to [ah]. The suffix
was -ה, regardless of the case of the governing noun.

SAMALIAN: Masc. -ה [(?)], as in אב(ו)ה "his father" (H 29; P 2,
etc.), מראה "his lord" (P 11.12), משבה "his throne" (P 2), and לה
"to him" (Kilamu Scepter 5).

Fem. -ה [(?)], as in כלה "all of it" (P 17).

AMMONITE: Masc. -ה[154] [uh, ih] < *-uhu or *-ihi, as in כרה "its
laver (?)" (Cit. 5).[155] The interpretation of this form and word is
disputed, however.

Fem. No evidence.

DEIR ALLA: Masc. -ה [(?)], as in עמה "his people" (I 4, II 17),
לבבה "his heart" (II 12), etc.

Fem. No evidence.

MOABITE: Masc. -ה [(?)],[156] as in בנה "his son" (Mesha 6.8),
ב(י)תה "his house" (Mesha 7.25), בה "over him" (Mesha 7), etc.

Fem. -ה [ăh], as in בה [băh] "in it" (Mesha 8, etc.) and
מגדלתה [magdalā/ōtăh] "its towers" (Mesha 22).

EDOMITE: No evidence.

HEBREW: Masc. The orthography of this suffix changed considerably throughout the history of epigraphic Hebrew. If the vocali-

zation of ירח as [yarḥô] "his month" is accepted for Gezer Cal. 3, etc.,[157] early Hebrew had a third person masc. sing. suffix in -∅. The suffix would therefore be derived from *-ahū̆ > [ô].[158] Yet the form of ירח cannot be interpreted with any certainty.

The first certain example of the third person masc. sing. suffix is ה-, pronounced [ô] < *-ahū̆.[159] See, for example, אשרתה "his Asherah" (Ajrud), [ע]בדה "his servant" (Lach. 2:5), אמתה "his maidservant" (Silwan B 2), etc. The identical suffix was represented by ו- in רעו [rēʿaw, rēʿô] "his fellow" (Shiloah 3); the waw was an alternate orthography for [ô] < *-aw < *-ahū̆.[160] The other suggested cases of the third person masc. sing. suffix ו-—Beit Lei A 2 לו "to him"[161] and Yavneh-Yam 1:6 קצרו "his harvest"[162]—may be misreadings of the text.[163]

Fem. No evidence.

Although there is little evidence for the vocalization of the third person masc. sing. possessive suffix, each dialect probably had its own pronunciation of the suffix. Nevertheless, the dialects can be arranged, at least superficially, into groups. Old Aramaic (and Samalian?) preserved a final vowel on the suffix. Standard Phoenician and Aramaic shared the genitive case as the connecting vowel; in Aramaic, the vowel [i] was frozen and used for all nominal cases, thus [ih (?)], whereas in standard Phoenician the vowel [i] was restricted to the genitive case of the noun. Standard Phoenician, however, exhibits a further development from the original *-hū̆ since palatalization of the he occurred, so that this *h following the genitive [i] became ו.[164] No other dialect exhibits this phenomenon.

The suffix [ô] < *-ahū̆ was characteristic of standard Phoenician when the governing noun was in the nominative or accusative case. The vocalization [ô] is also found in Hebrew, regardless of the case of the governing noun.

There were fewer variations of the third person fem. sing. suffix in the different dialects. Old Aramaic preserved an old ending [ah(a)]. Moabite had a simplified [ăh], and standard Phoenician was characterized by total syncopation of intervocalic he, thus [â]. This standard Phoenician form is found only on nominative and accusative sing. nouns. Palatalization of the he in the fem. sing. suffix, as in its masc. counterpart, occurred on genitive nouns: *-ihă > [iyā]. The final feminine [ā] was preserved. Further, there was a fem. sing. suffix [nnā (?)] in standard Phoenician found only on prepositions.

Standard Phoenician, then, exhibits, by far, the greatest number of (1) suffixes of the third person singular, and (2) phonetic variants of the original *-hŭ and *-hă. The suffixes of the other dialects are, to a large extent, traceable to forms found already in standard Phoenician.

9c. The first person plural.

PHOENICIAN: ן-, as in לן "for us" (Arsl.T. 1:9[165]). It is unclear whether the vocalization was [nū], like Hebrew and EA, or [ōn], like Punic.[166]

ARAMAIC: ן- [an, na], as in מראן "our lord" (Haza'el).[167] The orthography of the suffix does not indicate whether the suffix was pronounced [na], with short [a], thereby anticipating the later common Aramaic suffix [nā],[168] or [an], like the suffix in eastern Aramaic dialects which have lost final vowels.[169] In the Elephantine texts, however, the first person plural suffix of the verb was represented by both ן- and נא-, thus [nā].[170] The spelling with simple final *nun* may therefore reflect the old orthography. The pronunciation may have been [na] or [an] in the early texts.[171]

SAMALIAN: No evidence.

AMMONITE: No evidence.

DEIR ALLA: No evidence. Both examples cited by Hoftijzer[172]— ולן.שתי "and we have beverage (?)" (II 18) and בן "on (?) us" (II 20)—appear in passages too unclear to yield any meaning.

MOABITE: No evidence.

EDOMITE: No evidence.

HEBREW: (ו)נ- [nū], as in אי[נ]נו "we are not" (Arad 40:13/14) and שמרן "our keeper, protector" (Ajrud). While the Arad form shows the expected orthographic representation of [nū], the Ajrud form is an archaic spelling of the same suffix.

In NWS, and all Semitic languages, two forms of the first person plural possessive suffix appear. The old suffix, *nā,[173] appears in Aramaic dialects and other West Semitic languages. The other suffix, *nū, is found in Hebrew and (?) Phoenician; the final ū may have been borrowed from the ending of the independent pronoun.[174]

9d.   The third person masculine plural.

BYBLIAN: No evidence.

STANDARD PHOENICIAN: נם- [nōm],[175] when following a vowel, especially the genitive vowel [i], as for example לשבתנם "that they might dwell" (Karatepe A I 17), בנחת לבנם "in the tranquility of their heart" (Karatepe A I 18), etc. Otherwise, the suffix was ם- [ōm] < *-a-humu, as inferred from the later forms זרעם [zarʿōm] "their seed" (Eshmunazor 22 [accusative]), קלם "their voice" (KAI 47:4 [accusative]), etc. These two forms of the suffix, then, stood in complementary distribution.

ARAMAIC: הם- [hum], as in קרקהם "their fugitive" (Sf. III 19/20 [nominative]), להם "to, for them" (Sf. III 3.5, etc.), נבשהם "their soul" (Sf. III 5/6.6/7 [accusative]), etc. Another form, ם- [am], occurred only in the Fekh. text, as in כלם "all of them" (ll. 4.4).[176]

SAMALIAN: No evidence.

AMMONITE: No evidence.

DEIR ALLA: Two forms of the third person masc. plural suffix are attested in Deir Alla. One is הם- [hum (?)], found only in להם "to them" (I 5). The other is ם- [am (?)], possibly found in the uncertain form בלבבם "in their heart" (II 12).[177] On the basis of this little information, it appears that, as in Hebrew, the Deir Alla suffix [am] was used following consonants, while the other form [hum (?)] followed vowels. Cf. also standard Phoenician.

MOABITE: No evidence.

EDOMITE: No evidence.

HEBREW: ם- [ām] followed consonantal endings (e.g., ימם [yômām] "their day" [Ajrud] and אתם [ʾōtām] "them" [Arad 3:6]), whereas הם- [hem][178] followed vocalic endings (only in להם [lāhem] "for them" [Arad 1:8]).

Regardless of the syntax of the noun, Aramaic dialects generally had one suffix throughout the entire paradigm, [hum]. The remaining dialects, however, show a formal distinction between the postvocalic and postconsonantal suffix. Postconsonantally, *am appeared in Deir Alla, Hebrew (with tonic lengthening), Fekh.-Aramaic, and standard Phoenician (with tonic lengthening and *ā:[ō] correspondence).[179] Postvocalically, Deir Alla and Hebrew employed הם- (with different pronunciations), whereas Phoenician had a new form נם-. For this *nun*, cf. already the third person sing. suffix on mono-

consonantal prepositions ‑ן. Thus, standard Phoenician, Fekh.-Ar-
amaic, Deir Alla, and Hebrew formed one group; Aramaic-speaking
communities, other than Fekheriyeh, constituted another.

10a. The form of the possessive suffix attached to "plural" nouns: The second person masculine singular.

PHOENICIAN: No evidence.
ARAMAIC: ‑יך [ayk], as in שפתיך "your lips" (Sf. III 14/15).[180]
SAMALIAN: No evidence.
AMMONITE: No evidence.
DEIR ALLA: ‑יך [ayk], as in עלמיך "your eternities" (II 11).
MOABITE: No evidence.
EDOMITE: No evidence.
HEBREW: Two forms of this suffix appeared in the epigraphic
texts. The first, ‑יך, appeared in, for example, לפניך "before you"
(Arad 7:6), אליך "to you" (Mur 17 A 2), and אלהיך "your god" (Lach.
6:12/13). The other form, ‑יכה, appears now in אלהיכה "your god"
(Beit Lei A 1[181]). This second "long" form suggests that, as in BH,
the epigraphic form was pronounced [kā]. Although the two spellings
of this suffix may reflect dialectal differences, it is more likely that
the difference is merely orthographic. The "short" form was an
archaic spelling for [kā]; the "long" form was its phonetic spelling.[182]

All forms of the second person masc. sing. suffix are derived
from *-kā̆.[183] Southern Hebrew [aykā],[184] then, was inherited. In
Aramaic and Deir Alla, the form was [ayk]; the loss of final a is an
innovation which also occurs elsewhere in Semitic.[185] Neither form,
then, was an exclusively shared innovation.

10b. The third person masculine singular.

BYBLIAN: *‑ו [aw (?)], as inferred from the late Byblian form ימו
[yômaw (?)] "his days" (Yehawmilk 9). Since he did not syncopate in any NWS form of this suffix,[186] the evidence suggests
a development from *yômay-hŭ > (via regressive assimilation)
*yômaw-hŭ > *yômaw-wu > *yômaww > [yômaw (?)].

STANDARD PHOENICIAN: ‑י [êyū/ī], as in עלי [ʿalêyū/ī] "against him" (Kilamu 8) and למנערי "from his youth" (Kilamu 12) < *-ê-yū/ī < *-ay-hū̆. Like ‑י "his" attached to sing. nouns, this form of the suffix was used since it always followed a vowel. Cf. similarly the objective suffix on the infinitive absolute of final weak verbs, e.g. ובני אנך [banōyā] "and I built it" (Karatepe A II 11).

ARAMAIC: וה‑ [awh(i)], as in בנוה [banawh(i)] "his sons" (Sf. I A 5, II B 2'.6), שנוה "his years" (Fekh. 8), and קדמוה "before him" (Nerab 2:2). Another form of this suffix may appear in Halaf Ost. 4 Obv. 3, [ה]רבי "his elders."[187]

The development of the suffix in רבי[ה] is similar to that of standard Phoenician. Vocalized [ayh(i)], this suffix is composed of the masc. plural construct ending *ay + third person masc. sing. suffix *-hū̆ > [h(i)]. A similar suffix appears in the Uruk incantation as [ayhī] as well as [ēhī] in Eastern Aramaic.[188]

The development of the Old Aramaic form, וה‑, is uncertain. As Degen[189] observed, the theory that this suffix is a compound of *-ayhū̆ > *-ayhu > (with syncope of intervocalic he) *-ayu > (syncope of intervocalic yodh) *-aw + secondary suffix *-hu > *-awhu > [awh(i)] (via dissimilation)[190] is unfounded. First, there is no example of the syncope of intervocalic he in most Aramaic dialects.[191] Second, the addition of one suffix onto another, in this form, is otherwise unattested in the NWS dialects. Consequently, another explanation which would align the Old Aramaic form with those of the other NWS dialects is in order.

It is possible that the form of the suffix developed along the following lines: *-ay-hū̆ > (via regressive assimilation) *-aw-hū̆ > (dissimilation of u-u) [awhī]. The he, then, is part of the original form of the suffix and is not a secondary addition. If this development is correct, it not only conforms with generally accepted NWS phonetic changes but also follows the same development as forms of this suffix in the other NWS dialects.

SAMALIAN: There were two forms of this suffix in Samalian depending upon the syntax of the noun. When the noun was in the nominative case, the suffix was ה‑ [ūh(i/u)] (e.g., איחה [ʾayḥūh(i/u)] "his brothers" [H 30; P 17]). When, however, the noun was in the oblique case, the suffix was יה‑ [īh(u/i)] (e.g., איחיה [ʾayḥīh(u/i)] "his brothers" [H 27.28] and ביומיה [biyawmīh(u/i)] "in his days" [P 9]).

The presence of the yodh on oblique forms suggests that the suffix he began a new syllable. Since yodh was written for [ī] only in open syllables,[192] the *he* of the suffix could not have closed the preceding syllable (i.e. lacking a vowel) but rather began a syllable, leaving the preceding syllable open. If, however, the final vowel had been long, it would have appeared in the orthography. Thus the vowel following the *he* was probably short. The quality of the vowel is unknown.

AMMONITE: No evidence. Dion[193] suggested that the masc. plural construct noun + third person masc. sing. suffix appears in the Amman Citadel inscription, l. 4, as [ו]בצרה "with his enemies." Yet the last legible letter of this line is probably ק, not רה.[194] This word, then, is not an example of the third person masc. sing. suffix on a masc. plural noun.

DEIR ALLA: וה- [awh(u/i)], as in אלוה [ʾilawh(u/i)] "to him" (I 1.4) and possibly כפוה [kappawh(u/i)] "his palms" (IXa 3). The suffix in the Deir Alla dialect apparently developed in the same manner as that of Old Aramaic.[195] It is unclear, however, whether a final (short?) vowel was present in the Deir Alla suffix or whether it was already lost.

MOABITE: ה- [ôh(u/i) (?)], as in ימה [yômôh(u/i) (?)] "his days" (Mesha 8) and רשה [rōsôh(u/i) (?)] "its chiefs" (Mesha 20);[196] cf. the feminine counterpart in שעריה "its gates" (Mesha 22), with *yodh* in the suffix. The suffix probably developed from *yômay-hŭ > *-aw-hŭ > (contraction of the diphthong) [ôh(u/i) (?)]. This development most closely resembles that of Old Aramaic and Deir Alla.[197]

EDOMITE: No evidence.

HEBREW: ו- [āw], as in אנשו "his men" (Lach. 3:18) and possibly אלו "to him" (Yavneh-Yam 1:13). This suffix may also appear in the northern Hebrew text of Gezer, ירחו "his months" (Gezer Cal. 1.1.2).[198] Like other NWS forms, this suffix probably developed from *-ay-hŭ > *-aw-hŭ > *-aw-wu > *-aww > *-aw > (via stress-lengthening)[199] [āw]. It is possible, of course, that the suffix developed differently in northern and southern Hebrew,[200] although such a difference is not apparent in the epigraphic texts.

Lemaire[201] has suggested that another form of this suffix, יה-, appears in מצריה "his enemies" (el-Qom 3:3). The text of this passage, however, is uncertain. Dever[202] read the form as מארר "cursed," which appears to fit the context better. There is, then, no evidence for a form of the third person masc. sing. suffix on masc. plural nouns other than the single ו- [āw].

With the exception of the conservative form of this suffixed noun in Samalian,[203] the first-millennium NWS dialects form two major groups characterized by shared innovations. Standard Phoenician and the Aramaic dialect of Tell Halaf constitute one group whose suffixed noun developed from *-ayhŭ. The other group— most Old Aramaic dialects, Deir Alla, Moabite, Hebrew, and possibly Byblian—exhibit a suffixed form derived from *-awhŭ.[204] Within this second group, Hebrew and (?) Byblian exclusively share the progressive assimilation of he in *-awhŭ > *-awwu. The form of this suffixed noun in Ammonite and Edomite is unknown.

10c. The third person masculine plural.

BYBLIAN: הם-* [êhum (?)], as inferred from the later Byblian form עלהם [ʿalêhum (?)] "upon them" (Yehawmilk 6).

STANDARD PHOENICIAN: נם-* [ênōm], as inferred from its appearance only after vocalic endings in sing. nouns.[205] Cf. the third person plural objective suffix [nōm] following long vowels.

ARAMAIC: יהם- [ayhum], as in בתיהם [bâttayhum] "their houses" (Sf. II C 16) and יומייהם [yawmayhum] "their days" (Sf. II C 17). The connecting vowel of the masc. plural construct, [ay], remained uncontracted.

SAMALIAN: No evidence.

AMMONITE: No evidence.

DEIR ALLA: No evidence.

MOABITE: No evidence.

EDOMITE: No evidence.

HEBREW: הם-* [ay/ê-hem], as inferred from the forms in the Masoretic text. The connecting vowel was [ê] in the northern dialect and [ay] in the southern, conforming with the rules of phonetic change in these dialects.[206] The [e] of the suffix in the Masoretic form was transferred from the fem. plural form *hinna. Thus, masc. plural *humu lost [u] and adopted *i from the fem., producing [hem]. Cf. similarly the second person plural perfect suffix [tem] < *-tum.

All attested forms of the third person masc. plural suffix attached to plural nouns are derived from *-ay-hum, with some variations due to regular phonetic change. Thus [ayhum] appeared in

Old Aramaic, and [êhum (?)] (with diphthong contraction) in Byblian Phoenician. In standard Phoenician, the original *he* changed into *nun* after a vowel, so that this form appeared as [ênōm]. The tonic vowel also lengthened in this suffix.

In Hebrew dialects, the connecting vowel was [ay] and [ê] in southern and northern regions, respectively. The suffix itself was pronounced [hem], on analogy with its fem. plural counterpart. This particular analogy is idiosyncratic to Hebrew.

11a.   The objective suffixes: The third person masculine singular.[207]

BYBLIAN: In the oldest text, the suffix was ה- [hū], as in שתה [šōtahū] "he placed him" (Ahirom 1) < *šāta + hŭ.[208] In later Byblian, the suffix appeared as ו- in תחו "may she preserve him" (Yehawmilk 9); the form was pronounced, perhaps, [taḥawwēw] < *-êhŭ. The identical change in the form of this suffix occurred also in the possessive suffix, third person masc. sing., in this dialect: ה- > ו-.[209]

STANDARD PHOENICIAN: Two forms of this objective suffix were used in complementary distribution. When the verb ended in a vowel, the suffix was י- [yū/ī], as for example שתי [šōttīyū/ī] "I made him" (Kilamu 11) < *šattī + hŭ and the later form ישבני [yôšibnūyū/ī] "we caused him to dwell" (Eshmunazor 17) < *yôšibnū + hŭ. When the suffix was attached to the final consonant of a verb, it appeared as -∅ [ô], as may be inferred by the analogy with the possessive suffixes, and by the Punic forms ברכא [barakō][210] "he blessed him" (NP 8:2, etc.) and יברכא [yibrukō (?)] "he will bless him" (KAI 98:4/5); cf. the transcriptions ΒΑΡΑΧΩ "he blessed him" (KAI 175:4/5) and *felo* "he made it" (*Or Ant* 2:83,5), as well as the Phoenician form יברך "may he bless him" (KAI 38:2, etc.).[211] The possessive and objective suffixes of the third person masc. sing., then, followed the same pattern of complementary distribution: -∅ [ô] followed consonants, and י- [yū/ī] followed vowels.

ARAMAIC: ה- [ih (?)], as in היטבתה [hayṭibtih (?)] "I made it better" (Br-Rkb 1:12) and תשריה "may you release him" (Sf. III 18). In those verbal forms derived from "long" imperfects, the suffix was נה-, as for example יקתלנה "he will kill him" (Sf. I B 27), יהנסנה "he will remove it" (Zkr B 20), and יעברנה "he hates him" (Sf. III 17).

SAMALIAN: ה- [(?)], as in בכיה "they bewailed him" (P 17), תהרגה "you will kill him" (H 33), and לכתשה "may they pound him" (H 31). This suffix was attached to both vocalic and consonantal endings of the verb.

AMMONITE: No certain evidence. Cross[212] read אבחד[ה]ו֯ "I shall extirpate him" in Amman Cit. 3. Kutscher[213] read אבחדו⟨?⟩ "I shall destroy him." Either reading would require an objective suffix ו- or הו-. Since the reading of the line, and form, are so uncertain, it is prudent to abstain from drawing any morphological conclusions from this text alone.[214]

DEIR ALLA: ן- [(?)], as in תשנאן "you hate him" (II 10) and possibly תכסן "you will cover him" (II 10).[215] The context and text, however, are broken.

MOABITE: ה- [(?)],[216] as in ויגרשה "and he expelled him" (Mesha 19), ויחלפה "and he succeeded him" (Mesha 6), and (fem.) החרמתה "I consecrated it" (Mesha 17). There is no example of this suffix on nonconsecutive imperfect verbs in the extant texts.

EDOMITE: No evidence.

HEBREW: The suffix ה- [ô] < *-ahŭ followed consonantal endings, as for example לקחה [lᵊqāḥô] "he took him" (Lach. 4:6) < *laqaḥ + ô and שלחה [šᵊlāḥô] "he sent it" (Lach. 3:21). הו- [hū] followed accented vowels, as for example ויעלהו [way-yaᶜléhū] "and he brought him up" (Lach. 4:6/7). A third suffix, נו- [énnū] < *-en-hŭ, appeared in the epigraphic texts in שלחנו "send it!" (Arad 4:2), in which nun (cf. Aramaic and, probably, Deir Alla) preceded the ending [hū]. It has also been suggested in Yavneh-Yam 1:14 לא תדחנו "do not drive him away,"[217] although the reading is disputed.[218]

The NWS dialects exhibit two forms of the third person masc. sing. objective suffix. Perfect verbs took h-forms of the suffix (with regular phonetic variants), as in Old Byblian, standard Phoenician, Old Aramaic, Samalian, Moabite, and Hebrew. Other verbal forms, however, took two suffixes—an n-form and a h-form. When the verb originally ended in a vowel, as in the "long" imperfect or long imperative, the n-form was used; the n-form appeared in Old Aramaic (נה-), Hebrew (נו-), and probably Deir Alla (ן-?). In those verbs originally ending in a consonant, the h-form was used, as in the Old Aramaic jussive and Moabite consecutive imperfect. This distribution between n- and h-forms is apparently Proto-Semitic.[219]

In those dialects, however, which have lost the morphological distinction between indicative and jussive/"short" imperfects,[220] the *n*-form of the third person masc. sing. objective suffix has apparently disappeared as well. Thus standard Phoenician and Samalian had only *h*-forms. The other dialects, perhaps including Moabite, had both forms.

11b. The third person masculine plural.

BYBLIAN: No evidence.

STANDARD PHOENICIAN: Like the possessive suffix, the objective suffix was ם- [ōm] < *-a-humu* when attached to consonants (e.g., ירדם [yôridōm] "(I) exiled[221] them" and ישבם [yôšibōm] "(I) made them settle" [Karatepe A I 20 (both inf. abs. + suffix)]), and נם- [nōm] following vowels (e.g., ענתנם [ʿinnê/ītī-nōm (?)] "I subdued them" [Karatepe A I 20], שתנם [šōttī-nōm] "I placed them" [Karatepe A I 16], and the later form יסגרנם [yasgirū-nōm] "they will deliver them up" [Eshmunazor 21]). The two forms of this suffix were in strict complementary distribution.

ARAMAIC: הם- [hum], as in תרקהם "you will appease them" (Sf. III 6; cf. ארקהם "I shall appease them" [Sf. III 6]), תהשבהם "you will bring them back" (Sf. III 6), and תהסכרהם "you will hand them over" (Sf. III 2). This suffix הם- was attached to verbs ending in both consonants and vowels; the suffix, then, had achieved a frozen form.

SAMALIAN: No evidence.

AMMONITE: No evidence. Puech and Rofé[222] have tentatively identified a third person plural objective pronoun in Amman Citadel, l. 3 אבחדם, where ם- represents this suffix. Yet the reading and interpretation of this line are uncertain and cannot provide the basis for any dialectal conclusions.

DEIR ALLA: No evidence.[223]

MOABITE: הם- [hum (?)], as in ואסחב.הם "and I dragged them" (Mesha 18). Because of the presence of the word divider, the objective suffix was probably a form of the independent pronoun in Moabite;[224] the plural suffix had not yet been fused to the verb.

EDOMITE: No evidence.

HEBREW: The only suffix attested in the epigraphic texts is ם- [ām], which followed a consonant, as for example והבקידם "and he will hand them over" (Arad 24:14/15) and נתתם [nᵊtatt-ām] "you have given them''[225] (Arad 40:10). There is no suffix corresponding to the Aramaic-Moabite הם- or to an *n*-based form. In BH, this suffix ם- was also attached directly to vocalic endings,[226] although the vocalization was different.

Dialectal divisions based upon the form of the third person plural objective suffix are easily delineated. The old form הם- appeared in Aramaic and Moabite; a form in ם- < *-a-humu* was likewise found in standard Phoenician (one form) and Hebrew. These four dialects, then, constituted one dialect group which used the base *h-m* for the objective suffix; Hebrew and standard Phoenician formed a subgroup within this group.

The other standard Phoenician suffix, [nōm], was apparently unique. Yet the identical *nun* is found in third person sing. possessive and objective suffixes in several NWS dialects. On the objective suffix, the *nun* occurred in Aramaic, Deir Alla, and in Hebrew. On the possessive suffix, the *nun* appeared in standard Phoenician (on prepositions). In each instance, moreover, the *n*-form followed an original vowel; cf. also the possessive suffix [nōm] in standard Phoenician. On the one hand, then, the objective suffix [nōm] was isolated among the NWS dialects. On the other, the intrusive *nun* was common to these dialects and survived sporadically in different forms of the NWS third person suffixes. The *nun* was a common inheritance of all the NWS dialects, at least in the third person objective suffixes.

12. Numerals: The endings of the cardinal decades.

PHOENICIAN: ם-, as in תשעם ''90'' (Bronze Spat. 2).

ARAMAIC: ן-, as in שלשן ''30'' (KAI 219:3).

SAMALIAN: י-, as in והרג.שבעי 70 איחי.אבה ''and he killed seventy brothers of his father'' (P 3). The ending י- resembles those Semitic languages which form the decades by adding a dual suffix *ā* (nominative)/*ay* (oblique) onto the single digits; in Akkadian and Ethiopic, the decades end in [ā], and in ESA they end in -*(h)y*.[227] The Samalian form is very similar to that of ESA.[228] It is possible, though, that the final *yodh*, instead of marking the oblique dual [ay], was the sign of the masc. plural oblique [ī], corresponding to nominative [ū]; since ''70'' was the object of the verb, the decade may have been formed by adding a masc. plural ending onto the digit, ו-, which would be י- in the oblique case.[229] Nonetheless, the parallel between שבעי and the Akkadian/Ethiopic forms, especially the ESA form, is highly suggestive.

AMMONITE: No evidence.

DEIR ALLA: No evidence.

MOABITE: ן-, as in ארבען "40" (Mesha 8), חמשן "50" (Mesha 28), and שלשן "30" (Mesha 2).

EDOMITE: No evidence.

HEBREW: ם*-, as inferred from the form of the decades in BH.

Within the Semitic languages, there are two endings of the cardinal decades.[230] The decade can end in the nominal-adjectival masc. plural morpheme, as in Arabic, Hebrew, and Aramaic. Alternatively, it can end in the nominal-adjectival dual morpheme on analogy with the dual ending of "20," as in Akkadian, Ethiopic, and ESA. Most of the NWS dialects follow the model of Arabic; Phoenician, Aramaic, Moabite, and Hebrew added the masc. plural morpheme onto the digit to form the decade. The other NWS dialect which preserves a decade, Samalian, appears to have followed the pattern of Akkadian, Ethiopic, and ESA by adding the dual $*\bar{a}/*ay$ onto the corresponding digit. It is possible, however, that the final *yodh* on the Samalian form was the masc. plural oblique morpheme whose nominative would have been *waw*. The discovery of a nominative decade in this dialect would resolve this problem.

13.   The coordinating conjunction(s).

PHOENICIAN: ו- (passim).

ARAMAIC: Two conjunctions appeared in this dialect, ו- "and" (passim) and פ- "thus, therefore"[231] (Sf. II B 4.6; Br-Rkb 1:18).

SAMALIAN: Two conjunctions appeared in this dialect, ו- "and" (passim) and פ(א) "thus, therefore" (H 3.17, etc.; P 22). The meaning and function of these two conjunctions were identical to those of Old Aramaic.

AMMONITE: ו- (passim).

DEIR ALLA: ו- (passim).

MOABITE: ו- (passim).

EDOMITE: ו- (Ost. 2070 Rev. 3).[232]

HEBREW: ו- (passim).

The NWS dialects of the first millennium B.C.E. possessed two conjunctions, *wa "and" and *pa "thus, therefore." *wa occurred in all NWS dialects, as well as in all Semitic languages in general. *pa is a common West Semitic innovation.[233] Within the first-millennium NWS dialects, however, *pa is found only in Old Aramaic and Samalian. It was lost in Phoenician, Hebrew, and apparently in Ammonite, Deir Alla, Moabite, and Edomite as well. In these latter four dialects, however, the absence of *pa in the extant texts may be accidental.

14.   Negations: Nonexistence.

PHOENICIAN: No evidence.

ARAMAIC: ליש (Br-Rkb 1:16).

SAMALIAN: No evidence.

AMMONITE: No evidence.

DEIR ALLA: No evidence.

MOABITE: אן [ʾên] (Mesha 24).

EDOMITE: No evidence.

HEBREW: אין [ʾayn], as in Silwan B 1, Lach. 4:5.7/8 (plus pronominal suffix),[234] and Arad 40:13/14 (partially restored; plus pronominal suffix). The word is attested only in the southern dialect; in the North, the pronunciation would have been *[ʾên].[235]

Attestations of a term of nonexistence in these three NWS dialects suggest that the dialects can be divided into two groups. In Old Aramaic, the term ליש was used, literally translated "there is not," composed of the negative [lā] + "there is."[236] In Moabite and Hebrew, another term was used [ʾên, ʾayn]. *ʾayn, however, is not an exclusively shared lexical innovation, since it also appears in Ethiopic and Ugaritic.[237]

15a.   Particles: The *nota accusativi*.[238]

PHOENICIAN: אית, only in the Karatepe inscription during this period (Karatepe A I 3, III 3.14/15, etc.). The precise vocalization of this particle is unknown.

ARAMAIC: אית (Zkr B 5.16, etc.; Sf. I B 32, II C 5.5, etc.).

SAMALIAN: ות (H 28), only with possessive suffix. If this particle is related to Aramaic [lʾwāt] "toward" and [kʾwāt] "as, like,"[239] the pronunciation of the Samalian particle may have been *[wāt].

AMMONITE: No evidence. Although van Selms[240] believed he isolated a *nota accusativi* -ת in Cit. 5, the interpretation of the passage is too uncertain to provide evidence for the existence of this particle.

DEIR ALLA: No evidence.

MOABITE: את (Mesha 5.6.7, etc.). The vocalization of the Moabite particle is unknown. The absence of a medial *yodh*, however, separates the form of the Moabite particle from its Phoenician-Aramaic counterpart.

EDOMITE: No evidence.

HEBREW: את, with both nominal (e.g., Arad 16:4, 24:16, etc.) and pronominal objects (את + suffix, as in Arad 24:13; Lach. 3:12, 12:4 [partially restored], etc.).[241]

The forms of the *nota accusativi* in NWS are composed of pronominal suffix + *$\bar{a}t$.[242] Phoenician-Aramaic אית is derived from *iya + *$\bar{a}t$; cf. Akk. $y\bar{a}ti$ and Arabic [ˀīyā-]. Samalian ות developed from *hu + *$\bar{a}t$ > *$hu\bar{a}t$ (cf. Ugaritic *hwt*) > *$u\bar{a}t$ > [wāt]. Hebrew and Moabite, however, show a shared innovation. The old אית lost intervocalic *yodh*, producing את.[243]

15b. The conditional particles.

BYBLIAN: אל (Ahirom 2), cognate either to Hebrew אם > אילו < אילו[244] or to EA *allū*.[245] Another conditional particle, אם, is attested in Bronze Spat. 3;[246] in that context, אם may have functioned as an oath particle.[247]

STANDARD PHOENICIAN: אם (e.g., Karatepe A III 12.14.17, etc.).

ARAMAIC: הן (e.g., Sf. I B 28.31, etc.; Nerab 1:11).

SAMALIAN: There appear to have been two conditional particles in Samalian. One particle, אם, introduced verbal protases, whether the verb were imperfective (H 20 [?]) or perfective (H 29). The other conditional particle, הנ, introduced nominal protases (H 30.31.31 [?]). The particle הן, however, in הן.אם.שמת "now if I put" (H 29), is not a conditional particle, comparable to Aramaic [hen],[248] but is the interjection "behold" used to reinforce the condition.[249]

AMMONITE: No evidence.

DEIR ALLA: הן (II 10.10).

MOABITE: No evidence. The particle הן in והן.עשתי (Kerak frag. 3) is not the conditional "if" but the interjection "behold."[250]

EDOMITE: No evidence.

HEBREW: Two conditional particles were employed in epigraphic Hebrew. אם was followed by a perfect verb (e.g., Yavneh-Yam 1:11) or nominal predicate (e.g., Arad 2:7, 21:8 [?]). The other particle, הן, is found with perfect verbs (e.g., Arad 21:3, 40:9). The two particles, then, appeared in identical contexts and were probably semantically and grammatically equivalent.

The NWS dialects employed several conditional particles.[251] Some used the particle אם—Old Byblian (one possibility), standard Phoenician, Samalian (one possibility), and Hebrew (one possibility). Others used הן—Old Aramaic, Samalian (one possibility, with suffixed ו-), the Deir Alla dialect, and Hebrew (one possibility). Old Byblian alone used a second particle, אל, which did not spread to other NWS dialects. The distribution of אם and הן here and throughout the Semitic languages does not yield any classificatory scheme. The particle אל, however, may have been a Phoenician innovation.

Two conditional particles appeared in a single dialect. In Samalian, there appears to have been a syntactic and grammatical distinction between אם and הנו. In Hebrew, both particles interchanged freely. In Old Byblian, however, the evidence is insufficient to determine the grammatical relationship between אל and אם.

15c. The directive-terminative *he*.

PHOENICIAN: Not attested (?).

ARAMAIC: Not attested.

SAMALIAN: Not attested.

AMMONITE: No evidence.

DEIR ALLA: Not attested. While Hackett[252] tentatively identified three examples of this "adverbial *h*," none is certain. The final *he* in לילה "night" (I 1), whatever its origin,[253] was part of the word itself; cf. the same word in Aramaic, Moabite, and Samalian (with a different form), dialects which lacked the terminative *he*. The final *he* in שמה "there, thither" (II 13.14) is a reflex of the old adverbial *-at*, as in Ugaritic *ṯmt* "there, thither."[254] Finally, the form and meaning of אחראה "in the future (?)" (I 2) are uncertain.[255] There is no unambiguous example of this particle in the Deir Alla dialect.

MOABITE: Not attested (?).

EDOMITE: No evidence.

HEBREW: This particle appears in, for example, מצרימה "toward Egypt" (Lach. 3:16), העירה "toward the city" (Lach. 4:7, 18:2), and ביתה "toward the house" (Arad 17:2).

The terminative *he* is an old NWS suffix, found already in Ugaritic.[256] According to the present evidence, Hebrew alone preserved this particle. Yet its absence from other NWS dialects, particularly from the extant Phoenician and Moabite texts, may be coincidental.

15d.   The precative *lamedh*.

PHOENICIAN: Not attested. Although Albright[257] and others[258] have identified the precative *lamedh* in רח[מי ליפתח "may her womb be opened" (Arsl.T. 1:22–24), the correct reading of the text is אל יפתח "let it not be opened."[259] If the latter reading is followed, the text conforms to regular Phoenician grammatical usage,[260] and the only instance of the precative *lamedh* in this dialect is removed.

ARAMAIC: The precative *lamedh* appears only in the Tell Fekh. text, as for example להוי "may he be" (l. 12), ללקטו "may they gather" (l. 22), לשם "may he put" (l. 11), etc.[261] Its appearance only in the eastern Syro-Palestinian area—i.e. Fekheriyeh, and the Mesopotamian Assur ostracon—suggests an early isogloss between eastern and western Old Aramaic. As in Old Aramaic, the precative *lamedh* did not appear in later, western Aramaic dialects either.[262]

SAMALIAN: The precative *lamedh* regularly appeared in this dialect, as for example in למנע "may he prevent" (H 24), לתגמרו "may they be destroyed" (H 30), לכתשנה "may they pound her" (H 31), etc.

AMMONITE: No evidence. In Sir. 6, however, the jussive verbs, יגל וישמח "may he rejoice and be happy," lack the precative *lamedh*. This passage may indicate that in Ammonite the precative *lamedh* did not occur. The evidence, however, is meager.

DEIR ALLA: Not attested.

MOABITE: Not attested.

EDOMITE: No evidence.

HEBREW: Not attested.

The distribution of the precative *lamedh* between East and West Semitic indicates that it was common to the entire Semitic language group.[263] Within first-millennium NWS, it was absent from all but two dialects. It appeared only in Samalian and Fehkeriyeh (= eastern?) Aramaic. In later times, this feature became characteristic of eastern Aramaic as a dialect group.[264]

16a. Verbal conjugations: The *t*-stem of the *qal*.

BYBLIAN: Gt (infixed *t*-), as in תחתסף "may it be removed" (Ahirom 2) and תהתפך "may it be overturned" (Ahirom 2).

STANDARD PHOENICIAN: No evidence. Either the *t*-stem of the *qal* is not attested due to the paucity of Phoenician texts, or the *N*-stem had replaced the passive *t*-stem.

ARAMAIC: Two *t*-stems of the *peal* are attested in Old Aramaic. In most Aramaic-speaking communities, it was the tG (prefixed *t*-), as in יתחזה "it can be seen" (Sf. I A 28), יתשמע "it can be heard" (Sf. I A 29), and יתאחז "it is closed" (Nerab 2:4); the tG survived into later Aramaic dialects.[265] In the Aramaic speech form of Tell Fekheriyeh, however, there is one clear example of the Gt (יגתזר "may it be cut off" [Fekh. 23]).[266] And in Sf. I C 24/25—ואל־ ירתש ⌈ה⌉[ל]ה אשם[267] "may a name not be acquired by him"— Rosenthal[268] has tentatively identified another example of the Gt.[269] This conjugation is not attested in any other Aramaic dialect.

SAMALIAN: The only possible evidence of this conjugation is the form יתמר ב "it is said in . . ." (H 10) which, according to some,[270] is derived from *יתאמר. The *aleph* would have assimilated to the preceding *taw*, as occurs in various forms in Aramaic.[271] Yet such an uncertain example does not constitute proof that the tG stem appeared in Samalian. Additional evidence is needed in order to pronounce judgment.

AMMONITE: No evidence. Cross[272] analyzed the form תשתע "you are feared" (Cit. 6) as a Gt conjugation of *ṭʿy "to gaze; offer." The same form occurs in Ugaritic, where *ṭtʿ* means "to fear," and where the Gt conjugation is frequently found. Yet a *qal* conjugation of this verb is found as שתע "to fear" in Hebrew, Phoenician, and probably in Ugaritic as well; cf. especially the form נשתעם "feared" in Karatepe A II 4, where the triradical root *štʿ* takes the *niphal* conjugation. Thus, this form is not a Gt.[273] A Gt conjugation in Ammonite remains unproven.

DEIR ALLA: tG (?), if יתמלך "he will seek advice" (II 9) is the passive of the simple conjugation.[274] Two other examples of the tG, cited by Hoftijzer[275]—אתנתק "I am/he was pulled down (?)" (Vc 4) and אתיחדו "they have gathered" (I 5)—are most probably tD con-jugations.[276] Finally, the form יתעץ "he will seek counsel" (II 9) is morphologically uncertain. If the form is tD of *y‘ṣ, the first radical is missing; the derivation of this form from a middle weak root[277] is not convincing since it presents morphological difficulties.[278] The same obstacle would be apparent if the stem were tG (יתיעץ*) or Gt (ייתעץ*). This form then, remains unexplained. There is only one possible example of a *t*-stem of the simple conjugation in the Deir Alla dialect.

MOABITE: Gt, as in ואלתחם "and I fought" (Mesha 11.15), הלתחם "fight!" (Mesha 32), and בהלתחמה "when he fought" (Mesha 19).

EDOMITE: No evidence.

HEBREW: There is no trace of a *t*-stem of the *qal* in epigraphic Hebrew. A few forms in BH reflect an old use of the *t*-stem of the *qal*,[279] but this usage disappeared from the language very early.

The NWS dialects formed a *t*-stem of the simple conjugation in two ways. The *t* was either infixed to the root, as in Old Byblian, Sfire- (?) and Fekheriyeh-Aramaic, and in Moabite. The Gt also appears in Arabic and ESA.[280] Or the *t* was prefixed to the root, on analogy with the prefixed *t* of the *D*-stem. The tG conjugation was found in most Old Aramaic dialects, and possibly in Samalian and the Deir Alla dialect as well. It is unclear whether standard Phoe-nician and Ammonite once possessed either a tG or Gt stem which had died out by the time of the extant texts, or whether future ex-cavations will produce a text with such a form. In either case, the present evidence points to an emerging dialectal polarity between those dialects with analogical tG formations and those with Gt con-jugations, i.e. between Aramaic and Canaanite dialects. Although the Gt appeared at Tell Fekheriyeh, and possibly at Sfire, it did not survive into later Aramaic dialects.

16b. The presence/absence of the *N*-stem.

BYBLIAN: No evidence. The presence of a Gt passive conju-gation, however, may suggest that one function of the *niphal,* that of the *qal* passive, was usurped by the Gt; thus the *niphal* may have died out of the dialect, as in Aramaic. Or, the few extant Byblian texts have simply not preserved this conjugation; that a *niphal* and Gt conjugation can coexist is proven by Ugaritic and Akkadian, where both conjugations were used fully. The absence of a *niphal* in the extant Byblian texts, then, may be either significant or accidental.

STANDARD PHOENICIAN: The *niphal* conjugation was present in this dialect, as in נשתעם "feared" (Karatepe A II 4) and the later form נגזלת "I was stolen" (Eshmunazor 2.12).

ARAMAIC: As in other Aramaic dialects, there was no *niphal* conjugation in Old Aramaic.[281]

SAMALIAN: No evidence.

AMMONITE: A *niphal* conjugation may appear in Cit. 6. תשתע בבן.אלם "you are feared among the gods."[282] The evidence is contextual since there is no example of a *niphal* perfect verbal form.

Other suggested examples of *niphal* forms in Ammonite are less convincing. Krahmalkov[283] interpreted אשחת (Sir. 5) as a *niphal* of the root **šḥt* and translated "shall I be destroyed?" Instead, the form is to be interpreted, with most commentators,[284] as a noun "cistern" comparable to Moabite אשוח "cistern" (Mesha 9.23 [partially restored]); this latter interpretation better fits the context of the inscription. Albright[285] found a *niphal* in ילחם "it shall fight" (Cit. 4). But new readings of this passage show that these consonants do not appear and therefore that the form itself does not exist.[286] The only possible example of the *niphal* in Ammonite, then, is תשתע "you are feared" in Cit. 6.

DEIR ALLA: The *niphal* conjugation is present in this dialect, as for example in נאנח "it moans" (II 12.12).

MOABITE: No evidence. That the Moabite form הלתחם "to fight" (Mesha 11, etc.) corresponds to BH נלחם suggests that either the *niphal* conjugation was lost to the Gt (as in Aramaic) or the function of the Gt and *niphal* had merged.

EDOMITE: No evidence.

HEBREW: The *niphal* conjugation was present in this dialect, as for example in נשלחו[287] "they were sent" (Arad 13:4) and השמר "be on guard!" (Lach. 3:21).

The *N*-stem is a common Semitic conjugation.[288] In first-millennium NWS, it was preserved in standard Phoenician, Ammonite (?), the Deir Alla dialect, and Hebrew. It died out in Aramaic, and possibly in Byblian and Moabite too. Whether Samalian and Edomite preserved the *niphal* or not is unknown.

16c. The causative prefix.

BYBLIAN: No evidence. Friedrich and Röllig[289] claimed that the Byblian causative was *yiphil*, like that of standard Phoenician. Yet the examples which they cited, יארך "may they make long" (Yehimilk 3) and תארך "may she make long" (Elibaal 2; Shiptibaal 4), may be derived from a causative *hiphil* as well;[290] cf. for example BH ישמיד "he will annihilate" < *יהשמיד. Garbini[291] adduced one example of a *hiphil* causative in Byblian. Yet his example, העדית "you/she stripped bare" (Byblos 13:2), is an incorrect reading. One should read, with Cross,[292] העגזת (עצמי) "my mouldering bones;" the prefixed *he* is the definite article. Despite this lack of evidence, however, it is possible that the causative prefix was *he*, as in the third person sing. pronominal suffix.

STANDARD PHOENICIAN: -י, as in ירחב אנך "I widened" (Karatepe A I 4). Cf. the third person sing. possessive/objective suffix in ־י (following vowels).

ARAMAIC: -ה, as in המלכני "he made me king" (Zkr A 3), יהסכר "he will hand over" (Sf. III 3), and הושבני "they made me sit" (Br-Rkb 1:5). There are no examples of an *aphel* causative in Old Aramaic.[293]

SAMALIAN: -ה, as in הושבת "I settled" (H 19) and היטבה "he made it better" (P 9).

AMMONITE: -ה, as inferred from the PN הצלאל (Sir. 2), derived from *nṣl, with prefixed causative *he*.

DEIR ALLA: -ה, as in הקרקת "it chased" (I 15).[294]

MOABITE: -ה, as in החרמתה "I consecrated it" (Mesha 17), השעני "he saved me" (Mesha 4), and הראני "he made me see" (Mesha 4).

EDOMITE: No evidence.

HEBREW: -ה, as for example הכו "they struck" (Shiloah 4) and והבקידם "and he will hand them over" (Arad 24:14/15).

Most first-millennium NWS dialects exhibit the causative prefix *he*, i.e. Aramaic, Samalian, Ammonite, Deir Alla, Moabite, Hebrew, and possibly Byblian. In standard Phoenician, however, this *he* became -י; cf. the third person sing. suffixes [yū/ī, yā] < **-ihŭ*, **-ihă*.[295] All these dialects, then, preserved the identical morpheme, although its phonetic shape had changed in standard Phoenician.

17a. The strong verb: Inflection of the perfect. The first person singular.

PHOENICIAN: ת- [tī], as in פעלת [paʿaltī] "I did" (Kilamu 4) and שברת [šibba/irtī] "I smashed" (Karatepe A I 8), etc. For the final vowel [ī], cf. Punic כעתבתי "I wrote" (KAI 145:6) and the suffixed form ענתנם "I subdued them" (Karatepe A I 20) (instead of ענתם*).

In Arsl.T. 2:7, the form נעלת "I have locked" appears. Since this text regularly represents final long vowels,[296] the expected form here should have been נעלתי*. A variety of possibilities may explain this particular form. The spelling may have been historical, following the (contemporaneous) standard Phoenician model of the nonrepresentation of final vowels. Alternatively, the affix is to be vocalized according to the Aramaic pattern, -t(u/i), in which case, this morpheme was borrowed from the mutually intelligible Aramaic dialect spoken at Arslan Tash. Or, perhaps the form is not to be interpreted as "I have locked" but is another form altogether, such as a construct noun. Since, however, this text regularly does represent final (long) vowels, one of the latter two explanations is more probable than the assumption of a historical spelling.

ARAMAIC: ת- [t, tu/i],[297] as in כתבת [katabt(u/i)] "I have written" (Sf. I C 2), אחזת [ʾaḥadt(u/i)] "I seized" (Br-Rkb 1:11), and שמת [śāmt(u/i)] "I erected" (Zkr B 13). Had a final long vowel been part of this morpheme, it would have been represented in the orthography.[298] But since final short vowels were not represented, the suffix ת- does not necessarily indicate vowellessness.[299] Its pronunciation was either [t], as in later Aramaic dialects, [tu] as in Arabic, or [ti] as in Amorite.

SAMALIAN: ת- [t, tu/i], as in ישבת [yat̠/šabt(u/i)] "I sat" (H 8), שמת [śāmt(u/i)] "I put" (H 29; P 20), and הקמת [haqimt(u/i)] "I erected" (H 1.14 [partially restored]). A connecting vowel did not join the verbal base and personal suffix. If such a vowel existed, the long vowel in הקמת would have stood in an open syllable, *ha-qī-mVt; consequently, *ī would have been represented in the orthography.[300] Since *ī was not represented, it must have stood in a closed syllable. Thus ת- was not preceded by a vowel. It is also doubtful that a long vowel followed [t] since final long vowels were generally indicated in the orthography.[301]

AMMONITE: No evidence.

DEIR ALLA: No evidence.

MOABITE: תי- [tī], as in מלכתי [malaktī] "I ruled" (Mesha
2/3.28/29 [partially restored]), יספתי [yasaptī] "I added" (Mesha 29),
etc.

EDOMITE: No evidence.

HEBREW: תי- [tī], as in קראתי [qārā(ʾ)tī] "I read" (Lach. 3:12;
12:4 [partially restored]), מלכתי [mālaktī] "I ruled" (Arad 88:1), etc.

Another form of this suffix may have been ת- [tī (?)], found in
שלחת "I send" (Mur 17 A 1) and ברכת "I bless" (Ajrud). The absence
of final *yodh* is surprising. Either ת- was pronounced [tī], so that the
spelling without *yodh* is archaic. Alternatively, the morpheme could
have been pronounced differently in these two communities than in
most others. In view of the unanimity of the Masoretic vocalization
[tī], however, the former explanation is preferable.

According to all available evidence, the Proto-West Semitic first
person sing. perfect suffix was *-tŭ.[302] In Phoenician, Moabite, and
Hebrew, the first person sing. possessive suffix *ī was transferred
to *-tŭ, producing [tī]. In Old Aramaic and Samalian, the old suffix
*-tŭ was retained, shortened to [t], or became [ti] by analogy. Fi-
nally, in the Phoenician dialect of Arslan Tash, the suffix might have
been pronounced [t(u/i)]. If this interpretation is correct, the Arslan
Tash form reflects the penetration of Aramaic into the Phoenician-
speaking community; cf. the dual/masc. plural morpheme ן- in
Arslan Tash-Phoenician.

17b.   The third person masculine singular.

BYBLIAN: [qaṭala], as in פעל [paʿala] "he made" (Ahirom 1; Elibaal 1) and בני [banaya] "he built" (Yehimilk 1; Shiptibaal 1), etc.
The preservation of the final weak radical in the orthography indicates that the original, final short [a] of the perfect had not been lost
in early Byblian.[303]

STANDARD PHOENICIAN: [qaṭal],[304] as in מלך [malak] "he ruled"
(Kilamu 2), פעל [paʿal] "he accomplished" (Kilamu 3.3.4), etc.

ARAMAIC: [qatal], as in גזר [gazar] "he cut" (Sf. I A 7), נזר
[naḏar] "he vowed" (Br-Hdd 4), etc. Unlike later Aramaic dialects,
the pretonic short vowel in an open syllable had not been reduced
in this early period.[305]

SAMALIAN: [qatal (?)], as in הרג [harag (?)] "he killed" (P 3.3.7), אכל [ʾakal (?)] "it ate" (H 9), etc. As in Old Aramaic, the pretonic short vowel in an open syllable was not lost.[306]

AMMONITE: [qatãl], as in נתן "he gave" (Hesh. Ost. 4:6); cf. בנה "he built" (Cit. 1). It is unclear whether the base form *qaṭal was retained or whether the second a underwent stress-lengthening to *qaṭāl.[307]

DEIR ALLA: [(?)]; cf. אתה "he came" (II 14), etc.

MOABITE: [qaṭãl], as in מלך [malãk] "he ruled" (Mesha 2), אמר [ʾamãr] "he said" (Mesha 6), etc.[308]

EDOMITE: [qaṭãl] (see examples in Chapter 2, no. 7).

HEBREW: [qāṭal], as in ידע [yādaᶜ] "he knew" (Arad 40:13), נתן [nātan] "he gave" (Arad 17:8), etc. The pretonic short vowel characteristically lengthened in Hebrew.

All forms of the third person masc. sing. perfect qal are derived from *qatala;[309] all changes were, according to the present evidence, phonetic. Old Byblian preserved this old form [qatala]. Standard Phoenician, Old Aramaic, Samalian, and Hebrew (with pretonic vowel lengthening) preserved the old form as well, except that the final short [a] was lost, producing *qaṭal. Finally, the vocalization of this verbal form in Ammonite, Moabite, and Edomite was either *[qaṭal] (= standard Phoenician, Aramaic, and Samalian) or *[qaṭāl]. All forms of this verb, then, were phonetic variants of a single base.

17c. The third person feminine singular ending.

BYBLIAN: No evidence from this period. In later Byblian texts, the ending was -∅ [ā][310] (see Chapter 2, no. 18b).

STANDARD PHOENICIAN: -∅ [ā] (see Chapter 2, no. 18b).

ARAMAIC: ת- [at] (see examples in Chapter 2, no. 18b).

SAMALIAN: ת- [at] (see examples in Chapter 2, no. 18b).

AMMONITE: No evidence.

DEIR ALLA: ת- [at] (see examples in Chapter 2, no. 18b).

MOABITE: No evidence.

EDOMITE: No evidence.

HEBREW: *[ā], as inferred from the vocalization of the Masoretic text; there is, at present, no example of this verbal form in a strong verb.

Two endings of the third person fem. sing. perfect are attested in the NWS dialects. The old ending [at] was preserved in Aramaic, Samalian, and Deir Alla. A second form, in which *-at had been replaced by [ā], is found in standard Phoenician, Hebrew, and later Byblian. This replacement may have occurred independently in the dialects (cf. the correspondences of *-at) or may have spread by mutual contact.[311]

18a. The endings of the imperfect: The second person masculine plural (indicative and jussive).

PHOENICIAN: No evidence.

ARAMAIC: Depending upon the "mood" of the verb, there were two forms of this ending in Aramaic.[312] The indicative mood ended with ן- [ūn], as in [תשלמן] "you fulfill" (Sf. I B 24); cf. the final weak form [תא[תון][313] "you will come" (Sf. I B 32). The volitive mood ended with ו- [ū];[314] cf. the final weak form תפנו "do (not) pay attention" (Sf. III 7).[315] Thus the different endings ן- and ו- reflected a morphological difference in the verb itself.

SAMALIAN: ו- [ū], as in תהרגו "you kill(ed)" (P 5). The ending [ū] appeared regardless of the mood of the verb.[316]

AMMONITE: No evidence.

DEIR ALLA: No evidence.

MOABITE: No evidence.

EDOMITE: No evidence.

HEBREW: ו- [ū], as in the final weak form תעשו "you will do" (Lach. 6:9).

18b. The third person masculine plural (indicative and jussive).

BYBLIAN: No evidence.

STANDARD PHOENICIAN: -∅ [ū], as in יתלנן [yitlōn(i)nū][317] "they murmured" (Kilamu 10)[318] and יכבד "may they honor" (Kilamu 14.15). There was no distinction between the ending of the indicative vs. jussive verb;[319] both ended in [ū].

ARAMAIC: Like the forms of the second person masculine plural, the indicative verb ended in ן- [ūn] (e.g., ימלכן "they will rule" [Sf. I B 22], יצרן "they will guard" [Sf. I B 8], etc.),[320] whereas the volitive mood ended in ו- [ū] (e.g., יהפכו "may they overturn" [Sf.

I C 21], יצרו "may they guard" [Sf. I C 15], ללקטו "may they gather" [Fekh. 22], etc.).[321] The two different endings reflected, then, two different moods of the verb.

SAMALIAN: ו- [ū], as in יתנו "they give" (H 4), יקחו "they take" (H 12), and לתגמרו "may they be destroyed" (H 30) < *ל + יתגמרו.

AMMONITE: ן- [ūn], in ימתן "they will die" (Cit. 2) and possibly ילנן "they will lodge" (Cit. 4).[322] Since these are the only examples of the third person masc. plural imperfect in Ammonite, and since there are no examples of the second person masc. plural imperfect in this dialect, it is unclear whether Ammonite preserved the distinction between indicative and volitive verbs, as in Old Aramaic, or whether the ending [ūn] was frozen and used for both moods. The context of Cit. 2 and 4, although broken, suggests that the mood was not volitive but indicative.

DEIR ALLA: ו- [ū], as in ויאמרו "and they said" (I 2); cf. the final weak form יחזו "they will see" (II 13).[323] There is no evidence of the ending [ūn] in this dialect.[324]

MOABITE: No evidence.

EDOMITE: No evidence.

HEBREW: ו- [ū], as in יתנו "(may?) they give" (Ajrud), וילכו "and they flowed" (Shiloah 4), etc.

The endings of the second and third person masc. plural imperfect were identical. On the basis of the present evidence, the formal distinction between indicative and volitive moods was preserved only in Old Aramaic, represented by [ūn] and [ū] respectively. Standard Phoenician, Samalian, Deir Alla, and Hebrew employed [ū] in both functions. In Ammonite, only an indicative [ūn] is attested; it is unknown whether the corresponding jussive ended with [ū], as in Old Aramaic, or the identical [ūn]. In any case, the old indicative *-ūn survived in Old Aramaic and Ammonite. In standard Phoenician, Samalian, Deir Alla, and Hebrew, the indicative *-ūn had been replaced by the old jussive ending *-ū.

18c.   The third person feminine plural.

PHOENICIAN: No evidence.

ARAMAIC: ־ן -י [y . . . ān], in both indicative (e.g., יהינקן "they will nurse" [Sf. I A 22, etc.], ימשחן[ן] "they anoint" [Sf. I A 21], etc.) and volitive moods (e.g., יהרגן "may they kill" [Sf. I A 24],[325] להינקן "may they nurse" [Fekh. 20.20.21] < *li-yᵊhayn(a)qān, etc.).

SAMALIAN: י- -ן [y . . . ān], as in לכתשנה "may they pound her" (H 31). Like Old Aramaic, then, the third person fem. plural imperfect began with *yodh* and ended with [ān]. Cf., possibly, [רן   ] in H 31.[326]

AMMONITE: No evidence.

DEIR ALLA: ת-, -ן, as in תצמקן "they will wither (?)" (Xd 2) and תטפן "they drip (?)" (II 35.36). These passages, however, are very fragmentary.

MOABITE: No evidence.

EDOMITE: No evidence.

HEBREW: There is no epigraphic attestation of this verbal form. The form attested in BH, however, resembles that of the Deir Alla dialect, [tiqṭōlnā].

Two forms of the third person fem. plural imperfect competed in the NWS dialects.[327] The older form, with prefixed *yodh*, is attested in Old Aramaic and Samalian. Another form, however, arose in NWS and sporadically throughout the Semitic languages; the third person fem. plural imperfect gained a prefixed *taw* on analogy with its fem. sing. counterpart. In NWS, this analogy occurred in the Deir Alla dialect, and possibly epigraphic Hebrew as well. Since the *t* prefix was an analogical formation, it is of no value for classification.[328]

19a.   The infinitive: The *qal* infinitive construct.[329]

PHOENICIAN: לקטל *[liqṭōl], as inferred from the later forms לפעל "to make" (Yehawmilk 11) and *liful* (לפעל) "to make" (Poen. 935). The form of the third person sing. suffix attached to the infinitive, -י, suggests that a (genitive?) vowel connected the verb and suffix.[330]

ARAMAIC: Two forms of the inf. construct appeared in Old Aramaic. לקתל [(?)] appeared in, for example, לשגב "to strengthen" (Sf. I B 32.32). Another form, למקתל, is found in Fekh. (e.g., למלקה "to take" [ll. 9/10] and למלד "to remove" [l. 9]) and the Adon letter (e.g., למשלח "to send" [l. 7]); this *miqtal* infinitive may also appear in Sf. I B 34, but the reading of the form is not certain.[331]

SAMALIAN: לקתל [(?)], as in לאכל "to eat" (H 23), and possibly לנצב "to erect" (H 10).[332] In final weak verbs, the vocalization of this infinitive depended upon its construction in the sentence; the inf. bound to a following noun was vocalized one way, whereas the unbound inf. was vocalized another.[333]

AMMONITE: No evidence.

DEIR ALLA: לקטל [(?)], as in לחלק "to perish" (II 11).

MOABITE: *לקטל [(?)]. Cf. the פ״י infinitive לספת "to add" (Mesha 21).

EDOMITE: No evidence.

HEBREW: לקטל [liqṭōl], as in לשלח "to send" (Arad 40:14), etc.

The infinitive construct with prefixed *lamedh* took two consonantal shapes in NWS. The old form, לקטל, appeared in all dialects for which there is evidence of the form. A new *miqtal* infinitive appeared in the Fekh. text, Adon letter, and possibly in the Sfire inscription.[334] This latter form became the standard infinitive form of the *peal* in the later Aramaic dialects.

Whereas the *miqtal* infinitive was characteristic of Aramaic, standard Phoenician and Samalian each displayed a unique feature in the form of the *qal* inf. construct. In standard Phoenician, the inf. ended in [i] of the genitive case, as for example לשבתנם "that they may dwell" (Karatepe A I 17) vs. ישבם "(I) made them settle" (Karatepe A I 20).[335] In Samalian, the pronunciation of the bound inf. construct differed from that of the unbound inf. construct, at least in final weak verbs.

Thus, the infinitive form *l* + *qtl* occurred in all attested NWS dialects. The form *miqtal* was an innovation shared by a few Aramaic-speaking communities. The retention of a vowel between verb and suffix appeared only in standard Phoenician. And the difference between bound and unbound infinitives isolated Samalian from the other NWS dialects.

19b.   The *D*- and causative infinitive construct.

PHOENICIAN: There were no preformatives or suffixes on these derived infinitives, as for example in the later forms לשלם "to pay back" (KAI 60:7) and לשבת "to make cease" (CIS I 5510:3).

ARAMAIC: Two forms are attested in Old Aramaic. At Tell Fekheriyeh, the inf. construct had the same consonantal skeleton as in Phoenician and Hebrew (e.g., לכבר "to multiply" [l. 8],[336] and possibly לשלם "for the well-being" [ll. 8.8.8]); the vocalization of the

Fekh. forms is unknown.[337] At Sfire, the derived inf. construct ended in ת-, as for example לחבזתהם "to drive them out" (Sf. II B 7) and להמתת עקרי "to kill my offspring" (Sf. III 16). It is unclear whether the vocalization of this ending was [ūt], as in Syriac, Jewish Aramaic, etc., or [at] as in biblical Aramaic (Dan. 5:12; Ezr. 4:22).[338] The ending [ūt], however, is the more common among the Aramaic dialects.

SAMALIAN: No evidence.

AMMONITE: No evidence.

DEIR ALLA: No evidence.

MOABITE: No evidence.

EDOMITE: No evidence.

HEBREW: There were no preformatives or suffixes on these derived infinitives, as for example לדבר* "to speak" (BH) and להעיד "to warn" (Arad 24:18). The form is that of the imperative + prefixed *lamedh*.

The first-millennium NWS dialects can be divided into two groups on the basis of the form of the *D*- and causative inf. construct with prefixed *lamedh*. The present evidence indicates that the common form was *l* + verbal root. This infinitive appeared in Phoenician, Fekh.-Aramaic, and Hebrew, although the pronunciation may have differed from dialect to dialect. A deviation from this pattern appeared only in Sfire-Aramaic, where the inf. construct ended in ת-. Thus the Old Aramaic dialect spoken at Sfire, and perhaps most Aramaic-speaking communities in Syria-Palestine, constituted a dialectal island in this respect.

20.   The participle: The *qal* passive.

PHOENICIAN: No evidence.[339] הברך in Karatepe A I 1 is most likely a noun "official, steward."[340]

ARAMAIC: [qatīl], as inferred from the pronunciation of this form in later Aramaic dialects. The orthography in, for example, פתחה [patīḥā] "opened" (Sf. III 8/9), however, does not suggest any particular vocalization pattern.

SAMALIAN: [qatīl], as in קתילת [qatīlāt] "killed (women)" (P 8).

AMMONITE: No evidence.

DEIR ALLA: No evidence.

MOABITE: No evidence. The only form that may qualify as a *qal* passive participle, הרס (Mesha 27), is ambiguous. It may be a passive participle ("destroyed")[341] or a noun ("destruction").[342] In either case, the vocalization is unknown.

EDOMITE: No evidence.

HEBREW: [qāṭūl], as is evident from the *plene* writing in ארור [ʾārūr] "cursed" (Silwan B 2); cf. ארר "cursed" (Beit Lei; Nahal Yishai 1).[343]

According to the meager evidence, the *qal* passive participle was formed from two different bases in the first-millennium NWS dialects.[344] One base, *qatūl*, appeared in Hebrew (and Canaanite?; cf. EA[345]); this base also underlies the *qal* passive participle in Ethiopic and Arabic. The second base, *qatīl*, was found only in Aramaic and Samalian.[346] The distribution of these forms, then, suggests that *qatūl* was the older, and *qatīl* the more recent, *qal* passive participle. The vocalization of this participle in the other dialects is not known.

21a.   פ״י verbs: The *qal* imperfect of ישב* "to sit, dwell" and ידע* "to know."

PHOENICIAN: Forms such as ישב "he will sit" (Kilamu 14) appear in these texts. The vocalization is not known, however.

ARAMAIC: [yattib],[347] as in ישב [yattib] "he sits" (Sf. III 17). It is characteristic of the Aramaic dialects that the initial radical of ישב* and ידע* was lost, and that the second radical was doubled; this doubling occurred in the imperfect, infinitive, and nominal derivatives.[348]

SAMALIAN: *[yattib, yaššib], as inferred from the nominal form משב "throne" (H 8.15, etc.).[349] Since the *yodh* was lost, the second radical was probably doubled (vs. מושב*, following BH); such doubling presumably occurred in the imperfect as well.

AMMONITE: No evidence.

DEIR ALLA: No evidence.

MOABITE: The form וישב "and he dwelt" is preserved in Mesha 8.19. Its vocalization is unknown.

EDOMITE: No evidence.

HEBREW: *[yēšeb, yēdaʿ], as inferred from the vocalization in BH.

In the Aramaic dialects, the imperfect, infinitive, and nominal derivatives of יׁשב* "to sit, dwell" and ידע* "to know" exhibit loss of the initial weak radical as well as doubling of the second radical. This doubling also occurred in Samalian. In Hebrew, gemination did not occur, but the prefixed vowel was lengthened. There is no evidence for the vocalization of these forms in the remaining NWS dialects.

21b. The *qal* infinitive construct ending.

PHOENICIAN: ת-, as in לדעת "(to) know" (Ahirom Graff. 1), לשבת "to dwell" (Karatepe A I 17), and לתת "to give" (Karatepe A III 4) < *ytn.

ARAMAIC: -∅, as inferred from the later Aramaic dialects, as for example Syriac [(lᵓ)mettab] "to sit" and Mandaic מיתאב "to sit."

SAMALIAN: No evidence.

AMMONITE: No evidence.

DEIR ALLA: ת-, as in לדעת "to know" (II 17).

MOABITE: ת-, as in לספת "to add" (Mesha 21).

EDOMITE: No evidence.

HEBREW: ת-, as in כצאתי "when I left" (Arad 16:3), as well as BH forms like לדעת "to know" and לשבת "to sit, dwell."

According to the available evidence, the פ״י *qal* inf. construct had two endings in NWS. It could end in -∅, as inferred for Old Aramaic. Or it could end in ת-, as in Phoenician dialects, the Deir Alla dialect, Moabite, and Hebrew. The dialectal status of Samalian, Ammonite, and Edomite, in this respect, is unknown.

22a. Middle weak verbs: The *qal* infinitive absolute.

PHOENICIAN: No evidence.

ARAMAIC: הום [hawām (?)] "distraught" in Nerab 2:6, and possibly [   ]מותן "dying (?)" in Sf. I B 30.[350] In Aramaic, the original biradical root[351] had been restructured as a triradical root. The middle weak consonant was then treated as a strong radical letter.[352]

SAMALIAN: No evidence.

AMMONITE: מת [(?)] "dying" in Cit. 2. The original biradical root was not restructured according to the pattern of the strong, triradical root.

DEIR ALLA: If שם (I 6) is an inf. abs., "place!"[353] the original biradical root appears unmodified in this dialect.[354]

MOABITE: No evidence.

EDOMITE: No evidence.

HEBREW: *[qōm, śōm], as inferred from BH. The original biradical root was unmodified. The vowel [ō] may have arisen on analogy with [ō] of the strong inf. abs. [qāṭōl].[355]

The evidence of the first-millennium NWS dialects indicates two formations of middle weak *qal* infinitive absolutes. Ammonite, Hebrew, and (?) Deir Alla formed this inf. from the original biradical root [qV̄m, śV̄m]. In Old Aramaic, the biradical root was recast on the pattern of the strong, triradical root; [hawām, mawāt] arose on analogy to [qatāl]. This analogical formation was peculiar to Old Aramaic within the first-millennium NWS dialects.

22b. The formation of the *D*-stem.

BYBLIAN: No evidence.

STANDARD PHOENICIAN: *pōlel*, as in יתלנן[356] "they murmured" (Kilamu 10), with prefixed *t-*.

ARAMAIC: In Fekheriyeh, the form was *pālel*, as in כן "he erected" (Fekh. 10; cf. l. 11) < *kwn*. Another form may have appeared in Sfire, *qayyim*[357]/*kawwin*, in which the middle radical was treated as a strong consonant and was doubled like all *pael* verbs. Admittedly, the only example of this formation—יעורן "they will be aroused (?)" (Sf. II B 4 [*pual*])[358]—is in a broken passage and can be interpreted differently.[359] Nevertheless, the *qayyim/kawwin* formation survives throughout all the Aramaic dialects. The *pālel*, however, largely died out.[360]

SAMALIAN: No evidence.

AMMONITE: Evidence uncertain. The participle מסבב "surrounding" in Cit. 2 may be either a *pōlel* of a middle weak verb or a *D*-stem of an ע״ע root. Comparison with BH admits of either alternative.

DEIR ALLA: No evidence. Hackett[361] argued that יתעץ "he will seek counsel" (II 9) is a tD stem of *ʿwṣ. Yet if the root were middle weak, a tD stem would appear as *יתעצץ (*pōlel*) or as *יתעוץ (*kawwin*); these are the only two possible formations in NWS. Further, *ʿwṣ is a secondary root and appears only in BH. יתעץ cannot be a tD of *ʿwṣ.

MOABITE: No evidence.

EDOMITE: No evidence.

HEBREW: *pōlel, as inferred from the form found in Masoretic Hebrew.

The formation of the D-stem of middle weak roots divides the NWS dialects into two groups. In Sfire-Aramaic (?), and all later Aramaic dialects, the form was qayyim/kawwin; as in Arabic, the middle weak radical was treated like a regular, strong consonant and underwent consonantal gemination characteristic of the pael. In standard Phoenician, Fekh.-Aramaic, and Hebrew, the D-stem of middle weak verbs merged with the pālel/pōlel conjugation.[362] The distribution of this merger—Ugaritic,[363] Phoenician, Hebrew, and Fekh.-Aramaic—suggests that it occurred sporadically throughout NWS;[364] its appearance in these dialects may be due, in part, to parallel, independent development.

23a.   Final weak verbs: The qal first person singular perfect.

PHOENICIAN: [banêtī], as in the late form בנת "I built" (Eshmunazor 4, etc.). Evidence of the second root vowel appears in the Punic form caneth "I acquired" (Poen. 932),[365] in which [ê] was contracted from *ay. The proto-form of this Phoenician verb, then, was *banay-tī > [banêtī].[366]

ARAMAIC: [banayt(u/i)], as in בנית "I built" (Zkr B 10, etc.; Br-Rkb 1:20). Like Phoenician, then, the proto-form of this verb was *banay-t(u/i).

SAMALIAN: (vocalization unknown), as in בנית "I built" (H 14), and probably הוית "I became/let fall" (P 5). It is uncertain whether this form arose from *banay + *t(u/i) > *[banayt(u/i)] or from *baniy + *tu/i > *[banîtu/i]. The orthography of the Samalian texts admits of either possibility.

AMMONITE: No evidence.

DEIR ALLA: No evidence.

MOABITE: (vocalization unknown),[367] as in בנתי "I built" (Mesha 21, etc.) and עשתי "I made" (Mesha 23, etc.). It is impossible to determine whether this form was pronounced [banêtī], according to the Phoenician-Aramaic model, or [banîtī], according to the Hebrew model.

EDOMITE: No evidence.

HEBREW: [bānîtī], as in נקתי "I am guiltless" (Yavneh-Yam 1:11). The second root vowel [î] is inferred from the vocalization of this form in BH; the proto-form of this verb, then, was *baniy-tī > (with contraction) [bānîtī].[368] Cf. ba-ni-ti "I built" (EA 292:29 [Gezer]).[369]

The attested forms of the first person sing. perfect *qal* of final weak verbs divide the first-millennium NWS dialects into two groups. One group formed this perfect from *banay-, as Old Aramaic [banayt(u/i)] and Phoenician [banêtī]. The other group developed from *baniy-, as Hebrew [bānîtī]. The Hebrew form, then, differed from that of Phoenician and Aramaic by replacing the base *banay- with *baniy-; cf., however, the third person masc. sing. perfect *qal* בנה [bānâ] "he built" < *banaya. The dialectal affinities of Samalian, Ammonite, Deir Alla, Moabite, and Edomite, in this respect, are undetermined.

23b. The *qal* third person masculine singular perfect.[370]

BYBLIAN: [banaya], as in בני [banaya] "he built" (Yehimilk 1; Shiptibaal 1) and עלי ['alaya] "he attacks" (Ahirom 2); final short vowels had not been lost at this time.[371] It is uncertain whether a distinction between *qatala and *qatila perfects was maintained in this dialect.

STANDARD PHOENICIAN: [banō], as in חז [ḥazō] "he saw" (Kilamu 11.11.12) < *banấ < *banaa < *banaya.

ARAMAIC: [banâ], as in אתה ['atâ] "he came" (KAI 220:2) and comparable forms in later Aramaic dialects. The form is derived from *banaya > (syncope of intervocalic *yodh*) [banâ].[372]

SAMALIAN: [banâ], as in קן [qanâ] "he fashioned" (Kilamu Scept. 1) and שתא [šatâ (?)] "it drank" (H 9).

The vocalization of שתא, however, is uncertain. The final *aleph* may indicate [šatâ], since final *aleph* represents [ā] in זא [ḏ/zā(ʾ)] "this" (fem. sing.) (H 18) < *ḏā.[373] But if שתא is derived from *ša-tiya, as for example Syriac [ʾeštī], final *aleph* may represent [ê, ē].[374] As in Old Byblian, then, it is uncertain whether a distinction between *qatala and *qatila final weak perfects was maintained in Samalian.

AMMONITE: [banō], as in בנה [banō] "he built" (Cit. 1).[375] Like standard Phoenician, [banō] developed from *banaya > *banaa > *banâ > [banō].

DEIR ALLA: [banâ (?)], as in אתה [ʾatâ (?)] "he came" (II 14).

MOABITE: [banâ (?)], as in בנה [banâ (?)] "he built" (Mesha 18).

EDOMITE: No evidence.

HEBREW: [bānâ], as in עשה "he has done" (Arad 21:3; Lach. 4:3) and היה "it, he was" (Arad 111:5'; Yavneh-Yam 1:3; Shiloah 1.6). The vocalized forms in the Masoretic text support this vocalization.

The forms of the *qal* third person masc. sing. perfect of final weak verbs varied according to different phonetic changes in the individual dialects. Thus the old form *banaya was found in Old Byblian. The form [banâ] < *banaya occurred in Aramaic, Samalian, Deir Alla, Moabite, and Hebrew. And finally, a form [banō] < *banâ occurred in the two dialects exhibiting the regular correspondence *â:[ō],[376] standard Phoenician and Ammonite. It is unknown whether the individual dialects distinguished between *qatala and *qatila perfects in these forms of the final weak verb.

23c.   The *qal* third person masc. plural perfect.

PHOENICIAN: (vocalization uncertain). The Punic form בנא "they built" (KAI 101:1, etc.) may reflect either [banô] or [banū].[377] The vocalization of this form may correspond to either the Aramaic (with contraction) or Hebrew pattern.

ARAMAIC: [banaw], as in אתו [ʾataw] "they came" (Adon 4). The form in Old (and some later) Aramaic dialects developed from *banayū > (syncope of intervocalic *yodh*) *banaū > [banaw].

SAMALIAN: No evidence.

AMMONITE: No evidence.

DEIR ALLA: (vocalization uncertain), as in חזו "they saw" (I 14). On the basis of the orthography, this form could be vocalized either [ḥazaw] or [ḥazū].

If, however, שתיו (I 10) were a third person masc. plural perfect, "they drank,"[378] this form would constitute evidence that the Deir Alla perfect were vocalized like Aramaic; i.e. the form would have been pronounced [šatīw] < *šatiyū, similar to the later biblical Aramaic and Syriac forms. Yet this interpretation violates the orthographic pattern in these texts, for the *yodh* would constitute the only example of an internal *mater lectionis*. Alternatively, if the form were vocalized [šatiyū],[379] the final weak radical would have been preserved, contrary to all expectations; in all dialects, this consonantal *yodh* would have syncopated.[380] In light of these difficulties, it is preferable to follow Hoftijzer[381] in interpreting this form as a *qal* masc. plural imperative. It would therefore be vocalized [štayw].[382]

MOABITE: No evidence.

EDOMITE: No evidence.

HEBREW: [bānū], as in מנו "they counted" (Ophel "b" 2[383]); cf. הכו [hikkū] "they struck" (Shiloah 4). The pronunciation of this form is inferred from its vocalization in the Masoretic text. [bānū] probably developed from a monosyllabic base *ban* + verbal suffix *-ū*.

The evidence for the *qal* third person masc. plural perfect of final weak verbs suggests two different vocalizations and developments. In Old Aramaic, this verb developed from *banay* + *-ū*. In Hebrew, however, it developed from *ban* + *-ū*; the final weak radical was lost and a new biradical base was created. The vocalization of the Phoenician and Deir Alla forms is, however, uncertain; there is no internal evidence which suggests either the Aramaic or Hebraic model. Finally, evidence for the vocalization of this form in Samalian, Ammonite, Moabite, and Edomite is lacking.

23d. The *qal* third person masculine/feminine singular imperfect (indicative and jussive).[384]

PHOENICIAN: יגל "he uncovers" (Ahirom 2) and ימח "he wipes out" (Karatepe A III 13), both indicative. There is no evidence that the form of the jussive differed from that of the indicative.[385] The vocalization of either form, however, is unknown.

ARAMAIC: The indicative ended in ה- whereas the jussive ended in י-.[386] Examples of the indicative are יהוה "he will be" (Sf. II A 4) and יאתה "he will come" (Sf. I B 28, etc.). The jussive appears in תהוי "may it be" (Sf. I A 25, etc.), תהרי "may it become pregnant" (Sf. I A 21), and להוי "may he be" (Fekh. 12 [with precative *lamedh*]); cf. ויענני "and he answered me" (Zkr A 11).[387]

SAMALIAN: Both the indicative and jussive ended in י-, as in תלעי "it becomes weary" (H 32) and ירשי "he allows" (H 27.28) (both indicatives), and תשתי "may it drink" (H 22) and אל.ירקי "may he not be pleased" (H 22) (both jussives).

AMMONITE: No evidence.

DEIR ALLA: Like Old Aramaic, the indicative ended in -ה and the jussive in -י. For example, the indicative is attested in יבכה "he was weeping" (I 4); the jussive appears in אל.]תהגי[. "do not remove" (I 7) and ירוי "may he be satisfied" (II 6).

There is no certain example of a ל"ה consecutive imperfect in the third person singular. For example, ויעל (I 4) is not a final weak verb,[388] but an ע"ע root, "he entered."[389] Similarly, the form ויחז "he saw" (Ve 2)[390] is an uncertain reading on a small, plaster fragment. In any case, the expected form of this consecutive imperfect would be ויחזי*.

MOABITE: A final weak indicative does not appear in the Moabite texts. The consecutive imperfect, however, appears frequently and always exhibits recessive accent and loss of the final vowel,[391] as for example ויבן "and he built" (Mesha 10), ואעש "and I made" (Mesha 3.9), and וארא "and I saw" (Mesha 7).

EDOMITE: No evidence.

HEBREW: The indicative ended in -ה whereas the jussive lost this final syllable. The indicative occurs in יקרה "it befalls" (Arad 24:16), and perhaps ארצה "I will accept" (Beit Lei A 1[392]). The jussive appears in ויהי "that he may be" (Ajrud) and the causative ירא "may he let see" (Lach. 6:1); the final syllable, however, was lost only in certain persons and under certain syllabic conditions.[393] Whereas both Moabite and Hebrew formed the jussive by apocopation, this apocopation appears to have been more restricted in Hebrew than it was in Moabite.[394]

The indicative and jussive of final weak verbs divide the NWS dialects in two respects: First, the preservation or loss of distinction between indicative and jussive. This distinction was preserved in Old Aramaic, the Deir Alla dialect, Moabite, and Hebrew. In Phoenician and Samalian, however, this distinction was lost; one verbal form performed these two functions.[395] Second, the formal distinction between indicative and jussive. In Old Aramaic and the Deir Alla dialect, the indicative ended in -ה, and the jussive ended in -י; the Samalian ending -י may have been a survival of the jussive, now used in the indicative sense as well. In Hebrew (and Moabite?), the indicative had a final vowel, whereas the jussive lost this vowel and showed a recessive accent; in Hebrew, however, the apocopation of these verbs was more restricted than in Moabite.

In terms of dialectal groups, the preservation of a morphological distinction between indicative and jussive unites Old Aramaic, the Deir Alla dialect, Moabite, and Hebrew as one group, as opposed to Phoenician and Samalian, in which this distinction was lost. There is no evidence, however, suggesting that Phoenician and Samalian jointly innovated. Rather, this loss of morphological distinction developed independently, as in later Aramaic dialects. With respect to the specific shape of the indicative and jussive, Old Aramaic and Deir Alla constitute one group, Moabite and Hebrew another. The dialectal status of Ammonite and Edomite, in these respects, is unknown.

23e. The second/third person masculine plural imperfect ending.[396]

BYBLIAN: No evidence.

STANDARD PHOENICIAN: *[ô(n), ū(n)],[397] as inferred from the later form יקצן "they will cut down" (Eshmunazor 22). It is unclear whether the final vowel was [ū], as in Hebrew, or [ô] < *aw, as in Aramaic dialects.

ARAMAIC: [awn] < *ayūn,[398] as in יחיון "they will live" (Caquot 8[399]) and [תא]תון "you will come" (Sf. I B 32).[400] Cf. the jussive תפנו "do (not) pay attention" (Sf. III 7).

SAMALIAN: No evidence.

AMMONITE: [-n].[401] There is no evidence for the vowel preceding final *nun*.

DEIR ALLA: [aw (?)],[402] as in ויאתו "and they came" (I 1) and יחזו "they will see" (II 13). The vocalization of these imperfects can be inferred from שתיו "drink!" in I 10. Since this form is probably a masc. plural imperative, the *yodh* represented the diphthong [aw].[403] A diphthong, then, would have appeared in the masc. plural imperfect forms, following the pattern of these forms in the Aramaic dialects. Admittedly, there is no certain evidence for any particular pronunciation.

MOABITE: No evidence.

EDOMITE: No evidence.

HEBREW: [ū], as in יענו "they will act as witnesses" (Yavneh-Yam 1:10.11). The vocalization of these forms in the Masoretic text unanimously reflects the vowel [ū]. As in the third person masc. plural perfect, the verbal suffix *-ū was added to a new, biradical base.[404]

The ending of the second/third masc. plural imperfect of final weak roots took two forms in NWS.[405] Either the ending was derived from *-ayū, as in Old Aramaic and (?) the Deir Alla dialect. Or the ending *-ū was added to a biradical base without the final weak consonant; according to the present evidence, this form appeared only in Hebrew. There is no certain evidence for the quality of the vowel in Phoenician, and no evidence at all for Samalian, Ammonite, Moabite, and Edomite. The present evidence suggests, then, a two-fold dialectal division into an *-aw group and an *-ū group.

23f. The ending of the *qal* infinitive construct.

BYBLIAN: No evidence.

STANDARD PHOENICIAN: ת- [ōt], as in לבנת "to build" (Karatepe A II 11) and the later form לקצתנם "to cut them down" (Eshmunazor 9/10).

ARAMAIC: Evidence uncertain. The only possible example of this form is לחזיה "to see" (Sf. I A 13);[406] cf. the *peal* infinitive absolute as, for example, נכה "slaying" (Sf. III 12.13). It is difficult, however, to account for the *yodh* in this form.[407] Later Aramaic dialects show endings in either [ā] or [ê],[408] although a *yodh* is restored in determined forms ([ʾyā]).[409] Nonetheless, the vocalic ending of לחזיה resembles that of the final weak inf. in other Aramaic dialects; no Aramaic form has an ending in ת-.

Although Rosenthal[410] cited רקו (Sf. III 6) as a final weak infinitive, Degen[411] correctly interpreted this form as an imperative (plural) "appease!"

SAMALIAN: The ending of this inf. changed according to the syntax of the verb. When the inf. was not bound to a following noun, it was א-, as in לבנא "to build" (H 13.14); when bound to another word, however, it was י-, as in לבני (.כפירי) "to build (villages)" (H 10). א- and י- were not two different spellings of the identical sound;[412] rather, the two endings reflect a morphological distinction between unbound and bound forms.

AMMONITE: No evidence.

DEIR ALLA: No evidence.
MOABITE: No evidence.
EDOMITE: No evidence.
HEBREW: ת- [ōt], as in לעשת "to do" (Arad 1:8).

The ending of the final weak *qal* infinitive construct divides the NWS dialects into two groups. In standard Phoenician and Hebrew, this inf. ended in ת- [ōt]. In Old (and later) Aramaic and Samalian, this inf. ended in a vowel. Thus the distribution of these two forms supports the traditional division between a Canaanite and Aramaic branch of NWS.

Within the Aramaic-Samalian group, however, Aramaic had one infinitive form regardless of construction; Samalian exhibited two different forms, depending upon the syntax of the infinitive. While Samalian, then, shared the vocalic ending of the inf. with Aramaic, it uniquely exhibited two different forms of the inf., depending upon construction.

23g. The *qal* masculine plural (undetermined) participle.

PHOENICIAN: *[bōnêm], as inferred from בנם "builders" (KAI 100:2), as well as the *plene* forms בנאם "builders" (KAI 101:6) and בענים "builders" (KAI 140:6). The transcription, *bunem*, in *Or Ant* 2:75,3 suggests that the participle was formed in the same pattern as in Aramaic, i.e. *bānay-m* > *bōnay-m* > [bōnêm]; cf. Old Aramaic חזין "seers" (Zkr A 12).[413]

ARAMAIC: [bānay(i)n], as in חזין "seers" (Zkr A 12). The vocalization of this participle was either [ḥāzayn] or, with anaptyxis,[414] [ḥāzayin]. Had the participle been formed like *[ḥāziyīn],[415] the intervocalic *yodh* would have syncopated to *[ḥāzîn]. The presence of the *yodh*, then, argues for the diphthong [ay],[416] as in the form underlying the biblical Aramaic masc. plural undetermined participle.

SAMALIAN: No evidence.
AMMONITE: No evidence.
DEIR ALLA: No evidence.
MOABITE: No evidence.
EDOMITE: No evidence.

HEBREW: *[bōnīm], as inferred from the forms found in the Masoretic text. This form was either derived from participial *bāniy- + suffix (as in the masc. sing. בֹּנֶה). Or, in view of the fem. sing. בֹּנָה and fem. plural participles בֹּנוֹת, it was formed from a biradical base *bān- > *bōn- + suffix.

According to the present evidence, the *qal* masc. plural undetermined participle took two forms in the attested NWS dialects. In Hebrew it was *[bōnīm] < *bāniy- or *bān-. In standard Phoenician and Aramaic, *bānay- replaced old participial *bāniy- (*qātil-). The form of this participle in the remaining dialects is unknown.

23h.   The third person masculine singular perfect of the *D*- and causative stems.

BYBLIAN: (vocalization uncertain), as in חוי "he restored" (Yehimilk 2). Like the corresponding *qal* perfect, the presence of *yodh* indicates that the final short [a] had not been lost.[417] Whether the vowel preceding *yodh* was [a], as in Hebrew, or [i], as in Aramaic and Samalian, cannot be determined.

STANDARD PHOENICIAN: (vocalization unknown.) There are no unambiguous examples of this form in this dialect. Friedrich and Röllig[418] cited ען "he subdued" in Karatepe A I 18, although the construction וען אנך suggests that the verb may be more accurately interpreted as an inf. abs.[419] Further, the form כסי in Kilamu 12 can be interpreted either as a third person masc. sing. perfect *pual*, "he was covered,"[420] or more likely as a third person masc. sing. perfect *piel* with third person masc. sing. suffix, "it covered him."[421] The form and vocalization of the third person masc. sing. perfect of the *D*- and causative stems cannot be inferred from these examples.

ARAMAIC: *[bannî] and *[habnî], as inferred from the vocalization of these forms in the later Aramaic dialects. In Aramaic, all third person masc. sing. perfects in the *pael* and *haphel* conjugations end in [î][422] < *iy.[423]

SAMALIAN: *[bannî] and [habnî], as in הרפי "he released" (P 8). The single example of this form, הרפי, with final *yodh*, shows that, as in Aramaic, these derived conjugations ended in [î] in the third person masc. sing. perfect.[424]

AMMONITE: No evidence.

DEIR ALLA: No evidence.

MOABITE: No evidence.

EDOMITE: No evidence.

HEBREW: [binnâ] and [hibnâ], as in נסה [nissâ] "he tried" (Lach. 3:9), as well as BH גָּלָה "he uncovered," הִגְלָה "he exiled," etc. The final syllable in both conjugations is derived from *awa/*aya > *aa > [â].[425]

The first-millennium NWS dialects show two different endings of the D- and causative third person masc. sing. perfect of final weak verbs. In Hebrew, these forms ended in [â], whereas in Aramaic and Samalian they ended in [î]. It is difficult, however, to determine which form was inherited and which was innovative. If the proto-form were *bannaya,[426] as in Arabic and Ethiopic, Old Aramaic and Samalian innovated.[427] If, however, the proto-form were *banniya,[428] as in later Aramaic dialects, Hebrew constitutes the innovation. The problem is one of reconstruction.

23i.   The singular imperfect of the D-stem.

PHOENICIAN: No evidence for the vocalization.

ARAMAIC: [tibannê],[429] as in תרקה "you will appease" (Sf. III 18.19), as well as in biblical Aramaic, Syriac, and other Aramaic dialects.

SAMALIAN: No evidence.

AMMONITE: No evidence.

DEIR ALLA: No certain evidence. While Hackett[430] interpreted יענה (I 8) as a D-stem imperfect, "it sings out," it is also possible that the form is qal, "it will answer."[431] Also, Hoftijzer's[432] ירוי "may he be satisfied" (II 6) is better interpreted as a qal jussive.[433]

MOABITE: [yibannīw, yibannû], as in ויענו "and he oppressed" (Mesha 5) and אענו "I shall oppress" (Mesha 6). The form could be vocalized as [yiᶜannīw] < *yiᶜanniw < *yiᶜanniwu, in which the final short vowel was lost, creating a diphthong *iw > [īw].[434] Alternatively, the form could be vocalized [yiᶜannû],[435] derived either from *yiᶜanniwu > (syncope of intervocalic waw) *yiᶜanniu > *yiᶜannuu[436] > [yiᶜannû], or from *yiᶜanniwu > (loss of final [u]) *yiᶜanniw > *yiᶜannuw > [yiᶜannû]. In either case, the vocalization of the Moabite form differed from that of all other NWS forms.

EDOMITE: No evidence.

HEBREW: *[yᵊbannê], as inferred from the vocalization in BH.

The evidence of three NWS dialects, with respect to the form of the *D*-stem imperfect singular, suggests a twofold dialectal division. In Aramaic and Hebrew (and most other NWS dialects?), the imperfect ended in [ē]. In Moabite, it ended in either [ĩw] or [û]. While the forms in all these dialects were derived from the identical **yibanniy/wu*, a different sequence of phonological rules, as well as different vocalic assimilations, produced the unique vocalization in Moabite. Thus Moabite constitutes a dialectal island with respect to the vocalization of these forms in NWS.

24a.   The root הלך*: The *qal* imperfect.

PHOENICIAN: No evidence.

ARAMAIC: This root is not attested in Old Aramaic. Another root, **hwk*, found also in Ethiopic, was the regular verb "to go."[437]

SAMALIAN: No evidence.

AMMONITE: No evidence.

DEIR ALLA: No evidence.

MOABITE: ואהלך "and I went" (Mesha 14/15). The root **hlk*, then, was treated like a strong verb in the *qal* imperfect. Whether this form was the original construction,[438] or resulted from the (secondary) restoration of the *he* on analogy with the perfect,[439] is unknown.

EDOMITE: No evidence.

HEBREW: וילכו "and they flowed" (Shiloah 4), as well as similar forms without the first radical *he* in BH.

24b.   The *qal* imperative.

PHOENICIAN: Perhaps הלך "go (away)!" (fem. sing.) (Arsl.T. 1:21).[440] It is possible, however, that this form is an inf. absolute used as an imperative.[441]

ARAMAIC: No evidence. It is reasonable to assume, however, that the imperative, like the imperfect, was formed from **hwk*, not **hlk*.

SAMALIAN: No evidence.

AMMONITE: No evidence.

DEIR ALLA: לכו "go!" (masc. plural) (I 5). Like Hebrew, Moabite, and Ugaritic,[442] the imperative of the Deir Alla root **hlk* was formed from a secondary root **wlk*. The aphaeresis of the initial radical in the imperative is a regular morphological feature of פ״ו verbs.

MOABITE: לך "go!" (masc. sing.) (Mesha 14). The imperative of the Moabite verb *hlk was formed after the pattern of original פ״ו verbs.

EDOMITE: No evidence.

HEBREW: לך*, as inferred from the regular form of the imperative of *hlk in the Masoretic text. In Jer. 51:50,[443] however, the BH imperative of this root retained the initial *he*.

Since the form of the imperative and imperfect are morphologically related,[444] the forms of the imperative and imperfect of *hlk should be considered together. One isogloss separates Aramaic from Phoenician-Deir Alla-Moabite-Hebrew; Aramaic employed the verbal root *hwk to signify the verb "to go," whereas the remaining dialects used *hlk/*wlk. In this case, Aramaic was differentiated lexically from these dialects.

Within the Phoenician-Deir Alla-Moabite-Hebrew dialectal unit, further isoglosses can be drawn. In Hebrew, both the imperative and imperfect were formed from the secondary root *wlk; similarly, in Moabite and Deir Alla, the imperative was formed from *wlk. In Phoenician, however, the imperative may have retained the *he* of the original root *hlk, if הלך in Arsl.T. 1:21 is indeed an imperative. The use of a secondary root *wlk in the imperative and imperfect was an innovation shared by the Deir Alla dialect, Moabite, and Hebrew.[445]

In Moabite, however, the evidence is split between Phoenician and Hebrew-Deir Alla affinities. Whereas the imperative was formed from *wlk, the imperfect was formed from *hlk. Thus Moabite represents a transitional, dialectal area, with affinities to both morphological extremes of Phoenician (*hlk) and Hebrew-Deir Alla (*wlk). The language of the Mesha inscription reflects a time when the two roots *hlk and *wlk were still competing.[446]

In short, Aramaic stood apart from the other NWS dialects which attest a verb "to go," since it alone used the root *hwk instead of *hlk/*wlk. Within the *hlk/*wlk region, Phoenician lay at one dialectal end, using *hlk, while Hebrew and the Deir Alla dialect lay at the other, with *wlk. Moabite stood dialectally midway between Phoenician and Hebrew-Deir Alla. In this way, Moabite is a transitional dialect within the Phoenician-Hebrew/Deir Alla dialect group.

25a.   The root לקח*: The *qal* imperfect formations.

PHOENICIAN: *[yiqqaḥ], as inferred from the Punic form יקח "he will take" (KAI 69:20).

ARAMAIC: Two forms of the imperfect are found in Old Aramaic: (1) [yiqqaḥ], as in יקח "he will take" (Sf. I B 27), תקח "you will take" (Sf. III 2), and יקחן "they will be taken" (Sf. I A 42); and (2) [yilqaḥ], as in ילקח "he will take" (Sf. I B 35.35; Fekh. 17 [jussive]) and תלקח "may she take" (Fekh. 18).

Whereas [yiqqaḥ] is the regular NWS form,[447] [yilqaḥ] is unusual within this dialect group. On the one hand, the form with unassimilated *lamedh* may have been a survival of the Old Semitic form *yilqaḥ, like Akk. *ilqu* "he took." If so, the appearance of the specifically NWS form [yiqqaḥ] (only?) in Sfire suggests that, like other innovations within Old Aramaic,[448] the new formation [yiqqaḥ] first appeared in Aramaic at Sfire. The competition between [yiqqaḥ] and [yilqaḥ],[449] as well as the predominance of [yiqqaḥ] over the older [yilqaḥ], would therefore reflect the decline of the old form and the ascent of the innovation. On the other hand, the unassimilated *lamedh* in [yilqaḥ] may represent a restructuring of the imperfect *lqḥ on the model of the strong verb. Like [daqan]:[yidqan] "to be old," so [laqaḥ]:[yilqaḥ]. The *lamedh*, in this case, was treated as a regular, strong radical letter. Whether [yilqaḥ] was a survival of an old, dying verbal form, or a new formation on the pattern of the strong verb, it deviated from the NWS pattern of assimilating the *lamedh* in the imperfect of this root.

SAMALIAN: [yiqqaḥ], as in יקח "he will take" (H 10) and יקחו "they take" (H 12).

AMMONITE: No evidence.

DEIR ALLA: [yiqqaḥ], as in יקח "it will take" (II 13).

MOABITE: [yiqqaḥ], as in ואקח "and I took" (Mesha 17.19/20 [partially restored]).

EDOMITE: No evidence.

HEBREW: [yiqqaḥ], as in ויקח "and he took" (Yavneh-Yam 1:8), as well as similar forms in the Masoretic text. The form ילקח in Arad 111:4′ is, as Rainey noted,[450] a *niphal* imperfect; it is not comparable to יקלח in Sf. I B 35.35 and Fekh. 17.

The form [yiqqaḥ] was common to all NWS dialects. It is found in Phoenician, Aramaic, Samalian, the Deir Alla dialect, Moabite, and Hebrew. The only deviation appeared in Old Aramaic of Tell Fekheriyeh and, to a lesser extent, Sfire where the first radical, *lamedh*, was preserved in the imperfect construction. In these dialects, the form [yilqaḥ] was either a common retention or a new analogical formation.

25b. The ending of the *qal* infinitive construct.

PHOENICIAN: ת-*, as inferred from the Punic form לקחת (KAI 76 B 5).
ARAMAIC: -∅, for example למלקח (Fekh. 9/10).
SAMALIAN: No evidence.
AMMONITE: No evidence.
DEIR ALLA: No evidence.
MOABITE: No evidence.
EDOMITE: No evidence.
HEBREW: ת-, for example לקחת (Lach. 3:18).

The ending of the infinitive construct of *lqḥ* divides the first-millennium NWS dialects into two groups. In the Aramaic dialect of Fekheriyeh, no suffixal modifications were appended. In Phoenician and Hebrew, a final ת- was added to the verb. Thus Fekheriyeh-Aramaic lay at one dialectal extreme (conservative), while Phoenician and Hebrew lay at the other (innovative).

Notes to Chapter 3

1. The features listed in nos. 13–15 are not strictly morphological, but lexical in nature. They are included here since these features would commonly appear in the morphology section of a reference grammar.

2. The reading אנכי in P 19 has now been corrected by Joseph P. Healey, "The Archaic Aramaic Inscriptions from Zinjirli" (Ph.D. dissertation, Harvard University, 1981), pp. 62, 86.

3. As read by Frank M. Cross, "The Cave Inscriptions from Khirbet Beit Lei," in *Near Eastern Archaeology in the Twentieth Century*, ed. James A. Sanders (Garden City, N.Y.: Doubleday & Co., 1970), p. 301.

4. Carl Brockelmann, *GvG* 1:§104aδ.

5. I. J. Gelb, *Sequential Reconstruction of Proto-Akkadian*, Assyriological Studies, vol. 18 (Chicago: The University of Chicago Press, 1969), p. 177.

6. Eduard Y. Kutscher, *A History of Aramaic, Part 1, Old Aramaic, Jaudic, Official Aramaic (Biblical Aramaic excepted)* (Jerusalem: Akadamon, 1972), p. 24 (in Hebrew).

7. Paul-E. Dion, *La langue de Yaʾudi* (Waterloo, Ont.: The Corporation for the Publication of Academic Studies in Religion in Canada, 1974), p. 62.

8. See already S. Ronzevalle, "La langue des inscriptions dites de Hadad et de Panammū," in *Florilegium . . . Melchior de Vogüé* (Paris: Imprimerie Nationale, 1909), pp. 523–524. See below, no. 2a, for a complete discussion of (ה)זנ "this."

9. Joseph Naveh, "Old Hebrew Inscriptions in a Burial Cave," *IEJ* 13 (1963): 86. For a different reading, see Cross, in *Near Eastern Archaeology*, p. 302.

10. Brockelmann, *GvG* 1:§104cα.

11. See Stanislav Segert, *A Grammar of Phoenician and Punic* (Munich: C. H. Beck, 1976), §51.132.

12. André Dupont-Sommer, "Une inscription araméenne inédite de Sfiré," *BMB* 13 (1956): 27, 35.

13. J. T. Milik, in Joseph A. Fitzmyer, "The Aramaic Suzerainty Treaty from Sefire in the Museum of Beirut," *CBQ* 20 (1958): 462.

14. See Fitzmyer, "A Further Note on the Aramaic Inscription Sefire III.22," *JSS* 14 (1969): 198 with nn. 4–6; and Rainer Degen, *Altaramäische Grammatik der Inschriften des 10.–8. Jh. v. Chr.*, Abhandlungen für die Kunde des Morgenlandes, vol. 38/3 (Wiesbaden: Franz Steiner, 1969), p. 22 n. 88.

15. So, for example, J. Hoftijzer, "Interpretation and Grammar," in *Aramaic Texts from Deir ʿAlla*, ed. J. Hoftijzer and G. van der Kooij. Documenta et Monumenta Orientis Antiqui, vol. 19 (Leiden: E. J. Brill, 1976), p. 185; Fitzmyer, "[Review of Hoftijzer and van der Kooij, eds., *Aramaic Texts*]," *CBQ* 40 (1978): 94–95; and Jo Ann Carlton (Hackett), "Studies in the Plaster Text from Tell Deir ʿAllā" (Ph.D. dissertation, Harvard University, 1980), pp. 48–49, 139.

16. So André Caquot and André Lemaire, "Les textes araméens de Deir ʿAlla," *Syria* 54 (1977): 194; P. Kyle McCarter, "The Balaam Texts from Deir ʿAllā: The First Combination," *BASOR* 239 (1980): 52 (one possibility); and Stephen A. Kaufman, "[Review of Hoftijzer and van der Kooij, eds., *Aramaic Texts*]," *BASOR* 239 (1980): 73.

17. See Ziony Zevit, *Matres Lectionis in Ancient Hebrew Epigraphs*, ASOR Monograph Series, vol. 2 (Cambridge: ASOR, 1980), p. 28.

18. See Chapter 2, no. 19.

19. See Brockelmann, *GvG* 1:§104f, for comparative evidence.

20. See no. 1d, below.

21. Cf. E. Lipiński, "From Karatepe to Pyrgi. Middle Phoenician Miscellanea," *RSF* 2 (1974): 49–50.

22. Brockelmann, *GvG* 1:§104gγ.

23. Until recently, scholars have restored this form of the demonstrative in the Ur Box, [ז]ן ארן "this coffin" (e.g., Zellig S. Harris, *A Gram-*

mar of the Phoenician Language, American Oriental Series, vol. 8 [New Haven: American Oriental Society, 1936], p. 54; Johannes Friedrich and Wolfgang Röllig, *PPG*² §113b; and *KAI* 2:47). Ginsberg ("Ugaritico-Phoenicia," *JANES* 5 [1973]: 141), however, pointed out that since the third person singular pronominal suffix is ‎ʾ- in this text, it is unlikely that a specifically Byblian demonstrative should be restored. Thus, he restored ארן [ש]ן "(this) ivory box," which accords better with the dialect of the text. The Phoenician pronoun, זן, then, is found only in the Old Byblian dialect.

24. Franz Rosenthal, in Ginsberg, "An Aramaic Contemporary of the Lachish Letters," *BASOR* 111 (1948): 25 n. 4c; followed by Fitzmyer, "The Aramaic Letter of King Adon to the Egyptian Pharaoh," *Bibl* 46 (1965): 54, 44; John C. L. Gibson, *Textbook of Syrian Semitic Inscriptions,* 3 vols. (Oxford: Oxford University Press, 1971–1982), 2:113, 115; and Bezalel Porten, "The Identity of King Adon," *BA* 44 (1981): 36.

25. Ronzevalle, in *Florilegium . . . Melchior de Vogüé,* p. 524; Hans H. Schaeder, *Iranische Beiträge I,* Schriften der Königsberger Gelehrten Gesellschaft, Geisteswissenschaftliche Klasse, vol. 6, pt. 5 (Halle an der Saale: Max Niemeyer, 1930), p. 241; and Rosenthal, *Die Sprache der palmyrenischen Inschriften und ihre Stellung innerhalb des Aramäischen,* MVÄG, vol. 41, pt. 1 (Leipzig: J. C. Hinrichs'sche Buchhandlung, 1936), pp. 49, 51. Cf. Ginsberg, "Aramaic Studies Today," *JAOS* 62 (1942): 235 n. 29.

26. A. van Selms, "Some Remarks on the ʿAmmān Citadel Inscriptions," *BiOr* 32 (1975): 7.

27. So, for example, Horn, Cross, Albright, Kutscher, Puech and Rofé, Dion, and Fulco.

28. Published by Yigael Yadin et al., *Hazor II. An Account of the Second Season of Excavations, 1956* (Jerusalem: Magnes Press, 1960), pp. 71–72.

29. Jakob Barth, *Die Pronominalbildung in den semitischen Sprachen* (Leipzig: J. C. Hinrichs'sche Buchhandlung, 1913), §§42–47, 37a; and Brockelmann, *GvG* 1:§107 (especially §§d, f).

30. Ali Abou-Assaf, Pierre Bordreuil, and Alan R. Millard, *La statue de Tell Fekherye et son inscription bilingue assyro-araméenne* (Paris: Editions Recherche sur les civilisations, 1982), pp. 34, 48.

31. Brockelmann, *GvG* 1:§§107tα, vα.

32. Ibid., 1:§107tα.

33. Ibid., 1:§107pβ.

34. See Barth, *Pronominalbildung,* §28.

35. Rosenthal, "Canaanite and Aramaic Inscriptions," in *ANET*³, p. 658 with n. 1 (tentatively).

36. Caquot, "Observations sur la Première Tablette Magique d'Arslan Tash," *JANES* 5 (1973): 47. Cf. Frank M. Cross and Richard J. Saley, "Phoenician Incantations on a Plaque of the Seventh Century B.C. from Arslan Tash in Upper Syria," *BASOR* 197 (1970): 44 n. 7; and Röllig, "Die Amulette von Arslan Taş," *NESE* 2 (1974): 18, 21.

37. See examples listed by Brockelmann, *GvG* 1:§107vα.

38. Hoftijzer, in *Aramaic Texts,* pp. 189, 287.

39. Caquot and Lemaire, *Syria* 54 (1977): 194.

40. Carlton (Hackett), "Studies," p. 44.

41. For example, Baruch A. Levine, "The Deir ʿAllā Plaster Inscriptions," *JAOS* 101 (1981): 196; and Helga and Manfred Weippert, "Die 'Bileam'-Inschrift von *Tell Dēr ʿAllā,*" *ZDPV* 98 (1982): 84.

42. See Chapter 4, no. 2.

43. Barth, *Pronominalbildung,* §48a; and Brockelmann, *GvG* 1:§107g n. 1.

44. Barth, *Pronominalbildung,* §49.

45. Giovanni Garbini, *L'aramaico antico,* Atti della Accademia nazionale dei Lincei, Memoria. Classe di scienze morali, storiche e filologiche, Series VIII, vol. 7 (Rome: Accademia nazionale dei Lincei, 1956), pp. 266, 268, 275.

46. Additional citations in Degen, *Grammatik,* §40.

47. Degen, "Die aramaeischen Tontafeln vom Tell Halaf," *NESE* 1 (1972): 52. Cf. already Friedrich, "Denkmäler mit westsemitischer Buchstabenschrift," in *Die Inschriften vom Tell Halaf,* ed. J. Friedrich et al. AfO Beiheft, vol. 6 (Berlin: [private], 1940), p. 72.

48. Segert, *Altaramäische Grammatik* (Leipzig: VEB Verlag Enzyklopädie, 1975), §5.1.5.1.4; and Degen, *NESE* 1 (1972): 52 n. 4.

49. Rosenthal, *Die Sprache,* p. 51.

50. Dupont-Sommer, "Une inscription nouvelle du roi Kilamou et le dieu Rekoub-El," *RHR* 133 (1947–1948): 23; and Ginsberg, *JANES* 5 (1973): 147.

51. Felice Israel, "The Language of the Ammonites," *OLP* 10 (1979): 146. Cf. p. 65 n. 23.

52. Hackett, "The Dialect of the Plaster Text from Tell Deir ʿAlla," *Or* 53 (1984): 60.

53. So Hoftijzer, Fitzmyer, Caquot and Lemaire, Naveh, Levine, McCarter, and Kaufman. See especially the biblical passages cited by Weippert and Weippert, *ZDPV* 98 (1982): 84.

54. Cf. Hoftijzer, in *Aramaic Texts,* pp. 267, 287.

55. See above, p. 11.

55a. Evidence of the relative אשר in the Samaria texts is highly uncertain (*contra*, for example, E. L. Sukenik, "Note on a Fragment of an Israelite Stele found at Samaria," *PEQ* 1936: 156). The text in question is too broken to yield even speculative grammatical conclusions.

56. Garbini, *Il semitico di nord-ovest,* Quaderni della sezione linguistica degli Annali, vol. 1 (Naples: Istituto universitario orientale di Napoli, 1960), p. 105.

57. See Mitchell Dahood, "The Linguistic Position of Ugaritic in the Light of Recent Discoveries," *Sacra Pagina* 1 (1958): 269.

58. For relative **d,* see Barth, *Pronominalbildung,* §66.

59. For relative **t,* see Gelb, *Old Akkadian Writing and Grammar,* Materials for the Assyrian Dictionary, vol. 2. 2nd ed. (Chicago: The University of Chicago Press, 1961), pp. 134–136; and Harris, *Development of*

the Canaanite Dialects, American Oriental Series, vol. 16 (New Haven: American Oriental Society, 1939), p. 69.

60. Friedrich and Röllig, *PPG*² §120a.

61. N. Avigad, "New Moabite and Ammonite Seals at the Israel Museum," *EI* 13 (1977): 110 (in Hebrew); and Ruth Hestrin and Michal Dayagi-Mendels, *Inscribed Seals* (Jerusalem: Israel Museum, 1979), p. 134.

62. See also Naveh, "The Ostracon from Nimrud: An Ammonite Name-List," *Maarav* 2 (1980): 169.

63. With Hoftijzer, in *Aramaic Texts,* p. 174; and Caquot and Lemaire, *Syria* 54 (1977): 205.

64. Carlton (Hackett), "Studies," pp. 41, 106; and Levine, *JAOS* 101 (1981): 200.

65. See Naveh, "[Review of Hoftijzer and van der Kooij, eds., *Aramaic Texts*]," *IEJ* 29 (1979): 136; and Chapter 2, no. 16.

66. Brockelmann, *GvG* 1:§110c.

67. Garbini, *Il semitico,* p. 108.

68. For אָרָן זן. "this coffin" (Ahirom 2), see Chapter 4, no. 2.

69. *Inscriptions Reveal,* The Israel Museum Catalogue no. 100. 2nd ed. (Jerusalem: Israel Museum, 1973), no. 143.

70. Friedrich and Röllig, *PPG*² §117b; and Segert, *Grammar,* §§51.351, 51.351.1.

71. Richard S. Tomback, "Gemination in Punic," *JNSL* 5 (1977): 67–68.

72. Garbini, *Il semitico,* p. 123.

73. *KAI* 2:212.

74. Degen, *Grammatik,* p. 8 n. 40.

75. George A. Cooke, *NSI,* p. 189.

76. Gibson, *Textbook,* 2:97. Cf. Brockelmann, *GvG* 1:§245iα; and Segert, *Grammatik,* §5.2.6.3.5.

77. Dion, *La langue,* p. 137 (with earlier literature).

78. Segert, *Grammatik,* §5.2.5.1.5.

79. Schaeder, *Iranische Beiträge I,* p. 294. See also Segert, "Aramäische Studien V. Der Artikel in den ältesten aramäischen Texten," *ArOr* 26 (1958): 580.

80. Carlton (Hackett), "Studies," pp. 51, 168–169; and idem, *Or* 53 (1984): 59.

81. Hoftijzer, in *Aramaic Texts,* pp. 189, 300.

82. Caquot and Lemaire, *Syria* 54 (1977): 194–195.

83. McCarter, *BASOR* 239 (1980): 50, 52.

84. Carlton (Hackett), "Studies," p. 40, and *Or* 53 (1984): 59 n. 15. See also Levine, *JAOS* 101 (1981): 196; and Weippert and Weippert, *ZDPV* 98 (1982): 84, 102.

85. McCarter, *BASOR* 239 (1980): 50–51.

86. Caquot and Lemaire, *Syria* 54 (1977): 190; and Jonas C. Greenfield, "[Review of Hoftijzer and van der Kooij, eds., *Aramaic Texts*]," *JSS* 25 (1980): 251 (one possibility).

87. Caquot and Lemaire, *Syria* 54 (1977): 195; and McCarter, *BASOR* 239 (1980): 52, 50.

88. Hackett, *Or* 53 (1984): 59.

89. Segert, "Die Sprache der moabitischen Königsinschrift," *ArOr* 29 (1961): 218, 259.

90. Crystal-M. Bennett, "Excavations at Buseirah, Southern Jordan, 1972: Preliminary Report," *Levant* 6 (1974): 19; and Emile Puech, "Documents épigraphiques de Buseirah," *Levant* 9 (1977): 12–13.

91. Nelson Glueck, "The Topography and History of Ezion-Geber and Elath," *BASOR* 72 (1938): 11–13; and idem, "Tell el-Kheleifeh Inscriptions," in *Near Eastern Studies in Honor of William Foxwell Albright*, ed. Hans Goedicke (Baltimore/London: The Johns Hopkins University Press, 1971), pp. 237–238.

92. Israel, "Miscellanea idumea," *Rivista biblica italiana* 27 (1979): 180.

93. Sabatino Moscati, "Il semitico di nord-ovest," in *Studi orientalistici in onore di Giorgio Levi Della Vida*, Pubblicazioni dell'Istituto per l'Oriente, no. 52. 2 vols. (Rome: Istituto per l'Oriente, 1956), 2:212, 216; and Frank M. Cross and David N. Freedman, "Some Observations on Early Hebrew," *Bibl* 53 (1972): 418. Cf. Harris, *Grammar*, p. 56.

94. Cross and Saley, *BASOR* 197 (1970): 44 n. 10, 46 with n. 24; and Röllig, *NESE* 2 (1974): 18, 22, 25, 28.

95. Cf. Gibson, *Textbook*, 3:80.

96. See Chapter 2, no. 19.

97. Israel, *OLP* 10 (1979): 145.

98. For a discussion of mimation and nunation in the Semitic languages, see Werner Diem, "Gedanken zur Frage der Mimation und Nunation in den semitischen Sprachen," *ZDMG* 125 (1975): 239–258.

99. Cf. Dion, "The Language Spoken in Ancient Samʾal," *JNES* 37 (1978): 117.

100. Friedrich and Röllig, *PPG*[2] §225b.

101. So, for example, Friedrich, "Zur Stellung des Jaudischen in der nordwestsemitischen Sprachgeschichte," in *Studies in Honor of Benno Landsberger . . . 1965*, Assyriological Studies, vol. 16 (Chicago: The University of Chicago Press, 1965), p. 425.

102. See Chapter 2, no. 19.

103. For the ending [ê], see Dion, "Notes d'épigraphie ammonite," *RB* 82 (1975): 32 n. 55. For [ī], see Cross, "Notes on the Ammonite Inscription from Tell Sīrān," *BASOR* 212 (1973): 15.

104. Burkhart Kienast, "Das Possessivsuffix der 3.m.sg. am pluralischen Nomen des Maskulinum im Südostaramäischen," *Münchener Studien zur Sprachwissenschaft* 10 (1957): 72.

105. See Chapter 2, no. 8.

106. Dion, *RB* 82 (1975): 26–27.

107. See p. 76, n. 278.

108. Segert, *Grammar*, §§36.46, 43.412.1.

109. Friedrich, *PPG* §33*b; idem, in *Studies . . . Landsberger*, p. 427; and Dion, *La langue*, p. 134. Cf. Rosenthal, "[Review of Dion, *La langue*]," *JBL* 95 (1976): 155.

110. See Segert, *ArOr* 29 (1961): 220; and Joshua Blau, "The Parallel Development of the Feminine Ending *-at* in Semitic Languages," *HUCA* 51 (1980): 21–22, for a complete discussion.

111. Cf. Israel, *Rivista biblica italiana* 27 (1979): 183.

112. Blau, *HUCA* 51 (1980): 17–28; and idem, "Hebrew and North West Semitic: Reflections on the Classification of the Semitic Languages," *Hebrew Annual Review* 2 (1978): 33–34.

113. Friedrich and Röllig, *PPG*² §231; and Harris, *Grammar*, p. 60.

114. For this plural, see below.

115. Kaufman, "[Review of Segert, *Grammatik*]," *BiOr* 34 (1977): 94.

116. Segert, *Grammatik*, §5.2.3.5.3. See already Barth, "Beiträge zur Pluralbildung des Semitischen," *ZDMG* 58 (1904): 443–444.

117. Hoftijzer, in *Aramaic Texts*, pp. 290–291.

118. Caquot and Lemaire, *Syria* 54 (1977): 196; Carlton (Hackett), "Studies," p. 40; McCarter, *BASOR* 239 (1980): 51; Levine, *JAOS* 101 (1981): 196; and Weippert and Weippert, *ZDPV* 98 (1982): 87–88.

119. McCarter, *BASOR* 239 (1980): 55

120. So, for example, Weippert and Weippert, *ZDPV* 98 (1982): 100 n. 123.

121. Theodor Nöldeke, *Mandäische Grammatik* (1875; reprint ed., Darmstadt: Wissenschaftliche Buchgesellschaft, 1964), §134; and idem, *Kurzgefasste syrische Grammatik*, 2nd ed. (1898; reprint ed., Darmstadt: Wissenschaftliche Buchgesellschaft, 1966), §79.

122. Degen, *Grammatik*, §33, Anm. Cf. Cross and Freedman, *EHO*, p. 25.

123. See Nöldeke, *Neue Beiträge zur semitischen Sprachwissenschaft* (Strassburg: Karl J. Trübner, 1910), pp. 150–151. Cf. Abou-Assaf et al., *La statue*, pp. 35–36, 47.

124. Cf. Chapter 2, no. 18a.

125. So Cooke, Gibson, and Dion. KAI and Dupont-Sommer interpreted it as a singular noun.

126. See, for example, Aramaic מרמת "rebellion" (Sf. III 22) in Chapter 2, no. 18a.

127. William F. Albright, "The Phoenician Inscriptions of the Tenth Century B.C. from Byblus," *JAOS* 67 (1947): 158 n. 48.

128. Cross and Freedman, *EHO*, p. 13 n. 7.

129. For these forms, see Chapter 2, no. 16, and below, no. 10b.

130. Friedrich and Röllig, *PPG*² §238 with n. 2; and Segert, *Grammar*, §51.24. Cf. Cross and Freedman, *EHO*, p. 13 n. 7.

131. Cf. Hoftijzer, "La nota accusativi ʾt en phénicien," *Le Muséon* 76 (1963): 195–200.

132. Segert, *Grammar*, §63.41.

133. Dion, *La langue*, p. 153.

134. So Friedrich, *PPG* §38*.

135. Cf. Cross, "Epigraphic Notes on the Ammān Citadel Inscription," *BASOR* 193 (1969): 18 n. 13.

136. Nöldeke, *Die Inschrift des Königs Mesa von Moab* (Kiel: Schwers'sche Buchhandlung, 1870), p. 33 n. 2; and William L. Moran, "[Review of Cross and Freedman, *EHO*]," *CBQ* 15 (1953): 366.

137. Cross and Freedman, *EHO*, p. 41.

138. Barth, *Pronominalbildung,* §11a.

139. See Friedrich and Röllig, *PPG*[2] §234.

140. There are no examples of a singular noun with first person singular suffix on an accusative.

141. Translation of Rosenthal, in *ANET*[3], p. 654.

142. Friedrich and Röllig, *PPG*[2] §234.

143. For additional examples, see Degen, *Grammatik,* §36.

144. Cyrus H. Gordon, *UT* §6.6.

145. Wolfram von Soden, *GAG* §42g with nn. 1, 2.

146. The form is vocalized as if it were nominative, yet in the inscription it is genitive. See also pp. 40, 71 n. 146 on the derivation of אדת "lady."

147. There are no masculine singular nouns + third person singular suffix in the Old Byblian texts. For these feminine forms, see no. 8 above, and Friedrich, "Kleinigkeiten zum Phönizischen, Punischen und Numidischen," *ZDMG* 114 (1964): 226.

148. Ginsberg, *JANES* 5 (1973): 142, where the suffix is treated as an anceps vowel.

149. Rosenthal, "[Review of Harris, *Grammar*]," *Or* 7 (1938): 172.

150. Cf. Ginsberg, *JANES* 5 (1973): 145.

151. Hoftijzer, *Le Muséon* 76 (1963): 196 n. 9 (who interpreted the suffix as the first person singular). See also Friedrich and Röllig, *PPG*[2] §234 (p. 109).

152. Rosenthal, *Or* 7 (1938): 172.

153. Segert, *Grammar,* §51.261.

154. See Chapter 2, no. 16.

155. Cross, *BASOR* 193 (1969): 19 with n. 15; and Raphael Kutscher, "A New Inscription from ʿAmman," *Qadmoniot* 5 (1972): 28 (in Hebrew).

156. See Cross and Freedman, *EHO*, pp. 35 with n. 2, 37 n. 7, for a discussion of the possible vocalizations. See also Chapter 2, no. 16.

157. So ibid., p. 47.

158. *B-L* §25r.

159. Cf. Freedman, "The Massoretic Text and the Qumran Scrolls: A Study in Orthography," *Textus* 2 (1962): 93 (tentatively); and Cross, *Canaanite Myth and Hebrew Epic* (Cambridge: Harvard University Press, 1973), p. 102 n. 40.

160. See Chapter 2, no. 16 with n. 272.

161. Naveh, *IEJ* 13 (1963): 84 with n. 20.

162. Idem, "A Hebrew Letter from the Seventh Century B.C.," *IEJ* 10 (1960): 133 n. 6; and Zevit, *Matres Lectionis*, pp. 21–22.

163. Cross, in *Near Eastern Archaeology,* p. 301; and idem, "Epigraphic Notes on Hebrew Documents of the Eighth–Sixth Centuries B.C.: II. The Murabbaʿât Papyrus and the Letter Found Near Yabneh-Yam," *BASOR* 165 (1962): 43 with n. 31.

164. See Chapter 2, no. 17.

165. So, for example, Torczyner, Albright, Cross and Saley, Rosenthal, Gaster, Röllig, and Caquot.

166. Friedrich and Röllig, *PPG*[2] §112. Cf. Charles R. Krahmalkov, "Observations on the Affixing of Possessive Pronouns in Punic," *RSO* 44 (1969): 181–186.

167. Cf. KAI 219:2, ‏ז.זי.ק̇רבן‏[   ].

168. So Kutscher, "Aramaic," in *Linguistics in South West Asia and North Africa,* Current Trends in Linguistics, vol. 6 (The Hague/Paris: Mouton, 1970), p. 350; and J. J. Koopmans, *Aramäische Chrestomathie,* 2 vols. (Leiden: Nederlands Instituut voor het Nabije Oosten, 1962), 1:21.

169. So Cross and Freedman, *EHO,* p. 22 n. 10; and Gibson, *Textbook,* 2:5.

170. Schaeder, *Iranische Beiträge I,* pp. 240–241; Fitzmyer, *The Aramaic Inscriptions of Sefîre,* Biblica et Orientalia, vol. 19 (Rome: Pontifical Biblical Institute, 1967), p. 73; and Kutscher, in *Linguistics in South West Asia,* p. 350.

171. Cf. Kutscher, *A History of Aramaic,* p. 25.

172. Hoftijzer, in *Aramaic Texts,* p. 287.

173. So, for example, Nöldeke, "Untersuchungen zur semitischen Grammatik," *ZDMG* 38 (1884): 420 n. 6; and Brockelmann, *GvG* 1:§105dα.

174. Brockelmann, *GvG* 1:§105dβ.

175. For this vocalization, see Krahmalkov, "Studies in Phoenician and Punic Grammar," *JSS* 15 (1970): 181–185.

176. Abou-Assaf et al., *La statue,* pp. 29, 48.

177. See above, p. 87.

178. See no. 10c, for the vocalization [hem] < *$hum(u)$.

179. See Krahmalkov, *RSO* 44 (1969): 181–186, for the connecting vowel [ō] in Phoenician and Punic.

180. This form is a dual, but the outcome is identical to that of the masculine plural.

181. So read by Cross, in *Near Eastern Archaeology,* pp. 301, 305 n. 11.

182. Zevit, *Matres Lectionis,* p. 28.

183. Brockelmann, *GvG* 1:§105eα.

184. The presence of the diphthong in the Hebrew form results from the southern provenience of all attested forms; the northern form would have been *[êkā].

185. See Brockelmann, *GvG* 1:§105e, for evidence.

186. Cf. Cross and Freedman, *EHO,* p. 15.

187. So Friedrich, in *Tell Halaf,* p. 77; and Degen, *NESE* 1 (1972): 55 (tentatively).

188. Kienast, *Münchener Studien zur Sprachwissenschaft* 10 (1957): 73–76.

189. Degen, *Grammatik,* §36 (end).

190. See p. 75 n. 253 for references.

191. See Chapter 2, no. 16.

192. Dion, *La langue,* p. 407 n. 45.

193. Idem, *RB* 82 (1975): 32 with n. 55.

194. With Horn, Puech and Rofé, and Fulco.

195. So, for example, Hackett, *Or* 53 (1984): 63.

196. The suffix is masculine, as most interpreters have agreed (Cooke, *NSI,* p. 13; Cross and Freedman, *EHO,* p. 41; and Segert, *ArOr* 29 [1961]: 259).

197. Naveh, *IEJ* 29 (1979): 136; and Greenfield, *JSS* 25 (1980): 250. Cf. Cross and Freedman, *EHO,* p. 38.

198. Cross and Freedman, *EHO,* pp. 46–47 with n. 11. For other opinions, see Ginsberg, "[Review of Diringer, *Le inscrizioni*]," *ArOr* 8 (1936): 146; and Gibson, *Textbook,* 1:3.

199. See Chapter 2, no. 7.

200. So, for example, Cross and Freedman, *EHO,* pp. 47, 68–69.

201. Lemaire, "Les inscriptions de Khirbet el-Qôm et l'Ashérah de YHWH," *RB* 84 (1977): 599, 601.

202. William G. Dever, "Iron Age Epigraphic Material from the Area of Khirbet el-Kôm," *HUCA* 40–41 (1969–1970): 159; and idem, "Inscriptions from Khirbet el-Kom," *Qadmoniot* 4 (1971): 91 (in Hebrew). See also Zevit, *Matres Lectionis,* pp. 17–18 n. 6.

203. See above, no. 6b.

204. Cf. Cross, in Carlton (Hackett), "Studies," pp. 172–173.

205. See above, no. 9d.

206. Chapter 2, no. 8.

207. For the phonetic variants, see Chapter 2, nos. 16, 17.

208. So, for example, Hayim Tawil, "A Note on the Aḥiram Inscription," *JANES* 3/1 (1970–1971): 34 (earlier literature on p. 34 n. 13). Others emended to שׁ(ב)תה "his abode" (Albright, *JAOS* 67 [1947]: 155 n. 19; Rosenthal, in *ANET³,* p. 661; Naveh, "[Review of Friedrich and Röllig, *PPG²*]," *JAOS* 93 [1973]: 589).

209. See above, no. 9b.

210. The stem is *G,* not *D* (see Rosenthal, *Or* 7 [1938]: 170–171).

211. See Krahmalkov, "The Object Pronouns of the Third Person of Phoenician and Punic," *RSF* 2 (1974): 39–43, esp. p. 42.

212. Cross, *BASOR* 193 (1969): 17.

213. Kutscher, *Qadmoniot* 5 (1972): 27.

214. For other readings, see Emile Puech and Alexander Rofé, "L'inscription de la citadelle d'Amman," *RB* 80 (1973): 536; Dion, *RB* 82 (1975): 29–30; and William J. Fulco, "The ʿAmmān Citadel Inscription: A New Collation," *BASOR* 230 (1978): 41.

215. See Chapter 4, no. 1b. Cf. Caquot and Lemaire, *Syria* 54 (1977): 204, 205.

216. See above, no. 9b and n. 156.

217. So Cross, *BASOR* 165 (1962): 44 with n. 40; and *KAI* 2: 201.

218. Cf. Gibson, *Textbook,* 1:30.

219. See Robert Hetzron, "Third person singular pronoun suffixes in Proto-Semitic," *Orientalia Suecana* 18 (1969): 101–127, esp. pp. 119–120.

220. See below, nos. 18a, 18b, 23d, 23e.

221. For this translation, see Ginsberg, *JANES* 5 (1973): 144 n. 55.

222. Puech and Rofé, *RB* 80 (1973): 536.

223. Cf. Carlton (Hackett), "Studies," pp. 148, 140 (on לישבם [II 13]).

224. Cooke, *NSI*, p. 12. See also Cross and Freedman, *EHO*, p. 41.

225. Maybe [nᵊtattīm] "I have given them"?

226. *GKC* §58.

227. Brockelmann, *GvG* 1:§249e. Cf. von Soden, "Die Zahlen 20–90 im Semitischen und der Status absolutus," *WZKM* 57 (1961): 24–28.

228. See already D. H. Müller, "Die altsemitischen Inschriften von Sendschirli," *WZKM* 7 (1893): 43.

229. See Dion, *La langue*, pp. 247–248.

230. For the comparative evidence, see Brockelmann, *GvG* 1:§249e.

231. While scholars have proposed different meanings for -פ, the contexts in which -פ occurs suggest the meaning "thus, therefore, as a consequence thereof," or the like. For example, Fitzmyer (*Sefîre*, p. 87) interpreted -פ in פהן תשמע as "but if you obey" (Sf. II B 4). Yet the context indicates that the conditions preceding this one are identical to the condition in II B 4; the difference is that the preceding conditions were focused on a third party, while that of II B 4 is a direct indictment on "you." In other words, the conditions of ll. 2–4 were the background for that of l. 4. The translation should be "thus (according to the aforesaid), if *you* obey." The other attestations of -פ in Old Aramaic also have the meaning "therefore, thus."

232. Glueck, "Ostraca from Elath," *BASOR* 82 (1941): 7–11. Cf. idem, in *Near Eastern Studies . . . Albright*, p. 230.

233. See Brockelmann, *GvG* 1:§108f; and Garbini, "Il tema pronominale *p* in semitico," *AION* 21 (1971): 245–248, for the distribution.

234. As read by Albright, "Postscript to Professor May's Article," *BASOR* 97 (1945): 26 with n. 1; and Cross, "Lachish Letter IV," *BASOR* 144 (1956): 24 with n. 3.

235. See Chapter 2, no. 8.

236. Cooke, *NSI*, p. 184.

237. Brockelmann, *GvG* 1:§253Ac; and Gordon, *UT* §12.4.

238. For the use of this particle, see Chapter 4, no. 12.

239. See, for example, Cooke, *NSI*, p. 170; Brockelmann, *GvG* 1:314–315 n. 1; and *KAI* 2:222.

240. van Selms, *BiOr* 32 (1975): 6.

241. For the vocalization of BH את, see Harris, *Development*, p. 43.

242. On the development, see Paul Haupt, "Über das assyrische Nominalpräfix *na*," *BA* 1 (1889): 19–20 n. 28. See also Brockelmann, *GvG* 1:§§106b–e.

243. Harris, *Development*, p. 43.

244. *KAI* 2:3.

245. Moran, *CBQ* 15 (1953): 365–366.

246. So, for example, Albright, *JAOS* 67 (1947): 159; and Friedrich and Röllig, *PPG²* §324.

247. See the new reading and translation by P. Kyle McCarter and Robert B. Coote, "The Spatula Inscription from Byblos," *BASOR* 212 (1973): 19.

248. So, for example, Cooke, *NSI,* p. 170 (probable interpretation); and *KAI* 2:222.

249. So, for example, Charles-F. Jean and J. Hoftijzer, *Dictionnaire des inscriptions sémitiques de l'ouest* (Leiden: E. J. Brill, 1965), p. 66. Cf. Paul Joüon, *Grammaire de l'hébreu biblique* (Rome: Pontifical Biblical Institute, 1923), §167l.

250. So, for example, William L. Reed and Fred V. Winnett, "A Fragment of an Early Moabite Inscription from Kerak," *BASOR* 172 (1963): 9; and Gibson, *Textbook,* 1:84.

251. Brockelmann, *GvG* 2:§419.

252. Carlton (Hackett), "Studies," p. 148. See also McCarter, *BASOR* 239 (1980): 52, 59 n. 4.

253. See *B-L* §65s; and Joüon, *Grammaire,* §93g, for discussions.

254. Ronald J. Williams, *Hebrew Syntax: An Outline,* 2nd ed. (Toronto/Buffalo: University of Toronto Press, 1976), §61; Gordon, *UT* §11.2; and Chapter 2, no. 18b.

255. Contrast, for example, Hoftijzer, in *Aramaic Texts,* pp. 186–187, with Carlton (Hackett), "Studies," p. 54.

256. Gordon, *UT* §11.1.

257. Albright, "An Aramaean Magical Text in Hebrew from the Seventh Century B.C.," *BASOR* 76 (1939): 9–10 with n. 36.

258. *KAI* 2:46; and Segert, *Grammar,* §57.4 (tentatively).

259. Cross and Saley, *BASOR* 197 (1970): 46 with nn. 29–30; and Röllig, *NESE* 2 (1974): 19, 25.

260. See Friedrich and Röllig, *PPG*² §318.3a, for the use of אל.

261. Abou-Assaf et al., *La statue,* p. 49.

262. The loss of precative *lamedh* may be attributable to the coexistence of a "short" imperfect. In a construction like יהוי, the meaning is clearly "let him be"; a prefixed *lamedh* would be redundant, as it is in להוי. In the western dialects, then, the competition between "short" imperfect and precative *lamedh* + "short" imperfect led to the loss of precative *lamedh*; in the East, the precative *lamedh* was preserved, with and without precative force.

263. See Eduard König, "Das *l*-Jaqtul im Semitischen," *ZDMG* 51 (1897): 330–337.

264. Kaufman, *The Akkadian Influences on Aramaic,* Assyriological Studies, vol. 19 (Chicago/London: The University of Chicago Press, 1974), pp. 124–126.

265. Brockelmann, *GvG* 1:§257Haε.

266. Cf. Abou-Assaf et al., *La statue,* pp. 37, 46.

267. The autograph of this text reads ה[-]/⌐ה⌐שׁתרי, not ה[שׁ]/ירתשׁר (*KAI* and Fitzmyer).

268. Rosenthal, in *ANET*³, p. 660 n. 10.

269. For a different opinion, see Degen, *Grammatik,* §§10, 11, 25.

270. J. Halévy, "Nouvel Examen des inscriptions de Zindjirli," *RS* 7 (1899): 345; Gibson, *Textbook,* 2:63; and Dion, *La langue,* p. 206.

271. Dion, *La langue,* pp. 108–109.

272. Cross, *BASOR* 193 (1969): 19 n. 16 (preferred alternative); Garbini, *Le lingue semitiche. Studi di storia linguistica* (Naples: Istituto orientale di Napoli, 1972), p. 105; and Fulco, *BASOR* 230 (1978): 42 (tentatively).

273. Dion, *RB* 82 (1975): 31.

274. So Hoftijzer, in *Aramaic Texts,* p. 292; Carlton (Hackett), "Studies," p. 100 (one possibility). Cf. Levine, *JAOS* 101 (1981): 201.

275. Hoftijzer, in *Aramaic Texts,* pp. 292, 293.

276. Carlton (Hackett), "Studies," pp. 144, 145. See also Naveh, *IEJ* 29 (1979): 136.

277. So Hoftijzer, in *Aramaic Texts,* pp. 228, 293; and Carlton (Hackett), "Studies," pp. 100, 145.

278. See below, no. 22b.

279. Examples cited in *B-L* §38f.

280. Brockelmann, *GvG* 1:§257Haβ.

281. Gotthelf Bergsträsser, *Einführung in die semitischen Sprachen* (1928; reprint ed., Darmstadt: Wissenschaftliche Buchgesellschaft, 1977), p. 66.

282. Translation of Cross, *BASOR* 193 (1969): 19 n. 16; and idem, "Ammonite Ostraca from Heshbon: Heshbon Ostraca IV–VIII," *AUSS* 13 (1975): 12 n. 34, although the verb is analyzed as Gt.

283. Krahmalkov, "An Ammonite Lyric Poem," *BASOR* 223 (1976): 57. Cf. William H. Shea, "The Siran Inscription: Amminadab's Drinking Song," *PEQ* 1978: 109.

284. So, for example, Dion, and Zayadine and Thompson.

285. Albright, "Some Comments on the ʿAmmân Citadel Inscription," *BASOR* 198 (1970): 39.

286. For the readings, see Fulco, *BASOR* 230 (1978): 39–41.

287. For this reading, see H. Van Dyke Parunak, "The Orthography of the Arad Ostraca," *BASOR* 230 (1978): 25, 27–28.

288. For comparative evidence, see Brockelmann, *GvG* 1:§257Hf.

289. Friedrich and Röllig, *PPG*[2] §146.

290. Garbini, "I dialetti del fenicio," *AION* 27 (1977): 286 n. 16; and P. Swiggers, "[Review of Segert, *Grammar*]," *Lingua* 50 (1980): 384–385.

291. Garbini, "Il causativo *hqtl* nel dialetto fenicio di Biblo," *AION* 24 (1974): 411–412.

292. Cross, "A Recently Published Phoenician Inscription of the Persian Period from Byblos," *IEJ* 29 (1979): 41.

293. So, for example, Degen, *Grammatik,* pp. 19 n. 76, 25, 68 n. 54, 70 n. 58. Cf. Fitzmyer, *Sefîre,* pp. 106, 157.

294. Cf. Naveh, *IEJ* 29 (1979): 135.

295. For the development of the prefix, see Harris, *Grammar,* p. 43; and idem, *Development,* p. 74.

296. See Lipiński, *RSF* 2 (1974): 54; and Röllig, *NESE* 2 (1974): 36.

297. See Brockelmann, *GvG* 1:§262e.

298. Cross and Freedman, *EHO*, p. 31.
299. Cf. ibid., p. 27.
300. See above, pp. 107–108.
301. Dion, *La langue*, pp. 55–59.
302. Brockelmann, *GvG* 1:§262e.
303. See Chapter 2, no. 19.
304. For the vocalization, see Chapter 2, no. 7.
305. Klaus Beyer, "[Review of Degen, *Grammatik*]," *ZDMG* 120 (1970): 200.
306. Dion, *La langue*, pp. 104–105.
307. See Chapter 2, no. 7.
308. See Chapter 2, no. 7.
309. Harris, *Development*, pp. 45–46.
310. See p. 77 n. 283.
311. Cf. Blau, *HUCA* 51 (1980): 17, 27.
312. Degen, "Die Präfixkonjugationen des Altaramäischen," in *XVII. Deutscher Orientalistentag . . . Würzburg. Vorträge*, ed. Wolfgang Voigt, ZDMG Supplementa, vol. 1, pt. 2 (Wiesbaden: Franz Steiner, 1969), pp. 701–706; and idem, *Grammatik*, §§49–50.
313. For the ending [awn], see idem, *Grammatik*, p. 77 n. 78; and no. 23e below.
314. See below, no. 18b.
315. The ending is [aw] since the verb is final weak. See no. 23e below.
316. Cf. Nöldeke, "Bemerkungen zu den aramäischen Inschriften von Sendschirli," *ZDMG* 47 (1893): 102; Halévy, "Les Deux Inscriptions hétéennes de Zindjîrlî," *RS* 1 (1893): 254; and Dion, *La langue*, pp. 184–186.
317. This form was once read יתלון, a *(h)ithpael* conjugation of **lwy* (for example, Cross and Freedman, *EHO*, p. 18). More recently, however, scholars have agreed on the reading יתלנן, from **lwn* (so *KAI* 2:33, etc.).
318. For the translation, see Segert, *Grammar*, §54.364.
319. Friedrich and Röllig, *PPG*² §§135, 261, 264. *Contra* Friedrich, "Der Schwund kurzer Endvokale im Nordwestsemitischen," *ZS* 1 (1922): 6 n. 2; and Harris, *Grammar*, pp. 40–41. Cf. also Segert, *Grammar*, §§64.51, 64.531.
320. Cf. Garbini, *L'aramaico antico*, pp. 268, 275.
321. In the Nerab inscriptions, all third person masc. plural imperfect verbs end in ן-. Yet since these verbs were volitive, it is not known whether the corresponding indicative verbs ended in **-ūn* or the identical **-ū*. See Rosenthal, *Die Sprache*, p. 59.
322. So read by Fulco, *BASOR* 230 (1978): 41.
323. See n. 315.
324. Hackett, *Or* 53 (1984): 62.
325. Cf. Kaufman, *BiOr* 34 (1977): 94.
326. Dion, *La langue*, pp. 192, 463 n. 3.
327. For comparative evidence, see Brockelmann, *GvG* 1:§260Cg.
328. Blau, *Hebrew Annual Review* 2 (1978): 37.
329. For comparative evidence, see Brockelmann, *GvG* 1:§263Bb.

330. See Chapter 2, nos. 17, 19; and Chapter 3, nos. 11a, 11b.

331. Compare, for example, the readings of Fitzmyer (*Sefîre*, p. 18) with those of *KAI* and Degen (*Grammatik*, p. 15). See also Chapter 4, no. 10.

332. See above, pp. 42–43.

333. See no. 23f below.

334. See Müller, *WZKM* 7 (1893): 122.

335. See above, nos. 11a and 11b.

336. Cf. Abou-Assaf et al., *La statue*, p. 31.

337. For a discussion of these forms, see Kaufman, "Reflections on the Assyrian-Aramaic Bilingual from Tell Fakhariyeh," *Maarav* 3 (1982): 151.

338. Rosenthal, *Die Sprache*, p. 61; and Garbini, "[Review of Degen, *Grammatik*]," *AION* 20 (1970): 277.

339. Cf. Segert, *Grammar*, §§54.142, 54.252.2; and Friedrich and Röllig, *PPG*[2] §140b.

340. Rosenthal, in *ANET*[3], p. 653 n. 1; and Lipiński, *RSF* 2 (1974): 45–47. Cf. Helmuth T. Bossert, "Die phönizisch-hethitischen Bilinguen vom Karatepe," *Oriens* 1 (1948): 178 (on ארוך), and Albrecht Goetze, "Cilicians," *JCS* 16 (1962): 53 n. 42.

341. So Nöldeke, *Mesa,* p. 15; Cooke, *NSI,* p. 13; and Samuel R. Driver, *Notes on the Hebrew Text and the Topography of the Books of Samuel,* 2nd ed. (Oxford: Oxford University Press, 1913), p. xcii.

342. Segert, *ArOr* 29 (1961): 226, 233.

343. P. Bar-Adon, "An Early Hebrew Inscription in a Judean Desert Cave," *IEJ* 25 (1975): 228, 229.

344. Brockelmann, *GvG* 1:§263Ac.

345. See above, n. 339.

346. The vocalization of the *G* passive participle in Ugaritic is uncertain. For a possible *$qatīl$ passive participle, see *Ugaritica V* 137:II:39′.40′.

347. Or possibly [yittib]. See F. Philippi, "Die Aussprache der semitischen Consonanten ו und י. Eine Abhandlung über die Natur dieser Laute," *ZDMG* 40 (1886): 653.

348. Ginsberg, "The Classification of the North-West Semitic Languages," in *Akten des vierundzwanzigsten internationalen Orientalisten-Kongresses . . . 1957,* ed. Herbert Franke (Wiesbaden: Franz Steiner, 1959), p. 257; and idem, "The Northwest Semitic Languages," in *Patriarchs,* ed. B. Mazar. The World History of the Jewish People, vol. 2 ([New Brunswick, N.J.]: Rutgers University Press, 1970), p. 119.

349. Ginsberg, in *Akten . . . 1957,* p. 257; and idem, in *Patriarchs,* p. 119.

350. Segert, *Grammatik,* §5.7.6.4.6. Cf. Fitzmyer, *Sefîre,* p. 105.

351. Harris, *Development,* p. 57 (with earlier literature).

352. See, similarly, the formation of the middle weak *D*-stem in Old Aramaic, no. 22b.

353. So Carlton (Hackett), "Studies," pp. 67–68, 146. See Chapter 4, no. 7a.

354. Cf. Hoftijzer, Caquot and Lemaire, McCarter, and Levine, who interpreted שם as "there."

355. Joüon, *Grammaire,* §80c.

356. See above, nn. 317–318.

357. On the *yodh,* see Brockelmann, *GvG* 1:§270Gg; and Rosenthal, *A Grammar of Biblical Aramaic,* Porta Linguarum Orientalium, New Series, vol. 5 (Wiesbaden: Otto Harrassowitz, 1974), §139.

358. So Degen, *Grammatik,* p. 76 n. 76; and Segert, *Grammatik,* §5.7.6.7.2.

359. See Fitzmyer, *Sefire,* pp. 86–87.

360. For survivals, see Brockelmann, *GvG* 1:§270Gg, Anm.

361. See above, n. 277.

362. Blau, *Hebrew Annual Review* 2 (1978): 37.

363. Gordon, *UT* §9.36.

364. Cf. Ginsberg, in *Akten . . . 1957,* p. 256; idem, in *Patriarchs,* pp. 103–104; and Blau, *Hebrew Annual Review* 2 (1978): 37.

365. Harris, *Grammar,* p. 45; and Friedrich and Röllig, *PPG*² §176a. For the ending *-t* in Punic, see Nöldeke, *ZDMG* 38 (1884): 417 with n. 4.

366. Friedrich and Röllig, *PPG*² §86a.

367. Ibid., p. 84 n. 1.

368. *B-L* §57r.

369. Blau, *Hebrew Annual Review* 2 (1978): 36 n. 28.

370. See Chapter 2, nos. 15 and 6.

371. See Chapter 2, no. 19.

372. Segert, *Grammatik,* §§5.7.8.2.2–3.

373. Dion, *La langue,* p. 59.

374. See n. 31.

375. See p. 74 n. 238.

376. See Chapter 2, no. 6.

377. Friedrich and Röllig, *PPG*² §176d.

378. So, for example, Carlton (Hackett), "Studies," pp. 78, 146; and Weippert and Weippert, *ZDPV* 98 (1982): 97.

379. Carlton (Hackett), "Studies," p. 78.

380. Cf. Brockelmann, *GvG* 1:§271Hbβ.

381. Hoftijzer, in *Aramaic Texts,* p. 292. See further the citations in Weippert and Weippert, *ZDPV* 98 (1982): 97.

382. In either case, however, it is difficult to reconcile the form of שתיו with that of ראו (I 5), unless the latter is an infinitive (see below, n. 410). See McCarter, *BASOR* 239 (1980): 55–56.

383. Lemaire, "Les ostraca paléo-hébreux des fouilles de l'Ophel," *Levant* 10 (1978): 159.

384. See no. 18b.

385. Friedrich and Röllig, *PPG*² §§135, 261, 264.

386. See, for example, Degen, in *XVII . . . Orientalistentag,* pp. 701–706. Cf. Segert, *Grammatik,* §5.6.5.2.3, for possible vocalizations.

387. The jussive and consecutive imperfect are derived from the selfsame **yaqtul.*

388. Greenfield, *JSS* 25 (1980): 251 (tentatively).

389. So Fitzmyer, McCarter, and others.

390. For the reading, see Hackett, *Or* 53 (1984): 59 n. 15.

391. Cf. Segert, *Grammar*, §54.464.3 (on Phoenician).

392. As read by Cross, in *Near Eastern Archaeology*, p. 301.

393. *B-L* §§57d–h.

394. See Karl Jaberg, *Aspects géographiques du langage*, Société de publications romanes et françaises, vol. 18 (Paris: Librairie E. Droz, 1936), p. 94.

395. Cf. Dion, *JNES* 37 (1978): 117.

396. Cf. nos. 18a and 18b.

397. The final *nun* did not appear in the early period. See no. 18b.

398. Brockelmann, *GvG* 1:§271He.

399. Caquot, "Une inscription araméenne d'époque assyrienne," in *Hommages à André Dupont-Sommer* (Paris: Adrien-Maisonneuve, 1971), pp. 9–16.

400. See Degen, *Grammatik*, p. 77 n. 78.

401. For the final *nun*, see no. 18b.

402. Cf. Carlton (Hackett), "Studies," pp. 137, 136.

403. See no. 23c.

404. Bergsträsser, *Hebräische Grammatik*, 2 vols. (Leipzig: F. C. W. Vogel, 1918–1929), 2:§30l. Cf. *B-L* §57c.

405. The presence or absence of *-n* is not significant for this purpose.

406. For example, *KAI* 2:246; and Segert, *Grammatik*, §5.7.8.5.1.

407. So, for example, Fitzmyer, *Sefire*, p. 40; and Degen, *Grammatik*, p. 78 with n. 82. Because of this formal difficulty, Fitzmyer and Degen preferred to interpret לחזיה as a *pael* inf. Yet this interpretation poses two problems. First, a *pael* conjugation of חזה does not occur in the Aramaic dialects; the oft-cited example of the *pael* of this root, מחזה in Nerab 2:5, is instead a contraction of the interrogative [mā] + participle [ḥāzi(h)], i.e. "what do (I) see?" (Cooke, *NSI*, p. 190; and Rosenthal, in *ANET*[3], p. 661). Second, if the infinitive were *pael*, the expected syntax of the infinitive + nominal accusative would be a construct chain, as for example ולאבדת אשמהם "and to destroy their name" (Sf. II B 7) and (*haphel*) ולהמתת ברי "and to kill my son" (Sf. III 11); instead of the expected *לחזית עדי, this proposed *pael* infinitive appears as לחזיה. לחזיה, then, cannot be a *pael* infinitive.

408. Nöldeke, *Mandäische Grammatik*, §191 (end).

409. Brockelmann, *GvG* 1:§198c; and Rosenthal, *Grammar*, §149.

410. Rosenthal, "Notes on the Third Aramaic Inscription from Sefire-Sûjîn," *BASOR* 158 (1960): 29 n. 6.

411. Degen, *Grammatik*, p. 78 with n. 81.

412. *Contra* Dion, *La langue*, p. 57, with literature cited on p. 392 nn. 19, 22.

413. While it is possible that *e* in *bunem* represents the vowel [ī], the masculine plural participles *dobrim* "saying" (Poen. 935) and *iusim* "going out" (Poen. 939) show *i* for [ī]. In view of these examples, the *e* in *bunem* indicates a significant difference from the regular masculine plural morpheme. *e* is a contraction from *ay.

414. See Chapter 2, no. 11.

415. Cross and Freedman, *EHO*, p. 26 (one possibility).

416. See, for example, Degen, *Grammatik*, §7 (p. 28).

417. See Chapter 2, no. 15; and Chapter 3, no. 23b.

418. Friedrich and Röllig, *PPG*[2] §174 (p. 83).

419. So O'Callaghan, Donner and Röllig, and others.

420. So Harris, *Grammar*, pp. 42 with n. 17, 45; Friedrich and Röllig, *PPG*[2] §174 (preferred alternative); Rosenthal, in *ANET*[3], p. 655 (translation only); and Segert, *Grammar*, §54.351 (cf. ibid., §64.323).

421. So Cross and Freedman, *EHO*, p. 18 (with earlier literature, p. 18 nn. 39–40).

422. Ginsberg, in *Akten . . . 1957*, p. 257; and idem, in *Patriarchs*, p. 119. Cf. already Franz Praetorius, "Zur hebräischen und aramäischen Grammatik," *ZDMG* 55 (1901): 365.

423. Cf. Brockelmann, *GvG* 1:§271Hd; and Dion, *La langue*, pp. 327–328.

424. Ginsberg, in *Akten . . . 1957*, p. 257; idem, in *Patriarchs*, pp. 119, 270 n. 9; and Dion, *La langue*, pp. 220–221.

425. *B-L* §57k'.

426. So, for example, Goetze, "The So-Called Intensive of the Semitic Languages," *JAOS* 62 (1942): 1 n. 13; and Rudolph Meyer, *Hebräische Grammatik*, 3rd ed. 4 vols. (Berlin: Walter de Gruyter & Co., 1966–1972), 2:§66.3a.

427. Ginsberg, in *Akten . . . 1957*, p. 257; and idem, in *Patriarchs*, pp. 119, 270 n. 9.

428. So, for example, *B-L* §45f; and Joseph L. Malone, "A Hebrew Flip-Flop Rule and Its Historical Origins," *Lingua* 30 (1972): 422–448, esp. pp. 436–437.

429. For the prefix, see Richard C. Steiner, "*Yuqaṭṭil, Yaqaṭṭil*, or *Yiqaṭṭil*: D-Stem Prefix-Vowels and a Constraint on Reduction in Hebrew and Aramaic," *JAOS* 100 (1980): 513–518.

430. Carlton (Hackett), "Studies," pp. 73, 147.

431. So Hoftijzer, in *Aramaic Texts*, p. 292. Cf. McCarter, *BASOR* 239 (1980): 54–55.

432. Hoftijzer, in *Aramaic Texts*, p. 293.

433. See above under no. 23d.

434. See, for example, Cooke, *NSI*, p. 8; Cross and Freedman, *EHO*, p. 37; and Gibson, *Textbook*, 1:78.

435. Moran, *CBQ* 15 (1953): 366. Cf. Segert, *ArOr* 29 (1961): 227.

436. For this assimilation, see Brockelmann, *GvG* 1:§§40f, 70.

437. So Nöldeke, "Die aramäischen Papyri von Assuan," *ZA* 20 (1907): 142 with n. 1; Hans Bauer and Pontus Leander, *Grammatik des Biblisch-Aramäischen* (Halle an der Saale: Max Niemeyer, 1927), §46b; and Rosenthal, *Grammar*, §169. Cf. Degen, *Grammatik*, §64.3.

438. Blau, "Short Philological Notes on the Inscription of Mešaʿ," *Maarav* 2 (1980): 145.

439. Harris, *Development*, p. 71.

440. Friedrich and Röllig, *PPG*² §163. Cf. Caquot, *JANES* 5 (1973): 49 n. 14.

441. Cross and Saley, *BASOR* 197 (1970): 46 n. 23a. Cf. Röllig, *NESE* 2 (1974): 24; and Chapter 4, no. 7a.

442. See Harris, *Development,* pp. 33, 71.

443. Cf. the imperfect forms יהלך (Ps. 58:9, etc.), אהלך (Job 16:22), etc. See *GKC* §69x.

444. Brockelmann, *GvG* 1:§258A.

445. Cf. Blau, *Hebrew Annual Review* 2 (1978): 37.

446. Cf. idem, *Maarav* 2 (1980): 145–146.

447. See Harris, *Development,* pp. 8–9.

448. See Chapter 5 for the position of Sfire-Aramaic within the Aramaic dialects.

449. Cf. Segert, "Noch zu den assimilierenden Verba im Hebräischen," *ArOr* 24 (1956): 133–134.

450. Anson F. Rainey, "Three Additional Hebrew Ostraca from Tel Arad," *Tel Aviv* 4 (1977): 101.

CHAPTER FOUR

SYNTAX

1a.   The pronoun: The proleptic suffix.[1]

BYBLIAN: No evidence.

STANDARD PHOENICIAN: The proleptic suffix appeared regularly with the infinitive construct followed by a noun; the suffix was therefore subjective and redundant.[2] The suffix is found in לשבתנם דננים "so that they may dwell, (i.e.) the Danunians" (Karatepe A I 17/18) and לתתי בעל כרנתריש "so that he may give, (i.e.) Baal-*Krntryš*" (Karatepe A III 4). Cf. similarly later standard Phoenician, as for example למלכי מלך אשמנעזר "of his rule, (i.e. of) king Eshmunazor" (Eshmunazor 1).[3]

ARAMAIC: There was no proleptic suffix in Old Aramaic. In later eastern Aramaic dialects, the proleptic suffix is a characteristic feature.[4] A genitive particle, however, frequently separates the two members of the phrase, as in biblical Aramaic שרשוהי די אילנא "the roots of the tree" (Dan. 4:23).[5]

SAMALIAN: There does not appear to have been a proleptic suffix in Samalian.

AMMONITE: No evidence.

DEIR ALLA: A proleptic suffix does not seem to appear in the Deir Alla dialect. The decipherable material, however, is meager.

MOABITE: There was no proleptic suffix in Moabite, according to the present evidence.[6]

EDOMITE: No evidence.

HEBREW: Evidence uncertain. Skehan[7] has suggested that the proleptic suffix appeared in the Gezer Calendar, as for example in ירחו אסף "the two months of it, (i.e. of) gathering" (l. 1), ירחו זרע "the two months of it, (i.e. of) sowing" (ll. 1/2), etc. Similarly, Cross[8] identified the proleptic suffix in Arad 17:2, ביתה.אלישב "his house, (i.e. of) Elyašab." Finally, a proleptic suffix may have appeared in Beit Lei A 2, לו לאלהי ירשלם "his, (of) the God of Jerusalem."[9]

Yet each example is ambiguous. The passages cited in the Gezer Calendar are not clearly understood to date and therefore are not usable evidence. The passage in Arad 17 does not contain a proleptic suffix, but rather the directive *he* followed by an unbound name.[10] And the passage in Beit Lei A 2 may be read differently, as Cross[11] has done; this new reading removes the proleptic suffix altogether. Thus, there is no certain evidence for the proleptic suffix in epigraphic Hebrew.

The proleptic suffix is used throughout the West Semitic languages, though in different constructions, to anticipate a following noun.[12] In first-millennium NWS, only standard Phoenician showed a regular use of the proleptic suffix; it appeared only on infinitive constructs whose following noun was subjective. The other dialects apparently did not employ the proleptic suffix. On the one hand, then, this syntactic feature was unique to standard Phoenician among the first-millennium NWS dialects. On the other hand, standard Phoenician usage reflects common West Semitic syntax.

1b.   The form of the direct object pronoun of the finite verb (objective suffix vs. *nota accusativi* + suffix).

PHOENICIAN: The direct object pronoun always took the form of objective suffixes, as in פעלן "he made me" (Karatepe A I 3.12), עננתם "I subdued them" (Karatepe A I 20), שתי "I made him" (Kilamu 11.11), etc.

ARAMAIC: The direct object pronoun generally took the form of objective suffixes, as in בכוני "they bewailed me" (Nerab 2:5/6),

אחצלך "I will rescue you" (Zkr A 14), תשריה "may you release him" (Sf. III 18), היטבתה "I made it better" (Br-Rkb 1:12), etc. The author could give the direct object pronoun added emphasis by putting the object in the form of the *nota accusativi* אית + possessive suffix, as in הן אין[ת]י יקתלן "if it is me they kill"[13] (Sf. III 11) and תכה אי(ת)ה "you slay him" (Sf. III 13).[14]

SAMALIAN: The direct object pronoun was usually the objective suffix, as in הושבני "he made me sit" (P 19), בכיה "they bewailed him" (P 17), תהרגה "you will kill him" (H 33), and היטבה "he made it better" (P 9). This pronoun also took the form of the *nota accusativi* ות[15] + possessive suffix, as in ויקם.ותה "and he will erect it" (H 28). The semantic difference between these two notations of the direct object pronoun is unknown.

AMMONITE: No evidence. The example of objective suffixes recognized by Cross,[16] Kutscher,[17] and Puech and Rofé[18] are uncertain since the readings of these texts are difficult.[19]

DEIR ALLA: The direct object pronoun was an objective suffix in the extant texts, as in אחוכם "I shall tell you" (I 5) and תשנאן "you hate him"[20] (II 10).

MOABITE: The direct object pronoun was the objective suffix in the extant texts, as in ויחלפה "and he succeeded him" (Mesha 6), ויגרשה "and he expelled him" (Mesha 19), השעני "he saved me" (Mesha 4), ואחזה "and I captured it" (Mesha 11), etc.

EDOMITE: No evidence.

HEBREW: The direct object pronoun took two forms in epigraphic Hebrew. It was either an objective suffix, as for example ברכתך "I bless you" (Arad 16:2/3, 21:2, 40:3), והבקידם "and he will hand them over" (Arad 24:14/15), צותני "you commanded me" (Arad 18:7/8), ידעתה "you know it"[21] (Lach. 2:6, 3:8; Arad 40:9), etc. Alternatively, the direct object pronoun appeared as the *nota accusativi* את + pronominal suffix, as for example in ברכת.אתכם "I bless you" (Ajrud[22]), ושלחתם.אתם "and you will send them" (Arad 24:13 [parallel to והבקידם]), and קראתי.אתה "I read it" (Lach. 3:12, 12:4 [partially restored]). There appears to have been no difference, either syntactically[23] or semantically, between these two forms of the direct object pronoun.

As in all the Semitic languages,[24] the direct object pronoun took the form of either a suffixed objective pronoun or the *nota accusativi* + pronominal suffix. On the one hand, Phoenician, Moabite, and probably the Deir Alla dialect appear to have used the objective suffix alone; it is uncertain, however, whether the *nota accusativi* + suffix was used in these dialects but was not preserved in the extant texts. On the other hand, Old Aramaic, Samalian, and Hebrew texts show both the objective suffix and *nota accusativi* + suffix to signify this direct object.

Although the objective suffix and *nota accusativi* + suffix functioned as the direct object pronoun in Old Aramaic, Samalian, and Hebrew, these dialects do not necessarily exhibit identical usage. In Old Aramaic, as in Akkadian, Ugaritic, Ethiopic, and Arabic, the *nota accusativi* + suffix lent added emphasis to the direct object pronoun. In Hebrew, however, the emphatic nature of the *nota accusativi* + suffix had weakened considerably; the objective suffix and *nota accusativi* + suffix appear to have been interchangeable. Finally, the evidence for the distribution of the two forms in Samalian is too meager to admit any conclusions. The use of the *nota accusativi* + suffix, then, varied considerably within these dialects.

2. The demonstrative pronoun: The agreement or nonagreement between a noun and appositional demonstrative with respect to determination.[25]

BYBLIAN: Undetermined noun + demonstrative pronoun, as in ארן.זן "this coffin" (Ahirom 2).[26] The other example of a noun + appositional demonstrative in Old Byblian—כל.מפלת.הבתם אל "all the ruins of these houses" (Yehimilk 2/3)—may have been subject to different syntactic rules.[27]

STANDARD PHOENICIAN: Determined noun + simple demonstrative pronoun, as in הספר ז "this inscription" (Kilamu 15), הקרת ז "this city" (Karatepe A II 9.17, etc.), השער ז "this gate" (Karatepe A III 15.18), etc. In ועם ז "and this people" (Karatepe A III 7/8, C IV 7), however, the definite article syncopated between short vowels;[28] it does not contradict the general Phoenician rule that the demonstrative pronoun was preceded by a determined noun.

ARAMAIC: Determined noun + demonstrative pronoun, as in נצבא.זנה "this stele" (Zkr B 14.18.19; Sf. I C 17), ביתא.זנה "this house" (Br-Rkb 1:20), דמותא.זאת "this image" (Fekh. 15), etc.

SAMALIAN: "Undetermined" noun + demonstrative pronoun, as in נצב.זן "this stele" (H 1; P 1.20), אמרת.אל "these words" (H 29), etc.[29] The absence of a defined noun in this construction is not significant since Samalian had no definite article.[30] This Samalian construction, therefore, differed from parallel Old Byblian constructions since Old Byblian had a definite article but did not employ it in this construction.

AMMONITE: No evidence.

DEIR ALLA: Evidence uncertain. If the reading of I 2, proposed by Caquot and Lemaire[31] and McCarter[32] is correct, the syntax of כמל[י]א.אל "according to these words" would be determined noun + simple demonstrative pronoun. Yet the reading and interpretation of this passage are unclear.[33]

MOABITE: Determined noun + simple demonstrative pronoun, as in הבמת.זאת "this highplace" (Mesha 3).

EDOMITE: No evidence.

HEBREW: Determined noun + definite article + demonstrative pronoun, as in העת הזה "this season" (Lach. 6:2) and החדר.הזה "this room" (el-Qom 1:3). The definite article modifying the noun preceding the demonstrative was transferred to the demonstrative, on analogy with the model of the determined noun + determined adjective.[34] Thus, since "the good house" was הב(י)ת הטב, so too "this house" became ה.ב(י)ת ה-זה. Cf. קצרי זה "this harvest of mine" (Yavneh-Yam 1:9), in which the transference could not have taken place.

In the early period, however, Hebrew may have resembled Old Byblian if the reading בת ז{.}ה "this house/*bath*" (Hazor 3[35]) is correct. The analogical form הזה, then, would have developed between the mid-ninth and mid-eighth centuries B.C.E.

Three forms of the noun + demonstrative appeared in the first-millennium NWS dialects. An undetermined noun may have been followed by a simple demonstrative pronoun, as in Old Byblian, early Hebrew (?), and Samalian; in Samalian, the absence of determination is meaningless since the dialect had no definite article. In standard Phoenician, Aramaic, Moabite, and possibly the Deir Alla dialect, a definite article appeared before the modified noun; since the noun was determined by construction, the definite article was, strictly speaking, redundant.[36] The appearance of the article in comparable Arabic constructions suggests a common West Semitic development.[37] Finally, in Hebrew, a determined noun was followed by a demonstrative with prefixed definite article; this construction was an inner-Hebrew analogical formation.

3a.   The noun: The periphrastic genitive (nonconstruct state).[38]

BYBLIAN: No evidence.

STANDARD PHOENICIAN: There were two forms of the periphrastic genitive in standard Phoenician. In one, the relative particle was followed by the dative ל + PN, as in בעל.צמד.אש.לגבר "Baal-Ṣamad who (belongs) to Gabbar" (Kilamu 15) and בעל חמן.אש.לבמה "Baal-Ḥamman who (belongs) to *Bmh*" (Kilamu 16).[39] The other periphrastic genitive had a special genitive particle ש, as in the eighth-century seal חתם שצרי "the seal of *Ṣry*."[40] This use of a special genitive particle foreshadows the later Punic distinction between the relative אש and the genitive ש.[41]

ARAMAIC: The relative זי functioned as a genitive particle at Tell Fekheriyeh (e.g., דמותא.זי.הדיסעי "the image of *Hdysʿy*" [l. 1] and שבט.זי.נירגל "the scourge of Nergal" [l. 23]), Tell Halaf (e.g., . . . שערן זי אלמלך "grain of *ʾlmlk*" [Ost. 3 Obv. 1/2]), Palestine (זי מלך בבל "of the king of Babylon" [Adon 4][42]), and possibly at Deir Alla (זישרעא "of *Ṣrʿ*" [Clay Text 1][43]). All other examples of a genitive זי are dubious.[44] Further, the existence of a genitive ש has been conclusively disproven by Kaufman.[45]

SAMALIAN: There are no examples of a periphrastic genitive in Samalian.[46]

AMMONITE: No evidence.

DEIR ALLA: No evidence. For genitive זי in Clay Text 1, see above under Aramaic.

MOABITE: No evidence.

EDOMITE: No evidence.

HEBREW: Like BH,[47] a periphrastic genitive occurred in the relative particle + ל + proper name, for example [הו]אשר ⸢ל⸣אדן. גדי "which (belongs) to A. G." (Arad 71:2/3). If Naveh's reading[48] of Beit Lei A 1/2 is correct—הרי יהד לו לאלהי ירשלם "the mountains of Judah are his, the God of Jerusalem's"—the periphrastic genitive may have appeared without the relative particle. Admittedly, the reading and syntax of the inscription, as interpreted by Naveh, are difficult.[49]

According to the available evidence, the periphrastic genitive assumed three forms in the first-millennium NWS dialects. The relative particle functioned as a genitive particle in a few Old Aramaic dialects. The relative particle + dative preposition served this function in standard Phoenician and Hebrew; in Hebrew, the relative may even have been optional. Finally, a special genitive particle appeared only in standard Phoenician. Each of these forms of the periphrastic genitive appears in other Semitic languages,[50] and within NWS they probably developed independently or by mutual contact.

3b. The status of the noun before a relative particle/pronoun.[51]

BYBLIAN: Undetermined, as in ז. ארן "the coffin which" (Ahirom 1), ז.בת. "the house which" (Yehimilk 1), ז.קר. "the wall which" (Shiptibaal 1), etc.[52] In later Byblian texts, however, the nominal antecedent was determined, as in העפת חרץ אש "the golden bird (?) which" (Yehawmilk 5), etc.

STANDARD PHOENICIAN: The evidence is ambiguous. No definite article appeared in the nominal antecedent, but this absence does not necessarily imply that the nominal antecedent was undetermined. In עבד בעל אש "the servant of Baal, whom" (Karatepe A I 1/2) and פי.תם.אש.חורן.[א]שת "the wife of Hawron, whose voice (?) is pure" (Arsl.T. 1:16), the nominal antecedent of the relative clause was definite because עבד and [א]שת were bound to a proper name; a definite article would not appear in such a construction.[53] In ועם ז אש "and this people who" (Karatepe A III 7/8, C IV 7) and וזבח אש "and the sacrifice which" (Karatepe C IV 2), the absence of the definite article is attributable to the regular syncope of intervocalic *he*.[54] Nonetheless, the phrase ועץ אנך ארצת עזת . . . אש "and I subdued powerful countries which" (Karatepe A I 18/19) suggests that the nominal antecedent of a relative clause need not have had a definite article. Whether the nominal antecedent in standard Phoenician was determined by construction or by a definite article is as yet unknown.[55]

ARAMAIC: Determined, as in נצבא.זי "the stele which" (Br-Hdd 1; Zkr A 1), etc. The definite article is missing, however, in ביום זי "on the day that" (Sf. I B 31, C 20) and שבט.זי.נירגל "the scourge of Nergal" (Fekh. 23). The significance of these deviant constructions in Aramaic is unknown at present.[56]

SAMALIAN: "Undetermined," as in ז סמר "the *smr* which" (Kilamu Scept. 1).[57]

AMMONITE: No evidence.

DEIR ALLA: No evidence.

MOABITE: The evidence is ambiguous. The phrase בקרן אשר ''in (the) cities which'' (Mesha 29)[58] may conceal a definite article since, due to Moabite phonetic rules, the definite article *he* syncopated after the preposition *beth*.[59] Additional evidence is needed to resolve the question of the status of the noun.

EDOMITE: No evidence.

HEBREW: The nominal antecedent of the relative clause was either undefined (as for example in דבר.אשר ''something which'' [Lach. 2:6]) or defined (for example האדם אשר ''the man who'' [Silwan B 2] and את הרעה.אש[ר] ''the evil thing which'' [Arad 40:15]). Both epigraphic and biblical[60] Hebrew texts indicate that the presence or absence of the definite article was conditioned by the sense the author wished to convey, not by the construction alone.

In NWS, the nominal antecedent of a relative clause was either determined or undetermined. In Old Aramaic it was determined in every clause but two (Sf. I B 31 = I C 20; Fekh. 23); determination was demanded by the relative construction itself.[61] In Byblian, and twice in Old Aramaic, the nominal antecedent was undetermined. It is unclear, however, whether the noun was absolute or bound to the relative particle.[62] Finally, in Hebrew and (possibly) standard Phoenician, the presence or absence of a determined nominal antecedent was demanded not by mere construction, but by sense. The dialectal status of Moabite, in this respect, is unknown.

4a. Negations: The negation of the finite verb (nonprohibition).

BYBLIAN: No evidence from the early period. In a later Byblian text, however, the negative אבל < *ʾi + *bal[63] appeared, followed by an imperfect (Yehawmilk 13).

STANDARD PHOENICIAN: בל negated perfects[64] (Kilamu 2.3, etc.; Karatepe A I 19, II 16, etc.) and imperfects (Arsl.T. 1:6.8), as well as nouns (Karatepe A I 15).

ARAMAIC: ל- (Sf. I A 28.28, B 21, etc.; Nerab 2:6, etc.).

SAMALIAN: No evidence.

AMMONITE: No evidence.

DEIR ALLA: ל- (I 3 [?]; II 7.7.9.9).

MOABITE: No evidence.

EDOMITE: No evidence.

HEBREW: לא (Lach. 2:6, 3:8, etc.; Yavneh-Yam 1:12.14; etc.).

The scanty evidence of the negative of finite verbs in the first-millennium NWS dialects reflects a twofold dialectal division. The majority of dialects—Aramaic, Deir Alla, and Hebrew—used (א)ל[65] to negate finite verbs. Phoenician dialects, however, adopted different negatives—בל in standard Phoenician and אבל* in Byblian. While most Semitic languages use *lā in this function, other negations appear as well.[66] Each NWS negation, in fact, finds a counterpart in other languages in this usage.

4b. The negation of the participle.

BYBLIAN: No evidence.

STANDARD PHOENICIAN: In an early fifth-century text, אי negates the participle (Eshmunazor 5).[67] Whether אי negated participles in the early period, however, cannot be determined with any certainty.

ARAMAIC: ל-, as in Sf. II C 8.

SAMALIAN: No evidence.

AMMONITE: No evidence.

DEIR ALLA: No evidence.

MOABITE: No evidence.

EDOMITE: No evidence.

HEBREW: אין, in the construction אין + subjective suffix + participle, as in אינ[נו.יכלם.לשלח] "we are not able to send" (Arad 40:13/14) and אינ[נ]י.שלח "I cannot send" (Lach. 4:7/8). The construction is similarly found in BH.[68] No example of a simple negated participle is attested in the epigraphic corpus.

According to the scanty evidence, the NWS dialects did not negate participles uniformly. In Aramaic, the particle *lā was used. In standard Phoenician, it was אי (cf. Eth. [ʾī] "not" and Akk. aylê "may . . . not"). In Hebrew, the term for nonexistence, אין, served this function. This distribution suggests an independent syntactic usage in each dialect.[69]

4c.   The position of the term for nonexistence in the clause.

PHOENICIAN: No evidence.

ARAMAIC: Postpositive, as in ובי.טב.לישה "and a good house did not exist" (Br-Rkb 1:15/16). The term for nonexistence, with resumptive suffix, followed the subject of the sentence.

SAMALIAN: No evidence.

AMMONITE: No evidence.

DEIR ALLA: No evidence.

MOABITE: Postpositive, as in ובר.אן.בקרב.הקר "and a cistern did not exist in the city" (Mesha 24). Like the example from Br-Rkb 1:15/16, the term for nonexistence followed the subject.

EDOMITE: No evidence.

HEBREW: The term for nonexistence was always first in the clause, as for example אין פה כסף.וזהב "there is no silver or gold here" (Silwan B 1), אין.שם.אדם "there is no one there" (Lach. 4:5/6), and [אינ]ננו.יכלם.לשלח "we are not able to send" (Arad 40:13/14). It is possible, however, that the term for nonexistence appeared in alternative positions in epigraphic Hebrew texts which have not yet been discovered. In the Masoretic text, the term usually appears in initial position, although different positions are also possible, and prevalent.[70] The unanimity in the epigraphic Hebrew corpus, then, may be due to the small sample afforded by the texts.

According to the available evidence, the position of the term for nonexistence in NWS was either initial or postpositive. In Old Aramaic and Moabite, the term for nonexistence was postpositive; it immediately followed the clausal subject. In Hebrew, the term was always in initial position. Perhaps these different word orders reflect different grammatical conceptions of the term for nonexistence. It was treated as a copula, nominal element, or negative particle.

5.   The preposition: The repetition or nonrepetition of coordinated prepositions.

BYBLIAN: The only example of coordinated nouns in the extant Old Byblian texts is the special case of proper noun + appositional noun. In these cases, the preposition was not repeated before each noun, as for example לאחרם.אבה "for Ahirom, his father" (Ahirom 1) and לבעלת גבל.אדתו "for Mistress-of-Byblos, his lady" (Shiptibaal 3/4; Elibaal 2 [partially restored]). It is unclear, however, whether these examples are representative of Byblian syntax. At least in biblical Hebrew,[71] when a title precedes a proper name, the preposition is repeated, although it is not repeated when the title follows the proper name. Since, in the Byblian examples, the title followed the proper name, a coordination of prepositions would not be expected.[72]

STANDARD PHOENICIAN: The repetition of prepositions appears to have been the rule, as for example in בצדקי ובחכמתי ובנעם לבי "because of my righteousness and because of my wisdom and because of my peace of mind" (Karatepe A I 12/13), לדננים ולכל עמק אדן "for the Danunians and for the entire Adana plain" (Karatepe A II 8/9), and בשנאת וברע "because of hatred or because of evil" (Karatepe A III 17). See also Karatepe A II 11/12.12–14, III 10/11 = C IV 11/12, A III 19-IV 1. Cf. Kilamu 11/12.

Although each coordinated noun had a prefixed preposition in this dialect, there were two irregularities. First, the repetition of the preposition may have been optional. For example, in Karatepe A I 14, במקמם באש "in the places where," the preposition was repeated, whereas in Karatepe A II 3, במקמם אש "in the places which," it was not. Cf. similarly Karatepe C IV 12, בעבר בעל ובעבר אלם "because of Baal and because of the gods" (cf. Karatepe A II 11/12), in contrast to Karatepe A I 8, II 6, III 11, בעבר בעל ואלם "because of Baal and the gods." Clearly, the repetition of prepositions may have been determined by the stylistic preferences of the author.

The second irregularity appears also in other Canaanite dialects; the preposition was not repeated if a proper name preceded a title, as in לעפתא.אלת ססם "for ʿptʾ, (the) goddess of Ssm" (Arsl.T. 1:1/2). This particular nonrepetition of prepositions tallies with both Byblian and biblical Hebrew.

ARAMAIC: A preposition stood before each nominal unit, regardless of whether this unit was a single noun.[73] For example, the preposition was repeated in בארק ובשמין "on earth and in heaven" (Sf. I A 26; cf. l. 29) and מן בתיהם ומן יומיהם "as to their houses and as to their days" (Sf. II C 16/17; cf. I C 15/16). When the unit was a pair of nouns, the preposition stood before each pair, as for example in וקדם מרדך וזרפנת . . . . וקדם נרגל ולץ וקדם שמש ונר "and before

Marduk and Zerpanit . . . and before Nergal and *Lṣ* and before
Šamaš and *Nr*" (Sf. I A 8/9). When the unit was a combination of
single nouns and nominal pairs, the preposition stood before each
nominal unit, as for example ל[ברגאי]ה ולברה ולבר ברה ולעקרה "to Bar-
Ga'yah and to his son and to his grandson and to his offspring" (Sf.
III 25). When the nominal unit was even longer, a preposition ar-
ticulated each unit, as for example ועם ארם כלה ועם מצר ועם בנוה זי יסקן
באשר[ה] ו[עם מלכי] כל עלי ארם ותחתה ועם כל עלל בית מלך "and with all
Aram and with *Mṣr* and with his sons who will arise after him and
with the kings of all upper and lower Aram and with all who enter
the royal house" (Sf. I A 5/6). The preposition, then, stood before
each coordinated nominal unit.

Since each different nominal unit had a coordinating preposition, appositional modifiers were not treated as independent nominal
units but as adjuncts to the governing noun; one preposition governed
the entire unit. So, for example, לאבהי.מלכי.שמאל "for my fathers,
the kings of Samal" (Br-Rkb 1:16/17), עם מתעאל בר עתרסמך מלך [ארפד]
"with Matti'el, the son of Attarsamak, the king of Arpad" (Sf.
I A 1), למראן.חזאל "for our lord, Haza'el" (Haza'el), and אל מרא
מלכן פרעה "to the lord of kings, Pharaoh" (Adon 1). The only deviation
from this syntactic pattern is in Br-Hdd 3/4, למראה למלקרת "for his
lord, Melqart," in which *lamedh* appeared before both parts of the
nominal unit; the second *lamedh* appeared on analogy with the first
so that מלקרת was not treated as an appositional modifier to מראה.

SAMALIAN: The preposition was repeated before each noun in
a series of coordinated nouns, as in שי.להדד.ולאל.ולרכבאל.ולשמש "as
a gift for Hadad, and for El, and for Rakab-El, and for Šamaš" (H
18), בחכמתה.ובצדקה "because of his wisdom and because of his righteousness" (P 11), and קדם.אלהי.וקדם.אנש "before the gods and before
man" (P 23). Cf. similarly H 26.27/28 and 32/33.[74] The preposition
was also repeated before a title and an appositional modifier, as in
שם . . . לאבה.לפנמו "he erected for his father, Panammu" (P 1; cf.
l. 20 [partially restored]). The appositional element was therefore
treated as a separate unit and was preceded by a coordinating preposition.

AMMONITE: The one example in Sir. 7/8 indicates that coordinated nouns had a preposition before each unit, thus ביומת רבם ובשנת
רחקת "for many days and for distant years."

DEIR ALLA: The evidence is uncertain. The only instance where
a coordinating preposition could have been used is in ויאמרו.

בר בער.[בלעם]ל "and they said to Balaam, the son of Beor" (I 2; cf. l. 4). Yet the absence of a second preposition, coordinating the proper name and appositional patronymic, is not dialectally significant since the preposition is not repeated in the other NWS dialects which exhibit the sequence proper name + title/patronymic.[75] Whether the coordinating preposition appeared in the Deir Alla dialect is, at present, unknown.

MOABITE: The preposition was repeated before each coordinated noun, as for example וארא.בה.ובבתה "and I saw (defeat) over him and over his house" (Mesha 7), רית.לכמש.ולמאב "a spectacle (?) to Kemosh and to Moab" (Mesha 12), and בקרב.הקר.בקרחה "in the midst of the city, in *Qrḥḥ*" (Mesha 24). Cf. also Mesha 8.13/14. 21/22.[76] In Mesha 24, both "in the midst of the city" as well as the appositional "*Qrḥḥ*" bear a coordinating preposition.

EDOMITE: No evidence.

HEBREW: The preposition was repeated before each coordinated noun, as in בכרת.אתכם.ליהוה . . . ולאשרתה "I bless you by Yahweh and by his Asherah" (Ajrud) and שלח לשלם . . . ולשלם "he asks after the well-being of . . . and after the well-being of" (Arad 16:1/2, 21:1/2). In correspondence, the preposition was not repeated before two coordinated nouns when the title preceded the proper name; see, for example, אל אדני.יאוש "to my lord, Yauš" (Lach. 2:1, 6:1) and שלח.להג[ד.[ל[אד[נ]י יאו[ש] "he sends to say to my lord, Yauš" (Lach. 3:1/2). In biblical Hebrew, however, the repetition of the preposition is expected when the title precedes the proper name; it is not generally repeated when the title follows the proper name.[77]

All first-millennium NWS dialects repeated the preposition before each of a series of coordinated nouns. But when a proper name preceded an appositional modifier (title, patronymic, etc.), the preposition was generally not repeated before each part of the phrase. Both these syntactic features held true for all NWS dialects.

When a nominal modifier preceded the proper noun, however, the NWS dialects did not follow the same syntactic pattern. In epigraphic Hebrew and most cases from Old Aramaic, the preposition appeared only before the first member of the nominal unit. In Samalian, Moabite, and one example from Old Aramaic (Arslan Tash), the preposition was repeated before both the modifier and the proper noun. In this latter case, the second preposition appeared on analogy with the first; the title and proper noun thus functioned as independent nominal units.

6. The verb: The perfect. The consecutive perfect (in nonconditional sentences).

BYBLIAN: No evidence.

STANDARD PHOENICIAN: Not attested. In contrast to BH,[78] a precative verb was followed by an imperfect (Kilamu 15/16) or inf. absolute (Karatepe A III 2–7; cf. ll. 12–16). See also the sequence imperfect-imperfect in Kilamu 14.[79]

ARAMAIC: Not attested. A precative verb was regularly followed by an imperfect (e.g., Sf. I A 28/29).[80]

SAMALIAN: Not attested. All examples of the sequence imperfect-imperfect, however, probably lie in the protasis of conditions (H 15/16.20/21.25).

AMMONITE: No evidence.

DEIR ALLA: No evidence. The alleged consecutive perfect ונצבו "and they took their places" (I 6)[81] followed a simple perfect; it was probably a simple perfect as well. Also, ושמעו "and they heard" (I 13)[82] lies in a broken context.

MOABITE: No evidence. The sequence לך.אחז "go, capture!" (Mesha 14; cf. l. 32) does not necessarily argue against the existence of the consecutive perfect in Moabite. Although לך may be followed by a consecutive perfect in BH,[83] it is also possible that לך may be followed asyndetically by another imperative.[84]

EDOMITE: No evidence.

HEBREW: The consecutive perfect appeared in this dialect, as for example ושלחתם "and you will send" (Arad 24:13), והבקידם "and he will hand them over" (Arad 24:14/15),[85] and perhaps וגאלתי "and I shall redeem" (Beit Lei A 2).[86]

According to the available evidence, the consecutive perfect appeared only in Hebrew among the first-millennium NWS dialects. It is not attested in standard Phoenician, Old Aramaic, and probably Samalian. Since, however, the origin of the verb form is unknown, it is unclear whether its appearance in Hebrew is a survival[87] or innovation.[88]

7a. The infinitive: The infinitive as an imperative.

BYBLIAN: The infinitive construct appears to have functioned as an imperative in לדעת "attention, know!" (Ahirom Graff. 1).

STANDARD PHOENICIAN: Evidence uncertain. Cross and Saley[89] interpreted עבר "pass (away)!" (Arsl.T. 1:20) and הלך "go (away)!" (Arsl.T. 1:21) as infinitive absolutes functioning as imperatives. While this interpretation is possible, these verbs may have been imperatives as well.[90] Similarly, יצא in Arsl.T. 2:3 may have been a simple perfect,[91] not an inf. abs.[92] Further, Röllig[93] suggested that לרד (Arsl.T. 1:27) was an inf. construct of *rdd "to subdue" used as an imperative. In this case, though, the reading is either לדר "forever," composed of the dative preposition + דר (cf. BH [dōr]),[94] or simply לד "give birth!" < *wld.[95] Thus there are no unambiguous examples of the inf. (absolute) functioning as an imperative in standard Phoenician.

ARAMAIC: The infinitive never functioned as an imperative in Old Aramaic.

SAMALIAN: The infinitive does not appear to have functioned imperatively in Samalian. There is admittedly no infinitive absolute in the extant Samalian texts; all infinitives in these texts are construct.[96]

AMMONITE: No evidence.

DEIR ALLA: There is one possible example of the infinitive absolute used as an imperative.[97] In I 6, שם "place!" is parallel to the second person fem. sing. jussive תפרי "sew!" in the same line. Since this verb lacks a feminine ending, it cannot have been an imperative. Rather, שם may have been an infinitive absolute used as an imperative.[98]

MOABITE: The infinitive did not function as an imperative in the extant Moabite texts.[99] The present sample of infinitives, however, is too small to permit any definite conclusions.

EDOMITE: No evidence.

HEBREW: The infinitive absolute functioned as an imperative in the Arad letters, as seen in the form נתן "give!" (Arad 1:2, 2:1, etc.) used side by side with תן "give!" (Arad 3:2, 4:1, etc.).[100] This particular usage, however, is infrequent in epigraphic Hebrew.[101]

The use of the infinitive as an imperative is a common West Semitic feature.[102] This feature survived in Deir Alla and Hebrew, where the infinitive absolute functioned as an imperative. In Byblian, however, it was the infinitive construct which functioned as an imperative. In Aramaic and Samalian (and Moabite?), this feature did not survive.

7b.   The infinitive in temporal clauses.

BYBLIAN: The infinitive does not appear to have been used in forming temporal clauses in this dialect. The one possible example, כשתה "when he placed him" (Ahirom 1), is probably composed of the temporal conjunction כ + finite verb + objective suffix.[103] The evidence is too meager to draw any definite conclusions on this point, however.

STANDARD PHOENICIAN: In the extant texts, the infinitive is not used to form temporal clauses.[104]

ARAMAIC: The infinitive was not used to form temporal clauses in Old Aramaic. Temporal conjunctions marked the clause.[105]

SAMALIAN: The infinitive was not used, at least in the extant Samalian texts, to form temporal clauses.[106]

AMMONITE: No evidence.

DEIR ALLA: It does not appear that the infinitive was used to form temporal clauses in this dialect. The evidence is scanty, however.

MOABITE: The infinitive was used to form temporal clauses, as in בהלתחמה "when he fought" (Mesha 19).[107]

EDOMITE: No evidence.

HEBREW: The infinitive was used to form temporal clauses in epigraphic Hebrew, as for example in כצאתי "when I left" (Arad 16:3), בחתמך "when you sealed" (Arad 13:3), etc.

According to Isserlin,[108] the use of the infinitive in temporal clauses distinguishes Hebrew dialects. For him, the formation of temporal clauses with a preposition + infinitive was an "upper class" speech trait, whereas the use of temporal conjunctions (as in Yavneh-Yam 1:6.8) reflects "popular" speech. Yet it is impossible to draw such far-reaching conclusions from the evidence at hand. The initial distinction between "upper class" and "popular" speech (and texts) must be demonstrated for ancient Hebrew. Moreover, the distribution of these two types of temporal clauses is not clear; further examples are needed to chart the exact socioeconomic distribution of each construction in Hebrew. Isserlin's claim for a dialectal division of Hebrew on the basis of the form of the temporal clause, then, is unproven.

The use of the infinitive in temporal clauses is an old Semitic feature, found already in Akkadian[109] and Ugaritic.[110] In NWS, this feature was retained in southern dialects, i.e. Moabite and Hebrew. In the northern dialects of Phoenician, Aramaic, and Samalian, and probably in the peripheral dialect of Deir Alla, this feature was lost. Its survival in first-millennium NWS, then, was sporadic.

7c.   The use of the infinitive (absolute) as a finite verb.

BYBLIAN: No evidence.[111]

STANDARD PHOENICIAN: The infinitive absolute functioned as a narrative, past tense, present-future verb, or subjunctive. For the infinitive absolute used as a narrative tense, see no. 8. As a present-future verbal form, Karatepe A III 12–16 is especially instructive. There, the phrase אם . . . . אש ימח . . . . ושת . . . . ויסע . . . . ויפעל . . . . ושת "If (someone) who wipes out and places and rips out and makes and places" shows that the infinitive absolute maintained the tense of the preceding, present-future verbal form. The situation is similar in Karatepe C IV 13–16 and 17/18. The infinitive absolute also functioned as a subjunctive/precative verb in וברך בעל כרנתריש "and may Baal-*Krntryš* bless" (Karatepe A III 2/3, C III 16/17), וכן הקרת ז "and may this city be" (Karatepe A III 7, C IV 6), and in ומח בעל שמם "then may Baal-of-Heaven wipe out" (Karatepe A III 18 [apodosis of a condition]). The infinitive absolute in standard Phoenician, then, had a number of usages comparable to that of the finite verb.

ARAMAIC: The infinitive absolute did not function as a finite verb in Old Aramaic.

SAMALIAN: The infinitive did not function as a finite verb in Samalian.[112]

AMMONITE: No evidence.[113]

DEIR ALLA: The infinitive did not function as a finite verb in the Deir Alla dialect.

MOABITE: The infinitive did not function as a finite verb in Moabite.

EDOMITE: No evidence.

HEBREW: The infinitive does not function as a finite verb in the epigraphic Hebrew texts.[114] The one alleged example of the infinitive absolute used as a finite verb, ואסם in Yavneh-Yam 1:5[115] is doubtful. The converted imperfect appears four times in this text as the narrative, past tense; it would be odd for the author of this document to mix constructions. Thus, if ואסם is a verb,[116] it is preferable to interpret it as a simple perfect with prefixed conjunctive *waw*. In this way, grammatical consistency is maintained, and the harsh infinitive absolute construction is avoided.

The use of the infinitive absolute as a finite verb survived only in standard Phoenician. While a similar usage of the infinitive absolute appears in Ugaritic,[117] indicating the antiquity of the construction, the finite use of the infinitive absolute was absent from all first-millennium NWS dialects, with the exception of standard Phoenician. Within standard Phoenician, the only certain evidence for this particular function comes from the Karatepe inscription, found in the Syro-Palestinian periphery. Yet it is unlikely that this usage was a local tradition since the inf. absolute functioned as the historical past tense in several Phoenician-speaking communities.

8.   The narrative, historical past tense.

BYBLIAN: No evidence. Although Albright[118] stated that ויגל in Ahirom 2 was a consecutive imperfect, it is more likely that this verb was a simple imperfect, continuing the tense of the preceding protasis עלי . . . ואל "and if he attacks." ויגל, then, is a present-future tense; there is no example of a converted imperfect in this dialect.[119]

In later Byblian, the infinitive absolute functioned as the narrative past tense, as for example ויתן אנך "and I gave" (KAI 9 A 4), וקרא אנך "and I called" (Yehawmilk 2), and ופעל אנך "and I made" (Yehawmilk 3). Since this construction does not appear in the early texts, it is impossible to determine whether this syntactic feature was native to the Byblian dialect or was borrowed. If borrowed, this construction probably originated in standard Phoenician. This problem cannot be resolved without a narrative text in Old Byblian.

STANDARD PHOENICIAN: The infinitive absolute, as in ושכר.אנך "and I hired" (Kilamu 7/8), ועען אנך "and I subdued" (Karatepe A I 18), יחו אנך "I restored" (Karatepe A I 3), etc.[120] Cf. the suffixed forms[121] ואנך . . . ענתנם ירדם אנך ישבם אנך "and I subdued them, I exiled[122] them, I made them settle" (Karatepe A I 19/20).

ARAMAIC: The consecutive imperfect functioned as the narrative, past tense three times: ואשא.ידי "and I lifted my hands" (Zkr A 11), ויענני "and he answered me" (Zkr A 11), and ויאמר "and he said" (Zkr A 15).[123] Otherwise, the perfect expressed the historical past, as for example והוחד "and there united" (Zkr A 4), כנן.ויהב.לה

"he erected (it) and gave (it) to him" (Fekh. 10), ורצת "and I ran" (Br-Rkb 1:8), ושבת תלאים "and T. returned" (Sf. III 25), etc.[124]

The few attestations of the consecutive imperfect, in contrast to numerous examples of the historical perfect, suggest that the consecutive imperfect was already (becoming) obsolete by the ninth century (Zkr). Thereafter, the consecutive imperfect fell into total disuse. In this way, the syntactic situation in Old Aramaic of the ninth century is comparable to that of Hebrew in the sixth; the perfect usurped the function of the consecutive imperfect as a narrative, historical past tense. The occurrence of the perfect in the same syntactic position as the consecutive imperfect is especially curious. Whereas the consecutive imperfect was used only in initial position, the perfect later appears in this very position with the same "tense." In Old Aramaic, then, the perfect assumed the semantic and syntactic function of the consecutive imperfect.

SAMALIAN: The perfect,[125] as for example in ונתן.בידי "and (they) gave into my hands" (H 2; cf. l. 8), ו[ה]קמת "and I erected" (H 14), ופשש.מסגרת.והרפי "and he unlocked[126] the prisons and released" (P 8), etc. Alternatively, it is possible that the imperfect signified the narrative, past tense, as for example in תשמ[ו] חרב.בביתי.ותהרגו "you placed a sword in my house, and you killed" (P 4/5).[127] Yet the context of the passage is broken, and it is uncertain whether the verbs refer to past or present-future time. Furthermore, this clause may have been part of an apodosis, as inferred from the context, so that a prefixed verbal form would be expected.[128] If the imperfect did carry a historical past tense, the relation between yqtl-past and qtl-past, and the distribution of these two forms, are unclear. In any case, the perfect in Samalian was the regular narrative, historical past tense.

AMMONITE: No evidence.

DEIR ALLA: The consecutive imperfect,[129] as for example ויאתו "and they came" (I 1), ויאמרו "and they said" (I 2), ויקם "and he arose" (I 3), etc.

MOABITE: The consecutive imperfect,[130] as for example ואעש "and I made" (Mesha 3.9), ויבן "and he built" (Mesha 10), and ואהרג "and I killed" (Mesha 11.16).

EDOMITE: No evidence.

HEBREW: The consecutive imperfect, as for example וילכו "and they flowed" (Shiloah 4), ויקצר . . . ויכל "and he was harvesting and measuring" (Yavneh-Yam 1:4/5), and ויעלהו "and he brought him up'' (Lach. 4:6/7). During the course of the sixth century, however, the consecutive imperfect fell into disuse as the narrative, past tense.[131] The perfect took its place, as for example כתבתי ''I wrote'' (Lach. 4:3), השב ''he has returned'' (Lach. 5:6), etc. The loss of the converted imperfect to the simple perfect is recorded in the later biblical texts as well.[132]

Several verbal forms functioned as the narrative, historical past tense in the first-millennium NWS dialects. Most dialects—Old Aramaic (Zkr), the Deir Alla dialect, Moabite, and Hebrew—used the old consecutive imperfect; this distribution suggests that the consecutive imperfect was a common NWS verb form. In the other dialects, the consecutive imperfect was lost. It was replaced by the perfect in Samalian, most Old Aramaic dialects (post-ninth century), and in late Hebrew (sixth century on). This replacement probably occurred independently in the different dialects.[133] Finally, in standard Phoenician the consecutive imperfect was replaced by the infinitive absolute; with respect to the first-millennium NWS dialects,[134] the use of the infinitive absolute as the narrative tense was a Phoenician syntactic trait.[135]

One verbal form need not be the only form capable of signifying the historical past tense within each dialect. The linguistic situation in Old Aramaic and Hebrew indicates that one verbal form can be replaced by another over a period of time. Thus, while both dialects originally had the consecutive imperfect, they lost this form to the perfect. As these dialects changed over time, they tended to lose the consecutive imperfect.

9. The participle: The periphrastic tense ("to be" + participle).

BYBLIAN: A periphrastic tense does not appear in the extant texts.

STANDARD PHOENICIAN: The only possible example of the periphrastic tense in this dialect is Karatepe A II 3/4, ובמקממ אש כן לפנם נשתעם ''and in places which had formerly been feared.''[136] While the author could have conveyed a similar meaning by omitting כן, its inclusion served to emphasize the continuous state of fear which these ''places'' had in the past. Whereas the simple perfect נשתע* would have conveyed a one-time, past sense, the combination of

נשתעם + כן expresses an ongoing sense, comparable to the French *imparfait*.

ARAMAIC: There are no certain examples of the periphrastic tense in Old Aramaic. Greenfield[137] has cited one possible example in Sf. III 22, והוי חלפה "and be his successor!" Yet while this phrase is composed of "to be" + participle,[138] the participle is nominal, not verbal.[139] Thus, Sf. III 22 is not an example of the periphrastic tense but is equivalent to "be!" + noun.

SAMALIAN: No example of the periphrastic tense appears in the extant Samalian texts.

AMMONITE: No example of the periphrastic tense appears in the extant Ammonite texts. The size of the corpus, however, is small.

DEIR ALLA: No example of the periphrastic tense appears in the extant Deir Alla texts. The absence of a periphrastic tense may, however, be accidental.

MOABITE: No example of the periphrastic tense appears in the extant Moabite texts. The absence of a periphrastic tense may, however, be accidental.

EDOMITE: No evidence.

HEBREW: One example of the periphrastic tense appears in Yavneh-Yam 1:2/3,[140] עבדך קצר.היה.עבדך "as for your servant, your servant was harvesting." Like the periphrastic tense in Karatepe A II 3/4, this example in Hebrew stressed the continuousness of the action. While the simple perfect would have conveyed a single action at a single point in time, the periphrastic tense emphasized that the harvesting was a habitual action. Cf. similarly in Mishnaic Hebrew, as studied by Greenfield.[141]

Use of the periphrastic tense is sporadically attested during this period in the history of NWS dialects. Of the first-millennium dialects, only standard Phoenician and Hebrew show any trace of this feature. Each of these two dialects, moreover, exhibits only one example of the periphrastic tense. In the later periods, the periphrastic tense became common in Hebrew and Aramaic dialects independently.[142]

10. The verb "to be able" + complementary verb.

PHOENICIAN: יכל + infinitive. The only example of this construction is the uncertain passage in Karatepe A II 5/6, אשת תבל חד

ידל, which Gordon[143] and Rosenthal[144] translated "(where) a woman was able to stroll. . . ." If חד is cognate to Arabic *ḥyd "to stray,"[145] the complete construction תבלחד may be interpreted in two ways. The verbal form חד may be an infinitive absolute, or infinitive construct without prefixed *lamedh*.[146] Alternatively, the *lamedh* of תבל may have been shared, acting as both the final radical of *ykl and as the preposition "to" in the following infinitive; the *lamedh*, then, written once, acted as two letters.[147] In view of the complementary infinitive in ישתע אדם ללכת "a man feared to walk" (Karatepe A II 4), the latter interpretation is preferable.[148]

ARAMAIC: כהל + imperfect, as in פלאבכהל לאשלח "thus I will not be able to send" (Sf. II B 6), וליכהל . . . [ל]ישלח "and he will not be able to send" (Sf. I B 25), etc. This construction of כהל + asyndetic imperfect is also found in the later BMAP 2:13, 3:14.17, etc.[149]

A second construction, "to be able" + complementary infinitive, may be attested in Sf. I B 34. Most scholars[150] read . . . ליכ]הל למשלח "he will not be able to send," and interpreted the construction as כהל + infinitive; cf. the later Ahiqar 17 and Dan. 2:10.[151] Degen[152] was sensitive to the syntax of this construction. Observing that כהל is always followed by an imperfect in Old Aramaic, and also recognizing that the *mem* in למשלח is very faint, he proposed the reading לישלח. If confirmed,[153] this reading would remove the only possible example of כהל + infinitive in the Old Aramaic corpus.

SAMALIAN: No evidence. Cf., however, the complementary infinitive in [א]ל.יתן.לה.לאכל "may he not allow him to eat" (H 23) and קרני.לבנא "he summoned me to build" (H 13).

AMMONITE: No evidence.

DEIR ALLA: No evidence. The restoration ליכ]ל.לאכל "and he was unable to eat" (I 3)[154] is hypothetical.

MOABITE: No evidence.

EDOMITE: No evidence.

HEBREW: יכל + *lamedh* + infinitive construct, as in [אי]ננו. יכלם.לשלח "we are not able to send" (Arad 40:13/14), as well as similar constructions in BH.

The evidence of three dialects, with respect to the syntax of the construction "to be able to . . . ," suggests a bipartite division within NWS. In Phoenician, Hebrew, and possibly Samalian, the construction was יכל + infinitive construct. In Old Aramaic, the construction took the form כהל + (asyndetic) imperfect. And within

Old Aramaic, a new construction was possibly emerging, in which an infinitive followed the verb "to be able"; the reading of this particular passage, however, is uncertain. Since both constructions appear in other Semitic languages,[155] their appearance in NWS is most likely an inheritance.

11. The verbal sentence: The placement of the finite verb in main clauses.

BYBLIAN: The verb generally stood in initial position, as in תחתסף.חטר.משפטה.תהתפך.כסא.מלכה "may the scepter of his rule be removed, may the throne of his dominion be overturned" (Ahirom 2), יארך.בעל שמם "may Baal-of-Heaven lengthen" (Yehimilk 3), and תארך.בעלת גבל "may Mistress-of-Byblos lengthen" (Shiptibaal 4; Elibaal 2 [partially restored]). Yet in Yehimilk 2, and three times in Ahirom 2, S preceded V. Perhaps initial positioning of S was emphatic.[156]

STANDARD PHOENICIAN: The finite verb generally stood in initial position in the sentence (disregarding conjunctions, negations, etc.), as in Kilamu 2.3, etc., Karatepe A I 5, etc., and Arsl.T. 1:8/9.26.[157]

Two regular deviations from this verb-initial pattern occurred. (1) If the author used both the independent pronoun "I" and perfect verb, the verb always followed the pronoun[158] (e.g., Kilamu 13.4.9.10; Karatepe A I 16). (2) If the author wished to stress one syntactic element, that element was placed first, forcing the verb out of initial position (e.g., Arsl.T. 1:10/11.21; Karatepe A I 12, I 21–II 1, II 10/11; Kilamu 9/10). Neither of these two interpretations, however, explains the syntax of Karatepe A IV 1/2 = C V 5/6 (partially restored)—אפס שם אזתוד יכן—"however, the name of Azitawadda shall be." Cf. Karatepe A II 5/6.

ARAMAIC: The verb was generally placed in initial position in the texts from Syria.[159] Thus in Br-Hdd (ll. 4/5), Zkr (A 3.3.4.9, etc.), Sfire (I A 30.32; II C 4.5, etc.), and Br-Rkb (1:8.11.12, etc.), the verb appeared in initial position in the sentence. When another syntactic element was stressed, however, that element was placed first; the verb receded toward the end. Such emphatic positioning appears, for example, in Br-Rkb 1:4/5, Sf. I B 7/8, etc. Thus, with respect to the syntax of Syrian Aramaic texts, Old Aramaic and standard Phoenician are almost identical.

In the eastern and southern regions, however, the verb did not necessarily stand in initial position. In the Adon letter, for example, the verb followed the subject in ll. 4.6.8[160] although each passage was a main clause. In the Fekh. text, the verb appeared in medial (e.g., ll. 17.18.19, etc.) and final position (e.g., ll. 15.15, etc.).[161] And in Halaf Ost. 1 Rev. 1/2, the verb stood in final position. Similarly, in contrast to Nerab 1:11, 2:3.6 where the verb stood first, in Nerab 1:1/2.9.10/11, 2:4.5/6.7.9.10 the verb was not initial.[162] Cf. the Old Aramaic text published by Bordreuil,[163] where the verb stood first in ll. 6.10 and last in l. 2.[164] Whereas, then, western Old Aramaic texts had predominantly verb-initial syntax (excepting emphatic positioning), eastern and southern Old Aramaic texts reflect a fluidity in verb placement;[165] in these eastern and southern texts, the verb could appear in initial, medial, or final position, without any semantic difference.

SAMALIAN The verb predominantly stood in initial position in Samalian, as for example in H 2.3.4.8, etc., and P 2.3.3.4, etc.[166] When the verb was not initial, however, the word which stood in initial position received special stress, as for example in H 24, P 14, and 1/2. In P 1, the syntax O-V may reflect the added stress on the object. Alternatively, the clause may be an unmarked relative clause, "this stele (which) Br-Rkb set up." Thus Samalian syntax generally reflects the verb-initial pattern.

AMMONITE: The verb stood first in the sentence, as in Sir. 6–8 and Cit. 6. If, however, Horn's[167] restoration מ]לכם.בנה.לך "Milkom has built for you" (Cit. 1) is correct, S may have preceded V in Ammonite.

DEIR ALLA:[168] The verb generally stood first in the sentence, as for example in I 2.5.6, etc., and II 6.11.12, etc. In several cases, however, V followed S, without any apparent semantic difference. Thus מלכן.יחזו (II 13) appears to mean "(the) kings will see," and וקל.רחמן.יענה "and the voice of (the) vultures will answer" (I 8). Cf. similarly I 7/8 and (?) Xd 2. The S-V syntax in I 5, however, may reflect a subordinate clause. In short, while the Deir Alla syntax was usually verb-initial, V could follow S.

MOABITE: All main clauses in Moabite reflect verb-initial syntax, as in Mesha 5.6.7.8/9, etc. The only[169] deviation from this pattern appeared when the independent pronoun is found with the finite verb (Mesha 2/3. 21.22, etc.); in these cases, the pronoun always preceded the verb for emphatic stress. Cf. similarly Mesha 17.

EDOMITE: No evidence.

HEBREW: The verb generally stood in initial position in the epigraphic texts. Thus, in the texts from Arad (e.g., 2:1–4, 3:5/6, 5:2/3, etc.), Jerusalem (e.g., Shiloah 3.4), Lachish (e.g., 2:4, 6:13/14), and Ajrud (e.g., ברך.ימם), verb-initial syntax is apparent. When either the subject[170] or object[171] was placed before the verb, that particular element was given added emphasis. Yet there are very few examples of the postponement of the verb to either medial or final position in the Hebrew texts.

The NWS dialects of the first-millennium divide into two groups, depending upon the position the verb commonly occupied in main clauses. Most dialects exhibit verb-initial syntax; if preceded by any part of speech, the verb followed simple conjunctions or particles. This verb-initial syntax is found in Phoenician dialects, Old Aramaic from the (north-) western region, Samalian, Ammonite (?), the Deir Alla dialect, Moabite, and Hebrew. Comparative evidence suggests that verb-initial word order is the standard West Semitic pattern.[172]

In the eastern and southern regions of Old Aramaic, this verb-initial syntax was more flexible. The verb could appear in either medial or final position, in addition to the old initial position, without affecting the meaning of the main clause. This flexibility was also found in the Deir Alla texts, in which several examples of S-V syntax appeared in main clauses.

In view of the geographic position of Deir Alla in the south-eastern region of Syria-Palestine, and the other linguistic features it shares with Old Aramaic,[173] the freedom in the placement of the verb in Deir Alla can be related to the identical phenomenon in eastern and southern Syro-Palestinian Old Aramaic. In terms of dialect geography, this feature may have spread from eastern/southern Aramaic to Deir Alla, or from an external source to eastern/southern Aramaic and Deir Alla simultaneously[174] Alternatively, this syntax may have arisen independently in both dialects.[175]

12.   The marking or nonmarking of the definite, nominal direct object.

BYBLIAN: The definite, nominal direct object was unmarked in Old Byblian, as for example עלי.גבל.ויגל.ארן.זן . . . ואל ''and if he attacks Byblos and uncovers this coffin'' (Ahirom 2) and יארך . . . ימת.יחמלך.ושנתו ''may they lengthen the days of Yehimilk and his years'' (Yehimilk 3–5; cf. Shiptibaal 4–5). In later Byblian, this direct object could be introduced by the *nota accusativi*, as in standard Phoenician.[176]

STANDARD PHOENICIAN: The definite, nominal direct object was usually unmarked in standard Phoenician. In the Karatepe inscription, however, it was occasionally introduced by the *nota accusativi*. For example, when the author himself was the direct object of a verb, the *nota accusativi* introduced his name (Karatepe A III 3, C III 17). When, on the contrary, the author's enemies were the direct object, they were preceded by the *nota accusativi* (Karatepe A III 19–IV 1; cf. Yehawmilk 15). Or if the definite direct object was particularly contrastive, the object received the *nota accusativi* (Karatepe C IV 18/19). Finally, if the object was the focus, or emphasis, of the sentence, it was marked by the *nota accusativi* (Karatepe A I 3/4, III 14/15 = C IV 17). In standard Phoenician, then, the *nota accusativi* marked objects that were of particular interest to the author;[177] its use was subject to individual style.

ARAMAIC: As in standard Phoenician, the definite, nominal direct object was usually unmarked. The *nota accusativi* appeared only in the Sfire and Zkr inscriptions. In Sfire, the *nota accusativi* is found when the direct object was either Matti'el and his family (Sf. I B 32/33, II C 14; cf. III 13) or Bar-Ga'yah and his realm (Sf. II C 5/6). In Zkr's inscription, אית appeared only before nouns signifying Zkr's own achievements (Zkr B 5.10.11 [?].15.16/17; cf. Zkr B 19); one striking exception is אנה.ה.בני[ת].חזרך ''I built Hazrek'' (Zkr B 3/4), where the independent pronoun preceded the verb. According to present evidence, then, the *nota accusativi* in Old Aramaic functioned similarly to its standard Phoenician counterpart: It marked direct objects that were of particular interest to the author.

In one instance, the definite, nominal direct object may have been introduced by *lamedh*. In Sf. I C 4/5, לטבת[א].יעבד[ו] ''may they make good relations'' may exhibit O-V syntax, in which the direct object was preceded by *lamedh*.[178] Yet since this syntactic feature is common in later East Aramaic dialects,[179] it would be odd for it to appear in this early Aramaic text from the West.[180]

SAMALIAN: The definite, nominal direct object was unmarked, as for example in עד.יזכר.נבש.פנמו ''in order that he remember the soul of Panammu'' (H 17), והרג.אבה.ברצר ''and he killed his father,

Brṣr" (P 3), והרפי.שבי.יאדי "and he released the captives of *Yᵓdy*" (P 8), etc.

AMMONITE: No evidence.

DEIR ALLA: No evidence. Since no definite, nominal direct objects appeared in the extant texts, the absence of a *nota accusativi* may be accidental.

MOABITE: The definite, nominal direct object was marked or unmarked, with almost equal frequency. The definite object was not marked when the subjective independent pronoun accompanied the finite verb, as in אנך.בנתי.ערער "I built Aroer" (Mesha 26) and אנך.בנתי.בצר "I built Bezer" (Mesha 27);[181] cf. Zkr B 3/4. Otherwise, the *nota accusativi* introduced pláces oppressed (e.g., וירש.עמרי.את.כ[ל.אר]ץ.מהדבא "Omri took possession of the whole land of Medaba" [Mesha 7/8; cf. ll. 5.6.14]) and rebuilt (e.g., ואבן.את.בעלמען "I built Baalmaon" [Mesha 9; cf. ll. 9/10.10/11. 18/19]). Similarly, examples of great achievement were marked with את, as in ואהרג.את.כל.העם "and I killed the entire people" (Mesha 11) and ואשב.בה.את.את.אש.שרן.ואת.אש מחרת "and I settled in it *Šrn*-ites and *Mḥrt*-ites" (Mesha 13/14; cf. ll. 12.30/31). Apparently, examples of lesser achievement were unmarked, as ואעש.הבמת.זאת "and I made this highplace" (Mesha 3) and ואעש.בה.האשוח "and I made the cistern in it" (Mesha 9). Thus, use of the *nota accusativi* was not construction-bound,[182] since it appeared after various verbal forms in all three persons. Rather, the *nota accusativi* marked objects in which the author was particularly interested. In this way, the *nota accusativi* and independent subjective pronoun were mutually exclusive; both parts of speech were, in effect, emphatic.

EDOMITE: No evidence.

HEBREW: The *nota accusativi* usually introduced the definite, nominal direct object. Examples of the nonmarking of the object are relatively few, as for example וכתב.שם היום "and write the name of the day!" (Arad 1:3/4), השב.עבדך.הספרם "your servant has returned the letters" (Lach. 5:6/7), etc.[183] In the majority of cases, את introduced the object, as in ישמע יהוה.את אדני "may Yahweh cause my lord to hear" (Lach. 2:1/2, 8 Obv. 1, etc.), זכר.אדני.את.[ע]בדה "my lord remembered his servant" (Lach. 2:4/5), שלח את נחם "send Nahum!" (Arad 16:9/10), ושלחתי את ה[כ]סף "and I sent the silver" (Arad 16:4/5), לא נראה את.עזקה "we cannot see Azeqah" (Lach. 4:12/13), and especially אשר יפתח את זאת "who opens this" (Silwan B 2/3). These latter examples suggest that the category of "defi-

niteness" in the direct object alone provoked the appearance of את;
use of את had become grammaticalized.

Within the first-millennium NWS dialects, the marking or nonmarking of the definite, nominal direct object varied considerably.
At one extreme, the object was always unmarked in Old Byblian
and Samalian, at least according to the available evidence. In standard Phoenician, Old Aramaic, and Moabite, the definite, nominal
object was generally unmarked; use of the *nota accusativi* was subject to individual style. When it appeared, it seemed to focus particular attention on the object, for the purpose of emphasis, focus,
or contrast.[184] And finally, at the other syntactic extreme, the definite, nominal direct object in Hebrew was rarely unmarked, but
usually followed the *nota accusativi*. The *nota accusativi* had lost
all emphatic, or deictic, force; it had become a grammatical regu-
larity.

13.   The conditional sentence: The marking or nonmarking of the apodosis.

BYBLIAN: Unmarked, as in עלי.גבל.ויגל.ארן.זן.תחתסף . . . ואל "and
if he attacks Byblos and uncovers this coffin, (then) may it be
removed" (Ahirom 2). It is unknown, however, whether all Old
Byblian conditional sentences had unmarked apodoses or
whether there were alternate ways of signifying the apodosis.

STANDARD PHOENICIAN: Marked with *waw*, as in ואם . . . ומח בעל
שמם "and if . . . then may Baal-of-Heaven wipe out" (Karatepe A
III 12–18). Again, it is unclear whether this one example represents
the entire paradigm for the identification of apodoses in this dialect
or whether alternative constructions also existed.

OLD ARAMAIC: In almost every example, the apodosis was unmarked. So, for example, הן יאתה . . . יאתה "if he comes, (then) it
will come" (Sf. I B 28), הן לתהב . . . שקרת "if you do not give, (then)
you will have been false" (Sf. I B 38), והן תנצר . . . אחרה ינצר "and
if you protect, (then) in the future (yours) will be protected" (Nerab
1:11–13), etc.

In Sf. II B 4–6,[185] however, the apodosis was introduced by
פ-, פלאבהל . . . תאמר]ו[הן "and if you say, then I shall not be
able. . . ." On the basis of the use of פ- in Old Aramaic and Samalian,
פ- apparently means "thus, therefore, as a consequence thereof";[186]

in which case, the appearance of פ- in an apodosis would serve to mark the apodosis as a consequence of the preceding condition. The use of פ- in this context, then, was a new application of this conjunction. It was not a special marker of the apodosis.

SAMALIAN: Unmarked, as in אם . . . יאחז . . . יאמר "if he seizes, (then) he will say" (H 20/21), הן.אם.שמת . . . אמר "now if I put, (then) I shall say" (H 29/30), פהנו.זכר.הא.לתגמרו "thus, if he is male, (then) may they be destroyed" (H 30), etc. In H 15–17, however, the apodosis may have been introduced by פ(א), thus [אם] . . . יאחז . . . וישב . . . ויסעד . . . ויזבח . . . ויזכר . . . פא.יאמר "[if] he seizes and sits and supports (?) and does sacrifice and mentions, then (on account of all the aforementioned) he will say." If this interpretation of the passage is correct, the conjunction פ(א) performed the same function as in Sf. II B 6; it strengthened the apodosis and acted as a resumptive conjunction summarizing the preceding, long conditional protasis. It was, then, a new application of the conjunction "therefore, thus, as a consequence thereof."

AMMONITE: No evidence.

DEIR ALLA: Unmarked, as in הן.תשנאן.יאנש "if you hate him, (then) he will weaken" (II 10).[187] It is uncertain, however, whether this one example is representative of the syntax of the apodosis in the entire dialect.

MOABITE: No evidence.

EDOMITE: No evidence.

HEBREW: The only complete conditional sentence in the epigraphic corpus marked the apodosis with *waw*, ואם.עוד.חמץ.ונתת.להם "and if there is still vinegar left, then you will give (it) to them" (Arad 2:7/8). Yet the broken passages in Arad 40:9/10 and 21:3/4 may indicate that the apodosis could have been unmarked as well. In biblical Hebrew, too, the apodosis can be unmarked or introduced with *waw*.[188] The semantic and syntactic difference between the marked and unmarked apodosis is not certain.

All the NWS dialects either introduced the apodosis with a conjunction or left the apodosis unmarked.[189] The single conditional sentences in Old Byblian and Deir Alla showed unmarked apodoses. The only conditional sentence in standard Phoenician had a marked apodosis. In the other dialects—Old Aramaic, Samalian, and Hebrew—apodoses were marked and unmarked. Both treatments of the apodosis, then, were common NWS syntactic features.

Within that group of dialects which introduced the apodosis with a conjunction, different conjunctions were used. Old Aramaic and Samalian, which possessed the conjunction *pa "thus, therefore," used this conjunction to mark the apodosis. This use of *pa is a common West Semitic feature (cf. the Arabic *fa* of apodosis). In those dialects which lacked *pa, however, *wa performed this function, as in standard Phoenician and Hebrew. Here too, *wa is a common clausal conjunction. The particle used to mark the apodosis, then, depended upon the inventory of conjunctive particles in the individual dialects.

Notes to Chapter 4

1. See Helmer Ringgren, "A Note on the Karatepe Text," *Oriens* 2 (1949): 127–128.

2. André Dupont-Sommer, "Azitawadda, roi des Danouniens. Étude sur les inscriptions phéniciennes de Karatepe," *RA* 42 (1948): 171; idem, "Etude du texte phénicien des inscriptions de Karatepe," *Oriens* 2 (1949): 126; and A. M. Honeyman, "Phoenician Inscriptions from Karatepe," *Le Muséon* 61 (1948): 54. Cf. Stanislav Segert, *A Grammar of Phoenician and Punic* (Munich: C. H. Beck, 1976), §§74.262, 75.473, 64.624.2.

3. Additional texts are cited by Ringgren, *Oriens* 2 (1949): 127–128; and by Dupont-Sommer, *Oriens* 2 (1949): 126. Cf. Frank M. Cross, "Leaves from an Epigraphist's Notebook," *CBQ* 36 (1974): 489 n. 31.

4. Eduard Y. Kutscher, *A History of Aramaic*. Part 1: *Old Aramaic, Jaudic, Official Aramaic* (*Biblical Aramaic excepted*) (Jerusalem: Akadamon, 1972), pp. 117–118 (in Hebrew). Cf. Stephen A. Kaufman, *The Akkadian Influences on Aramaic*, Assyriological Studies, vol. 19 (Chicago/London: The University of Chicago Press, 1974), pp. 131–132.

5. Hans Bauer and Pontus Leander, *Grammatik des Biblisch-Aramäischen* (Halle an der Saale: Max Niemeyer, 1927), §90j.

6. Cf. Theodor Nöldeke, *Die Inschrift des Königs Mesa von Moab* (Kiel: Schwers'sche Buchhandlung, 1870), p. 35, against which see Chapter 3, nos. 23i and 11a.

7. In Frank M. Cross and David N. Freedman, *EHO*, p. 47 n. 11. See also *KAI* 2:181–182.

8. Cross, "The Cave Inscriptions from Khirbet Beit Lei," in *Near Eastern Archaeology in the Twentieth Century*, ed. James A. Sanders (Garden City, N.Y.: Doubleday & Co., 1970), p. 305 n. 3.

9. The reading is Naveh's, in "Old Hebrew Inscriptions in a Burial Cave," *IEJ* 13 (1963): 84.

10. See Yohanan Aharoni, *Arad Inscriptions* (Jerusalem: The Bialik Institute and the Israel Exploration Society, 1975), p. 34 (in Hebrew). For the identical BH usage, see *GKC* §90c.

11. Cross, in *Near Eastern Archaeology*, p. 301.

12. Carl Brockelmann, *GvG* 2:§152. For the Akkadian usage, see Kaufman, *Akkadian Influences*, pp. 131–132.

13. Note the translation of Franz Rosenthal, "Notes on the Third Aramaic Inscription from Sefîre-Sûjîn," *BASOR* 158 (1960): 29; and idem, "Canaanite and Aramaic Inscriptions," in *ANET*³, p. 661.

14. For the emphatic אית in Aramaic, see no. 12 below.

15. For a discussion of the form, see Chapter 3, no. 15a.

16. Cross, "Epigraphic Notes on the Ammān Citadel Inscription," *BASOR* 193 (1969): 17.

17. Raphael Kutscher, "A New Inscription from ʿAmman," *Qadmoniot* 5 (1972): 27, 28 (in Hebrew).

18. Emile Puech and Alexander Rofé, "L'inscription de la citadelle d'Amman," *RB* 80 (1973): 536.

19. See Chapter 3, nos. 11a and 11b.

20. So Jo Ann Carlton (Hackett), "Studies in the Plaster Text from Tell Deir ʿAllā" (Ph.D. dissertation, Harvard University, 1980), pp. 46, 140; and Baruch A. Levine, "The Deir ʿAlla Plaster Inscriptions," *JAOS* 101 (1981): 200.

21. On ידעתה, see Ziony Zevit, *Matres Lectionis in Ancient Hebrew Epigraphs*, ASOR Monograph Series, vol. 2 (Cambridge: ASOR, 1980), p. 31; and H. Van Dyke Parunak, "The Orthography of the Arad Ostraca," *BASOR* 230 (1978): 28.

22. Ze'ev Meshel and Carol Meyers, "The Name of God in the Wilderness of Zin," *BA* 39 (1976): 10, fig. 4.

23. Within the confines of the available evidence. For conditions requiring use of the *nota accusativi* + suffix, see *GKC* §117e.

24. For comparative evidence, see Brockelmann, *GvG* 2:§215.

25. See Zellig S. Harris, *Development of the Canaanite Dialects*, American Oriental Series, vol. 16 (New Haven: American Oriental Society, 1939), pp. 68–69.

26. The article began to be used with the noun in the later period. See, for example, המשכב זן "this coffin" (KAI 9 A 1), הערפת זא "this colonnade" (Yehawmilk 6), etc.

27. Thomas O. Lambdin, "The Junctural Origin of the West Semitic Definite Article," in *Near Eastern Studies in Honor of William Foxwell Albright*, ed. Hans Goedicke (Baltimore/London: The Johns Hopkins Press, 1971), pp. 328–329 with n. 23. Cf. Harris, *A Grammar of the Phoenician Language*, American Oriental Series, vol. 8 (New Haven: American Oriental Society, 1936), pp. 56, 66; and Johannes Friedrich and Wolfgang Röllig, *PPG*² §300.

28. See Chapter 2, no. 16.

29. See already J. Halévy, "Les Deux Inscriptions hétéennes de Zindjîrlî," *RS* 1 (1893): 143.

30. See Chapter 3, no. 5, for the NWS definite article.

31. André Caquot and André Lemaire, "Les textes araméens de Deir ʿAlla," *Syria* 54 (1977): 194.

32. P. Kyle McCarter, "The Balaam Texts from Deir ʿAllā: The First Combination," *BASOR* 239 (1980): 51, 52.

33. See Chapter 3, no. 2c with nn. 38–41.

34. Harris, *Development*, p. 69.

35. See above, p. 149 n. 28.

36. Lambdin, in *Near Eastern Studies . . . Albright*, p. 321.

37. Ibid., pp. 315–333, esp. pp. 321–324.

38. Excluding seals with ל + PN.

39. Segert, *Grammar*, §61.46. Cf. ibid., §15.1.

40. Published by Dupont-Sommer, "Deux nouvelles inscriptions sémitiques trouvées en Cilicie," *JKF* 1 (1950): 43–45. See also Giovanni Garbini, "I dialetti del fenicio," *AION* 27 (1977): 291 with n. 30. This interpretation presumes, of course, that ש was not part of the name.

41. See Harris, *Grammar*, pp. 63–64; and Segert, *Grammar*, §75.721.23. Cf. Stanley Gevirtz, "On the Etymology of the Phoenician Particle אש," *JNES* 16 (1957): 124 n. 8.

42. So, for example, Dupont-Sommer, "Un papyrus araméen d'époque saïte découvert à Saqqarah," *Semitica* 1 (1948): 49; H. L. Ginsberg, "An Aramaic Contemporary of the Lachish Letters," *BASOR* 111 (1948): 26 (translation only); and *KAI* 2:313.

43. J. Hoftijzer, "Interpretation and Grammar," in *Aramaic Texts from Deir ʿAlla*, ed. J. Hoftijzer and G. van der Kooij. Documenta et Monumenta Orientis Antiqui, vol. 19 (Leiden: E. J. Brill, 1976), p. 267. See also p. 11.

44. For the phrase זי סחרתי "of my vicinity" (Sf. III 7/8), see Kaufman, *Akkadian Influences*, p. 130 n. 74. A periphrastic possessive in זי + ל + suffix, as in Sf. III 20 and Nerab 1:14 (so Segert, *Altaramäische Grammatik* [Leipzig: VEB Verlag Enzyklopädie, 1975], §6.2.5.6) is also dubious since, instead of meaning "my, yours," etc., the construction is a verbless clause. In Sf. III 20, for example, הן השב זי לי means "if that which is mine is returned to me," and similarly Nerab 1:14 means "that which is yours will be protected." The relative זי functions as an independent relative, as the orthography with *yodh* shows. Both examples, then, are verbless clauses acting as the subject of the verb. The particle זי retains its relative force. Cf. Paul Joüon, *Grammaire de l'hébreu biblique* (Rome: Pontifical Biblical Institute, 1923), §§158l, 145a.

45. Kaufman, "Siʾgabbar, Priest of Sahr in Nerab," *JAOS* 90 (1970): 270–271; and idem, "[Review of Segert, *Grammatik*]," *BiOr* 34 (1977): 94.

46. Paul-E. Dion, *La langue de Yaʾudi* (Waterloo, Ont.: The Corporation for the Publication of Academic Studies in Religion in Canada, 1974), pp. 235–236.

47. *GKC* §129h.

48. Naveh, *IEJ* 13 (1963): 84.

49. See Cross, in *Near Eastern Archaeology*, p. 301.

50. Brockelmann, *GvG* 2:§§164–167.

51. Excluding the construction כל "every, any" + noun + relative.

52. See Lambdin, in *Near Eastern Studies . . . Albright*, pp. 318–319 with n. 7. Cf. Friedrich and Röllig, *PPG*[2] §293. For the determined sense, see Josh. 24:14 and I Sam. 24:6; cf. Ex. 21:28, Lev. 26:5, and Num. 21:9.

53. For this reason, the problematic הברך בעל (Karatepe A I 1) is best interpreted as cognate to Akkadian *abarakku*. See above, pp. 130, 161 n. 340.

54. See Chapter 2, no. 16.

55. Cf. Lambdin, in *Near Eastern Studies . . . Albright*, pp. 321–322.

56. For suggestions, see ibid., p. 318 n. 7; and Klaus Beyer, "[Review of Degen, *Grammatik*]," *ZDMG* 120 (1970): 202, on Sfire; and Kaufman, "Reflections on the Assyrian-Aramaic Bilingual from Tell Fakhariyeh," *Maarav* 3 (1982): 148 n. 27, on Fekh. 23.

57. The absence of a definite article on סמר is yet another feature which isolates the dialect of the Kilamu scepter inscription from standard Phoenician. For other traits, see Kaufman, *Akkadian Influences*, p. 8 n. 7.

58. See Francis I. Andersen, "Moabite Syntax," *Or* 35 (1966): 95–96, for a discussion of the possible interpretations.

59. See Chapter 2, no. 16.

60. Joüon, *Grammaire,* §158f.

61. Lambdin, in *Near Eastern Studies . . . Albright*, pp. 318–319, 321–322.

62. See above, nn. 52, 56.

63. Harris, *Grammar*, p. 62.

64. Cf. ibid.

65. Within that group of dialects which used a form of the *lamedh* as the negation, only Hebrew had a final *aleph* in this period. The presence of the final *aleph*, however, does not reflect a genetic difference from the Aramaic-Deir Alla -ל; it was merely a phonetic, syllable-closing *aleph*. Such a syllable-closing *aleph* is generally found after *a*-vowels in accented, final position (see Brockelmann, *GvG* 1:§§37dα, 107tα). For example, the Arabic-Ethiopic demonstrative [d̠ā, zā] appeared in late Byblian and Old Aramaic as זא "this" (fem. sing.), with final *aleph*; cf. Moabite, Hebrew, and Fekh.-Aramaic זאת "this" (fem. sing.). Similarly, the conjunction **pa* of Arabic and Ugaritic appeared in Samalian as פא three times, two of which were followed by a word divider, indicating the independent status of the word (Rosenthal, "[Review of Dion, *La langue*]," *JBL* 95 [1976]: 154). Further, the Hebrew particle of entreaty -נא is cognate to EA *-na*. These examples indicate that the final *aleph* in the Hebrew negation was merely a phonological development; when a word ended in [ā, a], and when that syllable was stressed, that final syllable could be closed with an *aleph*. This *aleph*, however, appeared only on words which themselves received an added stress, due either to the meaning or syntactic position of the word. Cf. Lambdin, in *Near Eastern Studies . . . Albright*, p. 323 with n. 14.

66. Brockelmann, *GvG* 1:§253A; 2:§§105–109.

67. Ginsberg, "[Review of Harris, *Grammar*]," *JBL* 56 (1937): 140; and idem, "Ugaritico-Phoenicia," *JANES* 5 (1973): 144 n. 58. Ginsberg credited Hoffmann (*Über einige phön. Inschriften*, p. 41) with first interpreting the syntax here correctly.

68. *GKC* §152m.

69. See also Brockelmann, *GvG* 2:§§57–59.

70. Ronald J. Williams, *Hebrew Syntax: An Outline,* 2nd ed. (Toronto/Buffalo: University of Toronto Press, 1976), §§406–411, 569.

71. Ibid., §70.

72. Cf. Segert, *Grammar,* §§75.462, 75.843.

73. See Joseph A. Fitzmyer, *The Aramaic Inscriptions of Sefîre,* Biblica et Orientalia, vol. 19 (Rome: Pontifical Biblical Institute, 1967), pp. 180–181.

74. Dion, *La langue,* p. 250.

75. See Ahirom 1 (Byblian), Arsl.T. 1:1/2 (standard Phoenician), Sf. I A 1 (Old Aramaic), and BH.

76. See already Andersen, *Or* 35 (1966): 88–89.

77. See p. 177.

78. *GKC* §112q.

79. Cf. ibid., §§112p, ii.

80. See also n. 149 below.

81. Helga and Manfred Weippert, "Die 'Bileam'-Inschrift von *Tell Dēr ꜥAllā*," *ZDPV* 98 (1982): 88. Cf. Carlton (Hackett), "Studies," p. 63.

82. Weippert and Weippert, *ZDPV* 98 (1982): 99.

83. See *GKC* §112r.

84. See Joüon, *Grammaire,* §177e.

85. Lemaire, "L'ostracon 'Ramat-Negeb' et la topographie historique du Negeb," *Semitica* 23 (1973): 14, 15.

86. As read by Cross, in *Near Eastern Archaeology,* p. 301.

87. So, for example, William F. Albright and William L. Moran, "A Re-interpretation of an Amarna Letter from Byblos (EA 82)," *JCS* 2 (1948): 244 n. 7.

88. So, for example, *B-L* §36s.

89. Frank M. Cross and Richard J. Saley, "Phoenician Incantations on a Plaque of the Seventh Century B.C. from Arslan Tash in Upper Syria," *BASOR* 197 (1970): 46 n. 23a.

90. See Chapter 3, no. 24b.

91. So, for example, Caquot, Gaster, and Röllig.

92. Cross, *CBQ* 36 (1974): 488 n. 21.

93. Röllig, "Die Amulette von Arslan Taş," *NESE* 2 (1974): 26.

94. So Cross and Saley, *BASOR* 197 (1970): 47 with n. 39.

95. So *KAI* 2:47.

96. Dion, *La langue,* p. 273.

97. See Chapter 3, no. 22a.

98. Cf., however, p. 162 n. 354.

99. For the Moabite infinitive, see Segert, "Die Sprache der moabitischen Königsinschrift," *ArOr* 29 (1961): 224.

100. Aharoni, "Hebrew Ostraca from Tel Arad," *IEJ* 16 (1966): 2 n. 2; and idem, *Arad Inscriptions,* pp. 12, 18 (in Hebrew).

101. See the examples cited by Joüon, *Grammaire,* §123u.

102. Brockelmann, *GvG* 2:§10a.

103. So, for example, Hayim Tawil, "A Note on the Aḥiram Inscription," *JANES* 3/1 (1970–1971): 34 (earlier literature on p. 34 n. 13). The prefixed כ, then, was the particle *kī.

104. See Friedrich and Röllig, *PPG*² §§323, 268.

105. See Rainer Degen, *Altaramäische Grammatik der Inschriften des 10.-8. Jh. v. Chr.*, Abhandlungen für die Kunde des Morgenlandes, vol. 38/3 (Wiesbaden: Franz Steiner, 1969), §§78, 93.

106. Dion, *La langue*, pp. 272–274, 318.

107. Cf. Andersen, *Or* 35 (1966): 106–108.

108. B. S. J. Isserlin, "Epigraphically attested Judean Hebrew, and the question of 'upper class' (Official) and 'popular' speech variants in Judea during the 8th–6th centuries B.C.," *AJBA* 2/1 (1972): 202–203.

109. Wolfram von Soden, *GAG* §150g.

110. Cyrus H. Gordon, *UT* §§9.26, 13.56.

111. Yet see below, no. 8.

112. Dion, *La langue*, p. 272.

113. Cf. Cross, *BASOR* 193 (1969): 18 with n. 8, although the form cited is probably a perfect (see Chapter 3, no. 23b).

114. The situation is more complex in BH, where the infinitive absolute did function as a finite verb, for which see John Huesman, "Finite Uses of the Infinitive Absolute," *Bibl* 37 (1956): 271–295, esp. pp. 284–295. The distinction between this use of the infinitive absolute and the consecutive imperfect remains to be studied.

115. Cross, "Epigraphic Notes on Hebrew Documents of the Eighth-Sixth Centuries B.C.: II. The Murabbaʿât Papyrus and the Letter Found Near Yabneh-Yam," *BASOR* 165 (1962): 44–45 n. 43; and *KAI* 2:200.

116. Shemaryahu Talmon ("The New Hebrew Letter from the Seventh Century B.C. in Historical Perspective," *BASOR* 176 [1964]: 30) and Albright ("Palestinian Inscriptions," in *ANET*³, p. 568 with n. 5), for example, understood אסם as a noun and linked the *waw* to the preceding verb.

117. Gordon, *UT* §9.29.

118. Albright, "The Phoenician Inscriptions of the Tenth Century B.C. from Byblus," *JAOS* 67 (1947): 156 n. 24, followed by Roger T. O'Callaghan, "The Great Phoenician Portal Inscription from Karatepe," *Or* 18 (1949): 190; Cross and Freedman, *EHO*, p. 14; Segert, *Grammar*, §64.444; and Joshua Blau, "Hebrew and North West Semitic: Reflections on the Classification of the Semitic Languages," *Hebrew Annual Review* 2 (1978): 38.

119. So Harris, *Grammar*, p. 40; and idem, *Development*, p. 47. Cf. Kaufman, *Akkadian Influences*, p. 155 n. 75; and Friedrich and Röllig, *PPG*², p. 134 n. 1.

120. For additional examples, see Dupont-Sommer, *RA* 42 (1948): 182; and Weippert, "Elemente phönikischer und kilikischer Religion in den Inschriften vom Karatepe," in *XVII. Deutscher Orientalistentag . . . Würzburg. Vorträge*, ed. Wolfgang Voigt. ZDMG Supplementa, vol. 1, pt. 1 (Wiesbaden: Franz Steiner, 1969), p. 194 n. 9. Cf. Friedrich and Röllig, *PPG*² §267 with n. 1 (p. 135).

121. O'Callaghan, "The Phoenician Inscription on the King's Statue at Karatepe," *CBQ* 11 (1949): 239. Cf. David Marcus, "Studies in Ugaritic Grammar 1," *JANES* 1/2 (1969): 59.

122. See above, p. 157 n. 221.

123. Degen, *Grammatik*, pp. 114–115 with n. 21 (with earlier literature); Kaufman, *Akkadian Influences*, p. 155; and idem, *BiOr* 34 (1977): 96.

124. Additional examples are listed by Degen, *Grammatik*, §74a. Cf. Fitzmyer, *Sefire*, p. 170.

125. Dion, *La langue*, pp. 259–260.

126. For the translation, see Rosenthal, *JBL* 95 (1976): 154.

127. So Dion, *La langue*, pp. 263–266.

128. See, for example, H 20ff.15ff.

129. So, for example, Hoftijzer, in *Aramaic Texts*, p. 296; Carlton (Hackett), "Studies," pp. 63, 150; and McCarter, *BASOR* 239 (1980): 50.

130. See already Nöldeke, *Mesa*, pp. 31–32. Cf. Segert, *ArOr* 29 (1961): 223, 229.

131. Harris, *Development*, p. 47; and Albright, "A Reëxamination of the Lachish Letters," *BASOR* 73 (1939): 21.

132. See *GKC* §112pp(a) with n. 2.

133. For other examples, see Brockelmann, *GvG* 2:§§77cβ, 78dα, 79cα.

134. This condition therefore excludes Ugaritic.

135. Ginsberg, "The Northwest Semitic Languages," in *Patriarchs*, ed. B. Mazar. The World History of the Jewish People, vol. 2 ([New Brunswick, N.J.]: Rutgers University Press, 1970), p. 105.

136. Segert, *Grammar*, §64.722.3. In Karatepe A I 15, עבד is nominal.

137. Jonas C. Greenfield, "The 'Periphrastic Imperative' in Aramaic and Hebrew," *IEJ* 19 (1969): 201.

138. Rosenthal, *BASOR* 158 (1960): 30 n. 12 (one possibility); and Fitzmyer, "A Further Note on the Aramaic Inscription Sefire III.22," *JSS* 14 (1969): 199–200.

139. Cf. Degen, *Grammatik*, §77.

140. James F. Ross, "Prophecy in Hamath, Israel, and Mari," *HTR* 63 (1970): 23 n. 80; and Albright, in *ANET*³, p. 568 (translation only). Cf. Dennis Pardee, "The Judicial Plea from Meṣad Ḥashavyahu (Yavneh-Yam): A New Philological Study," *Maarav* 1 (1978): 40–41, 36.

141. Greenfield, *IEJ* 19 (1969): 209–210.

142. Ibid., pp. 199–210.

143. Gordon, "Azitawadd's Phoenician Inscription," *JNES* 8 (1949): 114, 110.

144. Rosenthal, in *ANET*³, p. 654.

145. So Gordon, *JNES* 8 (1949): 114.

146. E. Lipiński, "From Karatepe to Pyrgi. Middle Phoenician Miscellanea," *RSF* 2 (1974): 48, though he translated the phrase differently.

147. See Wilfred Watson, "Shared Consonants in Northwest Semitic," *Bibl* 50 (1969): 525–533.

148. Cf. P. Swiggers, "Karatepe A II 5–6/B I 13–14/C III 3–4," *RSF* 9 (1981): 143–146.

149. Fitzmyer, *Sefire*, p. 66 (with list). The syntax of this construction, verb + complementary imperfect, is reminiscent of the Old Aramaic pur-

pose clause, in which a verb could be followed by an imperfect; see, for example, אתה + imperfect in the meaning "he came in order to . . ." in Sf. III 11/12.12.12 (asyndetic) and Sf. III 11 (syndetic). Yet also note the complementary infinitive in Sf. I B 32.32.

150. *KAI*, Fitzmyer, etc.

151. Segert, *Grammatik*, §6.6.5.6.1.

152. Degen, *Grammatik*, p. 15, §§84.1, 88, followed by Kaufman, *BiOr* 34 (1977): 95, and idem, *Maarav* 3 (1982): 151 n. 36.

153. The handcopy in the *editio princeps* shows only traces of this letter. While Degen's reading may therefore be the correct one, at least syntactically, the faint traces seem to indicate a *mem*. Only a new reading of this passage would clarify this difficulty.

154. So, for example, McCarter, *BASOR* 239 (1980): 51, 52; and Carlton (Hackett), "Studies," pp. 40, 157.

155. See Brockelmann, *GvG* 2:§§337–341; and von Soden, *GAG* §150e.

156. Segert, *Grammar*, §76.24.

157. Word order in the second Arslan Tash text is not yet clear. Compare, for example, the translations of Gaster and Cross (in Cross, *CBQ* 36 [1974]: 486–487 [Gaster's], 488–489 [Cross']).

158. Cf. Yehimilk 2.

159. Kaufman, *Akkadian Influences*, p. 132. Cf. Greenfield, "The Dialects of Early Aramaic," *JNES* 37 (1978): 94, 95.

160. See already Dupont-Sommer, *Semitica* 1 (1948): 52 with n. 2.

161. Note that here, and throughout these dialects, there was no syntactic difference between declarative and volitive clauses.

162. See Kaufman, *Maarav* 3 (1982): 154.

163. Pierre Bordreuil, "Une tablette araméenne inédite de 635 av. J.-C.," *Semitica* 23 (1973): 95–102.

164. Kaufman, "An Assyro-Aramaic *egirtu ša šulmu*," in *Essays on the Ancient Near East in Memory of Jacob Joel Finkelstein*, ed. Maria deJong Ellis. Memoirs of the Connecticut Academy of Arts & Sciences, vol. 19 (Hamden, Conn.: Archon Books, 1977), p. 120.

165. See idem, *Akkadian Influences*, p. 132.

166. Dion, *La langue*, p. 283; idem, "The Language Spoken in Ancient Sam'al," *JNES* 37 (1978): 118; and Segert, *Grammatik*, §7.3.3.4.1. See also Greenfield, "Dialect Traits in Early Aramaic," *Leshonenu* 32 (1968): 364 n. 29 (in Hebrew).

167. Siegfried Horn, "The Amman Citadel Inscription," *ADAJ* 12–13 (1967–1968): 83; idem, "The Ammān Citadel Inscription," *BASOR* 193 (1969): 8; and Puech and Rofé, *RB* 80 (1973): 532. Cf. Cross, *BASOR* 193 (1969): 18, 17; Albright, "Some Comments on the ʿAmmân Citadel Inscription," *BASOR* 198 (1970): 38, 39; Kutscher, *Qadmoniot* 5 (1972): 27; Dion, "Notes d'épigraphie ammonite," *RB* 82 (1975): 32; and William J. Fulco, "The ʿAmmān Citadel Inscription: A New Collation," *BASOR* 230 (1978): 42.

168. See the brief discussion by Hoftijzer, in *Aramaic Texts*, pp. 294–295.

169. The word order S-V in ll. 2.7.10.18.31 may reflect subordination. See the translation of Williams, "Moabite Stone," in *The Interpreter's Dictionary of the Bible*, 4 vols. (Nashville/New York: Abingdon Press, 1962), 3:420.

170. Ajrud (אמריו), Arad (18:2/3, 40:12), and Yavneh-Yam (1:10.11).

171. Arad (4:2/3; cf. 18:5/6) and Beit Lei B (according to Naveh's reading).

172. See Brockelmann, *GvG* 2:§92.

173. See Chapter 5.

174. See Kaufman, *Akkadian Influences*, pp. 132–133; and idem, *Maarav* 3 (1982): 154, on Aramaic.

175. See Brockelmann, *GvG* 2:§§92, 94.

176. See Yehawmilk 8 (oneself). 15 (one's adversary); Eshmunazor 4 (one's coffin), etc.

177. I thank Michael Covington for this formulation.

178. So Fitzmyer, *Sefire*, p. 74. Cf. Adon 8.

179. See Kutscher, "הארמית המקראית—ארמית מזרחית היא או מערבית?" *Leshonenu* 17 (1951): 122.

180. Yet cf. Brockelmann, *GvG* 2:§211.

181. Andersen, *Or* 35 (1966): 117–118 n. 4; and Masao Sekine, "The Subdivisions of the North-West Semitic Languages," *JSS* 18 (1973): 218 n. 2.

182. Cf. Blau, "Short Philological Notes on the Inscription of Mešaʿ," *Maarav* 2 (1980): 152–154.

183. Arad 2:5, 3:6–8, 40:4.12; Beit Lei A 2 (Cross' reading), B (Naveh's reading); Lach. 18:1; and el-Qom 3:1.

184. See also Brockelmann, *GvG* 2:§215.

185. Cf. Sf. II B 4.

186. See Chapter 3, no. 13, and n. 231.

187. So Caquot and Lemaire, *Syria* 54 (1977): 205; and Carlton (Hackett), "Studies," p. 46.

188. Williams, *Syntax*, §511.

189. See Brockelmann, *GvG* 2:§§430–432, 464–465.

THE DIALECTAL CONTINUUM OF SYRIA-PALESTINE

The table that follows summarizes the results obtained in Chapters 2–4. Each phoneme, phonetic feature, morpheme, and syntactic feature considered relevant to dialectal division is charted throughout the individual dialects. The table offers an overview of the Northwest Semitic dialects spoken in Syria-Palestine between 1000 and 586 B.C.E.

The dialects group, and regroup, according to the individual feature examined. For example, the correspondences of *d (2:1)[1] separate Old Aramaic, Samalian, and Deir Alla from the Phoenician dialects, Ammonite, Moabite, and Hebrew. The form of the first person singular independent pronoun (3:1a) unites Phoenician dialects, Samalian, and Moabite into one group, and Old Aramaic and Hebrew into another. Yet a third feature, the form of the relative pronoun/particle (3:3), joins Old Byblian, Old Aramaic, and Samalian into one dialectal unit, standard Phoenician and Ammonite into another, and Moabite and Hebrew into a third. No two linguistic features have the identical distribution among these dialects.[2]

Not all linguistic features, however, are equally significant in linguistic classification.[3] Since the goal of any classificatory scheme is the demonstration of a particular shared relation among speech forms, only those features reflecting shared innovations are useful

	BYBLIAN	STANDARD PHOENICIAN (Arsl. T.)	ARAMAIC (Zkr · Sfire · Nerab · Fekh. · Halaf · Adon)	SAMALIAN	AMMONITE	DEIR ALLA	MOABITE	EDOMITE	HEBREW N	HEBREW S
(2:1) Corresp. of *ḍ	צ*	צ	ק [(?)] (except קרן)	ק (exc.: ארק)	צ	ק	צ		צ	צ
(2:2) Corresp. of *ḏ	ז [z]	ז [z]	ז [d] (Fekh.)	ז	ז	ז	ז	ז	ז	ז
(2:3) Corresp. of *ṯ	צ [ṣ]	צ [ṣ]	ש [t] / ת [t]	ש*		ש	ש		ש	ש
(2:4) Corresp. of *ṭ	ש [š]	ש [š]	ע [ṭ] / ט (Adon)	ש	ש	ש	ש		ש	ש
(2:5) Corresp. of *â		[ō]	*[â]	*[â]	[ō]?		?		[ō]	[ō]
(2:6) Corresp. of *â		(*aʾ > â >) [ō] / (*awa >) [ō]	*[â]	*[âwa >] [â]?	[ō]				(*aʾ >) [â] / (*aʾ > â >) [ō] / (*awa >) [â]	
(2:7) Corresp. of *â		[ō] (nouns) / [â] (verbs)	[â]	[â]?			[ā̊]	[ā̊]	[â] (nouns) / [â] (verbs)	
(2:8) Corresp. of *aw / *ay	[ō] / [ē]	[ō] / [ē]	[aw] / [ay] (exc.: "long" impfs.; בן [Fekh. 17]; בנה? [Sf. III 18, etc.])	[aw, ō] / [ay, ē]	[aw] / [ē]	[aw] / [ay]	[aw] > [aj] > [ō] / [ay] > [aj] > [ē]	[aw] > [ō] / [ay]	[ō] < [aw] / [ē] < [ay]	
(2:9) *n + consonant	[cC] (exc.: n + laryng.) (incl. *bin + PN)	[cC]	[cC] (exc.: מן + X)	[cC] (exc.: מן + X)	[cC] (incl. מן + X)	[cC] (exc.: מן + X)	[cC] (incl. מן + X)	[cC] (incl. + X)	[cC] exc.: BH מנ, etc.	
(2:10) Dissim. of emph.	no	no	initial *q + emph. > k + emph.	קשט?		no?			no	
(2:11) Anaptyxis		incipient	incipient	no?					no?	

	BYBLIAN	STANDARD PHOENICIAN (Arsl. T.)	ARAMAIC (Zkr · Sfire · Nerab · Fekh. · Halaf · Adon)	SAMALIAN	AMMONITE	DEIR ALLA	MOABITE	EDOMITE	HEBREW N	HEBREW S
(2:12) Prothetic *ʾaleph*		אדרת (?) / אש	שם / אשם · אמר	אצב? / אמש? / אשם?	אשחת? / הדק? / אש	אמב	אשוה			yes / חרן?
(2:13) *CVʾ > [CVˊ]	no	yes		yes?	no?	no?	yes			yes
(2:14) Aphaeresis *ʾaleph*		in PNs, when 2 positions from accent	ח	ח	אש	ח	no	ח		
(2:15) Syncope intervocalic *yodh*	[banaya]	[banō] / בני/בנ / in caus. impf.	[banā] בנ / ליד?, etc. / ח-/ד-?	[banā] / בנ / לבנה	[banō] / בנ/בנה	[banā] / בנ	[banā (?)]	ח	[banā] / בנ	
(2:16) Syncope intervocalic *he*	in suff. / [waha]	always (exc.: after *i*-grade vowels)	no	in caus. impf.	[waha]	in caus. impf.?	in caus. impf.		in suff. and caus. impf. / [wᵊha]	
(2:17) Palat. *he*	no	*iḥ(V) > [iy(V)]	no	no	no	no	no		no	
(2:18a) Corresp. final *-āt*		[ōt]	[ā]	[ā]	נב	[ā]	חד		[ā]	
(2:18b) *-at*	חאת / שמעת*	חבת / בת	שנה	אלהת		שמה / החמה			זחה* / שמה / חכמה*	

	BYBLIAN	STANDARD PHOENICIAN (Arsl. T.)	ARAMAIC (Zkr, Sfire, Nerab, Fekh., Halaf, Adon)	SAMALIAN	AMMONITE	DEIR ALLA	MOABITE	EDOMITE	HEBREW N	HEBREW S
(2:19) Case endings	prob. in sing.	vestigial (gen. sing.)	no	masc. pl.		no	no		no	אני?
(3:1a) Ind. pronouns: 1st sing.	אנך*	אנך	אנה	אנך				אנך		אנך
(3:1b) 2nd m. sg.		[ʔattā]	[ʔatt(a)]	[ʔatt(a)]						[ʔattā]
(3:1c) 3rd m. sg.	הא [huʔa]	הא*	הא	הא		הא?	הא			הא
(3:1d) 3rd m. pl.		המת	המ[ו] / הם						הם* / המה*	
(3:2a) Demonst. pro.: m. sg.	ז	ז	זנ / זנה	זנ(ה)						זה
(3:2b) fm. sg.	זא*	ז	זא / זאת	זא				זאת		זאת
(3:2c) plur.	אל	אל*	אל / אלן	אל						אלה*
(3:3) Rel. pro./particle	ז	אש	ז(י)	ז(י)	אש			אשר		אשר*
(3:4) Pers. interrog. pronoun		מ	מנ	מ	[mi]	מנ?				מי
(3:5) Def. art.	ה-	ה-	א-	∅	ה-	ה-	ה-	ה-		ה-

	BYBLIAN	STANDARD PHOENICIAN Arsl. T.	ARAMAIC Zkr Sfire Nerab Fekh. Halaf Adon	SAMALIAN	AMMONITE	DEIR ALLA	MOABITE	EDOMITE	HEBREW N S
(3:6a) Noun: abs. m. pl./dual	־ם	־ם ־י	־י	[ū, ī]	־ם	־י	־י		־ם [ay]
(3:6b) m. pl. const.	[ē]	[ē]	[ay]	[ū, ī]	[ē, ī]	[ay]	[ē (?)]		
(3:6c) abs. fm. sg.	מתת חתת	־ת (incl. שׁת*)	־ה < *at ־ה < *āt שׁאת	־ה כבב	־ה	־ה	־ה (incl. שׁת)		־ה, ־ה שׁת שׁבת*
(3:6d) abs. fm. pl.		־ת	מת מאן	־ת	־ה	־ה	־ה		־ה
(3:7) Pl. final wk. nouns	like fm. sing.	מקר ילך	מתות- שׁן מאן	מתמה?		?	מתה		חתמה*
(3:8) Fm. pl. noun + suff.		like fm. sg.	like fm. sg.	?			like fm. sg.		like m. pl.
(3:9a) Poss. suff. on "sg." noun: 1st sg.	[i, iya]	[i, iya]	[ī]	[ī]		[ī]	[ī]		[ī]
(3:9b) 3rd m. sg.	[hū] > [aw, ō] *[nmū (?)]	[ō, iyū/ī]	[ih (?)]	־ה	־ה	־ה	־ה		[ō]
(3:9b) 3rd fm. sg.	*[hā]	[ā, iyā] [nnā (?)]	[ah(a)]	־ה			[āh]		
(3:9c) 1st pl.		[nū, ōn]	[an, na]						[nū]
(3:9d) 3rd m. pl.		[ōm, nōm]	[hum] [am] [hum]			־הם, ־ם			[ām, hem]
(3:10a) Poss. suff. on pl. nouns: 2nd m. sg.			[ayk]			[ayk]			[aykā]

Comparative linguistic table (rotated 90°). Columns left-to-right: row reference/label, BYBLIAN, STANDARD PHOENICIAN (Arsl. T.), ARAMAIC (Zkr, Sfire, Nerab, Fekh., Halaf, Adon), SAMALIAN, AMMONITE, DEIR ALLA, MOABITE, EDOMITE, HEBREW (N, S).

		BYBLIAN	STANDARD PHOENICIAN Arsl. T.	ARAMAIC	SAMALIAN	AMMONITE	DEIR ALLA	MOABITE	EDOMITE	HEBREW N	HEBREW S
(3:10b)	3rd m. sg.	ה-*[aw (?)]	ה- [éyū/ī]	ה- [awh(i)] ... [ה]- [ayhi(i)] ... ה-	[Vh(u/i)]		ה- [awh(u/i)]	ה- [ôh(u/i) (?)]			ו- [āw]
(3:10c)	3rd m. pl.	[éhum (?)]	*[énōm]	[ayhum]						*[é/ayhem]	
(3:11a)	Obj. suffix: 3rd m. sg.	[hū]	[ô, Vyū/ī]	ה(ו)-	ה-		ה-?	ה-	ה	[ô, Vhū] [émū]	
(3:11b)	3rd m. pl.		[ôm, nōm]	[hum]				[hum]?		[ām]	
(3:12)	Numerals: card. decades	ם-	ם-	ן-	ן-			ן-		ם-*	
(3:13)	Coord. conj.	ו-	ו-	ו-, פ-	ו-, פ-	ו-	ו-	ו-	ו-	ו-	
(3:14)	Neg.: nonexist.			לש	הן			אן			אן
(3:15a)	Particles: Nota acc.		את	את	הן			את		את	
(3:15b)	cond. particle	אך / אם	אם		אם / הן		הן			אם / הן	
(3:15c)	directive he	no?	no?	no	no		no	no?		yes	
(3:15d)	precative l-	no	no	no? / yes	yes	no?	no	no		no	
(3:16a)	Verbal conjugations: t- of qal	Gt		tG / Gt; Gt (one example); tG			tG?	Gt			
(3:16b)	niphal	?	yes	no		yes?	yes	no?		yes	

	BYBLIAN	STANDARD PHOENICIAN (Arsl. T.)	ARAMAIC (Zkr, Sfire, Nerab, Fekh., Halaf, Adon)	SAMALIAN	AMMONITE	DEIR ALLA	MOABITE	EDOMITE	HEBREW N	HEBREW S
(3:16c) causative pref.	-ה?	-י	-ה	-ה	-ה	-ה	-ה			-ה
(3:17a) Strong vb.: Perfect. 1st sg. ending		[tī] / [t(u/i)]?	[t(u/i)]	[t(u/i)]			[tī]		[tī]	
(3:17b) 3rd m. sg., qal	[qatala]	[qatal]	[qatal]	[qatal (?)]			[qatāī]	[qatāī]	[qātal]	
(3:17c) 3rd fm. sg., qal	*[ā]	[ā]	[at]	[at]	[qatāī]	[at]			*[ā]	[āt] (הָ◌)
(3:18a) Impf. endings: 2nd m. pl. indic. juss.			[ū]	[ū]					[ū]	
(3:18b) 3rd m. pl. indic. juss.		[ū] [ū]	[ūn] [ū]	[ū] [ū]	[ūn]	[ū] [ū]			[ū] [ū]	
(3:18c) 3rd fm. pl.			-ן -ʾ	-ן -ʾ		-ן -ה			-ה -ה*	
(3:19a) Infinitive: qal inf. const.		[liqtōl]	לקטל / לקטלה(ן) / לקטל	לקטל		לקטל	לקטל*		[liqtōl]	
(3:19b) D-/caus. inf. const.		לקטל	לקטל						לקטל* / לקטל	
(3:20) Participle: qal passive			[qatil]	[qatil]			?		[qātūl]	
(3:21a) I'ʾ verbs: qal impf. יֵרֵד/יֵשֵׁב		?	[yidda']	*[yidda']			?		*[yēdaʿ]	
(3:21b) qal inf. const.	-ה	-ה	*-ø		פה	-ה	-ה			-ה
(3:22a) Middle weak vbs.: qal inf. abs.			[mawāt]			שם?				[mōt, śōm]

	BYBLIAN	STANDARD PHOENICIAN (Arsl. T.)	ARAMAIC Zkr	Sfire	Nerab	Fekh.	Halaf	Adon	SAMALIAN	AMMONITE	DEIR ALLA	MOABITE	EDOMITE	HEBREW N	HEBREW S
(3:22b) D-stem		pōlel				pālel				?				pōlel	pōlel
(3:23a) Final weak vbs.: 1st sg. pf., qal		[banéti]		בניח?		[banayt(u/i)]			בנה					[bāníti]	[bānā]
(3:23b) 3rd m. sg. pf.	[banaya]	[banō]				[banā]			[banā]	[banō]	[banā (?)]	[banā (?)]		[bānā]	
(3:23c) 3rd m. pl. pf.		?				[banaw]			ל		?			[bānū]	
(3:23d) 3rd sg., qal indic. juss.	יבן	יבן				ה- / ל			ל / ל		ה- / ל	יבן		יהי / ה-	
(3:23e) 2/3 pl. impf.		*[ṓ/ū(n)]				[awn]				[-n]	[aw (?)]			[ū]	
(3:23f) qal inf. const.		ה-		מהלך?					לבנה, -נבל					ה-	
(3:23g) qal m. pl. (undet.) part.		*[bōném]				[bānay(ō)n]								*[bōním]	
(3:23h) 3rd m. sg. pf., D-/causative	יחר					[banni] / [habni]			[habni]					[binná] / [hibná]	
(3:23i) D-stem, impf. sing.						[tibanné]						[yibanniw, -ū]		[yᵉbanné]	
(3:24a) יהל: qal impf.												יאהל		יחל	
(3:24b) qal impv.		לך?									לך	לך		לך*	
(3:25a) לקח: qal impf.		*[yiqqah]	[yiqqah] / [yilqah]			[yilqah]			[yiqqah]		[yiqqah]	[yiqqah]		[yiqqah]	
(3:25b) ending of the qal inf. const.		ה-*				-∅								ה-	

	BYBLIAN	STANDARD PHOENICIAN Arsl. T.	ARAMAIC — Zkr, Sfire, Nerab, Fekh., Halaf, Adon	SAMALIAN	AMMONITE	DEIR ALLA	MOABITE	EDOMITE	HEBREW N	HEBREW S
(4:1a) Pronoun: proleptic suff.		yes							?	
(4:1b) form of the pron. direct object	obj. suff.	obj. suff.	obj. suff.; *nota accus.* + suff. (for emphasis)	obj. suff.; *nota acc.* + suff.		obj. suff.	obj. suff.		obj. suff.; *nota acc.* + suffix	
(4:2) Demonst. Pronoun: agreement or nonagreement bet. noun and demonst.	undet. noun + demonst.	det. noun + demonst.	det. noun + demonstrative	"undet." noun + demonst.		?	det. noun + demonst.		det. noun + def. art. + demonst.	
(4:3a) Noun: periph. gen.		PN + ל + אשׁ/ש	זי	no		?			PN + ל (+ אשׁר?)	
(4:3b) nominal state before rel.	undet.	?	det. (exc.: Fekh. 23; Sf. I B 31 = I C 20)	"undet."		?	?		det. or undet.	
(4:4a) Negations: neg. of finite vb.	בל*	בל	ל-			ל-			לא	
(4:4b) neg. of participle		אי*	ל-						אין	
(4:4c) position of term of nonexist.			postpositive				postpos.		initial	
(4:5) Preposition: repetition or nonrepetition before coordinated nouns	(?); not in PN + title	yes (generally)	yes (before each nominal unit); coord. of modifier + proper noun (only Arslan Tash)	yes (incl. modif. + proper noun)	yes		yes (like Samal)		yes (exc.: title + PN)	
(4:6) Verb: Pf. Consec. perf.		no	no	no					yes	
(4:7a) Infinitive: inf. as impv.	yes	?	no	no?		yes?	no		yes	

	BYBLIAN	STANDARD PHOENICIAN (Arsl. T.)	ARAMAIC (Zkr, Sfire, Nerab, Fekh., Halaf, Adon)	SAMALIAN	AMMONITE	DEIR ALLA	MOABITE	EDOMITE	HEBREW N	HEBREW S
(4:7b) inf. in temp. clause	no?	no	no	no		no	yes			yes
(4:7c) inf. as finite verb		yes	no	no		no	no		no	
(4:8) Narrative, past tense		inf. abs.	consec. imperf. / perfect	perf.		consec. imperf.	consec. imperf.		consec. impf. > perfect	
(4:9) Participle: periph. tense	no	1 example	no?	no	no?	no?	no		1 example	
(4:10) "to be able" + complem. vb.		inf.	inf. (1 example)? / imperfect	inf.?					inf.	
(4:11) Verbal sentence: position of finite verb	initial (generally)	initial (exc.: ind. pro. + perfect)	initial (exc.: emphasis) / initial and noninitial	initial (exc.: emph.)	initial	initial and noninitial	initial (exc.: emph.)		initial (exc.: emphasis)	
(4:12) Marking or nonmarking of definite, nominal direct object	unmarked	usually unmarked. marked only for "emphasis"	usually unmarked. marked only for "emphasis" ?? / unmarked	unmarked		?	unmarked; or marked for "emphasis"		usually marked	
(4:13) Cond. Sentence: marking or nonmarking of apodosis	unmarked	marked with waw (?)	marked once with -p / unmarked	unmarked; marked once with -p		unmarked			marked with waw (once)	

for this purpose.[4] It is necessary, then, to isolate those features which participated in common developments and to evaluate the types of changes which occurred to produce the resultant forms.

For this reason, linguistic retentions must be excluded from a classificatory scheme. Since retentions derive from the common stock of features in the proto-language, they do not participate in any linguistic change. They reflect no shared development.[5] Thus the masc. singular demonstrative pronoun זֶן* (3:2a) in Old Byblian, Aramaic (זנה), and Samalian (זנ[ה]) does not suggest any shared development among these dialects since *$\underline{d}$-n is a common Semitic form.[6] The absence of the definite article (3:5) in Samalian and Ugaritic does not reflect any particular relationship between these dialects; this morpheme was a secondary development in NWS absent from the proto-language.[7] Likewise, the presence of the *niphal* (3:16b) in the Deir Alla dialect does not facilitate classification since the *N*-stem was a Proto-Semitic feature.[8] Each of these features in the different Semitic languages was inherited from the proto-language.

Analogical formations must be excluded since they are the result of internal structural pressures, rather than common development.[9] For example, the first person singular perfect ending [tī] (3:17a) in Phoenician (except at Arslan Tash), Moabite, and Hebrew does not reflect a shared innovation but a well-attested analogical formation; cf. the ending [ti] in Amorite.[10] The form of the third person fem. plural imperfect (3:18c) with prefix -ת in Deir Alla and Hebrew resulted from an analogy with the feminine sing. prefix -ת; this analogical formation occurred sporadically throughout Semitic.[11] The appearance of the identical analogical formation in two or more speech forms, then, is coincidental.

Parallel, independent developments must be excluded from a classificatory scheme as well.[12] It must be demonstrated that an identical outcome resulted from a shared development, not from accident. In Akkadian, for example, *$\underline{d}$, *$\underline{\underline{d}}$ and *$\underline{t}$ merged with *$\underline{s}$, *z and *$\check{s}$, just as the identical merger took place in Hebrew.[13] Yet the geographic distance between the speakers of these two languages, as well as the chronological removal of Akkadian from Hebrew, preclude a shared innovation; the mergers occurred independently in Akkadian and Hebrew.[14] Similarly, the assimilation of *nun* to the following consonant (2:9) developed independently in Akkadian and NWS.[15] The *nota accusativi* אית (3:15a) in standard Phoenician and Aramaic arose independently as well.[16] Not only the outcome, but the history of the outcome, is important in linguistic classification.[17]

Finally, a feature must not be borrowed but must represent a native linguistic development.[18] For example, if יֹם "day" in southern Hebrew was borrowed from the northern dialect,[19] the absence of *waw* does not reflect any phonological feature of the southern dialect.[20] On the contrary, the absence of *waw* reflects the phonological pattern of the donor dialect. Since borrowings do not necessarily participate in the changes of the recipient dialect,[21] they must be excluded from a classificatory scheme.

Linguistic classification, or subgrouping, must begin with shared innovations. "A shared innovation is one which cannot be due to chance (i.e. to independent linguistic change) or to separate borrowing."[22] Only those features which reflect shared development provide the basis for a classificatory scheme.

Yet a single shared innovation in itself is insufficient, since the innovation may be coincidental.[23] In order to obviate this objection, it is customary to isolate sets of shared innovations;[24] the greater the number of innovations shared by certain speech forms, the smaller the likelihood of independent duplication. And the greater the number of shared innovations, the greater the likelihood of common linguistic development.

« »   « »

A preliminary evaluation of features examined in Chapters 2–4 suggests that classes of features are of different value in classifying the NWS dialects. Syntax, for example, is an unreliable tool. A syntactic feature may reflect a well-attested innovation and not demonstrate any particular shared history, as in the use of the perfect as the narrative, past tense (4:8), the appearance of a periphrastic tense (4:9), and the marking of apodoses (4:13). Analogical formations and extensions were also frequent, as for example the agreement between a noun and demonstrative pronoun (4:2) and probably the use of the *nota accusativi* to introduce nominal direct objects (4:12);[25] as in phonology and morphology, analogical formations and extensions in syntax do not reflect a shared linguistic development in the history of particular speech forms. Finally, syntactic retentions—the use of the infinitive to form temporal clauses (4:7b), the consecutive imperfect as the narrative tense (4:8), verb-initial syntax

(4:11), etc.—also do not demonstrate a shared development among speech forms, but rather a common ancestor. For the classification of these dialects, then, syntactic features have, at best, the effect of reinforcing the conclusions drawn from other linguistic features examined.

Phonological features are perhaps easiest to evaluate in classifying the NWS dialects. Having eliminated retentions, independent developments, and other features which do not contribute to classification, phonological innovations are a primary source for classifying these dialects.[26] The classification, however, would differ with each feature selected. For example, the correspondence *ḏ:p (2:1) aligned Samalian with Old Aramaic, whereas the contraction of final *ay (2:8) was a Phoenician (Canaanite) trait. So too, Fekh.-Aramaic showed *ḏ:p, yet intervocalic *he* syncopated in the third person plural possessive suffixes (2:16; 3:9d).

The same is true of morphological features.[27] Hebrew and standard Phoenician shared the form of the *qal* inf. construct [liqtōl] (3:19a), yet each dialect had new relative pronouns (3:3). Deir Alla shared the third person masc. singular suffix on masc. plural nouns, [awh(u/i)] (3:10b), with Old Aramaic, but its infinitive construct of initial weak verbs ended in ת- (3:21b). Similarly, Moabite exhibited the definite article *he* (3:5), like other Canaanite dialects, although its suffix [ôh(u/i)] < *awh- (3:10b) was native to the Aramaic dialect group.

From the present data base, it is difficult to choose whether phonological or morphological features are better aids to classification.[28] Either can, provided there is sufficient evidence, lead to a classificatory scheme. Yet all available features must be amassed, and the innovations must be separated from all others. Once these innovative features are recognized and isolated, classification can proceed easily. It appears, from the confines of the data from the first-millennium NWS dialects, that the assemblage of all phonological or morphological features should lead to the identical classification. Yet given the limited data base, the sum total of all phonological and morphological innovations, excluding those analogical formations, parallel, independent developments, and borrowings, should be brought to bear upon the problem of classification. A haphazard selection of features from the overall data base should be avoided. The classification of the NWS dialects should be based upon an evaluation of shared innovations, phonological and/or morphological.

« »   « »

Within these parameters, the distinctive innovations of each dialect can be categorized as follows:

OLD BYBLIAN

Analogical formations

The absolute masc. plural/dual nominal ending ם- (3:6a)

Independent developments

The assimilation of *nun* to all following nonlaryngeal consonants (2:9), and its extention to **bin* "son" + PN (2:9)
The correspondence **at*:[ā] in the later form שמע "she heard" (2:18b; 3:17c)

Shared innovations

The merger of **ḏ* and **ṣ* (2:1), **ḏ* and **z* (2:2), **ṭ* and **ṣ* (2:3), and **ṭ* and **š* (2:4).
The monophthongization of all diphthongs (2:8)
The syncope of intervocalic *he* in the third person masc. sing. suffix (2:16; 3:9b)
The definite article *he* (3:5)
The masc. plural construct ending **ay* (3:6b)
The third person masc. sing. suffix on masc. plural nouns [aw (?)] (3:10b) (attested only later)
The conditional particle אל (3:15b)
The ending of initial weak *qal* inf. constructs in ת- (3:21b)

Only these latter features facilitate the classification of Old Byblian.
    In the later phase of this dialect, certain phonological and morphological features had changed. For example, the *nun* in **bin* "son" no longer assimilated to the initial consonant of the following PN, the masculine sing. demonstrative pronoun זן (3:2a) was replaced by ז, and the relative pronoun -ז (3:3) was replaced by אש. Each of these changes in the later phase of Byblian was traceable to the influence of standard Phoenician.[29]

STANDARD PHOENICIAN

Analogical formations

The absolute masc. plural/dual nominal ending ם- (3:6a)
The first person sing. perfect ending [tī] (3:17a)

Independent developments

The assimilation of *nun* to the following consonant within a word
(2:9)
Incipient anaptyxis (2:11)
The complete absorption of syllable-closing *aleph* to the
preceding vowel (2:13)
The correspondence *at:[ā] in third person fem. sing. perfect
verbs (2:18b; 3:17c)
The form of the *nota accusativi* (3:15a)
The merger of indicative and jussive verbal forms (3:18a, 18b)
The merger of the middle weak *D*-stem and the *pōlel* (3:22b) (?)

Shared innovations

The merger of *$\d{d}$ and *$\d{s}$ (2:1), *$\d{d}$ and *z (2:2), *$\d{t}$ and *$\d{s}$ (2:3), and
*$\d{t}$ and *$\check{s}$ (2:4)
The change of *$\acute{\bar{a}}$ to [ó] (2:5), and its extention to all nonverbal
accented *a*-vowels (2:6–7)
The monophthongization of all diphthongs (2:8)
The usual syncope of intervocalic *yodh* (2:15)
The syncope of intervocalic *he* (even after the conjunction *wa)
(2:16), except after *i*-vowels (2:17, etc.)
The masc. sing. demonstrative pronoun ז "this" (3:2a) (?)
The relative particle אש (3:3)
The personal, interrogative pronoun מי (3:4)
The definite article *he* (3:5)
The masc. plural construct ending *ay (3:6b)
A special plural formation of final weak nouns (3:7)
The vocalization of the strong *qal* inf. construct [liqtōl] (3:19a)
The ending of initial and final weak inf. constructs in ת- (3:21b,
23f)
The replacement of *$b\bar{a}niy$- by *$b\bar{a}nay$- in the masc. plural
participle (3:23g)
The imperfect form [yiqqaḥ] (3:25a)
The ending of the *qal* inf. of לקח "to take" in ת- (3:25b)

While it appears that most Phoenician-speaking communities participated in these innovations, Arslan Tash[30] deviated from this pattern in two respects. The absolute masc. plural/dual nominal ending was ן-, and the first person sing. perfect morpheme may have been [t(u/i)]. These two features were, in all probability, borrowed from Old Aramaic which was spoken in this community at that time.[31]

OLD ARAMAIC

Analogical formations

The term for nonexistence ליש (3:14) (?)
The tG stem (3:16a)
The treatment of the middle weak radical as a strong root letter in certain verbal forms (3:22a, 22b)

Independent developments

The assimilation of *nun* to the following consonant within a word (2:9)
The correspondence *$át$:[å] (2:18a; 3:6c)
The loss of final short vowels (2:19; see also 3:9a)
The form of the *nota accusativi* (3:15a)
The position of the term for nonexistence in the sentence (4:4c)

Shared innovations

The correspondence *$\d{d}$:ק (2:1)
The dissimilation of emphatics: *q + emphatic > k + emphatic (2:10)
The aphaeresis of *aleph* in חד "one" (2:14)
The first person sing. independent pronoun אנה (3:1a)
The definite article -א (3:5)
The masc. plural construct ending *ay (3:6b)
A special plural formation of final weak nouns (3:7)
The third person masc. sing. suffix on plural nouns [awh(i)] (3:10b)
The loss of the *niphal* (3:16b)
The *pael* and *haphel* inf. construct of strong verbs ending in -ת (3:19b)
The *peal* passive participle *$qat\bar{i}l$ (3:20)

The loss of the initial radical and the doubling of the second in
   imperfect and certain nominal forms of ישב* "to sit, dwell"
   and ידע* "to know" (3:21a)
The form of the indicative and jussive sing. of final weak verbs in
   ה- and י-, respectively (3:23d)
The replacement of *bāniy- by *bānay- in the masc. plural
   (undetermined) participle (3:23g)
The *pael* and *haphel* of final weak roots, third person masc. sing.,
   in [bannî] and [habnî], respectively (3:23h) (?)[32]
The imperfect form [yiqqaḥ] (3:25a)

   While most Aramaic-speaking communities exhibited these innovations, there were certain speech variants in each community.[33]
   ALEPPO: In three passages of the Zkr Text, the consecutive imperfect functioned as the historical past tense (4:8). Since this usage
was a common NWS trait,[34] this feature was a retention here. It
does not suggest any dialectal affinities.[35]
   SFIRE:[36] Several dialectal variations resulted from analogy or
extention—the plural demonstrative pronoun אלן (3:2c), the absolute
fem. plural nominal ending ן- (3:6d), perhaps the imperfect form
[yilqaḥ] (3:25a), and the use of -פ to mark the apodosis of conditions
(4:13). Incipient anaptyxis (2:11), the prothetic *aleph* in אשם "name"
(2:12), and the possible loss of medial *aleph* in בירא "well (?)" (2:13)
are well-attested, Semitic phonetic developments. There is also one
possible example of an infinitive complement to כהל "to be able"
(4:10), and final weak nominal plurals were formed like strong plurals
(3:7). The combination of these features distinguished Sfire-Aramaic
from the other Old Aramaic dialects.[37]
   NERAB: Like other Old Aramaic dialects, initial *q* + emphatic
dissimilated to *k* + emphatic (2:10), and the third person masc. sing.
suffix on plural nouns was [awh(i)] (3:10b).[38] The position of the
verb in the sentence, however, was flexible (4:11).[39]
   FEKHERIYEH:[40] In addition to the innovations characteristic of
Old Aramaic, this dialect exhibited several others—the third person
plural possessive suffixes ם-/ן- (2:16; 3:9d) and the *peal* inf. construct
miqtal (3:19a). The flexibility in the placement of the verb in the
sentence (4:11) might be another Fekh. innovation shared with other
NWS dialects, unless it developed independently. Fekh.-Aramaic
did not, however, participate in every Old Aramaic innovation. For
example, the *t*-stem of the G was Gt in Fekh. (3:16a), not the an-

alogical tG. Further, the *pael* and *haphel* inf. constructs ended in -∅ (3:19b), not ת-. Both of these features were retentions in Fekh. Finally, other dialectal features at Fekh. were the precative *lamedh* (3:15d), the merger of the middle weak *D*-stem and the *pālel* (3:22b), the fem. sing. demonstrative pronoun זאת (3:2b), the imperfect formation [yilqaḥ] (3:25a), and the genitive particle זי (4:3a). These features were independent developments, analogical formations, or retentions.

HALAF: This dialect had a new form of the third person masc. sing. suffix on plural nouns [ayh(i)] (3:10b). This dialect also had a genitive particle זי (4:3a) and a great flexibility in the placement of the verb in the sentence (4:11). The suffixed form [ayh(i)] and flexibility in verb placement are features characteristic of later eastern Aramaic.

ADON LETTER (southern Palestine):[41] Like Fekh.-Aramaic, this dialect had a **miqtal peal* inf. construct (3:19a), the genitive particle זי (4:3a), and flexibility in the placement of the verb in main clauses (4:11).

SAMALIAN

Analogical formations

The cardinal decade ending in י- (3:12) (?)

Independent developments

The assimilation of *nun* to the following consonant within a word (2:9)
The use of the prothetic *aleph* (2:12)
The possible absorption of *aleph* to the preceding vowel (2:13)
The correspondence **át*:[ā́] (2:18a; 3:6c)
The loss of final short vowels (2:19; see also 3:9a)
The form of the *nota accusativi* (3:15a)
The merger of indicative and jussive verbal forms (3:18a, 18b, 23d)

Shared innovations

The correspondence **ḏ*:ק (2:1)
The monophthongization of final diphthongs (2:8)
The possible dissimilation of emphatics in קשת "truth" (2:10)

The aphaeresis of *aleph* in חד "one" (2:14) (unless borrowed)

The syncope of intervocalic *yodh* (except in ביד "in the hand [of]") (2:15)

The syncope of causative *he* in the imperfect (2:16)

The *peal* passive participle **qatīl* (3:20)

The loss of the initial radical and the doubling of the second in imperfect and certain nominal forms of ישב* "to sit, dwell" and ידע* "to know" (3:21a)

The ending of indicative and jussive final weak verbs, sing. persons in י- (3:23d)

The *pael* and *haphel* of final weak verbs, third person masc. sing., in [bannî] and [habnî], respectively (3:23h) (?)[42]

The imperfect form [yiqqaḥ] (3:25a)

AMMONITE

Analogical formations

The absolute masc. plural/dual nominal ending ם- (3:6a)

Independent developments

The assimilation of *nun* to any following consonant (2:9)

The use of the prothetic *aleph* before consonant clusters with initial sibilants (2:12)

Shared innovations

The merger of **ḏ* and **ṣ* (2:1)

The merger of **ā̤* and [ó] (2:5), and its extention to **ā:[ó] (2:6)

The monophthongization of **ay* (2:8)

The loss of intervocalic *yodh* (including the PN בדאל) (2:15)

The relative particle אש (3:3)

The personal, interrogative pronoun [mī] (3:4)

The definite article *he* (3:5)

DEIR ALLA

Analogical formations

The tG stem (?) (3:16a)

The third person fem. plural imperfect ת- -ן (3:18c)

Independent developments

The assimilation of *nun* to the following consonant within a word
    (2:9)

The possible use of the prothetic *aleph* (2:12)

The correspondence **át*:[ắ] (2:18a; 3:6c), and **at*:[ā] in שמה
    (2:18b)

The loss of final short vowels (2:19; see also 3:9a)

The merger of indicative and jussive verbal forms in the
    second/third persons plural (3:18a, 18b)

Shared innovations

The correspondence **ḍ*:ק (2:1)

The aphaeresis of *aleph* in חד "one" (2:14) (unless borrowed)

The syncope of causative *he* in the imperfect (2:16)

The masc. plural construct ending **ay* (3:6b)

The third person masc. sing. suffix on plural nouns [awh(u/i)]
    (3:10b)

The ending of initial weak inf. constructs in ת- (3:21b)

The form of the indicative and jussive sing. of final weak verbs in
    ה- and י-, respectively (3:23d)

The imperative of הלך* "to go" formed from the root ולך* (3:24b)

The imperfect form [yiqqaḥ] (3:25a)

The possible flexibility in the placement of the verb in main
    clauses (4:11) (unless an independent development)

MOABITE

Analogical formations

The first person sing. perfect ending [tī] (3:17a)

The imperfect form אהלך(ו) (3:24a) (?)

Independent developments

The assimilation of *nun* to any following consonant (2:9)

The use of the prothetic *aleph* before sibilants (2:12)

The absorption of syllable-closing *aleph* into the preceding vowel
    (2:13)

The loss of final short vowels (2:19; see also 3:9a)

The fem. sing. demonstrative pronoun זאת "this" (3:2b) (unless
    inherited)

The position of the term for nonexistence in the sentence (4:4c)

Shared innovations

The merger of *$\d$* and *$\ş$* (2:1)
The possible tonic lengthening of short vowels (2:7)
The gradual monophthongization of diphthongs (2:8)
The syncope of causative *he* in the imperfect (2:16)
The relative particle אשר (3:3)
The definite article *he* (3:5)
The masc. plural construct ending *ay* (3:6b)
The third person masc. sing. suffix on plural nouns [ôh(u/i) (?)]
    (3:10b)
The form of the *nota accusativi* את < *אית* (3:15a)
The possible loss of the *niphal* (3:16b)
The ending of initial weak inf. constructs in -ת (3:21b)
The apocopation of the final syllable in certain forms of final
    weak consecutive imperfects (3:23d)
The imperative of *הלך* "to go" formed from the root *ולך* (3:24b)
The imperfect form [yiqqaḥ] (3:25a)

EDOMITE

Independent developments

The assimilation of *nun* to any following consonant (2:9)

Shared innovations

The monophthongization of diphthongs (in later texts) (2:8)
The syncope of *yodh* in בד "through" < *ba/i-yad* (2:15)
The definite article *he* (3:5)

HEBREW

Analogical formations

The first person sing. independent pronoun אני (3:1a)
The absolute masc. plural/dual nominal ending -ם (3:6a)
The connecting vowel *ay* on feminine plural suffixed nouns (3:8)
The first person plural possessive suffix -נו (3:9c) (?)
The first person sing. perfect ending [tī] (3:17a)

The third person fem. plural imperfect ‏ת‎*- ‏נה‎ (3:18c)

Independent developments

The assimilation of *nun* to the following consonant (except in ‏ל״ן‎ verbs [BH]) (2:9)

The absorption of syllable-closing *aleph* into the preceding vowel (2:13)

The correspondence *át*:[ấ] (2:18a; 3:6c) and *at*:[ā] (2:18b; 3:1d)

The loss of final short vowels (2:19; see also 3:9a)

The fem. sing. demonstrative pronoun ‏זאת‎ "this" (3:2b) (unless inherited)

The merger of indicative and jussive verbal forms in the second/third persons plural (3:18a, 18b)

The merger of the middle weak *D*-stem and the *pōlel* (3:22b) (?)

Shared innovations

The merger of *$\underline{d}$* and *$ṣ$* (2:1), *$\underline{d}$* and *z* (2:2), *$\underline{t}$* and *$ṣ$* (2:3), and *$\underline{t}$* and *$š$* (2:4)

The correspondence *$\hat{a}$*:[ố] (2:5), and *$\hat{a}^{\,\prime}$*:[ố] (in doubly closed syllables) (2:6)

The tonic lengthening of nonverbal short vowels (2:7)

The syncope of intervocalic *he* in third person suffixes (under certain conditions) and in the causative imperfect (2:16)

The masc. sing. demonstrative pronoun ‏זה‎ "this" (3:2a) (?)

The relative particle ‏אשר‎ (3:3)

The personal, interrogative pronoun ‏מי‎ (3:4)

The definite article *he* (3:5)

The masc. plural construct ending *ay* (3:6b)

The third person masc. sing. suffix on plural nouns [āw] (3:10b)

The form of the *nota accusativi* ‏אית‎* < ‏את‎ (3:15a)

The vocalization of the strong *qal* inf. construct [liqṭōl] (3:19a)

The imperfect of ‏ישב‎* "to sit, dwell" and ‏ידע‎* "to know" as [yēšeb], etc. (3:21a)

The ending of initial (including ‏לקח‎ "to take") and final weak inf. constructs in ‏ת‎- (3:21b, 23f, 25b)

The replacement of *banay-* by *baniy-* in the first person sing. *qal* perfect (3:23a)

The use of a monosyllabic base *bă̆n-* in forming certain final weak verbal forms (3:23c, 23e [?], 23g)

The apocopation of the final syllable in certain forms of final
    weak jussives and consecutive imperfects (3:23d)
The imperfect and imperative of הלך* "to go" formed from the
    root ולך* (3:24a, 24b)
The imperfect form [yiqqaḥ] (3:25a)

The extent to which this analysis pertains to northern Hebrew,
as well as the southern dialect, however, is uncertain. Most direct
linguistic evidence came from texts of southern provenience, sup-
plemented by BH data. Where direct evidence for the northern dialect was available, it did not necessarily conform to the southern
speech pattern. For example, the northern dialect exhibited complete monophthongization (2:8) and a formation of "year" derived
from *šan-t (3:6c);[43] the southern dialect had uncontracted diphthongs and formed "year" from *šan-at. This analysis of Hebrew,
then, essentially reflects the southern, not the northern dialect.

        « »   « »

This analysis of shared innovations provides the basic information
necessary to establish a dialectal continuum of NWS spoken in
Syria-Palestine. Like a color spectrum,[44] the continuum is bordered
by two polar extremes. Between these extremes lie dialects with
intersecting linguistic elements, whose overall character displays
greater affinities to one or the other pole. The result is a series of
closely interrelated dialects which form a dialect chain.

According to the present evidence, the linguistic innovations in
first-millennium NWS cluster principally into two dialectal groups.
One set of innovations—the merger of $*\underline{d}$ and $*\d{s}$ (2:1), $*\underline{d}$ and $*z$ (2:2),
$*\underline{t}$ and $*\d{s}$ (2:3), and $*\underline{t}$ and $*\check{s}$ (2:4), the merger of accented a-vowels
and $*\acute{o}$ (2:5–7), monophthongization (2:8), the loss of intervocalic
he (2:16), the personal interrogative pronoun מי (3:4), the definite
article he (3:5), etc.—occurred, in differing degrees, in the Canaanite
dialects. Only standard Phoenician, however, had all these innovations, as well as several which did not spread beyond Phoenicia.[45]

The other set of innovations—the correspondence $*\underline{d}$:ק (2:1),
aphaeresis of $aleph$ in "one" (2:14), the definite article א- (3:5), the
third person masc. sing. suffix on plural nouns [awh(i)] (3:10b),[46]
the $peal$ passive participle *$qatīl$ (3:20), the loss of the initial radical

and the doubling of the second in imperfect and certain nominal forms of ישׁב* ''to sit, dwell'' and ידע* ''to know'' (3:21a), etc.—occurred, in varying degress, in Old Aramaic, Samalian, Deir Alla, and Moabite. Only the Old Aramaic dialects, however, bore the entirety of these innovations. Thus, standard Phoenician and Old Aramaic (as a dialect group) constituted the two major linguistic centers of Syro-Palestinian NWS. In terms of a dialect continuum, standard Phoenician and Old Aramaic were the linguistic extremes.

For those dialects lying between these two poles, standard Phoenician and Old Aramaic were competing forces. They are as follows:

AMMONITE: In addition to the features common to all Canaanite dialects—such as the correspondences *$\underline{d}$:[ṣ], *$\underline{d}$:[z], the definite article *he*, etc.—the correspondence *$\acute{a}$:[ó] (2:6) and the relative particle אש (3:3) strongly align Ammonite with standard Phoenician.[47] In terms of the available data, these two features were innovations shared exclusively between standard Phoenician and Ammonite.[48]

EDOMITE: The form of the preposition בד ''through'' < *ba/i-yad (2:15) allies this dialect with Ammonite (in the PN בדאל) and standard Phoenician. Further, if the correspondence *$\acute{a}$:[ā́] (2:7) is confirmed in Edomite, this feature forms a bond with Hebrew; in standard Phoenician, *$\acute{a}$:[ó].

HEBREW: The standard Phoenician affiliation of Hebrew is seen in the correspondences *$\acute{a}$:[ó] (2:5), *$\acute{a}$ʾ:[ó] (in doubly closed syllables) (2:6), the preservation of *$\acute{a}$ in verbs (2:7), the almost complete syncope of intervocalic *he* (2:16), the inf. construct of initial (including לקח ''to take'') and final weak verbs ending in -ת (3:21b, 23f, 25b), etc.

Several innovations, however, appear to have been native to this dialect. For example, the relative particle אשר (3:3), the *nota accusativi* את (cf. אית in standard Phoenician and Old Aramaic) (3:15a), and the apocopation of the final syllable in certain forms of final weak jussives and consecutive imperfects (3:23d) were innovations absent from standard Phoenician.

MOABITE: Although most of its phonological and morphological innovations were shared with Phoenician, Moabite possessed several Hebraic innovations: the possible tonic lengthening of short vowels (2:7), the relative particle אשר (3:3), the *nota accusativi* את (3:15a), and the apocopation of the final syllable in certain forms of final weak consecutive imperfects (3:23d). Moabite also shared the form of the third person masc. sing. suffix on plural nouns, [ôh(u/i)] (3:10b), with Old Aramaic. Further, an interesting feature connecting Moabite with northern dialects is the form of "year"—שת < *šan-t (3:6c), in which the fem. ending -t was added to the *CaC base; it is uncertain, however, whether this form was an innovation.[49]

DEIR ALLA: The Deir Alla dialect reflects the basic phonological innovations of Old Aramaic: the correspondence *ḏ:ק (2:1) and the aphaeresis of *aleph* in חד "one" (2:14) (unless borrowed). Further, the form of the third person masc. sing. suffix on plural nouns [awh(u/i)] (3:10b) is a morphological innovation aligning Deir Alla with Old Aramaic. Yet the syncope of causative *he* in imperfects (2:16), the ending of initial weak inf. constructs in -ת (3:21b), and the imperative of הלך* "to go" formed from ולך* (3:24b) were innovations native to Hebrew and standard Phoenician. Since no changes peculiar to standard Phoenician or Hebrew can be recognized in Deir Alla, the source of these innovations cannot be pinpointed.[50]

« » « »

At one linguistic extreme of the dialect chain is standard Phoenician, and at the other end is Old Aramaic. Of the dialects known, Ammonite was most closely related to standard Phoenician. Edomite was related to Phoenician as well as to Hebrew. On this dialectal continuum, Hebrew lies closer to standard Phoenician than it does to Old Aramaic. Moabite was most closely related to Hebrew; it also possessed distinctive Aramaic features. The Deir Alla dialect shared some features with Hebrew (and Canaanite), but most of its phonological and morphological inventory was derived from Old Aramaic. Finally, Old Aramaic lies at the end of the continuum.

In graphic form, this dialect continuum appears as:

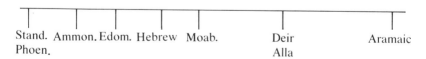

Stand. Ammon. Edom. Hebrew Moab.　　Deir　　　　Aramaic
Phoen.　　　　　　　　　　　　　　Alla

The position of Hebrew, however, in terms of this continuum, is unclear because it did not exhibit any diagnostic Aramaic traits. Rather, its unique characteristics suggest that Hebrew was a minor linguistic center within the Canaanite domain. While Hebrew participated in those changes which took place in Phoenician, Ammonite, and Edomite, it also displayed a series of independent innovations. Some of these innovations spread to neighboring Moabite and, perhaps, to Edomite. In terms of a proposed dialect chain within NWS, then, Hebrew might represent a slight break.[51]

The position of Edomite on the continuum is likewise uncertain. Since linguistic data from this dialect were so sparse, a reliable classification is unavailable. Yet the definite article *he* (3:5) was a Phoenician-Hebrew innovation, בד "through" (2:15) was Phoenician(-Ammonite), and stress-lengthening (2:7) was Hebraic(-Phoenician). In view of this distribution of features, Edomite lay between Hebrew and Phoenician on the continuum; more precisely, it probably lay between Ammonite and Hebrew.

It is impossible to account for the position of Old Byblian and Samalian, however, in terms of a dialectal continuum alone. For these dialects, a historical model is also necessary. For example, Old Byblian participated in many changes common to standard Phoenician and Hebrew. Yet its preservation of final short vowels in nouns and certain verbal forms (2:19; 3:17b), its relative pronoun -ז (3:3), the Gt stem (3:16a), the complete absence of the *nota accusativi* (3:15a; 4:12), and some of its other features deviated from the standard Phoenician-Hebrew model. All these dialectal features, however, are conservative; they reflect a time before Old Byblian participated in the changes of standard Phoenician. In fact, Old Byblian probably antedated the appearance of standard Phoenician altogether. Thus Old Byblian was an old Phoenician dialect which predated several innovations of standard Phoenician.[52]

Although Samalian was a contemporary of the first-millennium NWS dialects, it preserved several old linguistic features. On the one hand, Samalian participated in several Aramaic innovations, such as the correspondence *$\d{d}$*:ק (2:1), the *peal* passive participle *qatīl* (3:20), the loss of the initial and the doubling of the second radical in imperfect and certain nominal forms of *ידע*/*ישב* (3:21a), and perhaps the form of the *D*-and causative third person masc. sing. perfect of final weak roots as [bannî] and [habnî], respectively (3:23h).[53] On the other hand, the preservation of case distinctions on masc. plural nouns (2:19; 3:6a), the first person sing. independent pronoun אנך (3:1a), the absence of a definite article (3:5), the absence of a special masc. plural construct ending (3:6b), and the failure to mark definite, nominal direct objects (4:12) were retentions. They also appeared in, for example, Ugaritic.[54] Yet, unlike Ugaritic, Samalian was an eighth-century dialect. Samalian participated in many, but not all of the changes in Old Aramaic.[55] Samalian, then, developed from the same lineage as Old Aramaic, but its development was arrested at an early date. In terms of contemporary, eighth-century dialects, Samalian was therefore archaic.

In terms of the dialectal continuum of Syria-Palestine, a more accurate presentation of the linguistic situation is:

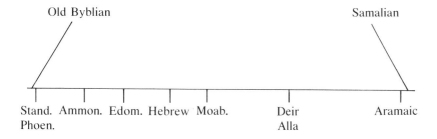

The dialect chain runs from standard Phoenician, through Hebrew and Moabite, to Old Aramaic. Old Byblian constitutes a dialect island on the Phoenician side, and Samalian forms another on the Aramaic extremity.

The preserved literature of this period supplements this view of NWS dialectal relations. II Kgs. 18:26 = Is. 36:11 relates that Hebrew and Old Aramaic, ca. 700 B.C.E., were not mutually intelligible. Further, according to Jer. 27:3, three-quarters of a century later, Jeremiah's speech was assumed to be understood by people knowing standard Phoenician, Ammonite, Edomite, and Moabite.[56] The Bible therefore indicates that dialects on the left side of this continuum—standard Phoenician through Moabite—were mutually intelligible.[57] Hebrew and Old Aramaic were not.[58] It would follow, then, that an Aramaic speaker did not understand any other Canaanite dialect lying to the left of Hebrew on the continuum either. Yet it is suggested that those dialects toward the center of the continuum, perhaps even Moabite and the Deir Alla dialect themselves, were, in fact, mutually intelligible. In other words, the farther away two dialects lay on the continuum, the smaller the chance of mutual intelligibility; the closer the proximity on the continuum, the higher the probability of mutual intelligibility.[59]

« »   « »

Nonlinguistic evidence further supports this view of the NWS dialectal continuum. For example, the overall character of a speech form can be correlated with its physical position on a map. The Samalian dialect, to take one case, was spoken in far north Syria. Samal was located in very rough terrain, and the Amanus mountains further blocked communication with neighboring communities.[60] The seclusion of this state, then, from principal Aramaic-speaking communities contributed to its arrested linguistic development.[61]

The inventory of linguistic features in Ammonite, also, was affected by its geographical position on the Transjordanian periphery. Ammonite, on the one hand, was a Phoenician-related dialect. On the other hand, it did not participate in all Phoenician innovations. The recognizable retentions—the preservation of *aw (2:8), the retention of initial and medial *aleph* (2:13, 14), the imperfect plural ending [ūn] (3:18b)—are probably attributable to its physical distance from Phoenicia; this Transjordanian dialect received some, but not all, innovations from the Phoenician center.[62] Interestingly, however, Ammonite showed no innovations shared exclusively with Old Aramaic.

In a similar fashion, the progressive monophthongization in Moabite can be understood by the gradual diffusion of this innovation from the source dialect; it took time to reach, and cover, all Moab. It took even more time for this innovation to reach Edom, for *aw did not contract until a very late period. Monophthongization in Ammonite affected only *ay. Finally, all diphthongs were preserved in Deir Alla. In Transjordan, then, monophthongization affected the dialects in different degrees; geographical removal from the innovating dialect was, at least in part, responsible for the different outcomes.

The location of southern Hebrew in southernmost Syria-Palestine promoted its rather unique character. Its several retentions— for example, the preservation of *â < *awa/*aya and *a> (2:6), the preservation of diphthongs (2:8), the directive *he* (3:15c), the use of the consecutive imperfect as the narrative tense (4:8), etc.—to some extent resulted from its geographical distance from the two principal linguistic centers. Further, the diffusion of several Hebraic innovations to neighboring Moabite, despite the barrier afforded by the Dead Sea, was facilitated, at least in part, by geographical proximity.

The development of southern Hebrew, and its relation to Moabite, then, were related to physical geography.

Physical geography also explains the recognizable deviations in northern Hebrew from the pattern of the southern dialect. Whereas southern Hebrew resisted monophthongization, the northern dialect followed the pattern of standard Phoenician, its neighbor. Also, the form of "year," שת, joins northern Hebrew and standard Phoenician (see also Moabite שת), in contrast to שנה* (BH). These features, then, spread into the neighboring Israelite state but stopped at the Judean border.[63]

Additionally, the presence of certain linguistic features in northern Hebrew can be inferred on the basis of its geographic position. Since this dialect lay physically between standard Phoenician (innovator) and Ammonite (recipient), the presence of innovations in the flanking regions would suggest their presence in the intermediate region as well.[64] For example, that both standard Phoenician and Ammonite shared the relative particle אש (3:3) suggests that northern Hebrew also had a relative ש(א).[65] Further, standard Phoenician and Ammonite exhibited the correspondence *$\hat{a}$:[ố] (2:6) in contrast, for example, to BH *$\hat{a}$:[ấ] (except *$\hat{a}$ < *$\hat{a}$ʾ in doubly closed syllables). Perhaps northern Hebrew deviated from the BH pattern and followed that of its lateral dialects; northern Hebrew, then, would have had the correspondence *$\hat{a}$:[ố] as well.[66] This dialect, then, might have shared several features with standard Phoenician-Ammonite which did not reach southern Hebrew or which are not preserved in BH.[67]

The relative isolation of the Aramean states in the North likewise had its effect upon the linguistic development of Aramaic. Its numerous phonological, morphological, and syntactic retentions—for example, the preservation of *$\underline{d}$ (2:2), *$\underline{t}$ (2:3), *$\underline{t}$ (2:4), all a-vowels (2:5–7), diphthongs (2:8), all initial and medial alephs (except in חד "one") (2:13–14), the preservation of intervocalic he (2:16), the personal, interrogative pronoun מן (3:4), the coordinating conjunction פ- (3:13), the distinction between indicative and jussive verbal forms (3:18a, 18b, 23d, 23e), the nonmarking of apodoses (4:13), etc.—may be explained by its geographical location; only in the far South was Aram bordered by NWS-speaking peoples. As was the case with Samalian, isolation facilitated these numerous retentions.[68]

In all these cases, however, physical geography was only indirectly responsible for the diffusion or arresting of linguistic change.

The degree to which physical geography affected human communication is the central issue, not simply the presence or absence of physical obstacles. A natural barrier may have corresponded to a language boundary only if it prevented communication.[69]

Just as physical geography sometimes affected linguistic relations among these NWS dialects, so too historical, political, and economic factors influenced their internal composition and interrelation. The degree of political unification, for example, may have affected the dialectal makeup of an area.[70] The contrast between the speech of the Aramean states and of Judah is especially telling in this respect. The Aramean states had a number of local dialects; in fact, according to the present evidence, no two Syrian Aramaic-speaking communities spoke the identical dialect in this period.[71] Geographically proximate dialects could be similar, as for example Aleppo- and Sfire-Aramaic. Or two neighboring Old Aramaic dialects could differ, as for example the dialects of Nerab and Aleppo. This heterogeneity may be traced, in some measure, to the lack of political unification among the Aramean states. Each state was largely independent, and the states joined forces for specific military needs. Afterward the union would dissolve. Throughout the early first millennium B.C.E., no single governmental system united all the Aramean states under one rubric.

The linguistic situation in Judah was very different. According to the present evidence, Judah was a single linguistic entity. The texts from Jerusalem, Arad, Yavneh-Yam, and Lachish (somewhat later) showed identical phonology,[72] morphology, and syntax. This linguistic unity may be accounted for, in some degree, by the political and religious centralization of the southern kingdom, beginning in David's time. Jerusalem was the cultural and political center, and it was this centralization which may have had its influence on linguistic development as well. In view of the overall sociopolitical structure of Syria-Palestine, however, this situation was very much atypical.

This unification of the South created a barrier between it and non-Judean communities. There were no major physical boundaries between North and South; rather, the religious/cultural differences which arose, already in the early first millennium, created a strong barrier between peoples. Linguistic differences therefore ensued.

Historical and political factors were also responsible, in part at least, for the linguistic similarity between southern Hebrew and

Moabite. By Saul's time, Moab had been captured by Israel (I Sam. 14:47–48). David left his parents in the care of the Moabite king (I Sam. 22:3–4); later, he too subjugated Moab, and all Transjordan, making it a vassal state (II Sam. 8:2). And by the time of Solomon, Israel and Moab were on friendly terms; Solomon even married Moabite women (I Kgs. 11:1). Israel, then, had won sway over Moab by this time, and the effect of this dominion may be seen in the linguistic similarity between Moabite and southern Hebrew.

Whereas polity and sociocultural factors influenced the NWS dialects at this time, economic factors were also important. For example, economic strength probably accounts for much of Phoenicia's linguistic control over southern Syria-Palestine. Since the inland communities were largely dependent upon the materials and goods arriving in the Phoenician ports, those ports became important economic and sociocultural centers. Linguistic changes could spread throughout the area via intricate trade routes crossing Palestine and Transjordan. In this way, such formidable geographical barriers as Mount Lebanon were largely overcome. And even after the decline of Phoenician inland trade, its linguistic hold over the area was already secure.[73]

Thus a number of factors influenced the linguistic complexion of first-millennium Syria-Palestine. Geographical proximity, or distance, from linguistic centers affected the degree to which changes were received. Political, economic, cultural-religious, and military factors likewise affected the dialectal makeup of the area. As in any area, the linguistic picture of Syria-Palestine resulted from an intricate series of linguistic, geographical, and historical factors.

Notes to Chapter 5

1. The numbers in parentheses indicate the chapter and section number where the feature was discussed.

2. Leonard Bloomfield, *Language* (New York: Holt, Rinehart & Winston, 1933), p. 328.

3. Cf. p. 3.

4. The classic formulation is that of Karl Brugmann, "Zur Frage nach den Verwandtschaftsverhältnissen der indogermanischen Sprachen," *Internationale Zeitschrift für allgemeine Sprachwissenschaft* 1 (1884): 226–256, esp. pp. 252, 253. See also C. Douglas Chrétien, "Shared Innovations and Subgrouping," *IJAL* 29 (1963): 66–68.

5. Joseph H. Greenberg, *Essays in Linguistics* (Chicago: The University of Chicago Press, 1957), p. 49.

6. For example, Sabatino Moscati, "Il semitico di nord-ovest," in *Studi orientalistici in onore di Giorgio Levi Della Vida,* Pubblicazioni dell'Istituto per l'Oriente, no. 52. 2 vols. (Rome: Istituto per l'Oriente, 1956), 2:215. Cf. Paul-E. Dion, *La langue de Yaʾudi* (Waterloo, Ont.: The Corporation for the Publication of Academic Studies in Religion in Canada, 1974), p. 325. See also Chapter 3, no. 2a with n. 29.

7. Dion, *La langue,* pp. 137–138 (earlier literature on pp. 437–438 n. 33). See also Chapter 3, no. 5, with n. 93.

8. See Chapter 3, no. 16b, with n. 288. Cf. Jo Ann Carlton (Hackett), "Studies in the Plaster Text from Tell Deir ʿAllā" (Ph.D. dissertation, Harvard University, 1980), p. 188; and idem, "The Dialect of the Plaster Text from Tell Deir ʿAlla," *Or* 53 (1984): 62, 65.

9. Greenberg, *Essays,* p. 51; and Theodora Bynon, *Historical Linguistics* (Cambridge: Cambridge University Press, 1977), p. 34.

10. See Chapter 3, no. 17a, and p. 31.

11. See Chapter 3, no. 18c, with n. 328.

12. On the phenomenon, see Antoine Meillet, *Linguistique historique et linguistique générale,* Nouveau tirage. 2 vols. (Paris: Édouard Champion, 1948–1951), 1:36–43; and more generally, Edward Sapir, *Language* (New York: Harcourt, Brace & Co., 1921), pp. 157–182.

13. Carl Brockelmann, *GvG* 1:§46a.

14. See pp. 26–27. Cf. *B-L* §2k'.

15. See Chapter 2, no. 9 with n. 165.

16. See Chapter 3, no. 15a.

17. See Robert A. Hall, "Bartoli's 'Neolinguistica,'" *Lg.* 22 (1946): 281. Cf. J. K. Chambers and Peter Trudgill, *Dialectology* (Cambridge: Cambridge University Press, 1980), pp. 163ff.

18. See, for example, Greenberg, *Essays,* p. 47.

19. See Chapter 2, no. 8.

20. Cf. p. 39.

21. See Bynon, *Historical Linguistics,* pp. 217–232; and Stephen A. Kaufman, *The Akkadian Influences on Aramaic,* Assyriological Studies, vol. 19 (Chicago/London: The University of Chicago Press, 1974), pp. 19–22.

22. Isidore Dyen, "[Review of Dahl, *Malgache et maanjan*]," *Lg.* 29 (1953): 580.

23. Greenberg, *Essays,* pp. 51, 53.

24. Bloomfield, *Language,* p. 342; Dyen, *Lg.* 29 (1953): 580–581; and Greenberg, *Essays,* p. 53.

25. On the latter, see Paul Joüon, *Grammaire de l'hébreu biblique* (Rome: Pontifical Biblical Institute, 1923), p. 368 n. 2.

26. See Henry M. Hoenigswald, "Criteria for the Subgrouping of Languages," in *Ancient Indo-European Dialects,* ed. Henrik Birnbaum and Jaan Puhvel (Berkeley/Los Angeles: University of California Press, 1966), pp. 6–7. Cf. Greenberg, *Essays,* p. 50.

27. Cf., for example, I. J. Gelb, "Thoughts about Ibla," *SMS* 1/1 (1977): 17.

28. On the methodological problems in Semitic, see Robert Hetzron, "Genetic Classification and Ethiopian Semitic," in *Hamito-Semitica*, ed. James and Theodora Bynon. Janua Linguarum, Series Practica, vol. 200 (The Hague/Paris: Mouton, 1975), pp. 103–121.

29. Giovanni Garbini, "I dialetti del fenicio," *AION* 27 (1977): 287. Similarly, several syntactic features in later Byblian may have originated in standard Phoenician, as for example the syntagms determined noun + demonstrative pronoun (4:2), determined noun + relative particle (4:3b), and perhaps the use of the *nota accusativi* to introduce certain nominal direct objects (4:12). Alternatively, however, these changes may reflect common West Semitic syntactic usage which developed late in this dialect.

30. On this dialect, see most recently S. David Sperling, "An Arslan Tash Incantation: Interpretations and Implications," *HUCA* 53 (1982): 1–10.

31. Cf. Frank M. Cross, "Leaves from an Epigraphist's Notebook," *CBQ* 36 (1974): 486 n. 4; and Wolfgang Röllig, "Die Amulette von Arslan Taş," *NESE* 2 (1974): 28, 36.

32. See Chapter 3, no. 23h with nn. 425, 427.

33. See, in general, Garbini, *L'aramaico antico*, Atti della Accademia nazionale dei Lincei, Memoria. Classe di scienze morali, storiche e filologiche, Series VIII, vol. 7 (Rome: Accademia nazionale dei Lincei, 1956), pp. 244–276; idem, "Unité et variété des dialectes araméens anciens," in *Akten des vierundzwanzigsten internationalen Orientalisten-Kongresses . . . 1957*, ed. Herbert Franke (Wiesbaden: Franz Steiner, 1959), pp. 242–244; Jonas C. Greenfield, "Dialect Traits in Early Aramaic," *Leshonenu* 32 (1968): 359–368 (in Hebrew); and idem, "The Dialects of Early Aramaic," *JNES* 37 (1978): 93–99, esp. p. 94, on "Early Standard Aramaic."

34. See Chapter 4, no. 8 with n. 123.

35. Cf. Joseph A. Fitzmyer, "The Phases of the Aramaic Language," in idem, *A Wandering Aramean: Collected Aramaic Essays*, SBLMS, vol. 25 (Missoula: Scholars Press, 1979), p. 67.

36. On this dialect, see Moscati, in *Studi . . . Levi Della Vida*, pp. 211 with n. 2, 217; and Garbini, "Nuovo materiale per la grammatica dell'aramaico antico," *RSO* 34 (1959): 53–54.

37. Cf. Fitzmyer, *A Wandering Aramean*, p. 67.

38. With Fitzmyer, ibid., pp. 66–67. Cf. Kaufman, *Akkadian Influences*, p. 10 n. 16.

39. Kaufman, *Akkadian Influences*, p. 132. Cf. Greenfield, *JNES* 37 (1978): 95.

If the indicative and jussive forms of the second/third persons plural had merged in this dialect (see above, p. 160 n. 321), this feature would also distinguish the dialect of Nerab.

40. On this dialect, see Ali Abou-Assaf, Pierre Bordreuil, and Alan R. Millard, *La statue de Tell Fekherye et son inscription bilingue assyro-araméenne* (Paris: Editions Recherche sur les civilisations, 1982), pp. 55–60; and Kaufman, "Reflections on the Assyrian-Aramaic Bilingual from Tell Fakhariyeh," *Maarav* 3 (1982): 145–173.

41. On the provenience, see now Bezalel Porten, "The Identity of King Adon," *BA* 44 (1981): 41–45.

42. See above, n. 32.

43. See already William F. Albright, "Ostracon C 1101 of Samaria," *PEFQS* 1936: 215. For other northern features recovered by inference, see below.

44. For the comparison, see Hugo Schuchardt, *Über die Klassifikation der romanischen Mundarten* (Graz: K. K. Universität-Buchdr., 1900).

45. See already Harris' "Coast Canaanite," in *Development of the Canaanite Dialects*, American Oriental Series, vol. 16 (New Haven: American Oriental Society, 1939), p. 98. Cf. idem, *A Grammar of the Phoenician Language*, American Oriental Series, vol. 8 (New Haven: American Oriental Society, 1936), pp. 67, 68–69.

46. Except at Halaf, where it was [ayh(i)].

47. Cf. p. 2.

48. For exclusively shared innovations, see Dyen, *Lg.* 29 (1953): 580.

49. On the classification of Moabite, see also Stanislav Segert, "Die Sprache der moabitischen Königsinschrift," *ArOr* 29 (1961): 250–259; and Masao Sekine, "The Subdivisions of the North-West Semitic Languages," *JSS* 18 (1973): 213–214.

50. For other opinions, see p. 2, and P. Kyle McCarter, "The Balaam Texts from Deir ʿAllā: The First Combination," *BASOR* 239 (1980): 50–51; Kaufman, "[Review of Hoftijzer and van der Kooij, eds., *Aramaic Texts*]," *BASOR* 239 (1980): 73; and idem, *Maarav* 3 (1982): 146 n. 22. Cf. Helga and Manfred Weippert, "Die 'Bileam'-Inschrift von *Tell Dēr ʿAllā*," *ZDPV* 98 (1982): 83 n. 26.

51. See already Ginsberg's division between "Phoenic" and "Hebraic" dialectal groups ("[Review of Harris, *Development*]," *JBL* 59 [1940]: 550; and "The Northwest Semitic Languages," in *Patriarchs*, ed. B. Mazar. The World History of the Jewish People, vol. 2 [(New Brunswick): Rutgers University Press, 1970], p. 102). Admittedly, a family-tree model would better represent this aspect of Hebrew.

52. Harris, *Development*, p. 97.

53. Ginsberg, "Aramaic Studies Today," *JAOS* 62 (1942): 235; Johannes Friedrich, "Kanaanäisch und Westsemitisch," *Scientia* 84 (1949): 221; and Dion, "The Language Spoken in Ancient Samʾal," *JNES* 37 (1978): 116.

54. For the comparison between Samalian and Ugaritic, see Friedrich, *Scientia* 84 (1949): 220–223; and idem, "Zur Stellung des Jaudischen in der nordwestsemitischen Sprachgeschichte," in *Studies in Honor of Benno Landsberger . . . 1965*, Assyriological Studies, vol. 16 (Chicago: The University of Chicago Press, 1965), pp. 425–429. Cf. Eduard Y. Kutscher, "Aramaic," in *Linguistics in South West Asia and North Africa*, Current Trends in Linguistics, vol. 6 (The Hague/Paris: Mouton, 1970), pp. 350–351; and idem, *A History of Aramaic. Part 1: Old Aramaic, Jaudic, Official Aramaic (Biblical Aramaic excepted)* (Jerusalem: Akadamon, 1972), pp. 61–63 (in Hebrew).

55. Franz Rosenthal, "[Review of Dion, *La langue*]," *JBL* 95 (1976): 154; and Dion, *JNES* 37 (1978): 118.

56. So D. S. Margoliouth, "Language of the Old Testament," in *A Dictionary of the Bible*, ed. James Hastings. 4 vols. (New York/Edinburgh: Charles Scribner's Sons/T. & T. Clark, 1900), 3:30.

57. See already Friedrich, "Zum Phönizisch-Punischen," *ZS* 2 (1923): 4–5; and Harris, *Development*, p. 94. Cf. Rosenthal, "[Review of Friedrich, *PPG*]," *JAOS* 72 (1952): 171–172.

58. For the lexical implication of mutual intelligibility, see Harold Hickerson, Glen D. Turner, and Nancy P. Hickerson, "Testing Procedures for Estimating Transfer of Information among Iroquois Dialects and Languages," *IJAL* 18 (1952): 1–8.

59. For a developmental view of the continuum, see Friedrich, *Scientia* 84 (1949): 220–223; and Moscati, in *Studi . . . Levi Della Vida*, p. 218. See also J. Hoftijzer, "Interpretation and Grammar," in *Aramaic Texts from Deir 'Alla*, ed. J. Hoftijzer and G. van der Kooij. Documenta et Monumenta Orientis Antiqui, vol. 19 (Leiden: E. J. Brill, 1976), pp. 300, 301.

60. Alkim, cited in Irene J. Winter, "On the Problems of Karatepe: The Reliefs and Their Context," *AS* 29 (1979): 134 n. 87.

61. Sekine, *JSS* 18 (1973): 215. See also Bloomfield, *Language*, p. 334.

62. See, generally, Wolfram von Soden, "Zur Einteilung der semitischen Sprachen," *WZKM* 56 (1960): 190.

63. See William L. Moran, "The Hebrew Language in its Northwest Semitic Background," in *The Bible and the Ancient Near East*, ed. G. Ernest Wright (Garden City, N.Y.: Doubleday & Co., 1961), p. 59.

64. For the reasoning, see Bloomfield, *Language*, p. 340; Hans Kurath, *Handbook of the Linguistic Geography of New England*, 2nd ed. (New York: AMS Press, 1973), p. 5; and Chambers and Trudgill, *Dialectology*, p. 109.

65. So, already, Brockelmann, *GvG* 1:§109gα. Cf. Gotthelf Bergsträsser, "Das hebräische Präfix ש," *ZAW* 29 (1909): 41–45. See also p. 150 n. 55a.

66. Could this general phonetic change be the origin of [ō] in BH ראש "head" and צאן "sheep"?

67. In terms of the dialectal continuum of Syria-Palestine, northern Hebrew may lie between standard Phoenician and Ammonite, in contrast to the position of southern Hebrew on the same continuum.

68. Interestingly, however, both standard Phoenician and Old Aramaic exclusively shared a special plural formation of final weak nouns (3:7) and jointly replaced **bāniy-* by **bānay-* in the masc. plural (undetermined) participle (3:23g).

69. So, for example, William Labov, in Pavle Ivić, "Structure and Typology of Dialectal Differentiation," in *Proceedings of the Ninth International Congress of Linguists . . . 1962*, ed. Horace G. Lunt. Janua Linguarum, Series Maior, vol. 12 (London/The Hague/Paris: Mouton & Co., 1964), p. 127.

70. For NWS, see, for example, Harris, *Grammar*, p. 69.

71. See already Rosenthal, *AF*, p. 1; Kaufman, *Akkadian Influences*, p. 9 (cf. ibid., p. 155); and the literature cited in n. 33 above. See also Harris, *Grammar*, p. 10.

72. The correspondences of medial *iy*, however, may have differed within southern Hebrew-speaking communities. See above, p. 70 n. 136.

73. See, generally, Bloomfield, *Language*, p. 343; and Bynon, *Historical Linguistics*, p. 183.

BIBLIOGRAPHY

Abou Assaf, Ali. "Die Statue des HDYS'Y, König von Guzana."
    MDOG 113 (1981): 3–22.

Abou-Assaf, Ali; Bordreuil, Pierre; and Millard, Alan R. *La statue
    de Tell Fekherye et son inscription bilingue assyro-araméenne.*
    Paris: Editions Recherche sur les civilisations, 1982.

Aharoni, Yohanan. *Arad Inscriptions.* Jerusalem: The Bialik Insti-
    tute and the Israel Exploration Society, 1975 (in Hebrew).

———. "The Hebrew Inscriptions." In *Beer-Sheba I. Excavations
    at Tel Beer-Sheba, 1969–1971 Seasons,* edited by Y. Aharoni,
    pp. 71–78. Tel Aviv: Tel Aviv University Institute of Archae-
    ology, 1973.

———. "Hebrew Ostraca from Tel Arad." *IEJ* 16 (1966): 1–7.

———. *The Land of the Bible: A Historical Geography,* translated
    by A. F. Rainey. 2nd ed. Philadelphia: The Westminster Press,
    1979.

———. "A New Ammonite Inscription." *IEJ* 1 (1950–1951): 219–
    222.

Albright, William F. "An Aramaean Magical Text in Hebrew from
    the Seventh Century B.C." *BASOR* 76 (1939): 5–11.

———. "New Light on Early Canaanite Language and Literature."
    BASOR 46 (1932): 15–20.

———. "The North-Canaanite Epic of 'Al'êyân Ba'al and Môt."
    JPOS 12 (1932): 185–208.

————. "The Northwest-Semitic Tongues before 1000 B.C." In *Atti del XIX congresso internazionale degli orientalisti . . . 1935,* pp. 445–450. Rome: Tipografia del Senato, G. Bardi, 1938.

————. "Notes on Ammonite History." In *Miscellanea Biblica B. Ubach,* edited by R. M. Díaz. Scripta et Documenta, vol. 1, pp. 131–136. Barcelona: Imprenta-Escuela, 1953.

————. "Notes on Early Hebrew and Aramaic Epigraphy." *JPOS* 6 (1926): 75–102.

————. "Ostracon C 1101 of Samaria." *PEFQS* 1936: 211–215.

————. "Palestinian Inscriptions." In *ANET*[3], pp. 320–322, 568–569.

————. "The Phoenician Inscriptions of the Tenth Century B.C. from Byblus." *JAOS* 67 (1947): 153–160.

————. "Postscript to Professor May's Article." *BASOR* 97 (1945): 26.

————. "Recent Progress in North-Canaanite Research." *BASOR* 70 (1938): 18–24.

————. "A Reëxamination of the Lachish Letters." *BASOR* 73 (1939): 16–21.

————. "Some Canaanite-Phoenician Sources of Hebrew Wisdom." In *Wisdom in Israel and in the Ancient Near East,* edited by M. Noth and D. Winton Thomas. VTS, vol. 3, pp. 1–15. Leiden: E. J. Brill, 1955.

————. "Some Comments on the ʿAmmân Citadel Inscription." *BASOR* 198 (1970): 38–40.

————. *The Vocalization of the Egyptian Syllabic Orthography.* American Oriental Series, vol. 5. New Haven: American Oriental Society, 1934.

Albright, William F., and Moran, William L. "A Re-interpretation of an Amarna Letter from Byblos (EA 82)." *JCS* 2 (1948): 239–248.

Andersen, Francis I. "Moabite Syntax." *Or* 35 (1966): 81–120.

Anttila, Raimo. *An Introduction to Historical and Comparative Linguistics.* New York/London: Macmillan Publishing Co./Collier Macmillan Publishers, 1972.

Avigad, N. "Ammonite and Moabite Seals." In *Near Eastern Archaeology in the Twentieth Century,* edited by James A. Sanders, pp. 284–295. Garden City, N.Y.: Doubleday & Co., 1970.

————. "New Moabite and Ammonite Seals at the Israel Museum." *EI* 13 (1977): 108–110 (in Hebrew).

————. "Two Ammonite Seals Depicting the *Dea Nutrix.*" *BASOR* 225 (1977): 63–66.

Baldacci, M. "The Ammonite Text from Tell Siran and North-West Semitic Philology." *VT* 31 (1981): 363–368.

Bar-Adon, P. "An Early Hebrew Inscription in a Judean Desert Cave." *IEJ* 25 (1975): 226–232.

Barnett, R. D. "Four Sculptures from Amman." *ADAJ* 1 (1951): 34–36.

Barth, Jakob. "Beiträge zur Pluralbildung des Semitischen." *ZDMG* 58 (1904): 431–446.

————. *Die Pronominalbildung in den semitischen Sprachen.* Leipzig: J. C. Hinrichs'sche Buchhandlung, 1913.

Bauer, Hans. "Die hebräischen Eigennamen als sprachliche Erkenntnisquelle." *ZAW* 48 (1930): 73–80.

————. *Zur Frage der Sprachmischung im Hebräischen. Eine Erwiderung.* Halle an der Saale: Max Niemeyer, 1924.

————. "[Review of Dhorme, *Langues*]." *OLZ* 36 (1933): 317–319.

Bauer, Hans, and Leander, Pontus. *Grammatik des Biblisch-Aramäischen.* Halle an der Saale: Max Niemeyer, 1927.

————. *Historische Grammatik der hebräischen Sprache des Alten Testamentes.* Halle: Max Niemeyer, 1922.

Bennett, Crystal-M. "Excavations at Buseirah, Southern Jordan, 1972: Preliminary Report." *Levant* 6 (1974): 1–24.

————. "Fouilles d'Umm el-Biyara. Rapport préliminaire." *RB* 73 (1966): 372–403.

Bergsträsser, Gotthelf. *Einführung in die semitischen Sprachen.* 1928. Reprint. Darmstadt: Wissenschaftliche Buchgesellschaft, 1977.

————. *Hebräische Grammatik.* 2 vols. Leipzig: F. C. W. Vogel, 1918–1929.

————. "Das hebräische Präfix ש." *ZAW* 29 (1909): 40–56.

————. "In Sachen meines 'Sprachatlas.'" *ZS* 1 (1922): 218–226.

————. "Mitteilungen zur hebräischen Grammatik." *OLZ* 26 (1923): 253–260, 477–481.

————. "Sprachatlas von Syrien und Palästina." *ZDPV* 38 (1915): 169–222.

Beyer, Klaus. *Althebräische Grammatik.* Göttingen: Vandenhoeck & Ruprecht, 1969.

————. "[Review of Degen, *Grammatik*]." *ZDMG* 120 (1970): 198–204.

Blanc, Haim. *Communal Dialects in Baghdad.* Harvard Middle Eastern Monographs, vol. 10. Cambridge: Harvard University Press, 1964.

Blau, Joshua. "Hebrew and North West Semitic: Reflections on the Classification of the Semitic Languages." *Hebrew Annual Review* 2 (1978): 21–44.

————. "On Problems of Polyphony and Archaism in Ugaritic Spelling." *JAOS* 88 (1968): 523–526.

————. "The Parallel Development of the Feminine Ending -*at* in Semitic Languages." *HUCA* 51 (1980): 17–28.

————. "Short Philological Notes on the Inscription of Mešaᶜ." *Maarav* 2 (1980): 143–157.

————. "Some Difficulties in the Reconstruction of 'Proto-Hebrew' and 'Proto-Canaanite.'" In *In Memoriam Paul Kahle,* edited by Matthew Black and Georg Fohrer. BZAW, vol. 103, pp. 29–43. Berlin: A. Töpelmann, 1968.

————. "'Weak' Phonetic Change and the Hebrew *śîn.*" *Hebrew Annual Review* 1 (1977): 67–119.

Bloomfield, Leonard. *Language.* New York: Holt, Rinehart & Winston, 1933.

Bordreuil, Pierre. "Inscriptions sigillaires ouest-sémitiques. I. Épigraphie ammonite." *Syria* 50 (1973): 181–195.

————. "Une tablette araméenne inédite de 635 av. J.-C." *Semitica* 23 (1973): 95–102.

Bossert, Helmuth T. "Die phönizisch-hethitischen Bilinguen vom Karatepe." *Oriens* 1 (1948): 163–192.

Brockelmann, Carl. *Grundriss der vergleichenden Grammatik der semitischen Sprachen.* 2 vols. 1908–1913. Reprint. Hildesheim: Georg Olms, 1966.

————. "[Review of Harris, *Grammar*]." *OLZ* 40 (1937): 527–529.

Brovender, Chaim. "Hebrew Language. Pre-Biblical." In *Encyclopaedia Judaica.* 16 vols., 16:1560–1568. Jerusalem: Keter Publishing House, 1971–1972.

Brugmann, Karl. "Zur Frage nach den Verwandtschaftsverhältnissen der indogermanischen Sprachen." *Internationale Zeitschrift für allgemeine Sprachwissenschaft* 1 (1884): 226–256.

Bynon, Theodora. *Historical Linguistics.* Cambridge: Cambridge University Press, 1977.

Caquot, André. "Une inscription araméenne d'époque assyrienne." In *Hommages à André Dupont-Sommer,* pp. 9–16. Paris: Adrien-Maisonneuve, 1971.

————. "Observations sur la Première Tablette Magique d'Arslan Tash." *JANES* 5 (1973): 45–51.

Caquot, André, and du Mesnil du Buisson, R. "La seconde tablette ou 'petite amulette' d'Arslan Tash." *Syria* 48 (1971): 391–406.

Caquot, André, and Lemaire, André. "Les textes araméens de Deir 'Alla." *Syria* 54 (1977): 189–208.

Carlton, Jo Ann. See Hackett, Jo Ann.

Chambers, J. K., and Trudgill, Peter. *Dialectology.* Cambridge: Cambridge University Press, 1980.

Chrétien, C. Douglas. "Shared Innovations and Subgrouping." *IJAL* 29 (1963): 66–68.

Cooke, George A. *A Text-Book of North-Semitic Inscriptions.* Oxford: Oxford University Press, 1903.

Coote, Robert B. "The Tell Siran Bottle Inscription." *BASOR* 240 (1980): 93.

Cowley, A. E. (ed.). *Aramaic Papyri of the Fifth Century B.C.* Oxford: Oxford University Press, 1923.

Cross, Frank M. "Ammonite Ostraca from Heshbon: Heshbon Ostraca IV–VIII." *AUSS* 13 (1975): 1–20.

————. *Canaanite Myth and Hebrew Epic.* Cambridge: Harvard University Press, 1973.

————. "The Cave Inscriptions from Khirbet Beit Lei." In *Near Eastern Archaeology in the Twentieth Century*, edited by James A. Sanders, pp. 299–306. Garden City, N.Y.: Doubleday & Co., 1970.

————. "Epigraphic Notes on Hebrew Documents of the Eighth-Sixth Centuries B.C.: II. The Murabbaʿât Papyrus and the Letter Found Near Yabneh-Yam." *BASOR* 165 (1962): 34–46.

————. "Epigraphic Notes on the Ammān Citadel Inscription." *BASOR* 193 (1969): 13–19.

————. "Heshbon Ostracon II." *AUSS* 11 (1973): 126–131.

————. "Heshbon Ostracon XI." *AUSS* 14 (1976): 145–148.

————. "Lachish Letter IV." *BASOR* 144 (1956): 24–26.

————. "Leaves from an Epigraphist's Notebook." *CBQ* 36 (1974): 486–494.

————. "Notes on the Ammonite Inscription from Tell Sīrān." *BASOR* 212 (1973): 12–15.

————. "An Ostracon from Heshbon." *AUSS* 7 (1969): 223–229.

————. "A Recently Published Phoenician Inscription of the Persian Period from Byblos." *IEJ* 29 (1979): 40–44.

Cross, Frank M., and Freedman, David N. *Early Hebrew Orthography*. American Oriental Series, vol. 36. New Haven: American Oriental Society, 1952.

————. "The Pronominal Suffixes of the Third Person Singular in Phoenician." *JNES* 10 (1951): 228–230.

————. "Some Observations on Early Hebrew." *Bibl* 53 (1972): 413–420.

Cross, Frank M., and Saley, Richard J. "Phoenician Incantations on a Plaque of the Seventh Century B.C. from Arslan Tash in Upper Syria." *BASOR* 197 (1970): 42–49.

Dahood, Mitchell. "The Linguistic Position of Ugaritic in the Light of Recent Discoveries." *Sacra Pagina* 1 (1958): 267–279.

Dajani, R. W. "The Amman Theater Fragment." *ADAJ* 12–13 (1967–1968): 65–67.

Davis, Lawrence M. "Dialectology and Linguistics." *Orbis* 26 (1977): 24–30.

Degen, Rainer. *Altaramäische Grammatik der Inschriften des 10.–8. Jh. v. Chr.* Abhandlungen für die Kunde des Morgenlandes, vol. 38/3. Wiesbaden: Franz Steiner, 1969.

————. "Die aramaeischen Tontafeln vom Tell Halaf." *NESE* 1 (1972): 49–57.

————. "Die Präfixkonjugationen des Altaramäischen." In *XVII. Deutscher Orientalistentag . . . Würzburg. Vorträge,* edited by Wolfgang Voigt. ZDMG Supplementa, vol. 1, pt. 2, pp. 701–706. Wiesbaden: Franz Steiner, 1969.

Dever, William G. "Inscriptions from Khirbet el-Kom." *Qadmoniot* 4 (1971): 90–92 (in Hebrew).

————. "Iron Age Epigraphic Material from the Area of Khirbet el-Kôm." *HUCA* 40–41 (1969–1970): 139–204.

Diakonoff, I. M. "Earliest Semites in Asia. Agriculture and Animal Husbandry According to Linguistic Data (VIIIth–IVth Millennia B.C.)." *AoF* 8 (1981): 23–74.

————. "Linguistic Data on the History of the Most Ancient Speakers of Afrasian Languages." *Africana* 10 (1975): 117–130 (in Russian).

————. "Problems of Root Structure in Proto-Semitic." *ArOr* 38 (1970): 453–480.

————. *Semito-Hamitic Languages. An Essay in Classification.* Moscow: Nauka Publishing House, 1965.

Diem, Werner. "Gedanken zur Frage der Mimation und Nunation in den semitischen Sprachen." *ZDMG* 125 (1975): 239–258.

Dion, Paul-E. "The Language Spoken in Ancient Samʾal." *JNES* 37 (1978): 115–118.

————. *La langue de Yaʾudi.* Waterloo, Ont.: The Corporation for the Publication of Academic Studies in Religion in Canada, 1974.

————. "Notes d'épigraphie ammonite." *RB* 82 (1975): 24–33.

Diringer, David. "Early Hebrew Inscriptions." In Olga Tufnell et al., *Lachish III (Tell ed Duweir). The Iron Age.* The Wellcome-Marston Archaeological Research Expedition to the Near East, vol. 3. 2 vols., 1:331–359. London/New York/Toronto: Oxford University Press, 1953.

Donner, Herbert, and Röllig, Wolfgang. *Kanaanäische und aramäische Inschriften.* 3rd ed. 3 vols. Wiesbaden: Otto Harrassowitz, 1971–1976.

Driver, G. R. "Seals from ʿAmman and Petra." *QDAP* 11 (1944): 81–82.

Driver, Samuel R. *Notes on the Hebrew Text and the Topography of the Books of Samuel.* 2nd ed. Oxford: Oxford University Press, 1913.

Dupont-Sommer, André. *Les araméens.* L'orient ancien illustré, vol. 2. Paris: A. Maisonneuve, 1949.

————. "Azitawadda, roi des Danouniens. Étude sur les inscriptions phéniciennes de Karatepe." *RA* 42 (1948): 161–188.

————. "Deux nouvelles inscriptions sémitiques trouvées en Cilicie." *JKF* 1 (1950): 43–47.

————. "Etude du texte phénicien des inscriptions de Karatepe." *Oriens* 2 (1949): 121–126.

————. "Une inscription araméenne inédite de Sfiré." *BMB* 13 (1956): 23–41.

————. "Une inscription nouvelle du roi Kilamou et le dieu Rekoub-El." *RHR* 133 (1947–1948): 19–33.

————. *Les inscriptions araméennes de Sfiré (stèles I et II).* Extrait des Mémoires présentés par divers savants à l'Académie des

Inscriptions et Belles-Lettres, vol. 15. Paris: Imprimerie Nationale, 1958.

―――. "Notes sur le texte phénicien." *Oriens* 1 (1948): 193–197.

―――. "Un papyrus araméen d'époque saïte découvert à Saqqarah." *Semitica* 1 (1948): 43–68.

Dyen, Isidore. "Lexicostatistics: Present and Prospects." In *Lexicostatistics in Genetic Linguistics II: Proceedings of the Montreal Conference . . . 1973*, edited by Isidore Dyen and Guy Jucquois. Cahiers de l'Institut de Linguistique de Louvain, vol. 3, pt. 5–6, pp. 5–28. Louvain: Imprimerie Orientaliste, 1976.

―――. "[Review of Dahl, *Malgache et maanjan*]." *Lg.* 29 (1953): 577–590.

Fitzmyer, Joseph A. *The Aramaic Inscriptions of Sefire.* Biblica et Orientalia, vol. 19. Rome: Pontifical Biblical Institute, 1967.

―――. "The Aramaic Letter of King Adon to the Egyptian Pharaoh." *Bibl* 46 (1965): 41–55.

―――. "The Aramaic Suzerainty Treaty from Sefire in the Museum of Beirut." *CBQ* 20 (1958): 444–476.

―――. "A Further Note on the Aramaic Inscription Sefire III.22." *JSS* 14 (1969): 197–200.

―――. "The Phases of the Aramaic Language." In idem, *A Wandering Aramean: Collected Aramaic Essays.* SBLMS, vol. 25, pp. 57–84. Missoula: Scholars Press, 1979.

―――. "[Review of Hoftijzer and van der Kooij, eds., *Aramaic Texts*]." *CBQ* 40 (1978): 93–95.

Freedman, David N. "The Babylonian Chronicle." *BA* 19 (1956): 50–60.

―――. "The Massoretic Text and the Qumran Scrolls: A Study in Orthography." *Textus* 2 (1962): 87–102.

―――. "A Second Mesha Inscription." *BASOR* 175 (1964): 50–51.

Friedrich, Johannes. "Denkmäler mit westsemitischer Buchstabenschrift." In *Die Inschriften vom Tell Halaf,* edited by J. Friedrich et al. AfO Beiheft, vol. 6, pp. 69–78. Berlin: [private], 1940.

―――. "Kanaanäisch und Westsemitisch." *Scientia* 84 (1949): 220–223.

―――. "Kleinigkeiten zum Phönizischen, Punischen und Numidischen." *ZDMG* 114 (1964): 225–231.

―――. *Phönizisch-Punische Grammatik.* Analecta Orientalia, vol. 32. Rome: Pontifical Biblical Institute, 1951.

―――. "Der Schwund kurzer Endvokale im Nordwestsemitischen." *ZS* 1 (1922): 3–14.

―――. "Zum Phönizisch-Punischen." *ZS* 2 (1923): 1–10.

―――. "Zur Stellung des Jaudischen in der nordwestsemitischen Sprachgeschichte." In *Studies in Honor of Benno Landsberger . . . 1965.* Assyriological Studies, vol. 16, pp. 425–429. Chicago: The University of Chicago Press, 1965.

Friedrich, Johannes, and Röllig, Wolfgang. *Phönizisch-Punische Grammatik*. 2nd ed. Analecta Orientalia, vol. 46. Rome: Pontifical Biblical Institute, 1970.

Fulco, William J. "The ʿAmmān Citadel Inscription: A New Collation." *BASOR* 230 (1978): 39–43.

———. "The Amman Theater Inscription." *JNES* 38 (1979): 37–38.

Garbini, Giovanni. *L'aramaico antico*. Atti della Accademia nazionale dei Lincei, Memoria. Classe di scienze morali, storiche e filologiche, Series VIII, vol. 7, pp. 235–283. Rome: Accademia nazionale dei Lincei, 1956.

———. "Il causativo *hqtl* nel dialetto fenicio di Byblo." *AION* 24 (1974): 411–412.

———. "I dialetti del fenicio." *AION* 27 (1977): 283–293.

———. *Le lingue semitiche. Studi di storia linguistica*. Naples: Istituto orientale di Napoli, 1972.

———. "Note sul 'calendario' di Gezer." *AION* 6 (1954–1956): 123–130.

———. "Nuovo materiale per la grammatica dell'aramaico antico." *RSO* 34 (1959): 41–54.

———. *Il semitico di nord-ovest*. Quaderni della sezione linguistica degli Annali, vol. 1. Naples: Istituto universitario orientale di Napoli, 1960.

———. "Studi aramaici—1–2." *AION* 19 (1969): 1–15.

———. "Il tema pronominale *p* in semitico." *AION* 21 (1971): 245–248.

———. "Unité et variété des dialectes araméens anciens." In *Akten des vierundzwanzigsten internationalen Orientalisten-Kongresses . . . 1957*, edited by Herbert Franke, pp. 242–244. Wiesbaden: Franz Steiner, 1959.

———. "[Review of Degen, *Grammatik*]." *AION* 20 (1970): 275–277.

Gaster, Theodor H. "A Canaanite Magical Text." *Or* 11 (1942): 41–79.

———. "A Hang-Up for Hang-Ups. The Second Amuletic Plaque from Arslan Tash." *BASOR* 209 (1973): 18–26.

Gauchat, L. "Gibt es Mundartgrenzen?" *Archiv für das Studium der neueren Sprachen und Literaturen* 111 (1903): 365–403.

Gelb, I. J. "The Early History of the West Semitic Peoples." *JCS* 15 (1961): 27–47.

———. "La lingua degli Amoriti." *Atti della Accademia nazionale dei Lincei. Rendiconti della Classe di scienze morali, storiche e filologiche*, Series VIII, vol. 13/3–4 (1958): 143–164.

———. *Old Akkadian Writing and Grammar*. Materials for the Assyrian Dictionary, vol. 2. 2nd ed. Chicago: The University of Chicago Press, 1961.

————. *Sequential Reconstruction of Proto-Akkadian.* Assyriological Studies, vol. 18. Chicago: The University of Chicago Press, 1969.

————. "Thoughts about Ibla." *SMS* 1/1 (1977): 3–30.

Gesenius, W. *Gesenius' Hebrew Grammar*, edited by E. Kautzsch and A. E. Cowley. 28th ed. Oxford: Oxford University Press, 1910.

Gevirtz, Stanley. "On the Etymology of the Phoenician Particle אש." *JNES* 16 (1957): 124–127.

Gibson, John C. L. *Textbook of Syrian Semitic Inscriptions.* 3 vols. Oxford: Oxford University Press, 1971–1982.

Ginsberg, H. L. "An Aramaic Contemporary of the Lachish Letters." *BASOR* 111 (1948): 24–27.

————. "Aramaic Studies Today." *JAOS* 62 (1942): 229–238.

————. "The Classification of the North-West Semitic Languages." In *Akten des vierundzwanzigsten internationalen Orientalisten-Kongresses . . . 1957*, edited by Herbert Franke, pp. 256–257. Wiesbaden: Franz Steiner, 1959.

————. "Lachish Ostraca New and Old." *BASOR* 80 (1940): 10–13.

————. "The Northwest Semitic Languages." In *Patriarchs*, edited by B. Mazar. The World History of the Jewish People, vol. 2, pp. 102–124, 270. [New Brunswick, N.J.]: Rutgers University Press, 1970.

————. "Notes on the Lachish Documents." *BJPES* 3 (1935): 77–86 (in Hebrew).

————. "Psalms and Inscriptions of Petition and Acknowledgment." In *Louis Ginzberg Jubilee Volume.* 2 vols., 1:159–171. New York: The American Academy for Jewish Research, 1945.

————. "Ugaritico-Phoenicia." *JANES* 5 (1973): 131–147.

————. "[Review of Diringer, *Le iscrizioni*]." *ArOr* 8 (1936): 145–147.

————. "[Review of Harris, *Development*]." *JBL* 59 (1940): 546–551.

————. "[Review of Harris, *Grammar*]." *JBL* 56 (1937): 138–143.

Glueck, Nelson. "Ostraca from Elath." *BASOR* 82 (1941): 3–11.

————. "Tell el-Kheleifeh Inscriptions." In *Near Eastern Studies in Honor of William Foxwell Albright*, edited by Hans Goedicke, pp. 225–242. Baltimore/London: The Johns Hopkins Press, 1971.

————. "The Topography and History of Ezion-Geber and Elath." *BASOR* 72 (1938): 2–13.

Goetze, Albrecht. "Accent and Vocalism in Hebrew." *JAOS* 59 (1939): 431–459.

————. "Cilicians." *JCS* 16 (1962): 48–58.

————. "Is Ugaritic a Canaanite Dialect?" *Lg.* 17 (1941): 127–138.

————. "Number Idioms in Old Babylonian." *JNES* 5 (1946): 185–202.

————. "The So-Called Intensive of the Semitic Languages." *JAOS* 62 (1942): 1–8.

Gordon, Cyrus H. "Azitawadd's Phoenician Inscription." *JNES* 8 (1949): 108–115.

————. *Ugaritic Textbook.* Analecta Orientalia, vol. 38. Rome: Pontifical Biblical Institute, 1965.

Greenberg, Joseph H. *Essays in Linguistics.* Chicago: The University of Chicago Press, 1957.

Greenfield, Jonas C. "Dialect Traits in Early Aramaic." *Leshonenu* 32 (1968): 359–368 (in Hebrew).

————. "The Dialects of Early Aramaic." *JNES* 37 (1978): 93–99.

————. "The 'Periphrastic Imperative' in Aramaic and Hebrew." *IEJ* 19 (1969): 199–210.

————. "[Review of Hoftijzer and van der Kooij, eds., *Aramaic Texts*]." *JSS* 25 (1980): 248–252.

Hackett, Jo Ann. "The Dialect of the Plaster Text from Tell Deir ʿAlla." *Or* 53 (1984): 57–65.

————. "Studies in the Plaster Text from Tell Deir ʿAllā." Ph.D. dissertation, Harvard University, 1980.

Halévy, Joseph. "Les Deux Inscriptions hétéennes de Zindjîrlî." *RS* 1 (1893): 138–167, 218–258, 319–336.

————. "Nouvel Examen des inscriptions de Zindjirli." *RS* 7 (1899): 333–355.

Hall, Robert A. "Bartoli's 'Neolinguistica.'" *Lg.* 22 (1946): 273–283.

Hallo, William W., and Tadmor, Hayim. "A Lawsuit from Hazor." *IEJ* 27 (1977): 1–11.

Harper, Robert Francis. *Assyrian and Babylonian Letters Belonging to the Kouyunjik Collection of the British Museum.* 14 vols. Chicago: The University of Chicago Press, 1892–1914.

Harris, Zellig S. *Development of the Canaanite Dialects.* American Oriental Series, vol. 16. New Haven: American Oriental Society, 1939.

————. *A Grammar of the Phoenician Language.* American Oriental Series, vol. 8. New Haven: American Oriental Society, 1936.

Haupt, Paul. "Über das assyrische Nominalpräfix *na*." *BA* 1 (1889): 1–20.

Healey, Joseph P. "The Archaic Aramaic Inscriptions from Zinjirli." Ph.D. dissertation, Harvard University, 1981.

Herdner, Andrée. *Corpus des tablettes en cunéiformes alphabétiques découvertes à Ras Shamra-Ugarit de 1929 à 1939.* Mission de Ras Shamra, vol. 10. 2 vols. Paris: Imprimerie Nationale, 1963.

Hestrin, Ruth, and Dayagi-Mendels, Michal. *Inscribed Seals.* Jerusalem: Israel Museum, 1979.

Hetzron, Robert. "Genetic Classification and Ethiopian Semitic." In *Hamito-Semitica,* edited by James and Theodora Bynon. Janua Linguarum, Series Practica, vol. 200, pp. 103–127. The Hague/Paris: Mouton, 1975.

———. "Third person singular pronoun suffixes in Proto-Semitic." *Orientalia Suecana* 18 (1969): 101–127.

Hickerson, Harold; Turner, Glen D.; and Hickerson, Nancy P. "Testing Procedures for Estimating Transfer of Information among Iroquois Dialects and Languages." *IJAL* 18 (1952): 1–8.

Hockett, Charles F. *A Course in Modern Linguistics.* New York: Macmillan Publishing Co., 1958.

Hoenigswald, Henry M. "Criteria for the Subgrouping of Languages." In *Ancient Indo-European Dialects,* edited by Henrik Birnbaum and Jaan Puhvel, pp. 1–12. Berkeley/Los Angeles: University of California Press, 1966.

Hoftijzer, J. "La nota accusativi ʾt en phénicien." *Le Muséon* 76 (1963): 195–200.

Hoftijzer, J., and van der Kooij, G. *Aramaic Texts from Deir ʿAlla.* Documenta et Monumenta Orientis Antiqui, vol. 19. Leiden: E. J. Brill, 1976.

Honeyman, A. M. "Phoenician Inscriptions from Karatepe." *Le Muséon* 61 (1948): 43–57.

Horn, Siegfried H. "The Amman Citadel Inscription." *ADAJ* 12–13 (1967–1968): 81–83.

———. "The Ammān Citadel Inscription." *BASOR* 193 (1969): 2–13.

Huesman, John. "Finite Uses of the Infinitive Absolute." *Bibl* 37 (1956): 271–295.

Inscriptions Reveal. The Israel Museum Catalogue no. 100. 2nd ed. Jerusalem: The Israel Museum, 1973.

Israel, Felice. "The Language of the Ammonites." *OLP* 10 (1979): 143–159.

———. "Miscellanea idumea." *Rivista biblica italiana* 27 (1979): 171–203.

———. "Un'ulteriore attestazione dell'evoluzione fonetica $\bar{a} > \bar{o}$ nel semitico di nord-ovest." *RSF* 7 (1979): 159–161.

Isserlin, B. S. J. "Epigraphically attested Judean Hebrew, and the question of 'upper class' (Official) and 'popular' speech variants in Judea during the 8th–6th centuries B.C." *AJBA* 2/1 (1972): 197–203.

Ivić, Pavle. "On the Structure of Dialectal Differentiation." *Word* 18 (1962): 33–53.

———. "Structure and Typology of Dialectal Differentiation." In *Proceedings of the Ninth International Congress of Linguists . . . 1962,* edited by Horace G. Lunt. Janua Linguarum, Series Maior, vol. 12, pp. 115–129. London/The Hague/Paris: Mouton & Co., 1964.

Jaberg, Karl. *Aspects géographiques du langage*. Société de publications romanes et françaises, vol. 18. Paris: Librairie E. Droz, 1936.

Jean, Charles-F., and Hoftijzer, J. *Dictionnaire des inscriptions sémitiques de l'ouest*. Leiden: E. J. Brill, 1965.

Johns, C. H. W. *Assyrian Deeds and Documents*. 2 vols. Cambridge/London: Deighton Bell & Co./George Bell & Sons, 1898–1901.

Joüon, Paul. *Grammaire de l'hébreu biblique*. Rome: Pontifical Biblical Institute, 1923.

Kaufman, Ivan T. "The Samaria Ostraca: A Study in Ancient Hebrew Palaeography." 2 vols. Ph.D. dissertation, Harvard University, 1966.

Kaufman, Stephen A. *The Akkadian Influences on Aramaic*. Assyriological Studies, vol. 19. Chicago/London: The University of Chicago Press, 1974.

————. "An Assyro-Aramaic *egirtu ša šulmu*." In *Essays on the Ancient Near East in Memory of Jacob Joel Finkelstein*, edited by Maria deJong Ellis. Memoirs of the Connecticut Academy of Arts & Sciences, vol. 19, pp. 119–127. Hamden, Conn.: Archon Books, 1977.

————. "The Enigmatic Adad-Milki." *JNES* 37 (1978): 101–109.

————. "Reflections on the Assyrian-Aramaic Bilingual from Tell Fakhariyeh." *Maarav* 3 (1982): 137–175.

————. "Si'gabbar, Priest of Sahr in Nerab." *JAOS* 90 (1970): 270–271.

————. "[Review of Hoftijzer and van der Kooij, eds., *Aramaic Texts*]." *BASOR* 239 (1980): 71–74.

————. "[Review of Segert, *Grammatik*]." *BiOr* 34 (1977): 92–97.

Kienast, Burkhart. "Das Possessivsuffix der 3.m.sg. am pluralischen Nomen des Maskulinum im Südostaramäischen." *Münchener Studien zur Sprachwissenschaft* 10 (1957): 72–76.

König, Eduard. "Das *l*-Jaqtul im Semitischen." *ZDMG* 51 (1897): 330–337.

Koopmans, J. J. *Aramäische Chrestomathie*. 2 vols. Leiden: Nederlands Instituut voor het Nabije Oosten, 1962.

Kraeling, Emil G. (ed.). *The Brooklyn Museum Aramaic Papyri*. New Haven: Yale University Press, 1953.

Krahmalkov, Charles R. "An Ammonite Lyric Poem." *BASOR* 223 (1976): 55–57.

————. "Comments on the Vocalization of the Suffix Pronoun of the Third Feminine Singular in Phoenician and Punic." *JSS* 17 (1962): 68–75.

————. "The Object Pronouns of the Third Person of Phoenician and Punic." *RSF* 2 (1974): 39–43.

————. "Observations on the Affixing of Possessive Pronouns in Punic." *RSO* 44 (1969): 181–186.

————. "On the Third Feminine Singular of the Perfect in Phoenician-Punic." *JSS* 24 (1979): 25–28.

————. "Studies in Phoenician and Punic Grammar." *JSS* 15 (1970): 181–188.

Kurath, Hans. *Handbook of the Linguistic Geography of New England*. 2nd ed. New York: AMS Press, 1973.

————. *Studies in Area Linguistics*. Bloomington/London: Indiana University Press, 1972.

Kutscher, Eduard Y. "Aramaic." In *Linguistics in South West Asia and North Africa*. Current Trends in Linguistics, vol. 6, pp. 347–412. The Hague/Paris: Mouton, 1970.

————. "הארמית המקראית—ארמית מזרחית היא או מערבית?" *Leshonenu* 17 (1951): 119–122.

————. *A History of Aramaic*. Part 1: *Old Aramaic, Jaudic, Official Aramaic (Biblical Aramaic excepted)*. Jerusalem: Akadamon, 1972 (in Hebrew).

Kutscher, Raphael. "A New Inscription from ʿAmman." *Qadmoniot* 5 (1972): 27–28 (in Hebrew).

Labov, William. *Sociolinguistic Patterns*. Conduct and Communication, no. 4. Philadelphia: University of Pennsylvania Press, 1972.

Lambdin, Thomas O. "The Junctural Origin of the West Semitic Definite Article." In *Near Eastern Studies in Honor of William Foxwell Albright*, edited by Hans Goedicke, pp. 315–333. Baltimore/London: The Johns Hopkins Press, 1971.

Landes, George M. "Ammon, Ammonites." In *The Interpreter's Dictionary of the Bible*. 4 vols., 1:108–114. Nashville/New York: Abingdon Press, 1962.

Landsberger, Benno. *Samʾal. Studien zur Entdeckung der Ruinenstaette Karatepe*. Veröffentlichungen der türkischen historischen Gesellschaft, Series 7, no. 16. Ankara: Türkische historische Gesellschaft, 1948.

Leander, Pontus. *Laut- und Formenlehre des Ägyptisch-Aramäischen*. 1928. Reprint. Hildescheim: Georg Olms, 1966.

Lemaire, André. "Les inscriptions de Khirbet el-Qôm et l'Ashérah de YHWH." *RB* 84 (1977): 595–608.

————. *Inscriptions hébraïques*, Tome 1: *Les ostraca*. Littératures anciennes du Proche-Orient, vol. 9/1. Paris: Les Éditions du Cerf, 1977.

————. "Les ostraca paléo-hébreux des fouilles de l'Ophel." *Levant* 10 (1978): 156–161.

————. "L'ostracon 'Ramat-Negeb' et la topographie historique du Negeb." *Semitica* 23 (1973): 11–25.

Levine, Baruch A. "The Deir ʿAlla Plaster Inscriptions." *JAOS* 101 (1981): 195–205.

Levine, Louis D. *Two Neo-Assyrian Stelae from Iran*. Royal Ontario Museum Art and Archaeology Occasional Paper 23. Toronto: The Royal Ontario Museum, 1972.

Lindsay, W. M. "The Carthaginian Passages in the 'Poenulus' of Plautus." *The Classical Review* 12 (1898): 361–364.

Lipiński, F. "From Karatepe to Pyrgi. Middle Phoenician Miscellanea." *RSF* 2 (1974): 45–61.

Maisler, Benjamin. "Two Hebrew Ostraca from Tell Qasîle." *JNES* 10 (1951): 265–267.

———. "הכתובות הפניקיות מגבל ושלשלת התפתחותו של הכתב האלפבית הפניקי העברי." *Leshonenu* 14 (1946): 166–181.

Malamat, Abraham. "The Aramaeans." In *Peoples of Old Testament Times*, edited by D. J. Wiseman, pp. 134–155. Oxford: Oxford University Press, 1973.

———. "Northern Canaan and the Mari Texts." In *Near Eastern Archaeology in the Twentieth Century*, edited by James A. Sanders, pp. 164–177. Garden City, N.Y.: Doubleday & Co., 1970.

Malone, Joseph L. "A Hebrew Flip-Flop Rule and Its Historical Origins." *Lingua* 30 (1972): 422–448.

———. "Wave Theory, Rule Ordering, and Hebrew-Aramaic Segolation." *JAOS* 91 (1971): 44–66.

Marcus, David. "Studies in Ugaritic Grammar 1." *JANES* 1/2 (1969): 55–61.

Margoliouth, D. S. "Language of the Old Testament." In *A Dictionary of the Bible*, edited by James Hastings. 4 vols., 3:25–35. New York/Edinburgh: Charles Scribner's Sons/T. & T. Clark, 1900.

Martinet, André. "Diffusion of Language and Structural Linguistics." *Romance Philology* 6 (1952): 5–13.

McCarter, P. Kyle. "The Balaam Texts from Deir ʿAllā: The First Combination." *BASOR* 239 (1980): 49–60.

McCarter, P. Kyle, and Coote, Robert B. "The Spatula Inscription from Byblos." *BASOR* 212 (1973): 16–22.

Meillet, Antoine. *Linguistique historique et linguistique générale.* Nouveau tirage. 2 vols. Paris: Édouard Champion, 1948–1951.

Meshel, Zeev. "Kuntilat ʿAjrud, 1975–1976." *IEJ* 27 (1977): 52–53.

———. *Kuntillet ʿAjrud. A Religious Centre from the Time of the Judaean Monarchy on the Border of Sinai.* The Israel Museum Catalogue no. 175. Jerusalem: Israel Museum, 1978.

Meshel, Ze'ev, and Meyers, Carol. "The Name of God in the Wilderness of Zin." *BA* 39 (1976): 6–10.

Meyer, Rudolph. *Hebräische Grammatik.* 3rd ed. 4 vols. Berlin: Walter de Gruyter & Co., 1966–1972.

Milik, J. T. "Textes hébreux et araméens." In P. Benoit et al., *Les grottes de Murabbaʿât.* Discoveries in the Judaean Desert, vol. 2, pp. 67–205. Oxford: Oxford University Press, 1961.

Moran, William L. "The Hebrew Language in its Northwest Semitic Background." In *The Bible and the Ancient Near East*, edited by G. Ernest Wright, pp. 54–72. Garden City, N.Y.: Doubleday & Co., 1961.

————. "[Review of Cross and Freedman, *EHO*]." *CBQ* 15 (1953): 364–367.

Moscati, Sabatino (ed.). *An Introduction to the Comparative Grammar of the Semitic Languages*. Porta Linguarum Orientalium, New Series, vol. 6. Wiesbaden: Otto Harrassowitz, 1969.

————. *The Semites in Ancient History*. Cardiff: University of Wales Press, 1959.

————. "Il semitico di nord-ovest." In *Studi orientalistici in onore di Giorgio Levi Della Vida*. Pubblicazioni dell'Istituto per l'Oriente, no. 52. 2 vols., 2:202–221. Rome: Istituto per l'Oriente, 1956.

————. "Sulla posizione linguistica del semitico nord-occidentale." *RSO* 31 (1956): 229–234.

Moulton, William G. "Structural Dialectology." *Lg.* 44 (1968): 451–466.

Müller, D. H. "Die altsemitischen Inschriften von Sendschirli." *WZKM* 7 (1893): 33–70, 113–140.

Naveh, Joseph. "A Hebrew Letter from the Seventh Century B.C." *IEJ* 10 (1960): 129–139.

————. "Old Hebrew Inscriptions in a Burial Cave." *IEJ* 13 (1963): 74–92.

————. "The Ostracon from Nimrud: An Ammonite Name-List." *Maarav* 2 (1980): 163–171.

————. "The Scripts of Two Ostraca from Elath." *BASOR* 183 (1966): 27–30.

————. "[Review of Friedrich and Röllig, *PPG²*]." *JAOS* 93 (1973): 588–589.

————. "[Review of Hoftijzer and van der Kooij, eds., *Aramaic Texts*]." *IEJ* 29 (1979): 133–136.

Naveh, Joseph, and Tigay, Jeffrey H. "A List of Ammonite Personal Names." Photocopy. N. P.: N.D.

Nöldeke, Theodor. "Die aramäischen Papyri von Assuan." *ZA* 20 (1907): 130–150.

————. "Bemerkungen zu den aramäischen Inschriften von Sendschirli." *ZDMG* 47 (1893): 96–105.

————. *Die Inschrift des Königs Mesa von Moab*. Kiel: Schwers'sche Buchhandlung, 1870.

————. *Kurzgefasste syrische Grammatik*. 2nd ed. 1898. Reprint. Darmstadt: Wissenschaftliche Buchgesellschaft, 1966.

————. *Mandäische Grammatik*. 1875. Reprint. Darmstadt: Wissenschaftliche Buchgesellschaft, 1964.

————. *Neue Beiträge zur semitischen Sprachwissenschaft*. Strassburg: Karl J. Trübner, 1910.

————. "Untersuchungen zur semitischen Grammatik." *ZDMG* 38 (1884): 407–422.

Nougayrol, Jean, et al. *Ugaritica V*. Mission de Ras Shamra, vol. 16. Paris: Imprimerie Nationale, 1968.

O'Callaghan, Roger T. "The Great Phoenician Portal Inscription from Karatepe." *Or* 18 (1949): 173–205.

———. "The Phoenician Inscription on the King's Statue at Karatepe." *CBQ* 11 (1949): 233–248.

Oded, B. "Ammon, Ammonites." In *Encyclopaedia Judaica*. 16 vols., 2:853–859. Jerusalem: Keter Publishing House, 1971–1972.

———. "Egyptian References to the Edomite Deity Qaus." *AUSS* 9 (1971): 47–50.

———. "Judah and the Exile." In *Israelite and Judaean History*, edited by John H. Hayes and J. Maxwell Miller, pp. 435–488. Philadelphia: The Westminster Press, 1977.

Pardee, Dennis. "The Judicial Plea from Meṣad Ḥashavyahu (Yavneh-Yam): A New Philological Study." *Maarav* 1 (1978): 33–66.

Parpola, Simo. *Neo-Assyrian Toponyms*. AOAT, vol. 6. Kevelaer/Neukirchen-Vluyn: Butzon & Bercker/Neukirchener Verlag des Erziehungsvereins, 1970.

Parunak, H. Van Dyke. "The Orthography of the Arad Ostraca." *BASOR* 230 (1978): 25–31.

Philippi, F. "Die Aussprache der semitischen Consonanten ו und י. Eine Abhandlung über die Natur dieser Laute." *ZDMG* 40 (1886): 639–654.

Poebel, Arno. *Das appositionell bestimmte Pronomen der 1. Pers. Sing. in den westsemitischen Inschriften und im Alten Testament*. Assyriological Studies, vol. 3. Chicago: The University of Chicago Press, 1932.

Pop, Sever. *La dialectologie. Aperçu historique et Méthodes d'enquêtes linguistiques*. Université de Louvain. Récueil de travaux d'histoire et de philologie, 3ᵉ Série, Fascicules 38/39. 2 vols. Louvain/Gembloux: [private]/J. Duculot, 1950.

Porten, Bezalel. "The Identity of King Adon." *BA* 44 (1981): 36–52.

Praetorius, Franz. "Zur hebräischen und aramäischen Grammatik." *ZDMG* 55 (1901): 359–370.

Pritchard, James B. (ed.). *Ancient Near Eastern Texts Relating to the Old Testament*. 3rd ed. with Supplement. Princeton: Princeton University Press, 1969.

Puech, Emile. "Documents épigraphiques de Buseirah." *Levant* 9 (1977): 11–20.

Puech, Emile, and Rofé, Alexander. "L'inscription de la citadelle d'Amman." *RB* 80 (1973): 531–546.

Pulgram, Ernst. "The Nature and Use of Proto-Languages." *Lingua* 10 (1961): 18–37.

———. "Spoken and Written Latin." *Lg.* 26 (1950): 458–466.

Rabin, Chaim. "Archaic Vocalisation in Some Biblical Hebrew Names." *JJS* 1 (1948): 22–26.

————. "Lexicostatistics and the Internal Divisions of Semitic." In *Hamito-Semitica*, edited by James and Theodora Bynon. Janua Linguarum, Series Practica, vol. 200, pp. 85–102. The Hague/Paris: Mouton, 1975.

————. "The Origin of the Subdivisions of Semitic." In *Hebrew and Semitic Studies Presented to Godfrey Rolles Driver*, edited by D. Winton Thomas and W. D. McHardy, pp. 104–115. Oxford: Oxford University Press, 1963.

Rainey, Anson F. "Three Additional Hebrew Ostraca from Tel Arad." *Tel Aviv* 4 (1977): 97–104.

————. "The Word 'Day' in Ugaritic and Hebrew." *Leshonenu* 36 (1972): 186–189 (in Hebrew).

Reed, William L., and Winnett, Fred V. "A Fragment of an Early Moabite Inscription from Kerak." *BASOR* 172 (1963): 1–9.

Rendsburg, Gary. "Evidence for a Spoken Hebrew in Biblical Times." Ph.D. dissertation, New York University, 1980.

Ringgren, Helmer. "A Note on the Karatepe Text." *Oriens* 2 (1949): 127–128.

Röllig, Wolfgang. "Die Amulette von Arslan Taş." *NESE* 2 (1974): 17–36.

Rofé, Alexander, *The Book of Balaam (Numbers 22:2—24:25)*. Jerusalem Biblical Studies, vol. 1. Jerusalem: Simor, 1979 (in Hebrew).

Ronzevalle, S. "La langue des inscriptions dites de Hadad et de Panammū." In *Florilegium . . . Melchior de Vogüé*, pp. 519–528. Paris: Imprimerie Nationale, 1909.

Rosenthal, Franz. *Die aramaistische Forschung seit Th. Nöldeke's Veröffentlichungen*. Leiden: E. J. Brill, 1939.

————. "Canaanite and Aramaic Inscriptions." In *ANET*[3], pp. 653–662.

————. *A Grammar of Biblical Aramaic*. Porta Linguarum Orientalium, New Series, vol. 5. Wiesbaden: Otto Harrassowitz, 1974.

————. "Notes on the Third Aramaic Inscription from Sefîre-Sûjîn." *BASOR* 158 (1960): 28–31.

————. *Die Sprache der palmyrenischen Inschriften und ihre Stellung innerhalb des Aramäischen*. MVÄG, vol. 41, pt. 1. Leipzig: J. C. Hinrichs'sche Buchhandlung, 1936.

————. "[Review of Cross and Freedman, *EHO*]." *JAOS* 73 (1953): 46–47.

————. "[Review of Dion, *La langue*]." *JBL* 95 (1976): 153–155.

————. "[Review of Friedrich, *PPG*]." *JAOS* 72 (1952): 171–173.

————. "[Review of Gordon, *Ugaritic Grammar*]." *Or* 11 (1942): 171–179.

————. "[Review of Harris, *Development*]." *Or* 11 (1942): 179–185.

————. "[Review of Harris, *Grammar*]." *Or* 7 (1938): 169–172.

Ross, James F. "Prophecy in Hamath, Israel, and Mari." *HTR* 63 (1970): 1–28.

Sapir, Edward. "Dialect." In *Encyclopaedia of the Social Sciences*, edited by Edwin R. A. Seligman and Alvin Johnson. 15 vols., 5:123–126. New York· Macmillan Co., 1930–1935.

———. *Language*. New York: Harcourt, Brace & Co., 1921.

Schaeder, Hans H. *Iranische Beiträge I*. Schriften der Königsberger Gelehrten Gesellschaft, Geisteswissenschaftliche Klasse, vol. 6, pt. 5. Halle an der Saale: Max Niemeyer, 1930.

Schuchardt, Hugo. *Über die Klassifikation der romanischen Mundarten*. Graz: K. K. Universität-Buchdr., 1900.

Segert, Stanislav. *Altaramäische Grammatik*. Leipzig: VEB Verlag Enzyklopädie, 1975.

———. "Aramäische Studien V. Der Artikel in den ältesten aramäischen Texten." *ArOr* 26 (1958): 578–584.

———. "Aufgaben der biblisch-aramäischen Grammatik." *Communio Viatorum* 1/2–3 (1958): 127–134.

———. *A Grammar of Phoenician and Punic*. Munich: C. H. Beck, 1976.

———. "Nach zu den assimilierenden Verba im Hebräischen." *ArOr* 24 (1956): 132–134.

———. "Die Sprache der moabitischen Königsinschrift." *ArOr* 29 (1961): 197–267.

———. "Zur Schrift und Orthographie der altaramäischen Stelen von Sfire." *ArOr* 32 (1964): 110–126.

Sekine, Masao. "The Subdivisions of the North-West Semitic Languages." *JSS* 18 (1973): 205–221.

Selms, A. van. "Some Remarks on the ʿAmmān Citadel Inscriptions." *BiOr* 32 (1975): 5–8.

Shea, William H. "The Siran Inscription: Amminadab's Drinking Song." *PEQ* 1978: 107–112.

Sherman, Merton E. "Systems of Hebrew and Aramaic Orthography: an Epigraphic History of the Use of *matres lectionis* in Non-biblical Texts to *circa* A.D. 135." Ph.D. dissertation, Harvard University, 1966.

Soden, Wolfram von. *Grundriss der akkadischen Grammatik samt Ergänzungschaft*. Analecta Orientalia, vol. 33/47. Rome: Pontifical Biblical Institute, 1969.

———. "Die Zahlen 20–90 im Semitischen und der Status absolutus." *WZKM* 57 (1961): 24–28.

———. "Zur Einteilung der semitischen Sprachen." *WZKM* 56 (1960): 177–191.

Speiser, E. A. "The 'Elative' in West-Semitic and Akkadian." *JCS* 6 (1952): 81–92.

———. "Secondary Developments in Semitic Phonology: An Application of the Principle of Sonority." *AJSL* 42 (1926): 145–169.

———. "The Shibboleth Incident (Judges 12:6)." *BASOR* 85 (1942): 10–13.

————. "The Terminative-Adverbial in Canaanite-Ugaritic and Akkadian." *IEJ* 4 (1954): 108–115.

Sperber, Alexander. *A Historical Grammar of Biblical Hebrew.* Leiden: E. J. Brill, 1966.

Sperling, S. David. "An Arslan Tash Incantation: Interpretations and Implications." *HUCA* 53 (1982): 1–10.

Starcky, Jean. "Une inscription phénicienne de Byblos." *MUSJ* 45 (1969): 257–273.

Steiner, Richard C. *The Case for Fricative-Laterals in Proto-Semitic.* American Oriental Series, vol. 59. New Haven: American Oriental Society, 1977.

————. "*Yuqaṭṭil, Yaqaṭṭil,* or *Yiqaṭṭil*: D-Stem Prefix-Vowels and a Constraint on Reduction in Hebrew and Aramaic." *JAOS* 100 (1980): 513–518.

Sukenik, E. L. "Note on a Fragment of an Israelite Stele found at Samaria," *PEQ* 1936: 156.

Swadesh, Morris. "Lexico-statistic Dating of Prehistoric Ethnic Contacts with Special Reference to North American Indians and Eskimos." *PAPhS* 96 (1952): 452–463.

————. "Towards Greater Accuracy in Lexicostatistic Dating." *IJAL* 21 (1955): 121–137.

Swiggers, P. "Karatepe A II 5–6/B I 13–14/C III 3–4." *RSF* 9 (1981): 143–146.

————. "[Review of Segert, *Grammar*]." *Lingua* 50 (1980): 381–391.

Sznycer, Maurice. *Les passages puniques en transcription latine dans le "Poenulus" de Plaute.* Etudes et commentaires, vol. 65. Paris: C. Klincksieck, 1967.

Talmon, Shemaryahu. "The New Hebrew Letter from the Seventh Century B.C. in Historical Perspective." *BASOR* 176 (1964): 29–38.

Tawil, Hayim. "A Note on the Aḥiram Inscription." *JANES* 3/1 (1970–1971): 32–36.

Tomback, Richard S. "Gemination in Punic." *JNSL* 5 (1977): 67–68.

Torczyner, Harry. "A Hebrew Incantation against Night-Demons from Biblical Times." *JNES* 6 (1947): 18–29.

Torczyner, Harry, et al. *Lachish I (Tell ed Duweir). The Lachish Letters.* The Wellcome Archaeological Research Expedition to the Near East Publications, vol. 1. London/New York/Toronto: Oxford University Press, 1938.

Tzori, N. "A Hebrew Ostracon from Beth-Shean." *Yediot* 25 (1961): 145–146 (in Hebrew).

Ugaritica V. See Nougayrol, Jean et al.

Ussishkin, David. "Excavations at Tel Lachish—1973–1977, Preliminary Report." *Tel Aviv* 5 (1978): 1–97.

Vattioni, Francesco. "I sigilli ebraici." *Bibl* 50 (1969): 357–388.

Watson, Wilfred. "Shared Consonants in Northwest Semitic." *Bibl* 50 (1969): 525–533.

Weippert, Helga and Manfred. "Die 'Bileam'-Inschrift von *Tell Dēr 'Allā.*" *ZDPV* 98 (1982): 75–103.

Weippert, Manfred. "Edom. Studien und Materialien zur Geschichte der Edomiter auf Grund schriftlicher und archäologischer Quellen." Inaugural-Dissertation, Eberhard-Karl-Universität, 1971.

———. "Elemente phönikischer und kilikischer Religion in den Inschriften vom Karatepe." In *XVII. Deutscher Orientalistentag . . . Würzburg. Vorträge,* edited by Wolfgang Voigt. ZDMG Supplementa, vol. 1, pt. 1, pp. 191–217. Wiesbaden: Franz Steiner, 1969.

———. "Menahem von Israel und seine Zeitgenossen in einer Steleninschrift des assyrischen Königs Tiglathpilesar III. aus dem Iran." *ZDPV* 89 (1973): 26–53.

Williams, Ronald J. *Hebrew Syntax: An Outline.* 2nd ed. Toronto/Buffalo: University of Toronto Press, 1976.

———. "Moabite Stone." In *The Interpreter's Dictionary of the Bible.* 4 vols., 3:419–420. Nashville/New York: Abingdon Press, 1962.

Winter, Irene J. "On the Problems of Karatepe: The Reliefs and Their Context." *AS* 29 (1979): 115–151.

Wunderlich, Clifford. "An Outline of the Grammar of Selected Hebrew Ostraca from Arad." Photocopy. Cambridge: Harvard University, 1978.

Yadin, Yigal, et al. *Hazor II. An Account of the Second Season of Excavations, 1956.* Jerusalem: Magnes Press, 1960.

Zadok, Ran. "Historical and Onomastic Notes." *WO* 9 (1977–1978): 35–56, 240–241.

———. "West Semitic Personal Names in the Murašû Documents." *BASOR* 231 (1978): 73–78.

Zayadine, Fawzi, and Thompson, Henry O. "The Ammonite Inscription from Tell Siran." *Berytus* 22 (1973): 115–140.

———. "The Tell Siran Inscription." *BASOR* 212 (1973): 5–11.

———. "The Works of Amminadab." *BA* 37 (1974): 13–19.

Zevit, Ziony. *Matres Lectionis in Ancient Hebrew Epigraphs.* ASOR Monograph Series, vol. 2. Cambridge: ASOR, 1980.

SUBJECT INDEX

*á, correspondences of, 33–35
*ã, correspondences of, 12, 30–32, 66–67 n. 59
*â, correspondences of, 30, 32–33; in northern Hebrew, 233
aleph: aphaeresis of, 50–52, 74 n. 226; prothetic, 47–48; syllable-closing, 83–84, 119 n. 65; syncope of, 49–50
Ammonite, classification of, 2, 228
Analogy, proportional, 95, 99, 171
Anaptyxis, 12, 45–47, 72 n. 179
Aramaic dialects, 221–222: Adon Letter, 222; Aleppo-Aramaic, 16 n. 39, 221; classification of, 227–228; Fekheriyeh-Aramaic, 221–222; Halaf-Aramaic, 222; Nerab-Aramaic, 221, 237 n. 39; Sfire-Aramaic, 221
*-at, correspondences of, 60–61
*-át, correspondences of, 59–60, 76 n. 278
*aw, correspondences of, 35–40, 41
*ay, correspondences of, 35–40

Bible, and NWS dialectal relations, 231

Canaanite: classification of, 4; coastal, 2, 4; inland, 2, 4; North, 2, 14 n. 6; South, 2
Canaanite vowel shift. See *ã
Case endings, 61–63
Classification: and analogical formations, 215; and borrowing, 216; choice of linguistic features used in, 2; criteria for, 4; and geography, 5; judgment by inspection, 2; and the lexicon, 6; and morphology, 217; and NWS, 2; and parallel, independent development, 215; and personal names, 12; and phonology, 217; and place names, 12–13; and retentions, 215; and syntax, 216–217; weighing of features in, 3, 205, 215–217. See specific entries for Ammonite, Canaanite, etc.
Conditional particles, 116–117

INDEX OF TEXTS CITED

Ezra
  4:22   130
  5:10   36

UGARITIC TEXTS

CTA
  3:B:7   96
  12 (= UT 75)   63 n. 1
  32:28   96
Ugaritica V
  137:II:39′   161 n. 346
  137:II:40′   161 n. 346

AKKADIAN TEXTS

ABL
  1112:8   34
ADD
  894:5   30

EA
  85:63   87
  94:12   87
  116:67   87
  141:44   30
  245:10   31
  245:35   52
  256:7   59
  256:9   31
  263:12   68 n. 84
  264:18   68 n. 84
  292:29   135
Fekheriyeh Akk. Text
  20   47
Nabunaid
  33.5   33

EGYPTIAN TEXTS

VESO
  X C 4   30
  X C 5   30

WORD INDEX

כברו, 93
כברת, 60
כלה, 102

לאכל, 49, 128
לבנא, 140
לבני, 140
לבגרי. See בלגרי
לה, 102
לילא, 36
לכתשה, 53, 111
לכתשנה, 118, 128
למנע, 53, 118
לנצב, 42, 128
לתגמרו, 118, 127

מודד, 36
מוקא, 23
מז, 82, 85
מחנת, 96
מלכו, 37, 62
מן, 42, 87
מראה, 102
משב, 69 n. 107, 131
משבה, 102
משבי, 100
משות, 96
מת, 42

עין, 36

פ(א), 114, 195, 196, 199 n. 65

צדי, 24, 66 n. 37

קירת, 95
קן, 135
קרני, 49
קשתה, 45
קתילת, 95, 130

רקה, 23
רש, 74 n. 216

שבי, 46
שבעי, 113
שי, 46
שמרג, 24
שמת, 123
שתא, 53, 135

תהרגה, 111, 169
תהרגו, 126, 185
תלעי, 137, 138
תשמ[ן], 185
תשתי, 138

AMMONITE WORDS

אכחד[ה]ו, 56, 111
אכחדו*, 111
אכחדם*, 112
[ʾĒl], 32
אלם, 89
אלעזר, 26
אש, 48, 65 n. 23, 85
אשחת, 48, 59, 121
את/סחר, 48. See also והאת/סחר

בדאל, 53. See also בידאל
בידאל, 53. See also בדאל
בן, 37, 91
בנה, 53, 125, 136
בצרה[ן]ו*, 108
בקש, 66 n. 50

גנת, 59. See also ה.גנת;וה.גנת

דבלכס, 65 n. 23
דשא, 29, 49

ה.גנת, 88. See also גנת;וה.גנת
הכרם, 88
הצלאל, 43, 122

והאת/סחר, 55. See also את/סחר
וה.גנת, 55. See also גנת;ה.גנת

חד*, 51

יומת, 37, 95
ילחם*, 121
ילנן, 127
ימתן, 127
י ן, 37
ירחעזר, 26

כחד, 51
כרה, 55, 102

לך, 82

מ, 87
מאלת, 43

BIBLICAL HEBREW WORDS

UGARITIC WORDS

AKKADIAN WORDS

Ka-ma-as-ḫal-ta-a, 31
Ka-am-mu-su-na-ad-bi, 31

Mil-ki-a-ša-pa, 33
mi-ya, 87
Mu/a-ʾa-b(a), 34

-na, 199 n. 65
nīnu, 51

Padā-yaw, 68 n. 82
Pa-na-am-mu-u, 62
Pu-du-il, 32

Qaus/Qauš, 38
Qauš-malaku, 34
Qusuyada, 38
Qusuyahab, 38

Ra-ḫi-a-nu, 23
Ra-qi-a-nu, 23
ru-šu-nu, 68 n. 84

Sa-la-ma-nu, 31
Sam-al, 30
Sa-am-al-la, 30
sinepû, 47, 73 n. 202
Si-pí-it, 72 n. 179
Si-pí-it-ti-bi-ʾi-il, 45
sú-ki-ni, 31
sú-ú-nu, 68 n. 84

ṣâḫu, 64 n. 12

Tu-ba-ʾ-lu, 50

-ūna/i, 12

EGYPTIAN WORDS

Bi-(ʾa)-ru-ta, 30
Q3ws, 38

ARABIC WORDS

[ʾīyā-], 116
*ḥyd, 188
[ḏā], 199 n. 65
[ḏalika], 82
ḏḥk, 64 n. 12
[ḍarra], 24, 66 n. 37
[ʿaẓuma], 27
[naḥnu], 51

EPIGRAPHIC SOUTH ARABIAN WORD

ḥmt, 82

ETHIOPIC WORDS

[šaḥaqa], 64 n. 12
[nᵊḥna], 51
[ʾī], 175
[ʾanā], 80
[zā], 199 n. 65

GREEK WORDS

θωρ, 28
ρω, 32, 49
Τυρος, 27